My Lords and Lady
of Essex: *Their State Trials*

Joseph Allen Matter

HENRY REGNERY COMPANY · CHICAGO

To My Wife

PREFACE

WHEN I was studying law at Northwestern University some forty-odd years ago, I paid part of my expenses serving as monitor of the law library. Poking around there in my spare time, I discovered Hargrave's British State Trials. There were eleven yard-high volumes, the leather crumbling and the pages musty.

The books fascinated me. Here were the official versions and trial transcripts of trials famous in English and American colonial history from 1388 well into the eighteenth century. The names of many of the persons involved had been familiar to me since grade school days. The trials ran the gamut of major crimes: high treason, regicide, sedition, slander, piracy, murder, rape, incest, sodomy, adultery, bigamy, divorce, heresy, witchcraft, practice of black magic and lesser felonies. Many of the decisions were key rulings in the evolution of the English common law which in part still controls our lives.

It seemed to me too bad that the more interesting and the more important of those trials could not be made available, with appropriate comment and background material, to the many persons who would enjoy reading them. I resolved (perhaps not too seriously) that some day I would see what I could do; it has taken those forty-odd years and my retirement from the active practice of law to bring that resolve to the partial fruition that this book represents.

I have selected these particular trials for this book because of their intrinsic interest and the insight they afford into the lives of the courtiers of Elizabeth and James I, and because, since they all involve the second and third Devereux Earls of Essex, they form a natural group.

Except for some abridgment, modernization of spelling, and the addition of some excerpts from other contemporaneous accounts,

My Lords and Lady of Essex

the trials appear here as they do in Hargrave. In the interest of easier reading, most of the contemporary letters, accounts and excerpts from early histories have also been modernized. In Elizabethan times, spelling was not standardized and was largely a matter of personal inclination. This was true of persons' names as it was of other words. To avoid confusion, I have made uniform throughout the book the spelling of each proper name.

About fifty years after the fourth Hargrave edition appeared, T. B. Howell brought out in more usable form a new edition, identical with Hargrave's except for its smaller format, some additional trials and some editorial comment. Because it is today more readily accessible, page references to the trials refer to Howell rather than to Hargrave. The trial excerpts are not placed in quotation marks, but are indented and set off from the main text. In these, and where interjected in direct quotations, my own comments or clarifying additions are placed in brackets or set in separate paragraphs.

The bibliography lists most of the books, manuscripts and documents that I have examined in my research, even though space has not permitted use of material from them all. I hope in this manner to make the bibliography more useful for students doing future research. Where the writer of any such book or document had special stature or was in position to have peculiar knowledge of that of which he wrote, I have indicated such qualifications in the bibliography. Several documents of real value and interest, but which because of space limitations had to be omitted or drastically abridged in the text, appear in the appendix.

Finally, I wish to acknowledge gratefully the fine assistance given me by members of the staff of the Newberry Library in Chicago, suggestions made by Norval Morris, Director of the University of Chicago Center for Studies in Criminal Justice, and the sympathetic understanding and uncounted hours of assistance in the writing of this book and its preparation for publication given me by my wife and by Fern Ferguson, my valued secretary for many years.

CONTENTS

DRAMATIS PERSONAE

Elizabeth I: Queen of England

James I: King of England

Walter Devereux: First Earl of Essex

Robert Devereux: Second Earl of Essex; son of Walter

Robert Devereux: Third Earl of Essex; son of Robert

Lady Lettice Knollys: Cousin of Queen Elizabeth; wife of Essex I, and by later marriages, wife of the Earl of Leicester and of Sir Christopher Blount

William Knollys: Earl of Banbury; brother of Lettice Knollys and hence uncle of Essex II

Lady Penelope Rich: Loyal sister of Essex II; faithless wife of Lord Robert Rich; loved by the poet Sir Philip Sidney and made famous by him as his "Stella"; mother of five children by Lord Mountjoy

Lady Frances Howard: Daugher of Thomas Howard; wife of Essex II; and by a second marriage, wife of the Earl of Somerset

Thomas Howard: Earl of Suffolk; father of Frances Howard; Admiral of the Fleet; Lord Chamberlain; Lord High Treasurer; convicted of embezzlement, fraud and extortion—his punishment ameliorated through influence of Buckingham

Henry Howard: Earl of Northampton; uncle of Thomas Howard and hence great-uncle of Frances Howard; learned bachelor; Privy Councillor; Lord Privy Seal; strongly influential with James I

Lady Katherine Howard: Wife of Thomas Howard and mother of Frances Howard

Charles Howard: Earl of Nottingham; Lord Chamberlain; as Lord High Admiral defeated the Spanish Armada; his wife, Catherine, Elizabeth's favorite

Henry Stuart: Son of James I; Prince of Wales

Robert Carr: Viscount Rochester; later Earl of Somerset

Anne Carr: Daugher of Robert Carr; married Lord Russell, the son of the Duke of Bedford

Sir Thomas Overbury: Poet and brilliant writer; close friend and confidential secretary of Robert Carr

Robert Dudley: Earl of Leicester; son of the Duke of Northumberland; brother-in-law of Lady Jane Grey; sentenced to death for his part in placing her on the throne, but pardoned; married Amy Robsart and, after her death under suspicious circumstances, Lettice Knollys, hence becoming stepfather of Essex II; long-time favorite of Queen Elizabeth

George Abbot: Archbishop of Canterbury; noted for his learning; favored the Puritans; bitter enemy of Northampton in the Council

Sir Francis Bacon: Son of Lord Keeper Bacon and nephew of William Cecil, Lord Burghley; noted barrister, scholar and philosopher; protégé of Essex II; rival of Sir Edward Coke for high judicial offices; became Lord Chancellor, confessed bribery, and died in disfavor

Thomas Seymour: Brother of Edward, Duke of Somerset and Lord Protector of England; Lord High Admiral; after death of Henry VIII married Catherine Parr, the dowager queen; executed for treason

Sir Edward Coke: Outstanding English jurist; Attorney General; Chief Justice of Common Pleas; Chief Justice of King's Bench

Sir John Popham: Chief Justice of King's Bench; Speaker of House of Commons; Attorney General; discharged his duties with humanity

William Cecil (Lord Burghley): Guardian of Essex II; although protégé of condemned Lord Protector Somerset, his life saved by England's need for his outstanding ability; Privy Councillor; Secretary of State; faithful and incorruptible servant to three children of Henry VIII

Robert Cecil: Earl of Salisbury; younger son of William Cecil, Lord Burghley; Secretary of State under Elizabeth and James I; under James, responsible for entire administration of England

Thomas Egerton (Baron Ellesmere): Solicitor General; Attorney General; Lord Keeper; Lord Chancellor; patron of Francis Bacon; warm friend of Essex II; high in confidence of both Elizabeth and James I

George Villiers: Duke of Buckingham; succeeded Robert Carr as favorite of James I

Sir John Harrington: Godson of Queen Elizabeth; protégé of Burghley; writer of "Nugae Antiquae"; popular but ribald court wit; knighted by Essex II in Ireland

Sir Christopher Hatton: Handsome courtier and graceful dancer; as one of Elizabeth's favorites became Gentleman of her Privy Chamber, Captain of her Bodyguard, Vice-Chamberlain of her Household, Privy Councillor, her mouthpiece in the House of Commons and Lord Chancellor

Hugh O'Neill: Earl of Tyrone; assisted Essex I in subduing Ireland but later led Irish rebellion against the English

Henry Wriothesley: Earl of Southampton; literature his chief interest; patron of Shakespeare and other writers; aided American colonization; close friend of Essex II

Sir Ferdinando Gorges: Naval and military commander; Governor of Plymouth; served under Essex II; founded American settlements, including New Plymouth, gaining name of "Father of English Colonization in America"; became Lord Proprietor of Maine

Sir Christopher Blount: Younger son of Lord James Mountjoy and younger brother of Lord Charles Mountjoy; attendant to Earl of Leicester and upon marrying Leicester's widow, Lettice Knollys, became stepfather of Essex II; short military career under Essex, his close friend

Sir Robert Cotton: Antiquary; student of William Camden; noted scholar; intimate with leading statesmen; protégé of Robert Carr, and hence of James I

Sir Robert Killigrew: Son of Queen Elizabeth's groom of the Privy Chamber; member of Parliament; Captain of Pendennis Castle

Sir Thomas Monson: Son of a knight and brother of an Admiral; Master of the Armory at Tower of London; M.A. from Oxford; falconer and favorite of James I

Sir John Lidcote: Brother-in-law of Sir Thomas Overbury

Sir John Davis: Friend and attendant of Essex II

Sir Charles Danvers: M.A. from Oxford; member of Parliament; outlawed for activity in family feud, but pardoned; Colonel under Essex II in Ireland; devoted friend of Southampton

Henry Cuffe: Noted Greek Scholar; Oxford professor; Secretary to Essex II

Sir Gilly Merrick: Son of a bishop; professional soldier, serving under Essex II on most of his expeditions; Steward of Essex II

Dr. Theodore de Mayerne: Noted Swiss physician; Court Physician to Henri IV of France and to James I

Dr. Simon Forman: Physician, charlatan, necromancer

Sir Gervaise Elwes: Nephew of Sheriff of London; Lieutenant of the Tower; friend of the Howards

Richard Weston

James Franklin

Anne Turner

ONE

THERE were three Devereux Earls of Essex. Walter Devereux was the first earl. Walter's son, Robert, and his grandson, also named Robert, were the second and third; it is they with whom we shall here be principally concerned. Each of the three was able, gifted and personable; each enjoyed the favors of his sovereign and served his country faithfully and sometimes well. Nevertheless, each died alone and unhappy: Walter had to beg protectors for his son, and as he died, he supplicated the boy to eschew public life; Robert died under the headsman's ax; and Robert's son never recovered from an early mischance for which he was not to blame. The engrossing story of the misfortunes of this family is brought vividly to light and life in the sixteenth- and seventeenth-century court records and other contemporary writings reporting the State Trials that we are about to examine — trials involving charges of adultery, impotency, black magic, murder and treason.

Two sons of the Norman Count of Rosmar and Mantelake went to England with William the Conqueror. One was Robert D'Evreux, who fathered the line to which the three earls belonged. William liberally rewarded his knights with confiscated Saxon fiefs; the Devereux family received an ample share.[1] By Walter's time the family had accumulated many titles, and royal blood ran in his veins. The Devereux bond with royalty was knit even more closely when Walter married Queen Elizabeth's cousin, Lettice Knollys. Later, this royal lineage, which could serve as a pretext for a claim to the throne, proved injurious to Walter's son.

After his marriage to Lettice, Walter, then Viscount Hereford, was called to public life, led troops which helped subdue a rebellion in the North and in 1572 was made Earl of Essex by a grateful

1

queen. The short remainder of his life was spent in attempts to extend the area of English control in Ireland. Elizabeth, always niggardly with her grants of money for war, permitted Walter to mortgage his estates to obtain money to pay his troops. His reward was the Earl-Marshalship of Ireland and the grant of some Irish land that produced no revenue. His requests to Elizabeth for assistance resulted only in confirmation of his earlier grant of Irish land. He sold most of his English property to pay some of his debts, but in 1576, then only thirty-five, he died of dysentery. The widely rumored adulterous connection between Lettice and the Earl of Leicester led to gossip that Walter had been poisoned. The subsequent marriage of Leicester and the widow lent color to the gossip, but it was probably unfounded.

Robert, Walter's elder son, was nine years old when his father died. At Walter's deathbed request, William Cecil, Lord Burghley, became Robert's guardian.² Burghley was a man of outstanding ability. In 1550 he was made one of the secretaries of state and a member of the Privy Council. For the following half-century he faithfully served three children of Henry VIII and probably came closer to running his country than any other non-sovereign in Europe. On his deathbed, Walter advised his son to refrain from the Court and not trust his ear with the flatteries nor his eye with the splendor of it.³

During his final illness Walter addressed a touching appeal to Queen Elizabeth:

> ... My eldest son, upon whom the continuance of my house remains, shall lead a life far unworthy his calling, and most obscurely, if it be not helped by your Majesty's bounty and favor, for the smallness of his living, the greatness of my debt, and the dowries that go out of my lands, make the remainder little or nothing towards the reputation of an Earl's estate. But if it please your Majesty to grant to him my poor offices in Wales, the leading of 100 horse, under controlment, ... and withal would pardon my debt to your Majesty, it would not only be more than a recompense to me, but a most strong obligation whereby to tie him everlastingly to so gracious a Prince .... I do not wish him my office of Earl-Marshal here, lest you should not think him worthy of the rest; but he is my son, and may be fit for more in his life, than his unfortunate father has in his possession at his death ... and therefore it is enough that to your Majesty I com-

mit him, with humble petition that my Lord Treasurer [Lord Burghley] and my Lord Chamberlain may direct his education. (Written from Dublin Castle.)[4]

Young Earl Robert was good at his lessons. He was taught to write in both Latin and English; his letter written in Latin in his ninth year to acknowledge Burghley's guardianship shows unusual maturity.[5] He lived from time to time on his various estates, and at fourteen he received a Master of Arts degree at Cambridge. He enjoyed hunting and kindred sports but was equally fond of scholarly pursuits. His only problem was his poverty: his grandfather Knollys told the boy that the lands he had inherited were insufficient to maintain the poorest earl in England. In one letter he complained to Burghley of the scantiness of his wardrobe.[6]

When at ten the young Essex made his first appearance at Court, Queen Elizabeth offered to kiss him, but the offer was rejected; in later times the two must have often laughed over this. The marriage of Leicester, the queen's acknowledged favorite, to Robert's mother was kept secret for two years, for Elizabeth disliked Lettice as a woman of questionable morality. When she learned of the marriage she was furious, but she soon relented, and upon agreement that Lettice live in retirement away from the Court, Leicester was returned to favor. Later, Lettice made Leicester unhappy because of her improper conduct with Sir Christopher Blount, whom she married immediately after Leicester's death. Since Elizabeth was not one to forget these things, Lettice's subsequent appeals to her for clemency for her son Robert (or Essex, as we shall now refer to him) when he was in disgrace were without influence.

With Leicester as his stepfather, Essex's advancement at Court was rapid. The anti-Burghley faction, seeing Elizabeth's obvious affection for him, hoped to build him up into a real obstacle to the Burghley ambitions and pushed his career. In 1585 Essex was made General of the Horse to an expedition sent under Leicester to aid Holland. There his boldness in combat earned him a knighthood, at nineteen. Elizabeth, then fifty-two, had fallen in love (perhaps maternally at first) with the brave, handsome young man. A year later she made him Master of the Horse, and in the following year she installed him Knight of the Garter. When an expedition was sent against Spain, Essex went along secretly, against the wishes of the queen. His offer to fight any of the Spanish garrisons in Lisbon in the name of his queen brought an angry letter from Elizabeth requiring his immediate return. He was forgiven, but Elizabeth required him to repay £3,000 she had loaned him. Although this necessitated the sale of one of his manors, Elizabeth offset his loss by granting him the monopoly on sweet wines that his stepfather had enjoyed.

Only a few aspects of his meteoric rise are essential to our understanding and evaluation of his treason and trial. One was his popularity with the common people, which became so great as to make him headstrong and to create fear in Elizabeth. He displayed reckless bravery as commander of an expedition sent to France to aid Henry of Navarre but angered the queen and Burghley by knighting 21 of his followers—a significant act because a similar action later got him in trouble. Recalled from Holland by Elizabeth to protect his life from his recklessness, Essex devoted himself to political and diplomatic chores for her, effectively aided by Francis and Anthony Bacon. Anthony's ability enabled Essex soon to rival the Foreign Office in the quality of its intelligence, impressing Elizabeth but hardly pleasing Secretary Cecil.

In partial command of an expedition sent to attack the Spanish coast, Essex captured Cadiz. Against his advice, the expedition returned without awaiting the arrival of the Spanish treasure fleet from the Americas. The fleet arrived in Spain two days after the English departed, and Essex was again credited for sagacity and judgment. When his ships returned to England with loot valued at £13,000, Essex was more than ever a popular hero, but, stingy as usual, Elizabeth complained of the smallness of the amount.

Essex was now the recognized favorite of the queen, and his influence was great. Characteristically, he underestimated her, thinking that he could manage her and continue in favor despite their frequent quarrels. He once said that in order to serve the queen he was forced, like the waterman, to look one way and row another. The untruthfulness of the Court was so notorious that Bacon advised Essex to take up measures he never intended to carry out, so that in dropping them he could appear to be bending to the royal will.[7] Bacon gave his patron other advice which it would have been well for Essex to have followed: appear modest; curb extravagance; strive for political rather than military favor; and recognize that popularity with the citizens is likely to jeopardize the confidence of the queen.[8]

Elizabeth's love for Essex lasted for most of his life. At first their life together was almost idyllic. In 1587 Anthony Bagot wrote to his father that when Elizabeth was abroad nobody was near her but Essex, and at night Essex was at cards or at one game or another with her, coming not to his own lodging till birds sing in the morning.[9] Nevertheless, theirs was a trying and often quarrelsome relationship. Essex was not an easy man to get along with, nor was Elizabeth noted for evenness of temper. According to William Camden, a shrewd observer of what was going on at Court,

> the Queen heaped upon Essex fresh honors and favors every day, and had a particular value for him, because he was a brave soldier, and cut out for a camp, [but as] soon as he had got a secure and real interest in the favor of his royal mistress, he made it his business to outstrip all persons, whether of his own or a superior rank; and this was a quarrel which the more politic courtiers had to him; especially when he took upon him to disparage all whose actions were not of his own square, . . . Nor was he excusable in his deportment to the Queen herself, whom he treated with a sort of insolence, that seemed to proceed rather from a mind that wanted ballast, than any real pride in him; though it looked the more ungrateful, because acted when he had more than once been restored to the Queen's favor, and received fresh instances of her bounty. However, this unhandsome carriage, and a way which he had of screwing (as it were) favors from her, joined with a coldness and disrespect towards her person, and backed by the sly management of some that wished him not well, failed not by degrees to lessen, and at the long run to extinguish entirely the Queen's affection for him. Indeed he was a person not rightly calculated for a Court, as being not easily brought to any mean compliances . . . so far was he from being capable of dissembling a resentment, that as Cuffe [Essex's secretary] used to complain to me, he carried his passions in his forehead, and the friend or the enemy were easily read in his face.[10]

Other writers, while recognizing the justice of parts of Camden's criticism, found in Essex a generosity, truthfulness and warmheartedness that made friends, and a quickness to admit it if he found himself in the wrong. He was thought unfortunate that the queen's love for him put him into positions for which he was not fitted.[11] Carte praised the beauty of his person, the frankness of his heart, the attachment he showed to his friends, the liberality he extended to all who wanted it and the zeal he manifested on all occasions for the service and glory of his country. Nevertheless, Carte recognized the inability of Essex to exercise his Privy Councillorship with art or prudence and thought him "not rightly cut out for a Court, since he knew not how to dissemble, cringe, or stoop to mean compliances."[12]

The Duke of Bouillon, the French envoy to Elizabeth, understood the relationship well. When Elizabeth complained to Bouillon that Essex was willful, rash and would not be ruled, but that she would bridle and stay him, the duke replied, as he later told Reynolds, Essex's secretary, that her Majesty, in his opinion, might easily govern his lordship, who was a man of virtue, wisdom, judgment and obedience, and whose actions were wholly destined to her service and the good of her state, but that she might not seek to rule him with an iron bridle, but with a golden bridle, not as sovereign only, but as mistress also. "Well," Elizabeth replied, "I will both rule him, and stay him."

At first their quarrels were quickly ended. After one in 1597 Essex wrote her, "Since I was first so happy as to know what love meant, I was never one day nor one hour free from love and jealousy, and, as long as you do me right, they are the inseparable companions of my life." In 1598 he wrote, "I do confess that, as a man, I have been more subject to your natural beauty than as a subject to the power of a king."

As time went on, however, their spats grew more frequent and more difficult to make up. A famous quarrel occurred in 1598. One present reported that it involved a pretty warm dispute between the queen and Essex about the choice of some fit and able person to superintend the affairs of Ireland. When the queen could by no means be persuaded to approve his choice, Essex quite forgot himself and his duty and turned his back upon his sovereign in a kind of contempt. The queen was not able to bear this insolence and so gave Essex a box on the ear and bade him go and be hanged. He immediately clapped his hand on his sword, and with the lord admiral's stepping in between, Essex swore a great oath that he neither could nor would put up with an affront of that nature, nor would he have taken it at the hands of Henry VIII himself. In a great passion, he immediately withdrew from Court.[13] Each was too stubborn for several months to move toward a reconciliation, but eventually they tired of the quarrel. Thus when Essex offered his services to assist in the projected Irish expedition, Elizabeth accepted, and they were soon together as much as always. Nevertheless, the scar remained.

We can understand the things which ended in Essex's trial for treason and can judge the justice of the verdict only in the light of the real relationship between Elizabeth and Essex. If we accept the theory that her love for him was frustrated by inability to consummate that love, or by knowledge that her love for no man could ripen into the bearing of children, her treatment of Essex becomes psychologically more understandable. She was constantly promising to marry, she was frequently in love, there was great talk about whether her offspring should be permitted to succeed to the throne, but always she drew back, sometimes at the last minute. Why? If no certain answer, we yet have clues.

When Henry VIII died, Elizabeth, then fourteen, was sent to live with the queen, Catherine Parr. Lord Seymour wished to marry Elizabeth. When the Council refused, Seymour accepted the next best chance at power and secretly married the queen. Seymour, although twenty years older than Elizabeth, was a dashing figure. Elizabeth saw him in a romantic aura, and Seymour lost no opportunity to fondle and make half-joking, half-earnest love to her. Wearing only his nightgown, he went frequently to Elizabeth's bedroom before she was up and threatened to crawl in with her. Finally, Catherine entered Elizabeth's room unexpectedly and found her in Seymour's arms: Elizabeth was sent to live elsewhere. Elizabeth Jenkins, who has devoted much study to the life and character of Elizabeth, thinks that this early warring of sexual excitement with dread of what might result did her nervous system and her sexual development an injury and created in her a psychotic fear of sex and motherhood from which she never recovered. Further, the fact, frequently mentioned later, that her monthly periods were few or none may have been accounted for by this shock and emotional strain.[14] Nevertheless, Elizabeth's affection, possibly even love, for Seymour was real, and it was popularly believed that she had been made pregnant by him.

Her longest and deepest love was for Robert Dudley, whom she made Earl of Leicester. He was her acknowledged favorite until his death thirty years after the start of their relationship. Even before the mysterious death of his wife, Amy Robsart, the Spanish envoy wrote that Elizabeth visited his apartment day and night. There is ample evidence that their relations were exceedingly intimate for at least ten years after she became queen. Many believed that they had two or more children and were probably secretly married. At one time when she thought she was dying, Elizabeth swore that nothing improper had passed between Leicester and her, but in the same breath she asked that a large pension be paid to the servant who slept in his bedchamber—a rather revealing request. It is quite possible that Elizabeth may have considered unchastity or impropriety to be reached only with actual commission of the sexual act and that she did not regard lying naked in bed with a man as "improper."

There is evidence that Elizabeth had a physical deformity which would have prevented conception or childbearing. William Drummond, close friend of Ben Jonson and relative of the Stuart kings, wrote, "She had a membrane on her, which made her incapable of man, though for her delight she tried many. At the coming over of Monsieur [the Duke of Savoy, a French suitor], there was a French surgeon who took in hand to cut it, yet fear stayed her. . . ."[15] This is also asserted by Froude. On the other hand, several physicians who examined her in behalf of various royal suitors certified that she could bear children, and this appears to have been the opinion of Burghley, who was in possession of as much evidence as anyone. Nevertheless, when Burghley told her that Mary Stuart had borne a son, Elizabeth almost wept and said, "The Queen of Scots is the mother of a fair son, and I am but a barren stock."[16]

Beyond question, Elizabeth wanted masculine admiration avidly. Her vanity demanded ardent courtship, and she was convinced of the charms of her body. When De Maisse, the French ambassador, was received by Elizabeth in 1597, he found her dressed with her gown open down the front like a dressing gown, under it a soft lawn chemise, also open, both held together at the waist by a girdle. Elizabeth, he said, repeatedly cast open the dress with both hands as though she were too hot, "et lui voyait-on tout l'estomac jusques au nombril."[17] De Maisse did not say whether he found this view of the ancient, royal stomach clear to the navel aesthetically pleasing.

The treaty prepared for her marriage to the Duke of Anjou contained detailed provisions about their children, on which subject Elizabeth took great care. Nevertheless, when she sat down with pen in hand to sign the contract, she threw it away in a great fury and, turning to the lords of her Council, asked them in a reproachful manner if they did not know that marriage would soon put an end to her days—which was generally interpreted to mean some bodily infirmity that rendered conception and childbearing exceedingly difficult. Since the queen was now in her forty-ninth year, this all seems pretty optimistic. Perhaps it is significant that a reservation was also added to the marriage contract signed by the commissioners, saying: "But Queen Elizabeth is not bound to consummate the marriage, till she and the Duke shall satisfy one another in certain points, and which shall be certified to the French King in writing within six weeks."[18]

In her early thirties, Elizabeth seemed to have fallen badly in love with young Lord Hatton, who either reciprocated her love or was a remarkable dissembler. His relations with her are said to have been very intimate, and certainly his letters were: "Would God I were with you but for one hour. My wits are overwrought with thoughts. I find myself amazed. Bear with me, my most dear, sweet lady. Passion overcomes me. I can write no more. Love me, for I love you."[19] When the queen's fancy turned to the Earl of Oxford, Hatton was crestfallen and reproachful. His friend Dyer gave him some good advice on self-control, one sentence of which may be meaningful: "For though in the beginning when her Majesty sought you . . . , she did bear with rugged dealing of yours, until she had what she fancied, yet now, after satiety and fullness, it will rather hurt than help you. . . ."[20] Mary Stuart once accused Elizabeth of having promised marriage with Leicester and with sleeping infinite times with him with all the license and extreme familiarity which can be indulged in between husband and wife, but of indubitably being not as other women. Hence, said Mary Stuart, it was complete folly on the part of those who would have her marry the Duke of Anjou to count on the marriage. Mary gave the Countess of Shrewsbury as her authority for saying that the queen made love so desperately to Hatton before the whole Court that he for very shame had to retire.[21] As to Mary's statement, "You are not like other women," Hallam quotes Camden as saying the people cursed Huic, the queen's physician, for having dissuaded the queen from marrying on account of some impediment and defect in her.[22]

What could be the most persuasive evidence of Elizabeth's ability to procreate was found some fifty years or more ago by Martin Hume in Volume Four of "The Spanish Calendar of Elizabeth" at Simancas, Spain. Briefly, a young Englishman was arrested in Spain in 1587 and accused of being a spy (the Spanish Armada was being assembled for the attack on England at that time). The young man claimed to be Arthur Dudley, son of Queen Elizabeth and Leicester, brought up by one Robert Southern. He gave many details of his early life and his connection with well-known persons of the Court. In 1583 Southern, apparently mortally ill, sent for Dudley and told him that he was the son of the queen by Leicester. He was sent to and spent several days with Leicester in England before returning to the Continent. In Spain, he offered his services to the King of Spain and suggested that he write to Leicester in the hope that Leicester would acknowledge him and help him to the English crown, after which he would cause England to make friends with Spain. This proposal held such possibilities of a terrific explosion that the king's English secretary recommended holding the young man tight in a monastery. Nothing further about him appears in the Spanish Calendar. Hume says the fact that Dudley, Leicester's son, did tell this story in Spain is substantiated by several records, and that the dates, persons and collateral details have all stood up when checked.[23]

TWO

Essex now began the series of mistakes which were to lead him to the scaffold. For years England had been attempting to subdue a rebellion in Ireland led by O'Neill, Earl of Tyrone, and backed by King Philip of Spain. The English had subdued Tyrone before and had accepted his promises of good behavior, which were never kept. Finally the Council decided it would compromise no longer and that Tyrone must be crushed. Essex was unwilling to approve any of the tentative selections of a leader for the proposed expedition. Finally, perhaps in hope of redeeming his father's misfortunes in Ireland, or perhaps because his jealousy would not permit him to see anyone else made lord lieutenant of Ireland, Essex persuaded Elizabeth to name him to the post. The office was the most exalted of all outside England, and in England only the lord treasurer had more power.[1]

Essex must have realized he was gambling. If he won, nothing could stop his success at home, but if he lost, his fortunes would suffer. His enemies on the Council, feeling that he might be in a trap, confirmed the appointment. Perhaps even Elizabeth was not certain of his capacity and loyalty. When Essex appointed Sir Christopher Blount and young Lord Southampton his chief aides, Elizabeth vetoed both appointments. Blount, perhaps because upon Leicester's death he had married her, now thoroughly disliked cousin Lettice, and Southampton because he had secretly married one of her ladies-in-waiting. Essex objected; the queen stood firm; the two men accompanied Essex to Ireland without official status and were used by him in the capacities he had originally intended.

Essex had been previously censured for making knights of too many men in his command. He was now specifically instructed not to do so. He requested sealed permission from Elizabeth to return at

11

will after a year, and Chamberlain wrote Carleton on March 15, 1599, that although the earl had all his demands, the queen showing herself very gracious and willing to content him, the clause of liberty to return at pleasure was not inserted in the patent, and it had to pass by virtue of the broad seal itself.[2]

Arriving in Ireland, Essex created fifty-nine more knights, for which he was later censured by the Council. "It is much marveled," Chamberlain wrote Carleton on August 23, "that this humor should so possess him, that, not content with his first dozens and scores, he should thus fall to huddle them up by half hundreds, and it is noted as a strange thing that a subject in the space of seven or eight years (not having been six months together in any one action) should upon so little service and small desert, make more knights than are in all the realm besides, and it is . . . [thought] that if he continue his course he will shortly bring in tag and rag, cut and long tail, and so draw the order into contempt."[3]

Sanderson noted Elizabeth's anger at this violation of her instructions and thought Essex was trying to build up adherents for an attempt against the government. Sanderson claimed to have seen letters about it between Essex and his uncle, Francis Knollys, "by which there appears, even from the beginning of that employment, a very plain and intentional resolution in Essex to make himself master of his own ambition, and by this ways and means to effect it."[4] We must take into consideration that Sanderson, strongly pro-sovereign, may have felt obligated to be anti-Essex.

At the suggestion of the English Council in Dublin, Essex disregarded his instructions from the Council in England (the higher authority) that he stay in Leinster and go after Tyrone. He made forays in other directions, usually successful, but costly in men. These losses, together with disease and desertions, reduced his army by three-fourths before Elizabeth, out of patience, ordered him to proceed immediately against Tyrone. Essex wrote her that he felt it wise to wait until he had more troops. She expressed to Bacon, who was with her when she read the letter, her passionate distaste of his lordship's proceedings in Ireland as unfortunate, without judgment, contemptuous and not without some private end of his own. Bacon replied:

> . . . I would think that if you had my Lord of Essex here with a white staff in his hand, as my Lord of Leicester had, and contin-

ued him still about you, for society to yourself, and for an honor and ornament to your attendants and court, in the eyes of your people, and in the eyes of foreign ambassadors, then were he in his right element. For to discontent him as you do, and yet to put arms and power into his hands, may be a kind of temptation to make him prove cumbersome and unruly.[5]

Essex finally encountered Tyrone on September 3. Tyrone declined to fight and cajoled Essex into a private interview. There is no record that anyone else was present at the meeting, and there is dispute as to exactly what was said, but there is in the Trevelyan Papers an account written by an apparently distant witness, probably amplified with information obtained later, which has the ring of authority. According to this account, the opposing forces were lined up on two hills about two miles apart. Each general rode down to the stream between the hills. Tyrone removed his head covering, did "his humble duty" to Essex and embarked on a long speech. He reminded Essex that he had married the sister of Sir Henry Bagnall and admitted that his attention to two other women had aroused her jealousy, whereupon she asked her brother to complain to the Council of Ireland and to "exhibit Articles against Tyrone." For this the Council proclaimed him a traitor, and Tyrone began the rebellion in order to save his head. He flattered Essex by claiming that until Essex was in command he had never dared trust his life to an English commander, but now because of his love for Elizabeth, for Essex's father and for Essex's reputation for honor and keeping his promises, he would yield himself to Essex, requesting him to ask the queen for mercy, after which he swore to be a most true and loyal subject.

Essex replied: "If I were sure you would not violate your oath and promise as heretofore you have already done, I would be very well content to speak to the Queen for you and in hope that you will keep your promise this time, I will send messengers with a written agreement which if you will sign and send pledges for its performance I will submit to the Queen and ask her to have mercy." The account says further that Articles were sent, were signed and were forwarded to the Court, as a result of which all hoped for peace and that Tyrone would become a true subject.[6]

Letters Essex now received from Elizabeth made it plain that the fat was definitely in the fire. Essex conceived that his only hope of forgiveness and justification lay in a personal meeting with Elizabeth. His first thought was to return to England at the head of a substantial part of his army, but Blount persuaded him that this action might be misinterpreted. On September 28, 1599, Essex, accompanied by six attendants and only a handful of soldiers, arrived in England. Spedding implies that Essex took so many soldiers with him on his return to London that had an attempt to arrest him been made, the Court would have been endangered, but Essex swore that not more than ten accompanied him after he reached shore and that only six men went with him to the Court.[7] One of Elizabeth's last letters had warned Essex not to leave Ireland without her specific permission, and his trepidation can be imagined.

Roland Whyte, in a series of letters written from the Court to Sir Robert Sidney, kept him up-to-date on Essex's misfortunes. Of the arrival of Essex at Court he wrote:

> Upon Michaelmas Eve, about ten o'clock in the morning, my Lord of Essex lighted at Court Gate in post, and made all haste up to the Presence, and so to the privy chamber, and stayed not till he came to the Queen's bedchamber, where he found the Queen newly up, the hair about her face; he kneeled unto her, kissed her hands, and had some private speech with her, which seemed to give him great contentment; for coming from her Majesty to go change his clothes in his chamber, he was very pleasant, and thanked God, though he had suffered much trouble and storms abroad, he found a sweet calm at home. 'Tis much wondered at here, that he went so boldly to her Majesty's presence, she not being ready, and he so full of dirt and mire that his very face was full of it. About eleven he was ready and went up again to the Queen, and conferred with her till half an hour after twelve. As yet all was well, and her usage very gracious toward him. He went to dinner, and during all that time discoursed merely of his travels and journeys in Ireland, of the goodness of the country, the civilities of the nobility that are true subjects, of the great entertainment he had in their houses, of the good order he found there. He was visited frankly by all sorts here of lords and ladies, and gentlemen: Only strangeness is observed between him and Mr. Secretary and that party.... Then he went up to the [apartment of the] Queen, but found her much changed in that small time, for she began to call him to question for his return, and was not satisfied in the manner of his coming away; and leaving all things at so great

hazard. She appointed the Lords to hear him, and so they went to Council in the afternoon.[8]

It is not hard to understand Elizabeth's inconsistent behavior. She was completely surprised when Essex burst in on her, and her first emotion may have been one of pleasure at seeing him again. This was doubtless succeeded by caution. She had no means of knowing how large a retinue he may have brought with him and whether her throne was in jeopardy. As he told his story, she must have begun to realize that she was not in present danger. After dinner, a daytime meal, she had opportunity to investigate, and once reassured she became less agreeable. She had an informal meeting with her Council, and before midnight Essex was under house arrest.

Whyte wrote Sidney that between ten and eleven o'clock at night on the day of his return, a command came to Essex from the queen to keep his chamber. On the next day the Council met in the morning. Essex was sent for at two o'clock. All rose to greet him, then sat down while he stood bareheaded as the secretary "in divers articles, delivered the offenses her Majesty conceived he had done against her." These were: his contemptuous disobedience of her Majesty's letters and will in returning; his presumptuous letters written from time to time; his proceedings in Ireland, contrary to the points resolved upon before he went; his rash manner of leaving Ireland; his overbold entrance on the previous day to her Majesty's presence in her bedchamber; his making of so many idle knights. It was said that never had man answered with more temper, more gravity or discretion than did Essex to these matters laid to his charge. The Council then reported to Elizabeth, who said that she'd think things over.[9]

After another day without any evidence of a popular uprising or other trouble, Elizabeth felt secure enough to commit Essex to the custody of his warm friend, Lord Keeper Egerton, at Egerton's residence, York House. After he had won a case against her some years before, Elizabeth had made Egerton solicitor general "to prevent its happening again." He subsequently became attorney general, lord keeper and finally lord chancellor, as which he presided over Essex's hearings, and later, as lord high steward, he presided over the murder trial of the third Countess of Essex.

On October 6 Whyte wrote that Lady Walsingham, the mother of Essex's wife, had made humble suit to the queen that "she would be pleased to give the Earl leave to write to his lady, who was newly delivered, and extremely troubled that she neither saw him, nor heard from him." At first the request was not granted, and he did not know if it had been yet. This, Whyte thought, showed that her Majesty's heart had hardened toward Essex. Further, Essex was said to be very ill and troubled with a flux; no man went to him, nor did he want to see any.[10]

Many weeks passed with no further action, during which Essex fretted himself more and more ill. His repentant letters to the queen, couched in the most affectionate and passionate language, went unanswered. In these letters he displayed extreme mortification with the sense of his condition, declared that he had discarded all the gaieties of life and drowned his ambition in his tears, and that he had but one request to make to Elizabeth — that she would let her servant depart in peace. One letter read in part:

> I come to consider how large a measure of his grace, and how great a resemblance of his power, God hath given you upon earth; and how many ways he giveth occasion to you to exercise these divine offices upon us, that are your vassals. . . . I acknowledge upon the knees of my heart your Majesty's infinite goodness in granting my humble petition [to spare him the humiliation of a Star Chamber trial]. God, who seeth all, is witness, how faithfully I do vow to dedicate the rest of my life, next after my highest duty, in obedience, faith, and zeal to your Majesty, without admitting any other worldly care; and whatsoever your Majesty resolveth to do with me, I shall live and die, your Majesty's humblest vassal, ESSEX.[11]

A letter to Essex from Tyrone, saying that he could not persuade O'Donnell to agree to the Articles of Peace, again aroused Elizabeth's anger. She refused to follow the Council's advice to release Essex, nor did his serious illness soften her. When John Harrington, her godson, returned from Ireland, where he had been commander of horse to Southampton, he waited for the queen to announce his return. He later wrote in his diary that when he entered her chamber, she exclaimed, "What, did that fool bring you too? Go back to your business." The entry continues:

She catched my girdle when I kneeled to her, and swore, "By God's Son I am no queen; that *man* is above me; — Who gave him command to come here so soon? I did send him on other business." It was long before more gracious discourse did fall to my hearing; but I was then put out of my trouble, and bid "Go home." I did not stay to be bidden twice; if all the Irish rebels had been at my heels, I should not have had better speed, for I did now flee from one whom I both loved and feared too.[12]

Elizabeth wanted to bring Essex to trial in the Star Chamber. It was becoming apparent that the people felt their idol unfairly treated, and Elizabeth wished to put on record and to publish the list of his offenses and the inadequacy of his answers. Both Bacon and the Council advised against it. As a compromise, a number of the Council members met in the Star Chamber on November 29 and made a public declaration of the reasons for the earl's confinement.

Essex was now so near death that his wife was allowed to see him. On December 15, 1599, Whyte wrote to Sidney:

Upon Thursday last, by her Majesty's command, hearing that the Earl of Essex was desperately sick, eight physicians of the best experience assembled and consulted what might speedily recover him to health; who sent in writing their opinion to her Majesty... that these things were required; to have his mind quieted; that he might take rest; that he might have recreation; that he might change the air, for they found his liver stopped and perished; that his entrails and guts were exulcerated, that they could not tell what now to minister, but gentle clysters to keep him clean within. Her Majesty very graciously understanding the state he was in, was very pensive and grieved, and sent Doctor James unto him with some broth. Her message was, that he should comfort himself, and that she would, if she might with her honor, go to visit him; and it was noted that she had water in her eyes when she spoke it. Some comfort it brought to the Earl, but it is thought and feared, that it comes very late, for nature is decayed, and he so feeble, that to make his bed he is removed upon sheets and blankets. Her Majesty commanded he should be removed from that chamber he was in, to my Lord Keeper's own chamber, in the same house.[13]

Essex began to make gradual improvement. On February 14, 1600, Whyte wrote that Essex had written a most submissive letter, delivered to the queen by Secretary Cecil, who did his best to dissuade her from having Essex called to the Star Chamber. He succeeded and was said to have won much honor and love by it. Whyte thought Cecil not so adverse to the earl as was supposed, but rather that it was Elizabeth who was wounded by the earl's contemptuous courses and was not easily to be satisfied.[14]

Elizabeth now permitted Essex to move into his own house in London but kept him in custody there. His wife was permitted to see him during the day, they walked and read to each other in the gardens and on the "leads,"[15] and he played an occasional game of tennis. He thanked Elizabeth by letter:

> ... Your princely and compassionate increasing of my liberty hath enabled me to wrestle with my many infirmities, which else long ere this had made an end of me. And now this farther degree of goodness in favorably removing me to mine own house doth sound in mine ears, as if your Majesty spoke these words, *Die not, Essex; for tho' I punish thine offense, and humble thee for thy good, yet I will one day be served again by thee.* And my prostrate soul makes this answer, *I hope for that blessed day.* All my afflictions of body or mind are humbly, patiently and cheerfully borne by, Your Majesty's humblest vassal, ESSEX.[16]

His letter sounded fine, but by May 20 Essex was again eaten with impatience for restoration of his honors and duties. He wrote Elizabeth, reminding her that he had been told several times that she meant to correct but not to ruin him, yet since she had said that, he had languished for four months, had almost died but, nevertheless, kissed her fair correcting hand and relied on her words. He told himself, he wrote, that there was no mean between ruin and her favor, that if she bestowed favor again she would give with it all things, but that it now looked to him as though he would have no means to care for his friends and faithful servants, that people who had once envied him his happiness now hated him and that the lowest people could say of him what they would and would shortly be caricaturing him on the stage. Further, although this was to him worse than death, it was still not the worst of his destiny, since Elizabeth regarded his eight months of imprisonment, illness, beggary and infamy too little punishment, rejected his letters and refused to hear of him, which to traitors she never did. It seemed that nothing remained for him but to beg her on his knees to conclude his misery and his life together so that he might go to his Saviour, whom he heard calling him out of the world in which he had lived too long and once thought himself too happy.[17]

The letter was not answered, but Elizabeth thought it time to end the impasse. She told Bacon that she had found him to be correct in advising against the earlier informal statement by the Council in the Star Chamber, that it had merely created factions among the people without deciding anything and that she now wanted a formal Star Chamber trial in which Essex would have to make his answer. After the verdict she could pardon him to an extent which would correct but not destroy him (the same expression she had used before). Bacon and the Council again dissuaded her but agreed to summon Essex to appear before a special commission to be assembled at York House.

Eighteen commissioners were appointed for the hearing. They included the Archbishop of Canterbury; Lord Keeper Egerton; the lord treasurer; the lord admiral; a number of peers; Essex's uncle, William Knollys; Secretary Cecil; the two chief justices; the lord chief baron; and two other justices. The hearing was held on June 5, 1600; the commissioners sat from eight in the morning until nine at night. At Essex's entrance, none of the commissioners gave any sign of courtesy. He kneeled at the upper end of the table, but having gone a while without a cushion, at last room was made for him and he was allowed a cushion but still was forced to kneel till the end of the queen's serjeant's speech, when with the consent of the lords he was permitted to stand up and afterward, upon the archbishop's motion, to have a stool.[18]

No full report of the hearing is available. Bacon later drew up an account, but only a fragment remains. Birch gives a rather detailed account taken from Fynes Morison's "History of Ireland." Few notes were ordinarily kept by the Council, even when it was sitting as a court. A Council was part of the household of any great magnate, including the king's, and its records frequently appeared only in the household books and ordinances.[19] However, Elizabeth's Council apparently kept some record of its proceedings, since she ordered that in this case there be "no register nor clerk to take this sentence, nor no record or memorial made up of this proceeding."[20] Nevertheless, when Essex was permitted to stand up, he found before him two clerks of the Council, the one to read, the other as a register. Any account which the register may have kept was not published or preserved; the following is the Morison-Birch report, somewhat abridged:

THE YORK HOUSE ARRAIGNMENT

The Lord Keeper Egerton first opened the cause of their meeting, and then directed the Queen's counsel at law, to inform against the Earl.

The Queen's serjeant, Christopher Yelverton, . . . began a short speech as a preface to the accusations. The sum of it was to declare her Majesty's princely care and provision for the wars of Ireland, and likewise her gracious dealing with the Earl before he went over thither, in discharging £10,000 of his debts, and giving him almost as much more to buy him horses, and provide himself, and especially in her proceedings in this cause, since after so great occasions of offense, as the consumption of a royal army, fruitless wasting of a vast sum of money, contempt, and disobedience to her express commandment, she notwithstanding was content to be so merciful towards him, as not to proceed against him in any of her courts of justice, but only in this private sort by way of mercy and favor.

The Attorney General Coke spoke next, whose speech contained the substance of the accusation, and was very severe. For besides the many faults of contempt and disobedience, with which he charged the Earl, he also inferred a dangerous disposition and purpose in his lordship, and this he aggravated by many rhetorical amplifications. . . . In his speech were contained five special crimes charged on the Earl: I. His making the Earl of Southampton General of the Horse; II. His going to Leinster and Munster, when he should have gone to Ulster; III. His making so many knights; IV. His conference with Tyrone; V. His return out of Ireland, contrary to her Majesty's command. . . .

The first was amplified by the Attorney General, because his lordship did it contrary to her Majesty's mind plainly signified to him in England: That he increased that offense by continuing the Earl of Southampton in the office, when her Majesty had by letters expressly commanded, that he should be displaced; . . . The second point of his southern journey was aggravated, as contrary to her Majesty's advised resolution agreed upon by her Council: . . . from which conduct of his followed the harrowing out and weakening of the most royal army, that ever went out of England, the wasting of a vast expense, and the overthrow of the whole action. The third point, the making of knights, was agreed to have been contrary to her Majesty's express commandment . . . that he should make but few, and those men of good ability, whereas he had made to the number of threescore, and those some of his menial servants; . . . The fourth point, his conference with Tyrone, was . . . shameful in the conclusion of it, that a wretched traitor should prescribe conditions to his sovereign, odious and abominable conditions, a public toleration of an idolatrous religion, pardon for himself and all the traitors in Ireland, and full restitution of lands and possessions to all sorts of them. . . . The fifth and last point, his return, was urged to be intolerably presumptuous, contrary to her Majesty's express commandment in writing. . . : That this return was also exceedingly dangerous, since he left the army divided between two, the Earl of Ormond and the Lord Chancellor, men whom [he] himself had excepted against as unfit for such a trust; and that he left this army in such a manner, that if God's providence had not been the greater, the ruin and loss of the whole kingdom had ensued thereupon.

This accusation was heightened in every part of it by all the rhetoric and bitterness of expression, which the Attorney General was master of, who concluded, that the ingress was proud and ambitious, the progress disobedient and contemptuous, and the regress notorious and dangerous. . . . He proposed in the end a precedent for the Earl's punishment, being forced, he said, to seek far for one gentle enough; and that was of William of Britten, Earl of Richmond, who refusing to come home out of France upon the king's letter, was adjudged to lose all his goods, lands, and chattels, and to endure perpetual imprisonment. . . .

The Solicitor General Fleming . . . [then spoke, after which] Mr. Francis Bacon concluded the accusation with a very eloquent speech; first, by way of preface, signifying that he hoped the Earl himself and all who heard him would consider that the particular bond of duty, which he did and ever would acknowledge himself to owe to his lordship, was now to be sequestered and laid aside. He then extolled her Majesty's singular grace and mercy, of which, he observed, the Earl was an eminent instance, upon whose humble suit she was content not to prosecute him in her court of justice, the Star Chamber, but, according to his earnest desire, to remove that cup from him (which he said were his lordship's own words in his letter) and now to suffer his cause to be heard *intra privatos parietes,* by way of mercy and favor only, where no manner of disloyalty was laid to his charge: For, added he, if that had been the question, this had not been the place. After considering particularly the Earl's journey into Ireland, he came to charge his lordship with two points not spoken of before. . . .

The special points of the whole accusation were afterwards proved by the Earl's own letters, and some of her Majesty's and the Council's, and by a letter of the Earl of Ormond, and others of the Council of Ireland, read by the clerk of the Council.

The accusation being ended the Earl, kneeling, began to speak for himself to this effect; that ever since it had pleased her Majesty to remove that cup from him (which he acknowledged to have been at his humble suit) and to change the course of proceeding against him, which was intended to be in the Star Chamber, he had laid aside all thought of justifying himself in any of his actions; and that therefore he had now resolved with himself never to make any contestation with his sovereign; that he had made a divorce betwixt himself and the world, if God and his sovereign would give him leave to hold it; that the inward sorrow and afflictions, which he had laid upon his soul privately betwixt God and his conscience for the great offense against her Majesty, was more than any outward cross or affliction which could possibly befall him; that he would never excuse himself either *a toto* or *a tanto* from whatsoever crimes of error, negligence, or inconsiderate rashness, his youth, folly, or manifold infirmities might lead him into. Only he must ever profess a loyal, faithful, unspotted heart, unfeigned affection, and desire ever to do her Majesty the best service he could, which rather than he would lose he would, if Christianity and charity permitted, first tear his heart out of his breast with his own hands. But this being always preserved untouched, he was most willing to confess whatever errors and faults it pleased her Majesty to impute to him.

The first part of his lordship's speech drew plenty of tears from the eyes of many of the hearers, for it was uttered with great passion, and the expressions well chosen and very forcible; and it plainly appeared that he had intended to have spoken no more for himself. But being touched, as it seemed, with the over sharp speeches of his accusers, he humbly desired their lordships that as he had observed many rhetorical inferences and insinuations thrown out by his accusers which might argue a disloyal, malicious, wicked and corrupt affection in him, they would give him leave, not in any sort to excuse himself, but only by way of explanation to lay before them those false guides which had deceived him and had led him into all his errors: And so he entered into a kind of answer to the Attorney General's speech from point to point in order. . . . That in making the Earl of

Southampton General of the Horse, . . . after he perceived her Majesty's mind plainly in her second letter, he displaced him the next day. . . . For his making of knights he pleaded the necessity and straits to which he was reduced, that being the only way which he had to retain the volunteers, the strength and pride of the army; that he had knighted but two of his servants, . . .

But before he had thus gone through half his answer, he was interrupted by the Lord Keeper [Egerton], who told him that this was not the course that was likely to do him good; that he began well in submitting himself to her Majesty's mercy and pardon, which he and the rest of the lords were glad to hear; and no doubt her princely and gracious nature was by that way most likely to be inclined to favor; that all extenuation of his offense was but the lessening of her Majesty's mercy in pardoning; that he, with all the other lords, would clear him of all suspicion of disloyalty; and that therefore he might do well to spare the rest of his speech, and save time, and commit himself to her Majesty's mercy. . . .

Then the Lord Treasurer began to speak, and clearing the Earl from all suspicion of disloyalty, confuted several of his other excuses.

Secretary Cecil next, after . . . acquitting his lordship of all thoughts of disloyalty, . . . examined his lordship's excuses, . . . He gave, however, the Earl his right always, and showed more courtesy to him than any other; but said, that the Earl in all his journey did nothing else but make, as it were, circles of errors, which were all bound up in the unhappy knot of his disobedient return. He gave the Earl free liberty to interrupt him at any time in his speech. But his lordship being contented with the opinion of loyalty so clearly reserved to him, was most willing to bear the whole burden of the rest of the accusation, and therefore never used any further reply, except a few words, on occasion of a question or two. . . .

In conclusion the Earl protested . . . that he yielded himself wholly to her Majesty's mercy and favor, and was ready to offer up his poor carcass to her, he would not say to do (for alas! he had no faculties) but to suffer whatever her Majesty should inflict upon him. He requested all the lords to make a just, honorable and favorable report of his disordered speeches, which had fallen from him in such sort as his aching head, and body weakened with sickness, would give him leave to use.

The lords then proceeded to the censure; and the Lord Keeper began with observing that the throne is established by justice and clemency; that her Majesty had reserved mercy to herself; but for the satisfaction of her justice she had appointed them to inquire into the cause. They were to examine only into these faults of contempt and disobedience laid to the Earl, and to censure him accordingly: but had nothing to do with mercy, which God only was to work in her Majesty's breast....The Lord Keeper concluded with this censure: "If this cause had been heard in the Star Chamber, my sentence must have been as great a fine as ever was set upon any man's head in that court, and perpetual imprisonment in that place which belongs to a man of his quality, the Tower. But now that we are in another place, and in a course of favor, my censure is, that he is not to execute the office of a Councillor nor to hold himself for a Councillor of State, nor to execute the office of Earl Marshall of England, nor of Master of the Ordnance; and to return to his own house, there to continue a prisoner as before, till it shall please her Majesty to release both this and all the rest."

After the Lord Keeper, all the rest in order gave their censures (amplifying her Majesty's clemency and the Earl's offenses), according to the manner in the Star Chamber; and all agreed to this censure, for so they called it, and not a sentence. The greater part of the day was spent in their censures, many of which were long, only those of the noblemen, not Councillors, were short....

They all seemed by their speeches to conceive a sure hope of her Majesty's releasing this censure; and the Earl himself was reasonably cheerful; only his body seemed weak and distempered with sickness; and now and then he showed most manifest tokens of sorrow for his offense to her Majesty, by tears in his eyes, especially in the first part of his own speech, and during that of the Lord Keeper. After they had all passed their censures, he desired them to intercede with her Majesty for grace and mercy, since there had appeared in his offenses no disloyalty towards her, only ignorance and indiscretion in himself. His behavior throughout the whole proceeding, and especially his patience in hearing all that was said against him, was admired by everyone present; and many were affected in a manner which drew tears from them.[21]

A later Devereux referred to the hearing as an unconstitutional and novel tribunal, but he may have been prejudiced. Novel it was, but it is doubtful that it was unconstitutional. The hearing was essentially a judicial act of the Council, represented by some of its members and some invited assistance from non-members. Judicial jurisdiction was one of the common functions of the Council.

At the time of the conquest, the King of England and the Duke of Normandy each had a central court or council made up of the country's important men. In England this council was known as the Witan and in Normandy as the Curia Ducia. This council, as Normanized in England, became the Curia Regis. Its functions were legislative, administrative and judicial. Legislation under Henry II, prescribing wide civil and criminal jurisdiction for the Curia Regis, merely confirmed its recognized status as a court.

The Council had exercised judicial power for 135 years after the Magna Carta without being supposed to have violated that charter. As trials grew more complex, the judicial sessions of the Curia Regis came to be attended only by the members and officials of the Court who were familiar with such matters. Henry VIII wanted to make more use of the Council for legislative and administrative deliberation, but it became so busy in the Star Chamber that he created a Privy Council to assist.[22] At his death, only nineteen of his Privy Council were nobles. Few or none of them took part in the judicial sessions except in the case of state trials, and not many participated even in those. The Council's judicial work came to be left mostly to the chancellor, the judges and the clerks, although the Privy Council maintained its right to participate in or reject Star Chamber judgments and to supervise judicial administration.

Nevertheless, the Star Chamber should not be thought of as a court apart from the Council. The Star "Chamber" was really a three-story building used by the Council for various purposes. The chamber in which the Council sat for most of its judicial sessions had a ceiling decorated with stars, hence those sessions gradually became known as Star Chamber sessions and finally as the Court of the Star Chamber, but the use of that name indicated no change in makeup or function. When the Council or the Privy Council (which was merely the inner circle of the Council) sat in the Star Chamber, serjeants, judges and attorneys usually attended, but only to give advice. The members of the Council were the judges. All members of the Privy Council were privileged to attend, and there were added such peers, bishops and judges as the chancellor saw fit to summon. In the time of Elizabeth and James I, the persons sitting there did so by virtue of "his (or her) Majesty's commission," and this was well accepted. It will, therefore, be seen that the Essex hearing, although held at York House rather than in the Star Chamber, since it was composed of commissioners appointed by her Majesty, followed a well-accepted judicial procedure.

The Court of the Star Chamber, finally abolished by the Long Parliament, was actually not a creature of statute, but rather a revered outgrowth of the Curia Regis, antedating Parliament itself.[23] Stephen suggests that the accepted judicial jurisdiction of the Privy Council and a statute of 3 Henry VII were together probably responsible for the origin of the Court of the Star Chamber,[24] but he would agree with Hallam that although its jurisdiction cannot be vindicated solely by statute, it had become so well established as a judicial arm of the Council by the time of Elizabeth as to pass without many audible murmurs.[25] In spite of its dictatorial methods and abuses in political trials, the Court of the Star Chamber accomplished great good, both in the cases which it tried itself and in its riding herd on the other courts of the country. Often without actually trying people for offenses triable at common law, it exacted heavy fines from those guilty of offenses against the State. For example, the Earl of Rutland was fined £30,000 for taking part in the Essex revolt.[26]

Entirely apart from the legal status of the York House hearing as an exercise of the judicial functions of the Council or as a sitting of the Court of the Star Chamber, it may well have been constitutional as the exercise of the Crown's right to innovate judicial procedures in order to preserve the king's peace. Bracton, the great thirteenth-century authority on English law, states as a general principle that strictly speaking the king is the proper judge for all temporal causes and that it was only the great mass of business that compelled him to delegate judicial power to his courts and ministers. Fleta, writing a little later, made the completely dogmatic statement that all judicial power is derived from the Crown.[27] The older textbooks dealing with criminal trials almost always entitled them "Pleas of the Crown," and only civil cases were called "Common Pleas." This distinction was commonplace in England for over 700 years. Originally the king's officers dealt only with causes, civil or criminal, which concerned the king or affected the king's peace and public order. The words used today, "against the peace of our Lord, the King, his crown and dignity," date back to the time when it was the king's business to handle matters which concerned his peace. By

Glanville's time, Pleas of the Crown had been considerably extended and included homicides.[28] It is by no means certain that in Elizabeth's time the Crown had no constitutional right to innovate judicial procedure. However, the question is really academic, since Essex was not in a position to raise the point.

THREE

Essex had conducted himself admirably at the hearing—his friends were pleased and the queen was touched. He stated firmly his reasons for his acts, professed his love and respect for his queen and yielded himself to her mercy. R. Adderly wrote to Bagot that Essex had showed himself to be a pretty fellow and had refused to yield to the pressure to confess guilt.[1]

The day after the trial, Francis Bacon was ordered by the queen to set down in writing all that had passed at York House. He did so and read it to her during two afternoons but persuaded her to agree that his account should not be made public. Elizabeth was much affected by Bacon's story and at this time was inclined to forgive Essex.

On June 21, Essex wrote to her: "I do too much reverence your Majesty's royal person (most dear and most admired sovereign) and know too well in whose place you sit here on earth, to be impatient at that which your Majesty will have me suffer. But since my cause hath been heard, and my submission humbly and publicly made, happy were it for me rather to be out of this world, than to have the world see your Majesty thought it fit to keep a guard upon my loyalty. It is not therefore a long life or a life accompanied with pleasure or plenty that I beg of your Majesty, but a life fit for a most dutiful, faithful subject, or an end of life."[2]

Elizabeth began to relent. On August 29 Secretary Cecil wrote to Sir George Carew to tell him that Essex had humbly petitioned from the queen permission to go into the country to improve his health. She granted him liberty to go into Oxfordshire to one of his uncle's houses, but with the command that, although she was satisfied to permit him to be under no guard but the guard of duty and discretion, he must in no way believe himself to be freed of her indignation, nor must he presume to approach the Court or her. That distinction of being free from guard but under indignation, Cecil added, "makes very few resort to him but those who are of his blood."[3]

Whyte informed Sidney that before Essex went into the country, he asked the Council to ask her Majesty if he might once present himself and kiss her hands, so that with some contentment he could go to his solitary life. It was thought, however, that he wouldn't hastily receive the favor.[4]

Still confident that if he could get into Elizabeth's presence he could sway her, Essex sent her a flattering and submissive letter by Lord Henry Howard.[5] She was very pleased but remarked that she heartily wished his actions would be in accordance with his words, that he had tried her patience a long while, and, therefore, she ought to take some time to receive proof of his submission. Her father would never have pardoned so much obstinacy, but she would not look back, for fear of incurring the fate of Lot's wife. All is not gold that glitters.[6]

Bacon continued to intercede with the queen for the earl's return to Court but succeeded only in vexing her. Hoping to have better opportunity to see her, Essex moved back to Essex House in London shortly before Michaelmas, on which date his ten-year monopoly of the tariff on sweet wines would expire. He badly needed the revenues, and furthermore, he began to regard renewal of the grant as the most certain sign of his chance of being restored to full favor. He wrote Elizabeth several affectionate letters, of which she said to Bacon, "My Lord of Essex hath written me some very dutiful letters, and I have been moved by them, but what I took for the abundance of the heart I find to be only a suit for the farm of sweet wines." She then sent Essex a short and cutting answer, saying that she must first learn the value of the sweet wine tariff and that benefits were not to be bestowed at random. After a month's hesitation she announced that the sweet wine revenues would be reserved for the Crown, and before long she granted them to another, saying that an un-governable beast must be stinted in his provender, so that he might be the better managed.[7]

Camden says that Essex was touched with these answers to the very quick, so that he let his emotions overcome his sense of reason and gave himself up to Cuffe (his secretary) and other close advisers who had been trying to persuade him to give up his attempt at ingratiation and to resort to force to restore himself to a place of power, and who did all they could to convince him that it was now apparent that the queen, the Council and his enemies were resolved to crush and sink him into the condition of a beggar. They told Essex that if he once was forsaken by the queen and his money, he must expect to lose his friends and be loaded with the scorn and reproaches of his enemies.[8]

His patience and hope both gone, Essex was not hard to persuade. Sir Walter Raleigh later said that one of his many accusations then made against the queen (that her mind had become as crooked as her carcass) "cost him his head, which his insurrection had not cost him but for that speech."[9] That Essex did make such a comment was confirmed by the Earl of Clarendon, who said after Essex's death that if ever the queen heard that uncouth speech—that she was as crooked in her disposition as in her carcass, since by chance there was a little unevenness in her shoulders—all his wonder at Essex's destruction left him, causing him to disbelieve the report that shortly after the earl's miserable end (which, indeed, deserved compassion from all hearts), the queen expressed much reluctance for his death.[10]

After a visit to Essex at this time, John Harrington, Elizabeth's godson, wrote in his diary:

> ... my Lord of Essex ... shifteth from sorrow and repentance to rage and rebellion so suddenly, as well proveth him devoid of good reason or right mind. In my last discourse, he uttered strange words bordering on such strange designs, that made me hasten forth and leave his presence. Thank heaven! I am safe at home, and if I go in such troubles again, I deserve the gallows for a meddling fool. His speeches of the Queen becometh no man who hath *mens sana in corpore sano*. He hath ill advisers, and such evil hath sprung from this source. The Queen well knoweth how to humble the haughty spirit; the haughty spirit knoweth not how to yield, and the man's soul seemeth tossed to and fro, like the waves of a troubled sea.[11]

To formulate something concrete out of their nebulous plans, a council was formed consisting of Southampton, Sir Charles Danvers (an intimate friend of Southampton), Sir Ferdinando Gorges (Governor of Plymouth), Sir John Davis and John Littleton. Sir Christopher Blount, Sir Gilly Merrick (a professional soldier serving un-

der Essex, and now his steward) and Henry Cuffe were active in
promoting the plotting. Negotiations were carried on with King
James of Scotland requesting his assistance in return for a promise
that he would succeed Elizabeth at her death. Efforts were made to
cultivate support in both the Puritan and Popish parties.[12] At one
time Blount's brother, Lord Mountjoy, now the lord deputy of
Ireland, had considered using the troops under his command to
assist the plotters, but by the time action was needed he had completed the subjection of Ireland, received Tyrone's submission and
was no longer interested. Essex's mother and his sister, Lady Rich,
who had lost the queen's favor for abusing her husband's bed,[13]
were constantly needling him to take action.

The throngs moving in and out of Essex House created suspicion, and on Saturday, February 7, Robert Sackville paid Essex a
visit to see what he could see.[14] Probably with the intention of
bringing matters to a head, Cecil on the same day sent a queen's
messenger to Essex requiring him to attend the Council. That was
enough. Feigning illness, Essex refused to go. Everyone panicked,
and it was determined to make the attempt to seize control the
following morning. The decision was in part prompted by a messenger (probably sent by the government to deceive him) offering Essex
the services of the sheriff, Sir Thomas Smith, with one thousand of
his militia to support the two hundred or three hundred knights
available to Essex. Accustomed to the applause of the citizens, Essex
easily believed the offer and was convinced that he had only to
appear in the streets to draw around him vast numbers of the
populace in his support.[15] He seems really to have believed that his
life was in danger. The die was cast, and Essex, headstrong and
ill-advised to the last, had sealed his fate.

The story of the easily thwarted attempt to seize the Court on
that Sunday morning (February 8, 1601) is sufficiently told in a letter
written two days later by Secretary Cecil to Sir George Carew in
Ireland and in the evidence which we shall see adduced at the
treason trials. The government, adequately warned, had stationed
troops in strategic locations. The sheriff could not be found, the few

people on the streets on this quiet Sunday morning did not respond to Essex's cries, and by midnight he and his principal followers were imprisoned in the Tower to be charged with treason. Cecil wrote:

> ... [I must] acquaint you with a most dangerous attempt which hath happened on Sunday last, wherein both her Majesty's own person and the usurpation of this kingdom were openly shot at.... If the queen had not put herself in strength that very morning, and barricaded Charing Cross and other places of the back-parts of Westminster, their resolution was to have been at Court by noon; ...but, being repulsed at Ludgate by a stand of pikes, and the city holding fast for the Queen, they and some 50 of their accomplices ran to the water and put themselves into Essex House, which the Earl had furnished with all manner of warlike provisions, and there defended themselves till towards six o'clock in the evening, at which time the Lord Admiral sent unto them if they would not yield that he would blow up the house, which he might have done sooner, but that the Lady of Essex and the Lady Rich were within it. Whereupon (nowithstanding their great braveries) they all yielded to her Majesty's mercy.[16]

It answered the purposes of Essex's enemies to keep the queen in a continual alarm and to persuade her that the danger was not over. The citizens were harassed and made to stand double watches at Court and in the city.[17] Even with Essex safely in the Tower and ample proof of his treason available, the Council feared his popularity with the people. According to Bishop Strype, one expedient adopted was to have certain prayers, written by those in authority, used three times a week in the churches. Strype sets out two of the five. This excerpt is illustrative of the exaggerated charges and florid style of them all:

> We, thy humble servants, bowing down the knees of our hearts, and prostrating ourselves before thy glorious throne, do render unto thee all praise, power, honor, and thanksgiving, for thy most gracious favor and most merciful deliverance of our most dread sovereign lady, thy vice-regent in her dominions, Queen Elizabeth ...from the traitorous attempts and desperate designments of sundry most unkind and disloyal-like persons, who forgetting their duty both to thee, O Lord, and towards thine annointed, have in the height of their pride ...sought in open rebellion, not only the destruction and extinguishment of thy

servant, our comfort, our health and our glory, but the utter ruin
also and tragical overthrow of this our native country.[18]

According to notes taken by someone present, Dr. Barlow in a
sermon at St. Paul's listed eleven items to convince the people of the
foul character of the rebellion and claimed that Essex had confirmed
all eleven in his presence. Many of these items were not once mentioned in the arraignment,[19] and Barlow later felt obliged to defend
himself by saying the sermon had been commanded by authority,
thus denying any personal malice against the earl.[20]

Like many others, the Earl of Clarendon resented these sermons,
which he called "two of the most pestilent libels against his fame that
any age hath seen published against any malefactor," concluding
that they would not have been so prescribed "had not there been
some sparks of indignation in the Queen that were unquenched
even with his blood."[21]

Although Essex was kept in ignorance of the fact prior to his
trial, his fellow plotters were persuaded to sign confessions. "It was
strange to see . . . noble and resolute men . . . fall in the end before
their deaths to such plague [of] confessions and accusations, one of
an other, that they seemed to strive who should draw one another in
deepest; and sought by all means to remove the blame and shame of
being the first movers and contrivers of their confessed treasonable
plot."[22]

In addition to some self-serving statements about the trial contained in Bacon's works, there are three reasonably complete known
reports. One is the official report contained in Hargrave's State
Trials and utilized again and commented upon by Howell. In many
instances, especially where a political crime was involved, Hargrave's
reports were colored somewhat by their writers to support the verdict and the Crown. Andrew Amos, a highly respected authority on
British criminal law in the early 1800's, regretted that in Hargrave
and Howell the reader is seldom furnished with any references to
the authorities from which the reports of the different trials are
taken. The reports of the more ancient trials in these collections, he
said, were most probably copies from publications prepared under
the inspection of the chief officers of state and of the law, sometimes
revised by the sovereign himself. He suggests as a comparison that
an account by the French Republic of the trial of Louis XVI could
hardly be expected to be given much credit.[23]

Obviously, without qualified reporters sufficiently skilled to take down a verbatim account and given an advantageous place in the room, it would have been impossible to obtain a complete account of any trial. The State Trials probably come as close to a complete account of the trials they cover as anything available, but at least one of the other available reports of the Essex trial is more complete and certainly less biased. Known as the Helmingham Manuscript, this report is written in what is thought to have been the court hand of the period, bears on its first page the inscription, "Lionel Tolmach-1600, of Bently," and was presumably written by a barrister of the time from his notes made during the trial. It has been in the possession of the Tollemache family ever since. The third report, taken from a manuscript in the State Paper Office, is that printed by Charles Knight in Volume One of his "Criminal Trials." The report used by Hargrave appears to be an abbreviated version of Knight's manuscript. It contains some material not in Hargrave and omits a little, but the differences involve relatively unimportant matters. Knight gives references to Bacon's account, to other papers in the State Paper Office and to Moor's Reports. Hargrave and Howell give no sources. William Camden, who was present at the trial, wrote a rather detailed narrative account in his "Life and Reign of Queen Elizabeth," which is useful in solving contradictions in the other accounts. The trial transcription in the next chapter follows the Helmingham Manuscript, clarified somewhat as to language and abridged to eliminate less important material but supplemented with material from the other two reports.

FOUR

THE ESSEX-SOUTHAMPTON
TREASON TRIAL

The arraignment, conviction and condemnation of Robert, Earl of Essex, and Henry, Earl of Southampton, held at Westminster the Nineteenth of February, 1600 [old style, actually 1601], before the Lord High Steward appointed for that day, being the Lord Treasurer of England [The Earl of Dorset], as followeth:

There was built for that day at the upper end of Westminster Hall a scaffold in form of a court or tribunal some two yards high and about six yards square, on the west part whereof was erected a Canopy of State, under which the Lord High Steward's grace, representing her Majesty's person, did sit as judge; on each side of that Chair of State were tapestry hangings without any other seats. On the south and north parts of this court were benches lined with green cloth, for the peers to sit upon, who were placed in their order, each observing a second course with the like on the opposite part. The most ancient in nobility or highest in dignity sat on the south part, being the right hand of the Lord High Steward, then the next most ancient on the north part, being the left hand, and so by turn to the lowest. On the east part, opposite the Chair of State, was framed a bar or pew railed round, for the two prisoners. On the north side of this was the entrance into the court, which was led to by a long gallery about ten feet wide, of equal height with the court, reaching as far as from the common place, where the ascent was some ten stairs. In the middle of this court was raised a square table about one foot higher than the ground of the scaffold, covered with green cloth, about which was let in a narrow place where the judges and Queen's Counsel sat, before the prisoners and peers: so they sat upon the same floor the peers and prisoners trod on. At the upper side of this table, before the Lord High Steward, was cut in a little pew for the Clerks of the Crown to sit in, which were

37

two; and the Sergeants of the Mace lay it upon the table, ready to summon the court and convey evidences as need required. The judges were divided, some sitting on the south, some on the north side of the table before the peers.

They were these:

The two Chief Justices [Popham and Anderson]	The Queen's Counsel sat before the prisoners and were:
Lord Chief Baron [Periam]	Serjeant Yelverton
Justice Gawdye	Mr. Attorney [Sir Edward
Justice Fenner	Coke, Attorney General]
Justice Walmesly	Mr. Solicitor Bacon
Baron Clarke	Mr. Recorder
Justice Kingsmill	

In the morning about eight or nine of the clock (most part of the peers being come before), the Lord High Steward repaired to the hall with seven maces and a long white rod borne before him, accompanied by the rest of the peers, saving the Lord Thomas Howard, Constable of the Tower, who about half an hour after the peers were seated brought Robert, Earl of Essex, with axe borne before him, the edge from him [It will, of course, be remembered that in a capital trial the axe was carried into the court just ahead of the accused, with its edge away from him. When the accused left the court after the verdict, the axe again preceded him, its edge toward him if he had been found guilty but away from him if innocent], and Sir William Woodhouse brought presently after him, Henry, Earl of Southampton. The Earl of Essex was apparelled in a black satin suit, a wrought velvet gown of the same color, a black felt hat faced with velvet, a ruff band with a single set, and a fall underneath it. The Earl of Southampton had on a sad colored suit of fustian or like stuff, a gown of cloth with long, slender sleeves wherein he held his hands for the most part of the day. When the Earls met they saluted each other at the Bar with kind and cheerful salutation. The Earl of Essex, his countenance was all that day very cheerful and confident. The other Earl was somewhat sad, but without dismay: when they were entered the Bar, the axe was set before them next to the Earl of Essex, and so continued.

The trial will be better understood by having some knowledge of the procedure, arising in remote times out of the powers of the old Curia Regis, prescribed for the trial of peers. The best-known clause

of the Magna Carta was, "No freeman shall be taken or/and imprisoned ... or in any way destroyed ... except by the lawful judgement
of his peers or/and by the law of the land." "Or/and" is the trans-
lation given to the word "vel" in the original, and there has been
great dispute about its intended effect. As used in the last clause of
the foregoing quotation, the word may well have been intended to
mean "and." "Except by the lawful judgment of his peers" meant
only that no freeman, whatever his rank, could be judged by his
inferiors in rank and had no reference to trial by jury. "In accordance with the law of the land" guaranteed that execution must be
preceded by a judgment of peers rendered according to the appropriate time-honored test, which at the time of Magna Carta could
mean battle, compurgation or ordeal and only later meant trial by
jury.[1]

In time, the clause assumed one meaning for peers and another
for commoners. To commoners it was interpreted to require trial by
jury. To the peers (lords), since almost all trials had to be handled by
the courts, and juries of peers were not practicable there, the words
were made applicable only to crimes involving forfeitures or capital
punishment. Eventually, in 1441, a statute made the requirement
applicable to the trial of peers only for treason and felony. As used
in the charter, "peers" probably meant only equals in rank, although
the nobles who extorted it from King John, interested mainly in
their own problems, may well have thought of the word as referring
only to themselves. Gradually, usage came to so accept the term, and
in England during Elizabeth's time a peer was any man entitled to
sit in the House of Lords except those sitting there by reason of
ecclesiastical office.

"Trial by peers" was undoubtedly an importation from continental
feudal law and was the solemn trial of a vassal by his fellow vassals in
the court of their lord. King John held his lands in France as a vassal
of the King of France and was himself once tried by his peers in the
court of the French king. Accordingly, in trying a peer the lords sat
in their ancient character as a seignorial court of vassals, each one
serving as a judge, the presiding officer being the lord high steward
of England. If Parliament was not in session, the trial took place
before the lord high steward, who then held the position of a true
judge, and the lords whom he summoned to serve as a jury were
known as the Lord Triers. In either case, it was customary to invite
professional judges and lawyers to advise the lord high steward on

points of law. Only the attorney general could prosecute in the lord high steward's court. The procedure was abolished in 1948.

William Sanderson, writing in 1653, described the procedure in use in the time of Essex:

> A Peer of the land hath the privilege upon treason or felony, indicted, to be tried by his peers: the King by Letters Patent assigns some sage Lord of the Parliament to be High Steward of England, for that day of his arraignment, who before that time makes precept to his Sergeant at Arms, to warn to appear before him a certain number of Lords of the Parliament, twelve at least, upon that day at Westminster. At which time the High Steward shall sit under the Cloth of State, and causeth his commission to be read; the same sergeant returns his precept, and calls the lords, who appearing by name and being set, the Lieutenant of the Tower is called, and brings his prisoner into the court to the Bar; the High Steward then declares to the people the cause, why the King hath assembled those lords and the prisoner, and persuades him to answer without fear freely, and commands the Clerk of the Crown to read the indictment unto him, and to ask him if he be guilty or not, to which he usually answers, "Not Guilty"; and [indicates willingness] to be tried by God and his peers. Then the King's Attorney and Serjeants at Law give evidence against him; whereto, when he hath given answer, the Lieutenant of the Tower is commanded to return with the prisoner from the Bar, while the lords do secretly confer in the court together, and then the lords rise out of their places, and consult among themselves, and what they affirm, shall be done upon their honor without oath.
>
> And being so agreed (or the greatest number), they return and take their places again in court; and the High Steward demands of the youngest lord first, if he that is arraigned be guilty or not, and so the next in order, and the rest, each one, answering "aye" or "nay." Then the prisoner is sent for to the Bar, to whom the High Steward recites the verdict of the peers, and doth give judgment accordingly (Stanford Pleas del Corona, lib. 3. Poult. 188). . . .
>
> And if a peer upon his arraignment of treason do stand mute, judgment shall be given upon his indictment, and yet shall he not be pressed to death [see the discussion of *"peine forte and dure"* in Chapter Nine], but saves the forfeiture of his lands (Statut.

Westm. Edw. 4. Dier 205). But if upon indictment of felony, he may be mute. . . .

. . . an Archbishop or Bishop, though Lords of Parliament, in such cases shall be tried by a jury of knights and other substantial persons, upon their oaths, because ecclesiastics cannot pass in like cases upon trial of other peers, for they are forbidden by the common and ecclesiastic laws, to be judges of life and death.

You see the great regard the law hath to the word of a peer, (heretofore) upon his honor, and yet how many ordinarily break their oaths in common?[2]

Although this procedure would seem designed to assure a peer a fair trial, no one in Elizabeth's time anticipated any verdict except "guilty." The life of Elizabeth was of paramount importance to the government, since during most of her reign her death would have meant a Catholic successor, who would not only have changed the system of government but would have replaced the ruling clique. The murder of the queen would not have been difficult. Other rulers of the period had been put out of the way for Catholic successors, and it could well be said that Elizabeth had rid herself of Mary, Queen of Scots, through the same means. Accordingly, the government regarded the lives of innocent or relatively innocent men unimportant if needed to reduce to a minimum plots against Elizabeth.[3] Evidence was easy to fabricate, and few people could hold out against the government. The accused themselves, knowing conviction inevitable, usually preferred a pleasant and "honorable" trial and execution to torture followed by just-as-certain death.

Hallam and other authorities are all censorious. The proceedings against Mary, Queen of Scots, Hallam said, were by no means exempt from the shameful breach of legal rules almost universal in trials for high treason during that reign. His language was almost intemperate. "Those glaring transgressions of natural as well as positive law . . . rendered our courts of justice in cases of treason little better than the caverns of murderers. . . . a virulent prosecutor, a judge hardly distinguishable from the prosecutor except by his ermine, and a passive pusillanimous jury. . . . perpetual interrogation of the prisoner, . . . the want of all evidence except written, perhaps unattested, examinations or confessions." When a conspirator against Elizabeth complained that two witnesses had not been brought against him as required by a statute of Edward VI, he was told by the chief justice that since he was indicted under an earlier act of Edward III, the requirement was not applicable—a blatant disregard of the intent of the later law.[4]

> The court being set, one of the Sergeants of the Mace made an Oyes [today's "Hear Ye"], saying: "The. Lord High Steward straightly chargeth and commandeth all persons present to keep silence, and hear her Majesty's commissions read, upon pain of imprisonment." Then were two commissions read: the first commission authorizing the Lord High Steward to be judge of their causes, the other of Oyer and Terminer of treasons, felons, etc., by virtue whereof the indictments were found.
> Then made he a second Oyes, saying: "The Lord High Steward chargeth and commandeth all justices, commissioners and other persons who have any writs to them directed by the Lord High Steward for the certifying of any indictments, that they return their writs, and bring in their indictments." . . .
> Then making another Oyes, he said: "All Earls, Viscounts, Barons, Peers of this Realm of England, summoned to be here this day for the trial of Robert Earl of Essex and Henry Earl of Southampton, answer to your names as ye shall be called," and about here the Earl of Essex said, "My Lords, I could have thought and wished that this matter might have been rather censured in the Star Chamber as a misdemeanor than heard here as a matter of treason." To which nothing was answered, but the lords called as followeth: . . .

The names of twenty-five peers were then called, and all were present. There were other peers in the House of Lords, but presumably these were the only ones available. All the peers were, of course, well known to Essex, although some were friendly and some were not. Some had participated in suppressing the revolt; Nottingham disliked Essex and had been charged with his arrest; Secretary Cecil had at one time been friendly but had been alienated through Essex's fault; and Grey was an admitted enemy.

> To their call they answered every one, "Here," and made their appearance; . . .
> Then the Earl of Essex desired to know of my Lord Chief Justice, whether he might challenge any of the peers . . . (we know to be our professed enemies); whereunto the Lord Chief Justice answered, "No," and Mr. Attorney General alleged a case

in Henry VIII's time, of my Lord Darcy. Whereupon the Earl bade them go on. When the Lord Grey was called, the Earl of Essex laughed with the Earl of Southampton, and jogged him by his sleeve. . . . After the call ended, the Earls were commanded to hold up their hands. The Earl of Essex with a bold countenance, first casting up his hand, said, "I have held up my hand to better purpose, and thought to have done so again"; then the Earl of Southampton held up his hand. [The foregoing passage is partly from Hargrave.]

In ordinary criminal trials it was well accepted that the defendant was entitled to challenge the jurors. As early as Fortescue's time the defendant had thirty-five peremptory challenges. Under Henry VIII the number was reduced to twenty, "except in treason, and it so remains."[5] Plucknett, in discussing the passage from Stephen, inter-prets the statute to mean that thirty-five challenges were still per-mitted in treason trials,[6] and Blackstone confirms this explanation.[7] It appears that these provisions for challenges in treason trials were not construed to apply to treason trials in the House of Lords. Peers were not required to be sworn before testifying, since it was pre-sumed that their honor would preclude lying. The same reasoning, if reasoning it can be called, would explain the refusal to permit a peer's impartiality and fairness as a Lord Trier to be challenged. The judges answered Essex's question by saying that the reputation and character of the peers of England were such that they were not obliged to take their oaths upon any trials, nor did any exception lie against them, and Essex accepted the ruling without question. I have seen no suggestion in any comment on his trial that the ruling was erroneous.

Then there were read the indictments . . . to this effect following, viz. Thou Robert Earl of Essex and thou Henry Earl of South-ampton stand indicted of High Treason in that you, contrary to your allegiance and fidelity unto our Sovereign Lady Queen Elizabeth, etc., not having the fear of God before your eyes and thereunto moved by the instigation of the devil, did upon the eighth day of February, in the forty-third year of the reign of our said Sovereign Lady the Queen, wickedly imagine, devise and compass to take her Majesty's person and deprive her of her throne and dignity, and to take away the life of her sacred Majesty and in her kingdom rebellion and sedition to raise, and thou the said Earl of Essex to exalt thyself and usurp the

Crown, to alter and change the present state of government and religion; and whereas her Majesty of her abundant grace and clemency the same eighth day sent to thee the said Earl of Essex, unto thy house the Lord Keeper of the Great Seal of England, the Lord Chief Justice, and Mr. Controller of her Majesty's Household, three of her said Majesty's Council of State, together with the Earl of Worcester and others, to admonish and to require you in her Majesty's name and upon your allegiance, to disperse your disordered companies and to repair to her Grace's Court, there to open your several grievances, you despising her Majesty's clemency, there at the said house imprisoned the said Councillors under the custody of Sir John Davis, Knight, Thomas Tresham, Owen Salisbury and others, with commandment that they should kill the said prisoners if they offered to escape out of their hands, or if thou the said Earl of Essex chanced to miscarry in this action of rebellion. And hereupon you the said Earls of Essex and Southampton, accompanied with divers earls, barons, knights, esquires and gentlemen, to the number of six score, armed with sundry shields, daggers, halberds and divers other unlawful weapons, the same morning issued into her Majesty's City of London with purpose there to raise tumults and gather numbers of people for the effecting of your traitorous attempt, and there, after sundry proclamations made to the contrary, you the said Earls continued in arms, killing divers of her Majesty's subjects and, returning to the house of the said Robert Earl of Essex, you there refused to yield to her Majesty's lieutenant, continuing in hostile manner to resist the force of her Majesty sent to repress and apprehend you, etc.

The sum of the second indictment was that they intended by force to remove from about her Majesty some of the nobility and Council, to surprise the Court and Tower of London, to possess themselves of the City of London and to carry the citizens in arms for their party against their Sovereign's forces.

In the time of the reading of these indictments the Earl of Essex behaved himself with a light and careless countenance, acting passions of admiration also, as lifting up his hands and shaking his head, blessing himself, as it were, at the strangeness of these accusations, though silent during the whole time, not uttering one word of interruption, only some private speeches he made to the Earl of Southampton, who carried a settled and sober countenance.

Here the Earls were willed to hold up their hands again, and being severally demanded as to the indictments what they could say for themselves answered, "Not Guilty," and by whom they would be tried, said, by God and their Peers. . . .

Then spoke the Queen's Serjeant upon the indictment repeating with very little difference the sum thereof, only at the latter end he aggravated the matter by showing the law on that point for, said he, "My good Lord, I beseech your grace, and you my Lords that be Peers, to understand that if any man do but intend the death of the King or to cause any sedition, it is treason and death by the law, for the King is the head of the Commonwealth, and his subjects as members ought to obey and stand with him, but as for this rebellion, it contains many branches of High Treason which will be directly proved and, being found to be so, you my Lords who are Peers are to find him guilty." Here he showed the Lord of Essex what great cause he had to carry himself gratefully and dutifully to her Majesty, having received so many high advancements and bountiful gifts from her, but contrarywise turning all her favors to a rebellious hand, the Earl had conspired in as great a conspiracy as Catiline, gathering all kinds of people to him like Catiline, especially discontented persons like atheists, papists, etc., to possess London, as Catiline did Rome; the difference was Catiline had many followed him in Rome, and London afforded none to follow the Earl, though he sought to creep into the common's favor and to make himself the people's minion. Ambition, he showed, so possessed him that he could never be satisfied; the more favors and honors he had, the more still he coveted, and this humor ever increased in him, as they say of the crocodile that he groweth still till his death. Then for my Lord's proceeding in the City he said, "You, my Lords Admiral and Cumberland, with others of these honorable peers, know how it was, which makes me wonder that they stand upon their trials without confession. The treasons being so apparent, for my part I conjecture that there is some further matter in it, but my hope is that God, who is merciful and hath revealed these treasons, will not suffer the rest or any other to the hurt of the state, or touch of her Majesty's royal person, whom I beseech God long to preserve from the hands of her enemies." "Amen," cried the prisoner Earls, "and confound their souls that ever wished otherwise to her sacred person."

Then Mr. Attorney [Sir Edward Coke], suddenly rising up, spoke to this purpose: "Whereas my Lord of Essex hath affirmed that he did nothing but that he was constrained unto by the law of nature and reason, I will prove it plainly that it is against the laws of nature, positive and divine, that which he intended to have done, viz. to take away the prince from the people and the Lord's annointed from that vice-regency upon earth which is bequeathed to such a sacred Majesty. May it please your Grace, the Lord Judges who are the fathers of the law do know that the intent of treason to the prince by the law is death, and it is my position that without controversy rebellion is more than high treason, for he that is guilty of rebellion is guilty of an intent by the laws of this land to seek the destruction of the prince, and that in two things: First, in that he will not suffer the prince to reign over the people as by right he ought; secondly, in that he himself usurpeth sovereignty which he hath no right to. This foundation laid, I am to prove rebellion to be in this act against which there is no color, he that doth usurp upon the prince's authority, the law intends that he purposeth the destruction of the prince. He that doth assemble power against the prince's commandment and continues in arms, no doubt is guilty of High Treason in usurping the prince's authority; he that doth levy forces to take any town, fort or hold against the prince, committeth treason.

"But my Lord of Essex intended to take by powerful hand not only a town, but a city, not a city alone but London, the chief city, and not only London but the Tower of London, the strength of the realm, and not only the Tower of London, but the royal palace and person of the prince, and take away her life, this is against the law of nature, and it is to be counted amongst the crying sins. *Res ipsa loquitur* [the thing speaks for itself]."

Here being long silent with wondering and passionate gestures the Earl of Essex spoke: "God let me never live or breath if ever I thought worse to my sovereign than to my own soul," but then the Lord High Steward, wishing the Earl not to be too confident till he heard all, he replied, that it was not affectation or vainglory, nor trust to the strength of his reason nor any opinion that philosophy had bred in him, but the innocence of his conscience that made him be confident. . . .

Coke has been criticized for mishandling the trial, neglecting pertinent evidence, using irrelevant evidence to abuse the defendants and arguing with the defendants in such manner as to create sympathy for them. There were only three items in the indictment—Essex's intention to surprise the Court, his going with his men into London to raise rebellion and his defending his house against the queen's forces. Coke devoted little time to these matters, but it must be admitted that his task in convicting Essex of treason was made more difficult. The reason is that for political reasons the government had considered it better to eliminate from the indictment Essex's casting about for the aid of Welsh troops and of English troops in Ireland and his intriguing with the King of Scotland for aid in return for assurance of his succession to the throne.

Mr. Attorney continued.... [I have omitted this part of Coke's speech. It served principally to blacken Essex, discussing the queen's goodness to him, his lack of gratitude, the queen's efforts to prevent his plotting and telling again the main features of the revolt.]
Then the Lord of Essex spoke: "Will your Lordships give us our turn to speak, for he playeth the orator, and abuseth your Lordships' ears, and us with slanders, and they are but fashions of corrupted states, or the corrupt instruments of corrupted states, banished out of other kingdoms [referring to Coke's many historical allusions], and I desire your Lordships that we may answer to the accusations in general, and then to the particular evidences, they being so many as will trouble ... [our] weak memories upon so short warning." If this might not be suffered, then desired he the company to suspend their judgments till they had their answers. His request was denied by the Lord High Steward, the Attorney desiring all for the Queen might first be delivered. But upon advice of the Lord Chief Justice it was granted. And the Earl spoke to this effect, that whatsoever he said that day he desired their Lordships and all the hearers present to accept graciously with equal censures of their consciences. And if ... [because of] the earnestness of his speech or default or weakness of his memory in that case among the multitude of his occasions of answer to all manner of oppositions and the variety of his examinations, [anything] should slip forth to his disadvantage which should be contrary to the truth of his sincere heart, that it might not be taken hold of with rigorous severity but charitably understood with just and true construction.... He said again that he protested before the Almighty God, before whom he should shortly appear, that he would not speak one word in hope or desire of life, for he much rather wished to die, and that speedily, even if it were on the morrow, and thereby he should gain the greatest good that might be, for he should be rid of a continual misery, and his enemies of their daily fear.... And for the wiping away of those foul spots and stains usually cast upon persons accused by their accusers, that he might clear that name of his, which he never desired should be other than honorable and untainted of all disloyalty....

Here began the evidence to be read, and first the examination of Witherington of the North, who, as he said, came to Essex House on Sunday morning the eighth of February and finding that assembly, sought to sever the Earl of Bedford from them but could not, and therefore went into the city with them, of purpose to withdraw the said Earl of Bedford, which he effected before the proclamation. [The "proclamation" referred to had been made by the government in several quarters of the city after Essex and his followers had arrived there in revolt. It declared all who continued in revolt to be traitors but promised amnesty to all citizens who returned peacefully to their homes.] In the meantime he had heard divers lewd and mutinous speeches by some of the Earl of Essex's company: Some of which speeches were rehearsed, as that he should hear some cry out, "Kill them, Kill them," meaning the Councillors, and that order was left by the Earl that they should be killed if he should miscarry in London.

To this the Earl of Essex answered that Mr. Witherington was not present himself, but his examination being taken he was sent, he knew not how, into the country. "Howsoever, Mr. Witherington did much disparage himself, if he said so, for I protest to God, upon my salvation, I never heard such words as, 'Kill them, Kill them,' and Mr. Witherington came to my house voluntarily, unsent for, and for anything I perceived . . . he was in the action as forward as any with the Earl of Bedford, and the first time I missed them was at our stand in Gratious Street. And further I desire your Lordships to consider what a man in danger and fear, as Mr. Witherington is, may speak, and for those speeches I hate and detest them, but these words being so openly spoken a hundred more might testify it." . . .

It is enlightening to note the differences between Witherington's testimony as it appears above and as it appears (doctored by Coke) in the official version of the State Trials. That version has Witherington saying that he told his uncle, who accompanied him to Essex House that Sunday morning, that he feared they were coming "into ill action," that when he perceived that the four members of the Council were there he feared danger to them, that when the earl left Essex House to go into the city an order was left that if his enterprise should miscarry in London, then the lord keeper and the lord chief justice were to be killed and that he went with the Essex forces into London only in order to desert the troops at his first opportunity.

The DECLARATION of the Lord Keeper, the Earl of Worcester, and the Lord Chief Justice of England.

Upon Sunday, being the eighth of February last past, about ten of the clock in the forenoon, the Lord Keeper of the Great Seal, the Earl of Worcester, Sir William Knollys (Controller of her Majesty's Household), and the Lord Chief Justice of England, being commanded by direction from the Queen's Majesty, did repair to the late Earl of Essex's house, and finding the gate shut against them, after a little stay they were let in at the wicket, and as soon as they were within the gate, the wicket was shut upon them, and all their servants kept out. At their coming thither, they found the court full of men assembled together in a very tumultuous sort: the Earls of Essex, Rutland and Southampton, and the Lord Sandys; Master Parker, commonly called Lord Mounteagle, Sir Christopher Blount, Sir Charles Danvers, and many other knights and gentlemen, and other persons unknown, which flocked together about the Lord Keeper, etc. And thereupon the Lord Keeper told the Earl of Essex that they were sent from her Majesty to understand the cause of this their assembly, and to let them know that if they had any particular cause of grief against any persons whatsoever, it should be heard, and they should have justice. Hereupon the Earl of Essex with a very loud voice declared that his life was sought, and that he should have been murdered in his bed; that he had been perfidiously dealt with; that his hand had been counterfeited, and letters written in his name; and that therefore they were assembled there together to defend their lives, with much other speech to like effect. Hereupon the Lord Chief Justice said unto the Earl that if they had any such matter of grief, or if any such matter were attempted or purposed against him, he willed the Earl to declare it; assuring him that it should be truly related to her Majesty, and that it should be ... heard, and justice should be done, whomsoever it concerned. To this the Earl of Southampton objected the assault made upon him by the Lord Grey. Whereunto the Lord Chief Justice said that in his case justice had been done, and the party imprisoned for it. And hereupon the Lord Keeper did will the Earl of Essex, that whatsoever private matter or offense he had against any person whatsoever, if he would deliver it unto them, they would faithfully and honestly deliver it to the Queen's Majesty, and doubted not to procure him honorable and equal justice, whomsoever it concerned; requiring him, that if he would not declare it openly, that he would impart it unto them privately, and doubted not but they would satisfy him in it. Upon this there was a great clamor raised among the multitude, crying, "Away, my Lord, they abuse you, they betray you, they undo you, you lose time." Whereupon the Lord Keeper put on his hat, and said with a loud voice, "My Lord, let us speak with you privately, and understand your griefs: And I command you all upon your allegiance, to lay down your weapons and to depart, which you ought all to do, being thus commanded, if you be good subjects and owe that duty to the Queen's Majesty which you profess." Whereupon they all broke out into an exceedingly loud shout and cry, crying, "All, all, all." And while the Lord Keeper was speaking, and commanding them upon their allegiance, as is before declared, the Earl of Essex and the most part of that company did put on their hats; and so the Earl of Essex went into the house, and the Lord Keeper, etc. followed him, thinking that his purpose had been to speak with them privately, as they had required. And as they were going, some of that disordered company cried, "Kill them." And as they were going into the great chamber, some cried, "Cast the Great Seal out of the window." Some other cried there, "Kill them," and some other said, "Nay, let us shut them up." The Lord Keeper did often call on the Earl of Essex to speak with them privately, thinking still that his meaning had been so, until the Earl brought them into his back chamber, and there gave order to have the farther door of that chamber shut fast. And at his going forth out of that chamber, the Lord Keeper pressing again to have spoken with the Earl of Essex, the Earl said, "My Lords, be patient a while, and stay here, and I will go into London, and take order with the mayor and sheriffs for the city, and will be here again within this half hour." And so departed from the Lord Keeper, etc., leaving the Lord Keeper, etc. and divers of the gentlemen pensioners in that chamber, guarded by Sir John Davis, Francis Tresham and Owen Salisbury, with musket-shot, where they continued until Sir Ferdinando Gorges came and delivered them, about four of the clock in the afternoon. In the meantime we did often require Sir John Davis and Francis Tresham to suffer us to depart, or at the least to suffer some one of us to go to the Queen's Majesty to inform her where and in what sort we were kept. But they answered that my Lord (meaning the Earl of Essex) had commanded that we should not depart before his return, which (they said) would be very shortly. [Signed] THOMAS EGERTON. C.S. EDWARD WORCESTER. JOHN POPHAM.

All which the Lord Chief Justice Popham attested, *viva voce.*

The foregoing declaration by the three members of the Council is taken from the State Trials. Note that the statement was not under oath and was merely attested by the lord chief justice *viva voce*. It is hardly necessary to comment on the incongruity of the lord chief justice's testifying in a trial at which he was acting as official prosecutor.

To this the Earl of Essex answered, desiring that the circumstances might be weighed: What time it was, and in what company ... [that they had had warnings] both the night before and that present morning of preparation by their enemies for assault to be made upon him in his own house, and therefore what he did was but to secure them [the queen's four emissaries] lest in the midst of those tumults which were like to ensue between him and his enemies, these Lords should have perished. "Otherwise," said he, "what reason had I in the world to purpose mischief against them, whereof the one was my uncle [Knollys], the other my best honorable friend [Egerton], such as I protest before God I hold so dear that if anything had been enterprised by me against any of the nobility, they should have been the last."

Here Mr. Attorney excepted against those words of the Earl, but the peers disliked his exception, and thought they were well spoken.

The Earl continued that what was said or done in that kind was against his will, and though he could not restrain some hotheads from uttering irreverent speeches, yet he withheld them from doing any violence. Then protested he that whensoever they uttered unto him any such devises as their heads had feigned, and would wish him to follow, he so coldly entertained them that oftentimes he checked them for their rashness. And for that the Lord Keeper spoke to them upon their allegiance to disperse their assembly, he answered and protested he never heard of it till it was too far past, that they showed no warrant from the Queen, and besides at the time of their issuing forth, if they could have known how they might possibly have found all the Council together, they would directly have gone to them, but they feared they should have been intercepted by their enemies to their uttermost danger.

Here Mr. Attorney spoke, "My Lord, your grace sees that this is without color or question, for my Lord Chief Justice and Mr. Witherington have proved it plain that they would not dissolve their company that was up in arms, being [so] commanded upon their allegiance by the Lord Keeper."

The Earl of Essex said that it was no marvel, considering that the people abroad in the streets with a great and sudden outcry said we should all be slain, and considering our other intelligences.

The Earl of Southampton answered [that] for as much as concerned him of that evidence of Mr. Witherington, he neither heard the Lords deliver such message to the Earl, neither heard any of these speeches mentioned by the Lord Chief Justice and him.

At this point the report in the State Trials contains considerable irrelevant material not in the Helmingham Manuscript, including bickering about whether certain of Essex's adherents were Papists. It was at about this point in their trial that Essex and Southampton learned that their confederates in the plot had made full confessions. It must have come as quite a shock to them, after coming into the trial imagining that things had hitherto been kept pretty much in the dark, to learn that their co-conspirators had broken down and signed confessions largely proving the charges made in the indictment. A significant change in their attitude appears to have resulted.

Then was brought in Sir Ferdinando Gorges's confession against them, who deposed that in January last he received a letter from the Earl of Essex complaining of his unfortunateness and desiring the said Sir Ferdinando to come to London to him where, when he was come, the Earl uttered his grievances and the injury done him by his enemies, which he could not endure, and he said he had many earls, barons and gentlemen that would join with him against his enemies. Further his confession revealed the consultation at Drury House, where was moved the taking of the city, the Tower and the Court . . . ,[but nothing was resolved through these consultations, and the matter was] referred to the Earl of Essex his own ordering, by reason Mr. John Littleton and himself misliked the plot; himself, he said, as well for the horror that afflicted his mind as also for the impossibility to effect it. . . .

The account of Gorges's confession in the State Trials is obviously colored. Neither the State Paper Office version nor the Helmingham version contains the statement appearing in the State Trials account that Essex had written Gorges that he purposed

shortly to free himself of the miserable estate in which he stood, that
120 earls, barons and gentlemen participated in his discontented
humor, that he hoped "to have a good party in Wales," that Gorges
advised Essex to give up his plans and to submit himself to the
queen's mercy, that at his advice Essex sent him back to release the
lord chief justice but that he took advantage of the opportunity to
liberate all four councillors from their confinement in Essex House.

After Gorges's deposition was read, Essex said, "I desire to have
Sir Ferdinando Gorges face to face," and he was then summoned.
Essex wanted to be confronted with the hostile witness, an occurence
which would, of course, be routine today in criminal trials. At that
time, what is currently the fundamental rule of English
law — insisting on *viva voce* examination of sworn witnesses — was then
either as yet still unknown or at least dispensed with in political
trials.[8] Although it was realized that a written confession was not
reliable, about the only protection one being tried for treason had
was the requirement that two lawful witnesses were necessary to
convict him unless the treason were confessed. Obviously in recogni-
tion of the small value of confessions obtained under duress (a point
made by Essex himself later in the trial), a statute was later adopted
under William III requiring the defendant's confession to be made
in open court. We must keep constantly in mind in reading these
treason and political trials that the lord high steward's court was
merely a loaded device to assure a verdict of guilty.[9]

While waiting for Gorges to come, Essex spoke further on his
lack of intent to harm the queen and said his only object in
attempting the Court was to obtain access to the queen in order to
accuse Raleigh, Cobham and Cecil of having told her falsehoods to
persuade her to withdraw her favor from Essex and his associates.
He was satisfied, he said, that if he could just tell Elizabeth of these
things, his enemies' plots against him and the way in which those in
her confidence were abusing their power to harm her kingdom, then
nothing more would be necessary. Thereupon:

> Lord Cobham stood up and said, for those imputations on his
> soul and conscience he was innocent, neither used he any such
> means of accusing the Earl to the Queen as the Earl of Essex
> pretended against him, and so desired to know why the Earl so
> charged him. The Earl answered that he had forgiven all the
> world, and therefore the Lord Cobham needed not to justify

himself; indeed, said he, "I have heard and thought that you used such means with the Queen, but I envy you not, my Lord."

Here came in Sir Ferdinando Gorges to justify what he had delivered in his examination.

... and there he delivered his statement, *viva voce,* as aforesaid, adding further, "that he advised the Earl, at his return out of the City to his house, to go and submit himself to her Majesty."

Essex. Good Sir Ferdinando, I pray thee speak openly whatsoever thou dost remember; with all my heart I desire thee to speak freely; I see thou desirest to live, and if it please her Majesty to be merciful unto you, I shall be glad and will pray for it; yet I pray thee, speak like a man.

Sir F. Gorges. All that I can remember I have delivered in my examination, and further I cannot say.

Essex. Sir Ferdinando, I wish you might speak anything that might do yourself good; but remember your reputation, and that you are a gentleman; I pray you answer me, did you advise me to leave my enterprise?

Sir F. Gorges. My Lord, I think I did.

Essex. Nay, it is no time to answer now upon thinking; these are not things to be forgotten; did you indeed so counsel me?

Sir F. Gorges. I did.

Essex. My Lords, look upon Sir Ferdinando, and see if he looks like himself. All the world shall see, by my death and his life, whose testimony is the truest.

Southampton. Good Sir Ferdinando, satisfy the court what was intended amongst all our conferences and consultations.

Sir F. Gorges. Some delivered their minds one way, some another; but by the oath I have taken, I did never know or hear any thought or purpose of hurt or disloyalty intended to her Majesty's person. . . .

[As Gorges concluded his recital,] said the Earl of Essex, Sir Ferdinando speaks as a man desirous to live; he hath done her Majesty good service and may do so again. I pray God give him joy of his life, so I shall be glad; yea, if I may conceive hope that he shall prosper here and speed well in his conscience hereafter, I shall be glad, yet I would that all these bystanders which behold us do but observe this man's life to come and my death.

The above report of the unsworn *viva voce* testimony and the following colloquy between Southampton and Attorney General Coke (referred to in our Helmingham Manuscript as "Mr. Attorney") are from the State Paper Office version. Camden, commenting on Essex's remark about Sir Ferdinando's appearance, said that

Essex "bestowed upon Gorges several smart and severe reflections, and endeavored to invalidate the credit of his evidence by the paleness and discomposure of his looks."[10]

After Essex's death, Gorges was accused of treachery to him by having warned Raleigh of the approaching revolt, of having liberated the members of the Council and of having given evidence against Essex on his trial. Raleigh had sent a message to Essex House that Sunday morning asking that Gorges meet him at a spot by the river, and Gorges left the house long enough to do so. The only thing definitely known about their conversation is that Raleigh advised Gorges to return immediately to his post at Plymouth Fort if he wished to avoid serious trouble. In the Gatehouse where he was imprisoned after the revolt, Gorges on June 14, 1601, wrote his defense against the charges. It is today among the Cotton manuscripts. In it Gorges says he advised against any attempt at the use of force and that he had released all the hostages, despite Essex's instructions to release only the chief justice, because the chief justice refused to accompany Gorges to the queen unless the lord keeper was also released. During their interview by the river all he did was reply to Raleigh's inquiry concerning the reason for his being in London by saying that there were two thousand men who had resolved that day to live or die free men. According to an item in "Archaelogia," it is not known whether he released the prisoners as the result of a warning from Raleigh or through a misunderstanding of Essex's orders. Almost from the start, the government seems to have regarded Gorges as its own witness rather than a guilty participant in the uprising. After the trial he was released and returned to his duties.

Gorges's defense ends, "But I must say no more, for he is gone, and I am here; I loved him alive, and cannot hate him being dead; he had some imperfections — so have all men; he had many virtues — so have few; and for those his virtues I loved him; and when time, which is the trial of all truths, hath run his course, it shall appear that I am wronged in the opinion of this idle age. In the meantime, I presume this that I have said is sufficient to satisfy the wise and discreet; for the rest, whatever I can do is but labor lost, and therefore I purpose not to trouble you nor myself at this time any farther."[11] Gorges was a highly respected man and so influential in furthering American colonization that he has been called the "Father of English Colonization in America."

Southampton. I protest I bear all loyalty in my heart towards her Majesty; and in that I have offended her, I am heartily sorry, and do in all humbleness crave her pardon. But as touching the consultation at Drury House, many things indeed were propounded, but nothing performed or even resolved upon, all being left in the end to the Earl of Essex himself. It was advised both to surprise the Court and take the Tower at once; yet neither of these two were done; how can this be made treason? It is true we did consult at Drury House about the securing of my Lord of Essex's free access to her Majesty out of imprisonment, and that for no other end but to prostrate ourselves at her Majesty's feet, humbly submitting ourselves to her mercy, and laying forth our grievances to herself, whereof we thought she had not so true information of others. And I confess that I could have been well content to have adventured my life in my Lord of Essex's quarrel against his private enemies. This was the whole scope and drift of all our meetings, and that this was not with any treasonable thought, for my own part, I take God to witness. My Lords, I desire the opinions of the Judges, whether a thing consulted upon and not executed, and another executed, not spoken of, nor known, be treason; for we talked of going to the Court; the Tower also was spoken of, but both rejected; and we went forth into London, a matter not spoken of at all; and this you will have to be treason. For my own part, I knew nothing of my Lord's intent to go into London in the morning when I came to Essex House; I had no arms, but my sword which I usually wear; and I was accompanied by only ten of my servants, and they were footmen and lackeys. When I was in London, I heard nothing of the Proclamation, for I was not near by the length of a street. Let my Lord Burghley speak, if he saw me in London, I never drew my sword all the day.

Attorney General. My Lord you say you had no other weapon with you but your sword; it hath been confessed that you had a pistol when you were in the City.

Southampton. Mr. Attorney, it is the most uncivil thing in the world to interrupt a man who is speaking for his life. But touching a pistol, I carried none out with me; but being in the street, I saw one having a pistol, and I desired it of him and had it, but it had no flint, nor could it hurt a flea. At my return to Essex House, I did there what I could to hinder the shooting, and to that end sent Captain White about the house to stay them. From this kind of behavior can be gathered no thoughts of treason. I beseech you, therefore, my Lords, not to judge of me according to the strict letter of the law, but as in your own consciences you are persuaded of me. If in this business I was too far carried away with the love I bore to my Lord of Essex, I confess I have offended; but that which I have before rehearsed was the whole end and scope of all my purposes.

Attorney General. My Lord of Southampton, is this no treason, to force the Queen in her own house, to set guards at her gates, in her chamber, and in all parts of the house, to the end that having her in your power you might do what you listed?

Southampton. Good Mr. Attorney, let me ask you what, in your conscience, you think we would have done to her Majesty if we had gained the Court?

Attorney General. I protest upon my soul, and in my conscience, I do believe she should not have lived long after she had been in your power. Note but the precedents of former ages: How long lived King Richard the Second after he was surprised in the same manner? The pretense there also was to remove certain Councillors; but it shortly after cost the King his life. Such is the unquenchable thirst of ambition, never satisfied so long as any greatness is unachieved. But I know this for certain, that to surprise the Court or take the Tower by way of defense from private enemies, is plain treason.

Southampton. The taking of the Tower was rejected as ridiculous to be thought on; neither was the surprising of the Court meant but for a quiet access to her Majesty.

Then the Judges being thereto required by the peers to deliver their several opinions concerning the question before propounded by the Earl of Southampton, . . . argued it severally and they agreed to the following resolutions [these Resolutions are taken from Moor's Reports, p. 621]:

First, they resolved that the Earl of Essex, in going with a troop of persons from Essex House into the City, and there calling upon the citizens to aid him in defending his life, and forcing himself into the Queen's presence, with power sufficient to remove certain of his enemies in attendance upon the Queen, was guilty of High Treason, inasmuch as the action threatened force and restraint to the person of the Queen.

Secondly, they resolved that the Earl's proceedings in the City of London amounted to actual rebellion, though he might intend no corporal harm to the Queen's person.

Thirdly, they resolved that the adherence of the Earl of Southampton to the Earl of Essex in the City, although he might be ignorant of any other purpose than to revenge a private quarrel of the Earl of Essex against certain of the Queen's servants, was High Treason in him, because the acts of the Earl of Essex amounted to rebellion.

Fourthly, they resolved that all persons going with the Earl of Essex from Essex House into the City, whether they were privy to his design or not, or whether they departed upon proclamation made or not, were traitors; but that those who joined him suddenly in the City, and dispersed as soon as the Proclamation was made, were within the terms of the Proclamation, and entitled to a pardon.

Here my Lord of Essex being forced with that speech of his touching his fear of the seeking of his life by these his enemies, was constrained to make a proof of some part thereof, "for," said the Lord High Steward, "you speak these things without probability."

"Nay," said Mr. Attorney, "the Lord Essex tells us he feared Raleigh and took up all these arms against him when he might have killed him every day walking by his door," whereupon the Earl of Essex, suddenly speaking, asked, "Who? I fear Raleigh? No, I fear not this," laying his hand therewith on the axe. "But I, understanding many ways how they prepared against me and what they could procure in their places, I could not be ignorant; besides I had intelligence upon intelligence, as my Lord Southampton can tell, of their preparations that day." ...

And here Sir Walter Raleigh desired on his knees to satisfy for that point, and having leave was ready to swear, when vehemently the Lord of Essex cried out, "Look what book it is he swears on"; and the book being in *decimo sexto* (the smallest volume), was ... changed to a book in folio of the largest size.

And then Sir Walter Raleigh with a settled countenance related that upon private occasions, sending to Sir Ferdinando to speak with him, "Sir Ferdinando appointed to meet me upon the water, where I came only with one boy, not mistrusting any this matter, and I protest before God and his holy angels, after I had delivered my mind unto him about repairing into the country, where he had a charge and whither her Majesty would have him go, Sir Ferdinando thanked me, but answered that these were no times for going, for the Earl of Essex stood upon his guard. Whereat I wondered, as never having word of it before, as I shall be saved, told Sir Ferdinando, 'If you return then are you a lost man,' and this was all the speech and intelligence I had of this matter or else let me be reputed a traitor to her Majesty."

And here my Lord of Essex spoke, "It was told us otherwise." ...

There followed some discussion of an assault made by Lord Grey on Southampton, in which discussion Grey participated despite his being one of the Lord Triers. Then Coke questioned Essex about a statement Coke said he had made that Secretary Cecil favored selling the state to Spain by making the Spanish Infanta heir to the Crown. Essex answered that he had not come to accuse others but to defend himself, although both Southampton and he had been informed that Secretary Cecil had mentioned to one of his fellow councillors "the title of the Infanta to be best after her Majesty's death and, in a manner, before."

Whereat the Mr. Secretary coming forth from behind the hanging where he had stood, fell on his knees and humbly besought the Lord High Steward that he might be suffered to break course and clear himself of this slander. Leave being granted, he stood up and began: "I have just cause to rejoice that this day, being to speak before this honorable assembly, my part is better than yours, Lord of Essex, for I speak under the person of a traitor. I will not compare with you for wit, and for the sword you have the advantage of me, but I have my innocence, my loyalty, my faith, all which you have forfeited, to defend me against the sting of slanderous tongues and of aspiring hearts. Your proud and turbulent thoughts have brought you to be a spectacle this day, and could you but have contented yourself within the bonds of charity, as we whom you have termed your enemies have always done towards you, you might have lived in safety, a peaceable subject.... I protest before God, I never hated your person, nor envied your greatness, and after you had utterly cast down yourself, by your own too much climbing and other follies, so that her Majesty was highly displeased with you, I continually pitied you, and was an earnest suitor for your restitution, often telling her Majesty [that] I have verily thought this, your cross and affliction, might make you fitter to do her Majesty better service. And I made not doubt, had you not thus hostilely thrust yourself into this violent and disloyal action, her Majesty would graciously have received you, if not into the former height, yet into a competent place in her favor." . . .

To this the Earl of Essex said little, but with a strange kind of smiling somewhat disdainfully, he would shake his head sometimes, which was answered with the like behavior in the Secretary. Only the Earl once said he thanked God for his humbling that day, but he envied not the Secretary.

Mr. Secretary continued, "And for that you have too slanderously touched my faith, and allegiance to her Majesty and my country by your seditious and false giving out in London, and this offensive affirming that Secretary Cecil had betrayed the State to the Spaniard, and offered to persuade a Councillor that the Infanta's title was next her Majesty, I defy all those that will say it of me; if you ever heard me speak of it, speak; if you heard it of others, name the author if you dare, tell his name if you dare, name him, name him, if you dare."

... the Earl of Essex said that indeed he heard not the Councillor himself report it, but it was told him by others, that Mr. Secretary used those speeches to a Councillor whom the Earl of Southampton could name as well as he....

Then after the Earl of Southampton turned his countenance to speak to the Earl of Essex..., he named Sir William Knollys.... [The court, in response to Cecil's passionate plea that Knollys be sent for immediately, did so, although this whole matter was, of course, completely lacking in pertinence.]

Here came in Mr. Controller [Knollys] and Mr. Secretary demanded of him, whether he had at any time heard him maintain the Infanta's title to the Crown of England before other. The Controller ... confessed how in Greenwich Garden Mr. Secretary had speech with him about it the last summer; and he remembered well the Secretary had cited a book, going under the name of Dolemans, wherein that title was preferred before any others, and offered to show him the book, but never persuaded him of the truth thereof....

Then said Mr. Secretary, "I thank God of this day that I stand cleared before my enemies." ...

Here Mr. Attorney urged the Earl with the small proof against Mr. Secretary. The Earl answered, "Oh, I have other proofs if you will have me utter them," to which nothing was replied.

Then Mr. Bacon entered into a speech much after this fashion. ...

Accounts of Bacon's speech differ. He flattered the intelligence of the lords, assumed their knowledge of former ages and histories, which made it plain that every traitor attempting to overthrow his liege prince always colored his attempt with some plausible pretense, recalled that Cain had outfaced with impudence the murder of his brother and likened Essex's defense to such flimsy excuses. After some classical allusions, Bacon affirmed that Essex had never been in the danger he pretended to fear and that in any event he should not have been so forgetful of his allegiance to and his favors from the queen, thus he should be confessing, not justifying. Essex answered that he would call forth Mr. Bacon against Mr. Bacon, that Bacon had written for him two letters stating the reasons for Essex's discontent and that either of those reasons had been just and true or else Bacon had been guilty of false and injurious counterfeit. Bacon ended by saying, "Well, my Lord, I have spent more hours in vain in the study how to make you a good servant to her Majesty and the State than I have done in anything else."

After this were read the examinations of Sir Charles Danvers, Sir Christopher Blount, Sir John Davis, the Earl of Rutland, Lord Cromwell, Lord Sandys, the three first being of the consultation at Drury House, and confessing in substance as much as Sir Ferdinando had before. . . .

The evidence of these witnesses is set out comparatively in full by Howell. Salmon, in his abridgment of Howell's "Trials," points out that the despositions of Essex's accomplices which were read as evidence against him in this trial were certainly not legal evidence; they were altogether unnecessary since there was abundant evidence against the prisoners and, indeed, the facts were so notorious that there was no denying them.[12] The depositions added little to the evidence given by Gorges and are omitted here.

An instance of official doctoring of evidence appears in a letter in the Essex papers in the State Paper Office, written by Secretary Cecil to Coke, telling him, in reading Blount's confession at the trial, to omit certain words which might have reflected unfavorably on the government. Again, in reading Blount's confession at the trial, his answer to the question whether Essex had not told him that if Essex came to authority there should be a toleration for religion was read as saying that he "should have been to blame to have denied it." There was not read the remainder of the sentence, in which was the explanation: "for in the Earl's usual talk he was wont to say that he liked not that any man should be troubled for his religion." These words had been marked for omission by Coke, and similar omissions were frequent. What is set forth as Lord Cromwell's confession cannot be found in the State Paper Office, and a version by Bacon dated subsequent to the trial differs totally from that used at the trial.

The depositions were followed by a long speech by Essex, in which he earnestly asserted that he was not a Papist, Puritan or atheist but was a firm believer in the doctrines of the Church of England. Spedding, in discussing Essex's religious beliefs, described them as simple, earnest and unaffected, also saying that the tone in which Essex replied to this charge and solemnly affirmed the sincerity of his faith in the religion which he had all his life professed contrasted strangely with the weakness and inconsistency of his answers upon the questions really at issue, making a corresponding impression on the court.[13]

The following two paragraphs, reporting Coke's statement at the conclusion of the evidence and Essex's rejoinder, are from the State Paper Office report of the trial.

> Mr. Attorney. Now, my Lord, I beseech your Grace, and you, my Lords, that be the Peers, let the due consideration of these several examinations and depositions enter into your hearts; and do but note how they have all agreed together in each particular point, notwithstanding these persons were all severally examined: But I must needs tell you that it is the just judgment of God, in his mercy towards our Sovereign, to have the truth so miraculously revealed, coming from these witnesses of their own accords, without either rack or torture to any of them.
>
> Essex. Mr. Attorney, I answer for that point; the self-same fear and the self-same examiner, may make the several examinations agree all in one, were they ever so far distant; but, good my Lord, let me desire your Grace to note who they be, and in what state they be that testify thus against me; my Lord, they are men within the danger of the law, and such as speak with a desire to live; and I wish that what they speak may purchase life unto them, for I never meant to endanger any of them; but I think they have much to answer for between God, their souls, and me.

I am here omitting a lengthy passage in which Coke irrelevantly again accused Essex of pretending to any religion which suited his purpose of the moment and in which Essex with great earnestness and sincerity maintained his devotion to the Church of England: "God forbid that I who have been esteemed a man of religion and zeal, now in the declining state of my life and fortunes should incline to hypocrisy or atheism"; the court finally refused to hear Coke further on the point. There followed some inconsequential testimony on minor incidents of the revolt.

And he the Earl of Southampton, who had hitherto spoken but little, began to answer the accusations in general as they concerned him. ... [The first part of Southampton's defense merely repeated his previous claim to good intentions and lack of knowledge, in going to Essex House on Sunday morning, that anything unusual was going on.]

"Afterwards," said the Lord Southampton, "I went with my Lord into the City as his friend in a private quarrel." Here the Attorney excepted against it, and said, "This is plain treason, my Lord, I will prove it; for any subject to rise with a company of armed men with intent to revenge a private quarrel, it is plain treason." "Oh, Mr. Attorney, give me leave," said the Lord Southampton, "why say you 'armed men'? I protest before God, I had no more weapon about me than my rapier and dagger." "That is enough weapon, enough to make an armed man," [said Mr. Attorney]. "Oh," said the Earl of Essex, "say you so, Mr. Attorney? By this you prove yourself to be a better lawyer than a soldier." ...

Mr. Attorney said he was guilty of those speeches that were given out in my Lord of Essex's house. The Earl of Southampton said, he thought no, for what was it to him when he was none of them that either spoke or heard. [Southampton's argument was that there was so much noise and confusion at Essex House when he arrived there that he could hear little, that he heard no proclamation made after their arrival in the City and that he thought he was merely going along with his close friend Essex to assist him in a private quarrel.] Mr. Attorney would prove he was, and then he drew out his evidence that did not convince him in the point in question, whereto the Earl of Southampton said it was uncharitably forced by Mr. Attorney, and absurdly.

"I thank God," said he, "that you are not my judge. ... her Majesty may, if she please, take my life, yet I know her Majesty is gracious and merciful and therefore may please to pardon me. And I do humbly crave her Majesty's pardon for my error. And I do rely upon her mercy. And though in nice points and quirks in law I be found a traitor, yet in heart I am none, for I had no evil intent."

Then the Lord Admiral, being the uppermost of one side of the court, stood up and said, all the lords of his party were desirous that for that point the Lord Chief Justice and the other judges would deliver their opinion of the law, whether their rising to go to the Court with such a company only to present the Lord of Essex his complaints without all manner of purpose of violence to the person of her Majesty or any other, whether this were treason; . . . the Earl of Southampton [continuing to insist that his presence with the others was purely accidental] put the case after this sort, whether such a tumultuous act, without any intent of treason, were to be adjudged treason. Mr. Attorney stood up and answered, "Who doubts it?" The Earl of Essex replied that the act was to be judged by the intent in conscience. "Nay," said Mr. Attorney, "our law judgeth the intent by the overt act." "Well," said the Earl, "plead your law, and we will plead conscience."

Then the Lord Chief Justice began and gravely stated his opinion that the act made it treason alone, and so the other judges for the most part. . . .

Both the State Trials and the Helmingham Manuscript give parts of Bacon's final speech, but a manuscript in the Bodleian Library is more complete and probably more honest. With one sentence added from Jardine, Bacon is quoted as saying in part, "I have never yet seen in any case such favor shown to any prisoner; so many digressions, such delivering of evidence by fractions, and so silly a defense of such great and notorious treasons." After repeating the various opinions of the judges, for fear the peers might have forgotten some, he proceeded, "Now put the case that the Earl of Essex's intent were, as he would have it believed, to go only as a suppliant to her Majesty. Shall their petitions be presented by armed petitioners? This must needs bring loss of liberty to the prince. Neither is it any point of law, as my Lord of Southampton would have it believed, that condemns them of treason (but it is apparent in common sense). To take secret counsel, to execute it, to run together in numbers armed with weapons — what can be the excuse? Warned by the Lord Keeper, by a herald, and yet persist! Will any simple man take this to be less than treason?" Bacon then answered Essex's statement that if he had intended to move against any other than his private enemies he would not have stirred with so slender a company by saying, "It was not the company you carried with you, but the assistance which you hoped for in the city which you trusted unto." Bacon could hardly have tried harder to convict his friend and benefactor.

And here my Lord Admiral mentioned his promise to the Earl of Essex when the Earl yielded to him, namely, that he should have an honorable hearing and trial, which he demanded the Earl whether he had or not now performed.

The Earl of Essex answered, "You have used me honorably my Lord." . . .

Now [after some further argument between Coke and the defendants] the peers being ready to go together about the verdict, the Earl of Essex detained them with a speech . . . [part of which, as reported in the State Trials, went,] "My Lord, I must confess it was my fault to stand out, and to maintain my house with defense and resisting; but I will not deny but that my Lord of Southampton and Sir Charles Danvers did persuade me to parley with my Lord General: which I hope your Lordship will remember I did yield upon some indifferent terms and conditions; which were, 1. That I might have an honorable trial. 2. That I might deliver my griefs myself to the Queen. 3. That I might go in safety. 4. That I might have my minister with me. And, lastly (which I chiefly beg of her Majesty), that she would be pleased to redeem some that were with me in the house, and guiltless, for knowledge, intent or action, of which was by me purposed. All which I thought good to remember, and so humbly submit the same to her Majesty's gracious pleasure." . . .[14]

Chamberlain, in a report to Carleton on February 24, gives us an informed spectator's reaction to the impression made by the two defendants:

This was the sum of his [Essex's] answer, but delivered with such bravery and so many words that a man might easily perceive that, as he had ever lived popularly, so his chief care was to leave a good opinion in the people's minds now at parting. But the worst of all was his many loud protestations of his faith and loyalty to the Queen and State, which no doubt caught and carried away a great part of the hearers; but I cannot be so easily led to believe protestations (though never so deep) against manifest proof, yet I must needs say that one thing sticks much in many men's minds that, whereas divers preachers were commanded the Sunday before to deliver to the people, among his other treasons, that he had complotted with Tyrone, and was reconciled to to the Pope; . . . there was no such matter once mentioned at his arraignment, and yet there was time enough for it from nine o'clock in the morning till almost seven at night. At his coming to the Bar his countenance was somewhat unsettled; but, after he was once in, I assure you I never saw any go through with such boldness and show of resolution and contempt of death; but

whether this courage were borrowed and put on for the time, or
natural, it were hard to judge. But I hear he begins to relent,
and, among other faults, to acknowledge and be sorry for his
arrogant (or rather, as Mr. Secretary well termed it to his face)
his impudent behavior at his arraignment. . . . The Earl of Southampton spoke very well (but methought somewhat too much, as
well as the other): and as a man that would fain live, pleaded
hard to acquit himself, but all in vain, for it could not be, whereupon he descended to entreaty and moved great commiseration;
and, though he were generally well-liked, yet methought he was
somewhat too low and submissive, and seemed too loath to die
before a proud enemy.[15]

Secretary Cecil's comment on his own knowledge of things
brought out at the trial is interesting. In a letter to Sir George Carew
he wrote, "He (Essex) pretended also an intention he had to have
removed me, with some others, from the Queen as one who would
sell the kingdom of England to the Infanta of Spain, with such other
hyperbolical inventions." Cecil, of course, referred to Essex's accusation, to refute which Cecil sent for Knollys. Gardiner discovered
shortly before writing his "History of England 1603-1616" that Essex's accusation was probably not so groundless as Cecil made believe. There are printed in Appendix III to his History letters
showing that, from the time of the accession of James I to Cecil's
death, Cecil received annually large sums of money from the king
of Spain. Since Cecil was accepting bribes during that period, it is
not unreasonable to suspect that he may have been on the Spanish
payroll even earlier, at a time when Spain was particularly anxious in
regard to the succession.

One other statement in Cecil's long letter should be quoted. It
will be remembered that the revolt was brought on earlier than
intended because the Council had sent for Essex, who feared imprisonment. In referring to Essex's fear of being imprisoned if he
obeyed the Council's summons, Cecil wrote, "which (summons),
upon my faith to you (to whom I will not lie) was only to have
reproved him for his unlawful assemblies, and to have wished him to
leave the city and retire into the country."[16]

And both the prisoners were commanded from the Bar to the
Lieutenant of the Tower, where the Earl of Essex continued
pleasant and cheerful. And the peers withdrew them into a little

room built at the Chancery Bar, where having consulted and called for the judges to resolve them on some points, after half an hour they returned and placed themselves in their order. Then the Lord High Steward demanded of them severally their verdict, beginning at the puny [lowest in rank] and so upward, first upon the Earl of Essex, after this sort. The Sergeant called the Lord Thomas Howard by his name as before, who standing up uncovered, attended the Lord High Steward's demand, delivered with such words: "You have heard Robert Earl of Essex this day indicted of High Treason, and arraigned. How say you, is he guilty or not? My Lord? Speak upon your honor." His answer was, "I hold him guilty of High Treason upon my honor," laying his hand upon his breast withal. In this form was it demanded of the rest, who gave their verdicts in like manner, as after they did upon the Earl of Southampton. Their verdicts being given and the prisoners at the Bar again, after a little pause the Lord High Steward said: "Robert, Earl of Essex, and Henry, Earl of Southampton, you have been here arraigned and indicted of High Treason; you have pleaded not guilty and for your trial put yourselves upon God and your peers; the nobility here who have heard the evidence and your objections and answers in your defense, have found you guilty. Now what can you say for yourselves why I should not proceed in judgment?" . . .

Essex replied, "I only say this, that since I have committed that which hath brought me within the compass of the law, I may be counted the law's traitor in offending the law, for which I am willing to die, and will as willingly go thereto as ever did any; but I beseech your Lordship and the rest of the Lords here to have consideration of what I have formerly spoken, and do me the right as to think me a Christian, and that I have a soul to save, and that I know it is no time to jest: Lying and counterfeiting my soul abhorreth, for I am not desperate nor void of grace, now to speak falsely. I do not speak to save my life, for that I see were vain: I owe God a death, which shall be welcome, how soon soever it pleaseth her Majesty. And to satisfy the opinion of the world, that my conscience is free from atheism and Popery, howsoever I have been in this action misled to transgress the points of the law in the course and defense of private matters, and whatsoever through the weakness of my wit and dullness of memory, or through violent courses (if there be any violent that seek either life or death), or if I have omitted or may have uttered anything otherwise; yet I will live and die in the faith and true religion which here I have professed."

Then the Clerk of the Crown demanded of Henry, Earl of

Southampton, what he could say for himself, why judgment of
death should not be pronounced against him.

The Earl of Southampton said, "For my part I must say as
before I have, I perceive my ignorance of the law hath made me
incur the dangers of it. Therefore I desire you my Lords that can
witness I am condemned by the letter of the law, that you will
truly inform the Queen of what I say and my penitence for this
my fault. I have been brought up from a child under her Majesty
and employed my whole time in her service, and have spent most
of my patrimony therein. I never became suitor in my own behalf
to her Majesty for anything, neither ever did I to my knowledge
fall into any offense against her Majesty before now; so if anything of my service past may move her Majesty to a gracious
consideration of me, or if there be anything in me that may
hereafter in any sort be turned to her Majesty's service, I humbly
entreat your graces' favor so far as to give me my life, and I hope
your Lordships will signify to her Majesty this my humbleness
and sorrow of heart for my offense, and my suit for pardon. I
humbly rely on her Majesty's merciful disposition." . . .

Essex's reply as set forth above is that given in the State Trials.
The lord high steward is there stated to have attempted to persuade
Essex, in view of the great favors the queen had accorded him, to
submit himself to her mercy, to acknowledge his offenses and thereby, no doubt, to find her merciful. Camden, who was present, says
Essex's reply was that he was loath, however, to be represented to
the queen as a person who despised her clemency, though he should
not, he believed, make any cringing submissions for it.[17] The Helmingham Manuscript, in reporting Essex's two replies, does not
contain the admission that he "may be counted the law's traitor" and
makes his reply to the lord high steward's request less stubborn and
more gracious than reflected in the State Trials.

Now the Lord High Steward proceeded to pronounce judgment against them . . . : "Robert, Earl of Essex, and Henry, Earl
of Southampton, you are here indicted, arraigned and convicted
of High Treason. Now you must go to the place from whence
you came, there to be laid on a hurdle, drawn to the place of
execution, hanged and cut down ere you be dead, then your
members to be cut off and burned before your faces, your heads
to be cut off and your bodies to be quartered and dispersed at the
Queen's pleasure, and the Lord have mercy on your souls."

Judgment pronounced, the Earl of Essex said, "I could have wished that my quarters might have been reserved to have done her Majesty better service, but howsoever, if it be her pleasure that they shall be thus bestowed, I shall be content if they may do her service though but in this kind. I desire not to live, nor crave her gracious pardon; not that I contemn her favor, but because I desire to die, and perhaps the example of my punishment may be made profitable in her government; yet I humbly request that a true relation may be made of my serious protestation this day of my innocent and loyal heart to her Majesty, and I hope the sprinkling of my blood will wash away my offenses and her Majesty's displeasure against me for them."

Here again, we find some tampering in the official report in the State Trials. The part of the sentence that the defendants be "cut down ere you be dead, then your members to be cut off and burned before your faces, your heads to be cut off" was omitted, presumably because it might cause the government to appear revengeful. Essex is there made to say in response to the sentence that he was not a whit dismayed to receive that sentence and that death was as welcome to him as life.

He confessed then, he had been misled and persuaded to transgress the laws; otherwise he had never entered into this offensive action. Then he made a petition to the Lord High Steward that he might have his own preacher. It was answered that it was not so convenient for him at that time to have his own chaplain as another. The Earl replied that if a man in sickness would not willingly commit his body to an unknown physician, he hoped it would not be thought but a reasonable request for him at that time to have a preacher who hath been acquainted with his conscience, to whom he might more boldly open his heart; further he desired the Lord High Steward that he would be a petitioner to her Majesty that the Earl of Southampton and himself, who loved, lived and now stood condemned together, might continue in the company of one of another till the time of her Majesty's pleasure for their execution, which the Earl of Essex, for his part, desired might be as speedy as it should please her Majesty. He desired a gracious consideration might be had of those lords and gentlemen which were fallen into this action merely of good will towards him. He said before his death he would make something known that should be acceptable to her Majesty in point of State. To these petitions the Lord High

Steward said he could not grant them but would move her Majesty in his behalf. Then the Sergeant at Arms stood up with his mace on his shoulder, making an Oyes and saying: "All peers and other persons appointed to be here this day may depart to take their ease, for the Lord High Steward is pleased to dissolve his commission. Then the white rod was broken, the court voided, and the prisoners committed back to the Tower, whither the axe was carried before them with the edge towards them. God save the Queen.

The official version contains one additional paragraph: As the lords were rising, the Earl of Essex said, "My Lord Delaware and my Lord Morley, I beseech your Lordships to pardon me for your two sons that are in trouble for my sake: I protest upon my soul they knew not of anything that was or should have been done, but came to me in the morning, and I desired them to stay, and they knew not wherefore. And so farewell, my Lords."[18]

FIVE

COKE, as attorney general, had been in charge of the prosecution of Essex. His conduct in preparing the case, in suppressing and distorting evidence and during the trial must be severely criticized. Lord Campbell, himself a chief justice, said Coke incurred never-dying disgrace by the manner in which he insulted his victims at the bar of a criminal court, that the first revolting instance was the Essex trial, that the young earl, although technically guilty of treason, was not guilty of evil intent, that although Yelverton opened the case with becoming moderation Coke followed with a most inflamed and exaggerated statement of the facts and that Bacon covered himself with still blacker infamy by volunteering to be counsel against his friend and benefactor and resorting to every mean art for the purpose of bringing him to the scaffold.[1]

Coke prepared the trial for prosecution like a playwright writing a scenario. In the Collier collection of manuscripts there is a memorandum in Coke's handwriting outlining the trial procedure, assigning parts and suggesting the arguments.[2] This was not of itself reprehensible, but when Elizabeth asked Bacon to write the "Declaration," Coke actually rewrote the evidence and gave Bacon twenty-five papers to use in supporting the verdict. Bacon himself wrote "Om." (omit) in several places in the papers to eliminate facts favoring Essex,[3] and in the government's publication of the evidence against Essex issued after his execution the material was substantially doctored.[4]

Not much needs to be said about the confession which was drawn from Essex after his trial in order to eliminate public objection to his execution. A letter written by the Earl of Nottingham to Lord Mountjoy in Ireland said that at Essex's request, he and Secretary

Cecil were sent to him the day after his trial, that Ashton, Essex's chaplain, was also with him and that Essex said that Ashton in a few hours had made him know his sins against the queen and God.[5] Ashton may well have been a selfish hypocrite. Birch prints an anonymous letter written on May 30 to Anthony Bacon calling Ashton a man base, fearful and mercenary, who had wormed his way into the confidence of Essex, who, being most religious, might easily be deceived. The letter tells how Ashton worked on Essex to make the confession by persuading him that his chances of salvation depended on it.[6]

The so-called confession, as partially contained in Nottingham's letter, is so completely inconsistent with everything Essex up to the time had been and said as to bear out the charge that it was written for him and his signature extorted under threat of eternal damnation. "[I] must confess to you, " it read in part, "that I am the greatest, the most vilest, and most unthankfullest traitor that ever was born in this kind. And therefore, if it shall please you, I will deliver now the truth, though yesterday at the Bar, like a most sinful wretch, with countenance and words I maintained all falsehood." Then he explained the plan for the "suppressing" of her Majesty and the Court and named those who were at the conference at Drury House (the Earl of Southampton's lodging), saying that these were the men appointed by him to consider how the plan should be executed. "And now," the confession incredibly says, "I must accuse one who is most nearest to me, my sister [Lady Rich], who did continually urge me on."

Camden thought that Essex could think of nothing but damnation unless he confessed the whole scheme and named his accomplices. While making his confession, Essex told Cecil and the other officials that the queen could never be safe as long as he lived and that he desired only to suffer privately in the Tower. He very much blamed some of his accomplices for aiming at nothing else except the ruin of their country and wanted particularly to speak with Blount and Cuffe. To Cuffe he said: "Be sure you ask pardon of God and the Queen and behave yourself so as to procure it. As for my own part, I have fixed my thoughts upon a better world, and have resolved to deal sincerely before God and man: And I must tell you plainly, that this instance of disloyalty is purely owing to your advice." Essex similarly impeached several persons not previously thought implicated. Lord Mountjoy was included, but because

Mountjoy was so successfully administering Ireland, the queen was prudent enough to forget what she had heard about him.[7]

Andrew Amos, in criticizing the measures adopted to obtain the confessions of Essex and the others for use in molding public opinion, questions both the sincerity of the confessions and the fidelity with which they were communicated to the public. Essex, he says, was visited on the day after his trial by the Dean of Norwich, who was sent to him by the Council, and afterward by his own chaplain, Ashton, and other clergymen. He had also a meeting in the Tower with Secretary Cecil, the lord keeper, the lord admiral and the lord treasurer, but no friend — not even his wife or mother — was allowed to interview him. A letter by Cecil in Winwood's Memorials says that Essex signed a written confession but that the contents of the document were never made public. Instructions to the constable, the lieutenant of the Tower and the clergymen who were to be present at the execution directed them to have "a very great and vigilant care" that Essex should not at his execution "excuse or justify himself" but should keep his speech within the limits already prescribed.[8]

T.G., in his contemporary but semifictional narrative, wrote that Essex expected a pardon until the date of his execution was fixed, that knowing of the power the Countess of Nottingham had over Elizabeth, he persuaded the countess to visit him and on his knees asked her to intercede with Elizabeth, giving her the ring Elizabeth had given him for use whenever he needed her help, but that after promising Essex she would do so, the countess went to Cecil and told him the story, after which they both went to Elizabeth and reported Essex haughty, unyielding. T.G. further says that at the last minute Elizabeth sent an officer to stop the execution but that Cecil, expecting her to do this, had pushed up the hour for the execution, and the message was too late.[9] We find no support for this story elsewhere.

That the queen was in extreme agitation of mind and very irresolute regarding the execution of the sentence and that she at first countermanded it but afterward, being provoked by Essex's obstinancy in not asking her mercy and alarmed by his declaration that his life would be dangerous to her safety, sent Darcy with an order for his death is confirmed by Birch on Camden's authority. Birch further confirms that the Earl and Countess of Nottingham did have a hand in preventing a stay of execution and that they intercepted Essex's application for clemency. This fact, he says, is agreed upon by both Francis Osborne and D'Maurier on the authority of Sir Dudley Carleton, who related it in Holland to the French ambassador. However, probably the better view is that Essex was too proud to send his queen the request for mercy for which she was anxiously waiting. The famous story of the ring is thought to be apocryphal. Elizabeth undoubtedly gave the ring to Essex during the early period of her love for him, but there is no acceptable evidence to support the story that it was given to Lady Nottingham, who withheld it but confessed to the queen on her deathbed what she had done and that the queen replied: "God may forgive you, madam, but I never can." Both Camden and Clarendon deny it.

Southampton, who didn't have such haughty pride as Essex, asked for clemency and was pardoned, but only after an extended imprisonment.

In the Collier collection of manuscripts relating to Essex there are several letters written to the lieutenant of the Tower by officers of the Council and endorsed by Secretary Cecil, "24 Feb 1600 [1601, new style]: Letters for the execution of my Lo. of Essex." Some words are indecipherable (handwriting in Elizabethan times appears to have been even worse than it is today), but in substance the letters advised the lieutenant that two executioners were being sent to him secretly (two because one might fail), that further instructions would follow and that the queen would name seven or eight noblemen to be present who would give the lieutenant the necessary warrants. He was asked to have an officer at the gates in the early morning to let in both the executioners and the two clergymen he had requested the Archbishop of Canterbury to send to the Tower at six in the morning.

A second letter of the same date advised the lieutenant that he was to signify to the clergymen "her Majesty's pleasure unto them that they be both present at the execution of the late Earl of Essex, as well to give all comfort unto his soul, the which her Majesty's great care and infinite desire is he might receive, as also that both you, Mr. Lieutenant, and both the divines do with all care and circumspection take heed that the said late Earl of Essex at the time of execution . . . [limit his speech to matters of penitence, religious faith and desire for God's pardon]." "But," the instructions continued, "if he shall enter into any particular declaration of his treason or the accusation of any of those that have been his adherents and participants therein, you shall forthwith break him from that course.... Likewise if he shall fall into any excuse or justification of himself... both you and the divines must utterly divert him from that course...." The lieutenant was to exercise "great and vigilant care" to that end, because the government still feared the people's reaction to Essex's execution.

A final letter to the lieutenant, signed by Cecil, Buckhurst and Nottingham, enclosed the queen's warrant for the execution. The lieutenant was told to go to Essex a half-hour after he had eaten and remind him that he would have been executed the Saturday after his trial except for the delay in his confession. The lieutenant should add that since all those matters had been sufficiently dealt with, and since Essex realized that his execution was for the safety and pre-servation of her Majesty, upon whom so many depended, he should know that on the next day, between six and seven, he would receive the execution of his judgment and that, therefore, he must continue in his firm resolution and prepare himself accordingly, in order to release his soul from the miseries of this wicked world. How well the lieutenant remembered all this we do not know, but it is a matter of record that he did not tell Essex of the time fixed for his execution until one in the morning of the day designated.

Many persons who watched the earl's execution have written accounts of it, but perhaps the one contained in the Helmingham Manuscript is the most accurate. Somewhat abridged, it says:

Upon Ash Wednesday in the morning about one of the clock the Lieutenant of the Tower gave warning to the Earl of Essex, being then in his bed, to prepare himself to his death, which should ensue that present day. Immediately upon notice thereof taken the Earl arose, and shortly after Doctor Momford and Doctor Barlow were sent to him, whom, together with his own chaplain Mr. Ashton (that had been with him all the time from his judgment), he desired to join with him in those exercises that might fit him to his end, now so near approaching, praying God so to bless them as they came to comfort him. And the divines being with him for that purpose willingly submitted to his request. Their exercises were prayer, confession and preaching; the latter was performed by Mr. Ashton at the entreaty of the other two as being best acquainted with the Lord's state. In the meantime was prepared for the execution a scaffold raised in the High Court toward the church, that was some four feet high and three yards over, railed round with small poles; in the midst thereof lay the block, being a piece of timber of some half a foot over [wide], and two feet long, rounded at the upper side. Between the hours of seven and eight of the clock the Earl was brought by the Lieutenant of the Tower, attended by some 16 of the guard, to the place of execution, being appareled in a black velvet gown, a satin suit of the same color, and silk stockings; he was in his slippers and neither girt nor trussed. He had on a black felt hat, and a ruffband with a single set. Thus he ascended the stairs of the scaffold (having the three divines with him only). At his coming up his countenance was neither light nor dejected, but with a constant and settled gait, he stepped into the middle where the block lay and with little motion of his body, he lightly put off his hat to the lords, viz, the Earls of Cumberland and Hartford, Lord Thomas Howard, Viscount Bynden, Lords Darcy and Compton, who were seated on a form on the north side of the scaffold some three yards from it, many knights, gentlemen and others to the number of 100 persons standing round beside them.

After his curtsey the Earl, having paused a little, drew towards the Lords, desiring the ministers to stand by him [so that] if he should wander or err in speech or behavior they might tell him of it, and so wholly putting off his hat with a distinct and serious delivery, . . . [The first part of his speech—a homily on Christian living, confession of sin, prayer for forgiveness and profession of faith—is omitted]. Then he paused a little and said, "I desire your Lordships and you my Christian brethren to join your spirits with mine, for now will I give myself in prayer to God, which I will perform on my knees so that all of you may hear that it will please God to give me an humble heart, and to assist me in this greatest temptation of my death, for I am not able to endure without his special grace, this last conflict." Here the ministers put him in mind to say his Creed, which he did (having first thanked them for reminding him, as they had done once before) for, said he, "Satan is most busy now." At the end of his Creed he added, "Lord Jesu receive my spirit," then giving away his hat out of his hand and putting off his gown and ruff-band he kneeled down in the straw which [had been] strewed before the block for that purpose, using these words, "Here Lord I submit myself in obedience and humility to thy commandment in obedience to thy ordinance, to thy will, O God, I submit myself to my deserved punishment," and then with his hands lifted up before him, and joined, his eyes most earnestly fixed on Heaven, whence they never removed, he began his prayer in this manner,

" . . . Give me patience and strength to endure this last judgment inflicted upon me by so honorable a trial. Grant that my flesh may not tremble or show resistance at the stroke of death. Let thy spirit seal up my soul in the assurance of thy mercies, and lift it up above all earthly cogitations that in this dissolution of mine I may have thee only before my eyes, even to the last breath." Thus he concluded with the Lord's Prayer, in pronouncing whereof all the assembly joined with him in tongue and voice, as before they had done in. heart, all (I think) present shedding abundant tears, casting out loud sobs. . . . In uttering the petition of forgiveness of sins, he spoke with great vehemence, "Forgive us our trespasses in Christ Jesus": His prayer ended, he asked for the executioner, who, kneeling down, asked him forgiveness. The Earl said, "Thou art welcome; God forgive thee, thou art the minister of justice"; then he desired him to tell him how he should fit himself for the block, for he knew not. And then the executioner directed him to pull off his doublet and falling-band; under his doublet he had a red waistcoat embroidered in front with a border of gold. [For a moment, tall, splendid, bareheaded, with his fair hair about his shoulders, he stood before the world for the last time.[10] Then,] bowing down himself he said, "I prostrate myself here before thee, O Lord God, beseeching you that thy blessed angels may be ready to receive my soul up into heaven as soon as it is departed from my body. And I pray you all here present to join with my spirit when my arms are stretched out," for he said [he] would only stretch them out when the executioner should do his office. He was willed here by one of the Doctors to say the beginning of the Fifty-first Psalm - "Have mercy upon me, O God, etc." When he had said two verses, the executioner being ready, he was called upon to say, "Lord, into thy hands I commit my spirit." Then laying his head on the block, and his body at full length, his arms stretched out, without muffle [muffled sound] he patiently received the stroke of the executioner, who performed his office ill, having an ordinary axe wherewith he struck three blows. Howbeit, neither body, arms nor head ever stirred after the first. The executioner took up his head and [said], "God save the Queen." All the time of his being on the scaffold the Earl never uttered worldly thought, taking no notice or leave of any person more than other.

SIC ITUR AD ASTRA

[These words are roughly erased in the original, in ink that is not the same as that in which the other words are written but is ancient.]

Among the spectators was Raleigh, for the purpose, if he is to be believed, to answer for himself if Essex made any accusations against him. Some of those present thought Raleigh had come "to feast his eyes upon the tragedy of the Earl's sufferings." Upon request, Raleigh retired to the armory and watched the execution from there. "This was the fatal, but withal pious and Christian end of Robert D'Evereux, Earl of Essex, in the 34th year of his age; tho' the French Marshal Biron, and some other lewd persons, did ridicule his piety, as a way of dying fitter for a gown-man [clergyman] than a soldier; as if a Christian might not startle at the terrors of hell, without forfeiting his courage."[11]

Essex was buried in the Tower. In 1679 a broadside was printed for Thomas Basset containing the official report of the trial later used by Hargrave. The broadside ends with:

HIS EPITAPH

Here sleeps Great Essex, Darling of Mankind,
Fair Honor's Lamp, Foul Envy's Prey, Art's fame,
Nature's pride, Virtue's Bulwark, lure of Mind.
Wisdom's Flower, Valor's Tower, Fortune's shame,
England's Son, Belgia's light, France's star,
    Spain's thunder,
Lisbon's lightning, Ireland's cloud, the whole
    World's Wonder.

A man named Robert Pricket, who had seen military service under Essex and who eked out a living writing verses and pamphlets, published a poem in 1604 (now in the Bodleian) called "Honor's Fame in Triumph Riding." Pricket was imprisoned because of the publication of this praise of Essex, but Cecil helped him to be released.

It is a long narrative poem, sufficiently pertinent to tempt printing here more than space permits. Perhaps three or four stanzas will suffice to give the poem's flavor. After discussing the Irish campaign and attributing the earl's lack of success to bad luck and unwillingness to stoop to deceit rather than to lack of bravery or ability, the author continues: "Harmless in thought when he a peace had made,/ He back returns to his beloved Queen,/ Thinking to rest secure under her shade,/ To whom she had a gracious mistress been:/ But wanting warrant for his back return,/ Displeased anger softly gan to burn:/ And some that did a flame desire,/ Threw flax and oil into the fire," The plotting against Essex continued: "Mole- hills were to mountains raised." The people and the Queen wanted a public trial where he could be cleared, but "All this was yet but labor lost,/ For policy that course had crossed." Sure that everything could be righted if he could just get to see the queen, "Guarded with friends, untimely forth he goes,/ to raise a force so strong his part to take:/ As that he might remove his settled foes,/ and to his Queen a quiet passage make./ . . . He died for treason; Yet no Traitor. Why?"

The trial and speeches on the scaffold are given in detail, then follows a graphic picture of the actual execution: "Base wretch, whose hand true honor's blood should spill,/ Death's axe did first into his shoulder strike:/ Upreared again he strikes a blow as ill,/ Nor one nor other were directed right./ Honor ne're moved, a third blow did divide/ The body from the world's admired pride:/ Was that the way to lose a head,/ To have an Earl so butchered?" The peroration is in the style much admired in that period: "Where God and Christ, and holy ghost combined,/ Environed are with glory more, than if/ Ten hundred thousand suns at once all shined,/ And clearly showed their radiant splendence guise./ Amidst that glory the soul of Essex stands,/ In endless joy upheld by angels hands;/ Then mourn no more, heaven hath his spirit,/ Whose life on earth such praise did merit."[12]

The earl's principal co-conspirators, Danvers, Blount, Davis, Merrick and Cuffe, were tried in Westminster Hall on the fifth of March. The Hargrave account is based on a manuscript in the Le Neve collection. It is very wordy, and since much of the evidence and material in the confessions duplicates that used at the earl's trial, it is here abridged considerably.

TRIAL OF THE CO-CONSPIRATORS

A fuller Account of the Trial of Sir Christopher Blount, Sir Charles Davers [Danvers], Sir John Davis, Sir Gilly Merrick, and Henry Cuffe. From a MS. purchased at the Sale of the MSS. of Peter Le Neve, Esq., Norroy King at Arms.

The Commissioners were the Earl of Nottingham, Lord High Admiral; the Lord Hunsdon, Lord Chamberlain; Mr. Secretary Cecil; the L. C. Justice Popham; Sir John Fortescue, Chancellor of the Exchequer; Mr. Secretary Herbert, with divers of the Judges.

The defendants hardly received a fair break in having as two of the commissioners before whom they were to be tried men who were their active opponents in the revolt: Lord Chief Justice Popham, who was one of the four men imprisoned at Essex House, and Nottingham, who was in charge of the queen's forces sent to capture the conspirators. Nevertheless, at that time this was accepted procedure. Remember that in a treason trial the judges were there not to acquit but to convict.

The commission being read, the court proceeded to the indictment, which was in substance as follows:

That on the eighth day of February last, at Essex House, they conspired the death and disinheritance of the Queen's Majesty, and on that day caused an insurrection of the subjects, and made war in London against the Queen and intended altering the government, state, and religion now established, and to surprise the Court at Whitehall. The Queen understanding of their intended treasons, for preventing thereof, upon the eighth of February sent the Lord Keeper, the Earl of Worcester, Sir William Knollys, and the Lord Chief Justice, to Essex House; they there commanded the Earls of Essex and Southampton upon their allegiance to desist from their purposes, to disperse their forces assembled, and to demean themselves as dutiful subjects. But they refused to obey their command; and committed them the said Lord Keeper, Earl of Worcester, Sir William Knollys, and the Lord Chief Justice, to be strictly kept and detained in Essex House, by the said Sir John Davis, keeping them in by force; and these words being used by some, "Kill them! Kill them!" and the Earl of Essex, upon his going out of the house, commanded that if they should offer to deliver them out of their custody, or if the said Earl should miscarry in London, then they should kill the said Privy Councillors and the Earl of Worcester. And that the same day they, with the number of 300 men, went into the City of London, seeking to stir up such citizens as they could move to their rebellion. And that the said Sir Charles Davers, Sir Christopher Blount, and Sir John Davis, on the said eighth day of February, together with the Earl of Essex, did fortify the said house, and armed themselves against the Earl of Nottingham, the Queen's Lieutenant, and against the Queen's army and forces sent for the suppressing of the said rebels.

The prisoners being demanded, whether they were guilty or not guilty of the several treasons whereof they were indicted, Sir Christopher Blount confessed several of the things contained in the indictment, and would have pleaded not guilty to the rest but the court told him he must plead general, either guilty or not guilty to the whole indictment, and upon evidence excuse himself in what parts he can. Whereupon he pleaded to the indictment, "Not Guilty," and put himself for his trial to God and his country. Sir Charles Davers made the like protestation, but was directed by the court to plead to the indictment, and so he pleaded, "Not Guilty." Sir John Davis said, his case was different from the rest, but seeing he must plead negatively to all, he pleaded, "Not Guilty." Sir Gilly Merrick and Mr. Cuffe were arraigned upon another indictment, but upon the points of the former indictment, save for levying of war in London and assaulting the Queen's forces there, and conspiring and plotting at Drury House.

Bacon later wrote, "The reason of . . . [Blount's] question was, as they confessed, in respect of the clause laid in the indictment, 'That they intended and compassed the death and destruction [disinheritance?] of the Queen's Majesty,' unto whose person (although they confessed at the bar, as they had done in their examinations, that their meaning was to come to her in such strength as they should not be resisted, and to require of her divers conditions and alterations of government, such as in their confessions are expressed), nevertheless they protested they intended no personal harm to herself. . . . "[13]

Yelverton, the Queen's Serjeant, began the evidence and opened the indictment, showed the act itself to be treason by the Statute of 25 Edw. 3, therefore for the prisoners to pretend an intent to another purpose, is no excuse. To alter the state, change the religion, enforce the prince to settle power, and for subjects to sway things at their list, is *crimen laesae majestatis*; and all indictments term this treason: For that subject that will rule his prince, will never be ruled by his prince; and to rule with his prince, the world may as well bear two suns as the state suffer two such governments. For particular proofs and plain convincing of the parties, there need no other but their confessions; which he protested, as he would be credited in the world, came voluntarily from every man examined, no man being racked or tormented. . . .

Yelverton then expatiated on the gravity of Essex's offenses in Ireland, the queen's clemency and her unnecessary kindnesses to him after his return and his subsequent plotting against her, yet all of these details were completely without pertinence in this trial. One of Elizabeth's kindnesses to Essex, Yelverton said, was her request to him to appear before her Privy Council in order that he might be warned to cease his plotting and disband his followers, a request Essex refused. The same night Essex sent for his supporters. The queen hearing of this, Yelverton continued, sent the lord keeper, the Earl of Worcester, Sir William Knollys and the lord chief justice to him. These men, finding the house guarded, ordered the earl to lay down his arms and requested a private conference with him, which he refused, saying he had to go to London and confer with the mayor and sheriffs but would return promptly, "so confident he was of his own strength and favor of the city."

> Mr. Attorney General Coke, coming to urge the evidence, desired, because the Bar was pestered, to have Sir Gilly Merrick and Mr. Cuffe removed for a time, which was done. . . .
> Sir Christopher Blount said hereupon, that he was now a man that through weakness of his hurt and through grief of his action, [was] not himself, scarce *compos mentis*; therefore desired not to be concluded by what he said, for he hoped the lords had called him thither rather to confess his faults, than to excuse or defend them. . . . Blount desired them to proceed against the others, for he would confess all that had been said. But Mr. Attorney desired to be heard against him. . . .

Coke first explained that the intent to use force against the queen, although not to injure her, constituted treason. He cited several examples from the law books: laborers in Kent started an insurrection for an increase of wages, contrary to a statute, which was held to be treason; London apprentices, resenting a sentence that some of them be whipped, agreed to whip the mayor for permitting it, and this was held to be treason; farmers in Oxfordshire, resenting the fencing in of farm land, destroyed the fences to restore tillage, and this was adjudged to be treason against the person of the queen. The London apprentices and the Oxfordshire men, Coke observed, were hanged, drawn and quartered, and he emphasized how much greater treason the actions of the defendants in the present case had been. Popham concurred that force to compel the prince in any government is treason.

After comparing these conspirators to Catiline, Coke, taking advantage of the popular dislike of Catholicism, thundered that although conspiracy against the queen was bad enough, this conspiracy contemplated the toleration of religion—and "this of all things concerns most!" He then rambled on that the attack by the Spanish Armada had grown out of the desire to restore Catholicism, that this had involved many treacheries against the queen herself, that the queen would rather lose her crown than see Catholicism restored and that an attempt under Edward II to change the religion resulted in the smothering of the king and the putting to death of the treasurer and chancellor. He was attributed the imprisonment and death of Richard II to the same cause. As for the allegation that Walter Raleigh intended the death of Essex, it was not only untrue but, on the contrary, the conspirators intended to kill Raleigh. Finally getting back to the point, Coke then asked the judges to affirm his statement that all assisting in a treasonable action, though not knowing treason was intended, were guilty of treason and that aiders and abettors in such a matter, even though the law did not charge them in this point with direct treason against the person of the prince, were offenders in treason. The judges concurred in both points, adding that the indictment must so charge them. Coke evidently had some concern about the lack of pertinence of his proof to the charges actually made in the indictment.

Now, Coke went on, for proof against every person then arraigned, he would first begin with Sir Christopher Blount, using his own confession as evidence. There was no necessity for Coke's repeating and commenting on all the facts which had been stated in the confessions, but he was a great show-off and could not resist the opportunity. He may also have had in mind the fancied necessity for keeping Essex's guilt before the public.

Coke next repeated Gorges's story about his meeting with Raleigh by the river but claimed that Gorges said Blount had advised him to kill Raleigh and had sent four shots with him when he went to speak with Raleigh. Blount replied that Gorges wronged him in so saying but confessed he did not like Gorges to go to the interview unarmed. Mr. Secretary asked Blount whether he thought either Lord Cobham or Raleigh had intended to kill the earl, and Blount admitted that he did not believe this was their intention.

In further statements, Coke, meeting with some denials and explanations by Blount, maintained he saw "some shiftings" in Blount's answers and told him to confess things plainly or otherwise he would prove him guilty of the earl's death. Blount replied that he wished his death were worthy to restore the earl to life again but that his confessions had been full and plain from the first. He asked Mr. Secretary to verify that fact, and Mr. Secretary acknowledged that he had always found Blount to deal honestly and plainly.

Coke now dwelt again upon Elizabeth's sending Mr. Secretary Herbert to invite Essex to appear before the Council, and on Herbert's offering to go in the coach with him alone, without any light, or to take a boat and go by water so that they could go and come without being seen, and as how Essex still refused. Blount said that he wished to God he had insisted on the earl's going. In spite of Essex's refusal, Coke said, Elizabeth chose to send to Essex House to investigate the assembly there four of Essex's best friends and nearest allies he had in the Court. To Coke's charge that Essex's followers, nevertheless, threatened to kill the queen's emissaries and that Blount advised the earl to imprison them, Blount replied that his advice to Essex was that the courtyard was an unfit place to talk and that he should conduct the emissaries to a more private place. Here Chief Justice Popham interrupted to give his own version of what had happened at Essex House, and a narrative by the lord keeper was then read.

When Popham asked Blount why his followers had stood outside the chamber door with muskets and matches, as he had seen through the keyhole, Davis spoke up and said that since Essex had charged him with the custody of the emissaries, he instructed Captain Salisbury, who was in charge of the muskets, not to permit their use and that he went in to the emissaries to assure them that no force would be offered. Popham replied to Davis that he had no reason to think the emissaries were in fear, that he told Davis that if he would take their lives it only was cutting off a few years and that when Gorges came and would have let Popham alone go, he refused to go unless they were all released. Davis then added that in order to assure the lords that no harm was meant them, he asked the Countess of Essex to join them, which she did, and dinner was served to them. Popham, still fiery, wanted it known that he had refused to eat any of Essex's meat.

Hereupon Mr. Secretary told Sir Christopher that the Earl had confessed that he [Sir Christopher] had been a principal instigator of him to these acts, and a mover of him to plots more pernicious to the state than these. Sir Christopher Blount said, "Hath my Lord that gone is, said so by me? Well, since I am so nearly touched in honor, and my reputation so far charged, I will tell you, Mr. Secretary, what I have counselled him, and what I have kept him from." Mr. Secretary said, "The Earl for part of his sacrifice to God, had left under his own hand all that he could disclose of all confederation in this matter."

Sir Christopher Blount seemed ready at the Bar to have disclosed further matter against the Earl, but referred to my Lord Admiral and Mr. Secretary, whether he should there utter it, or privily deliver it to them two; which afterwards he did, being brought into the Court of Wards to them after judgment was given.

Mr. Attorney proceeding with his evidence: . . .

Now was read some parts of the Earl's last confession, which contained four sheets of paper, all written with the Earl's hand; and it being showed to Cuffe at the Bar, he acknowledged it to be the Earl's handwriting. Out of the Earl's confession this only was read: That Blount, Cuffe, Temple, and some others, though they were not present at Drury House, yet they were privy to more dangerous practices and plots than these. And Cuffe being brought face to face before the Earl, the Earl charged him to call to God for mercy, and deal truly with the Queen; for he being to go out of the world, must deal truly with his soul . . . . And Cuffe denied not, but being confronted by the Earl, the words aforesaid were used to him. . . .

An abstract of Essex's confession was then read, in which he thanked God that his revolt had been unsuccessful, although men would wonder if they knew how often he had been requested to remove the evils of the Commonwealth. He confessed that the rebellion was first plotted when he was prisoner at the lord keeper's house and that, after having obtained control of London, he had intended to call a Parliament to enact needed reforms. Calling himself a burden on the Commonwealth, Essex desired his life to be shortened because he knew that the queen could not be safe so long as he himself was living, and he desired only that he might have a private death, thereby avoiding the acclamations of the people.

Mr. Attorney proceeding, said the Queen had charged those of her counsel to say nothing in this business, but what might plainly be proved, if it were objected; for she would go with her justice untouched: Therefore he would open matters, which though they of the jury need not to take as any part of their evidence yet because they were true, and fortified the matter divulged and proclaimed through the realm, for the honor of the Queen, though against an Earl that was executed, he would disclose unto them how this treason had a deeper root than most were aware of: . . .

The rest of Coke's speech and some evidence introduced to support it were completely irrelevant and are omitted here. Much was said about Essex's negotiations with Tyrone, about certain actions of a man named Lee (an emissary of Essex) and about confessions touching upon the Irish affair. Since it had been decided by the government and Elizabeth not to include Essex's conduct of affairs in Ireland or any subsequent negotiations with Tyrone as grounds on which he was to stand trial for treason, Coke had no excuse for bringing up those actions except the government's policy to blacken Essex's reputation as far as possible.

And here the evidence ended against Sir Christopher Blount.

And then Mr. Solicitor General urged new evidence against Sir Charles Danvers. . . . [There was not much "new" evidence presented. Danvers's long connection with the plotting was alleged, and it was said that Essex would not even confer about the revolt unless Danvers were present. Danvers's principal defense was that his actions were done out of the great love he had for Southampton, who had obtained already for him a pardon and his life for offenses Danvers had committed during the course of a family feud. Danvers's confession was repeated, in which he went somewhat more completely into the details of the plot and the part each participant was to take than had been done before. It all looked very neat on paper. After taking over the Court, Blount was to have had the gate, Merrick the hall, Davis the great chamber and Danvers the privy chamber, after which it was expected that various of the lords would come out of the queen's presence to salute him and to welcome him to the Court, whereupon the earl with ten or twelve noblemen was to proceed to the privy chamber to placate the queen; the city was then to be satisfied and a Parliament called.]

Mr. Secretary said that since this is a world wherein princes must be accountable for their doings to their subjects, that men should not marvel why like proceedings were not had against Sir

Ferdinando Gorges as these; the reason of forbearance was not that he had deserved better, or was otherwise conceited of, than to be an arch traitor, but because he was the instrument of saving and letting go those that were sent from the Queen to Essex House; and for this cause divers of her Majesty's Privy Council had been suitors to her Majesty for sparing his life for a time, though for their opinions of him, they held him an original and principal traitor; and that he advised more mischievously than any other, for he would have had the Court fired upon the taking of it. . . . .

Danvers still claimed that although he had participated in the plotting, he had never been an instigator. Blount, still attempting to clear himself, said he knew nothing of the plot until he arrived in London at the earl's request and reminded the lord commissioners what natural considerations tied him to Essex, since he had married Essex's mother, and how prodigal he had previously been in fulfilling the obligations of love through repeatedly venturing his life in the service of Essex and the queen. Mr. Secretary promised to remind the queen of this.

Against Sir John Davis, Mr. Francis Bacon urged the evidence, . . . [Bacon did not show much better grace in his effort to secure the execution of these lesser figures in the revolt than he did in urging the evidence against his long-time friend and protector, the Earl of Essex. However, his rivalry with Coke was such that he must outshine him and he made the most of his opportunity. Except for some classical allusions, we miss little by the omission of his speech.] Sir John Davis hereupon told Mr. Bacon, "If with good manner I might, I would long since have interrupted you, and saved you a great part of labor; for my intent is not to deny anything I have said, or excuse that I have done, but to confess myself guilty of all, and submit myself wholly to the Queen's mercy.". . .

Davis's confession was really the only evidence submitted. During the part of his confession that related to the detaining of the four lords at Essex House, the lord admiral, who had been given the duty to demolish the Essex House with cannon fire if it did not surrender, became excited and interrupted to say that the four lords really were in great danger, "for by God," he swore, "though these Councillors had been in the house, yet being as I was, general of the forces, and sent to force the house, I must and would have battered and blown it up, though it had been the death of them as well as the rest, and had all my own sons been there, I would have done it."

Then Mr. Attorney took in hand the evidence against Sir Gilly Merrick and Mr. Cuffe. To Cuffe, Mr. Attorney said that he was the arrantest traitor that ever came to the Bar; he was Poly — — [sic] the very seducer of the Earl; and since he was a scholar and a sophister, he would frame him a syllogism, and bade Cuffe deny what part he would. The syllogism was this, "Whosoever commits rebellion, intends the Queen's death; ... you committed rebellion; ergo, you intended the Queen's death.". . .

Disrespect for Cuffe was common. He was largely blamed for having fomented the unrest in Essex's mind which resulted in the revolt. Coke gave him pretty rough treatment while telling of his part in instigating Essex to rebel, but we can afford to omit his speech. It was followed by Secretary Cecil's story of Essex's confession and the manner in which it was obtained, but again the account appears irrelevant to the trial of the conspirators before the bar and to have been designed only to convince the people of the justice of Essex's execution.

Whereupon Mr. Secretary said that he must needs speak of a difference he found between noble and generous-minded men and others baser born: From the Earls and other the gentlemen of birth and of good house, all their confessions came freely and liberally from them without concealment or covering anything with untruths. By Cuffe, and some others of baser sort, nothing would be confessed but what they were convicted of, and shadowed with untruths so far as their wits could do it. . . .

Cuffe being willed to speak for himself, said the matters objected against him were many, and forced against him with all force of wit: Therefore for the help of his weak memory, he would reduce all unto two heads: things plotted and things acted. "For the first, in them Mr. Attorney thinks he hath concluded me in mood and figure; but my answer is, that if a man may be excused of treason by committing nothing, I am clear. . . .But whereas your argument, Mr. Attorney, is this, that whosoever intends treason, and the same is afterwards acted by others, there the intender as well as the actor is a traitor; but I intended treason, and others acted it; ergo, Mr. Attorney, it is not your *major* that I deny, because my Lords the judges have determined that; but I deny your minor, for if the thing intended was the going to the Court, yet the thing acted was the going into London."

But Mr. Attorney taking him short upon his own confession concluded him a traitor; for in treason the very intent is treason, if the same can be proved. Now, it is confessed by Mr. Cuffe that he intended the taking of the Court, which in itself is treason. . . .

Against Sir Gilly Merrick, Mr. Attorney urged first, that he was the man who fortified Essex House against the Queen's forces; and if God had not otherwise guided it, that day he had been the death of a noble person, the Lord Burghley, for he set one with a musket-shot to shoot at him, but missing the Lord Burghley, Captain Lovell's horse was killed under him at Essex Gate with that shot. . . . [Several confessions and examinations were then read, describing Merrick's part in the revolt.]

And here ended the evidence against Sir Gilly Merrick and the rest. . . .

Now the jury went out to agree upon the verdict, which after half an hour's time and more, they brought in, and found every of the five prisoners severally guilty of High Treason. The verdict being entered, and the jury discharged, the Queen's Serjeant prayed judgment. The Chief Justice then demanded of the prisoners, what they had to say for themselves, why judgment should not be given against them. . . .

All of the defendants next confessed their guilt, expressed their love for her Majesty and threw themselves upon her mercy. In respect for their high military standing, Blount and Danvers asked to be beheaded rather than hanged. Davis requested that his wife's estate not be seized, and Cuffe asked that he be permitted to retain his same apartment in the Tower pending his execution, that he be attended by a divine and that he be permitted pen and paper. It was allowed that "he should have means to write what he would."

Here ended all that passed before judgment.

The Lord Chief Justice of England (Sir John Popham), being now to pronounce judgment, used these words: "I am sorry to see any so ill affected to this state as to become plotters and practicers against the state, and that so strongly as you and others in this action have done. And my grief is the more in this, men of worth, service and learning are the actors in that conspiracy! Shall it be said in the world abroad, that we Englishmen, now after 43 years peace under so gracious and renowned a prince, are become weary of the government of such a Queen, whom all the world else admires for her government?" . . .

The lord chief justice then condemned all defendants to death. They were all hanged at Tyburn except Blount and Danvers, who, being nobly descended, were beheaded on Tower Hill. Each man made an appropriate speech on the scaffold. Cuffe moralized and asked pardon of those he had injured. Merrick once or twice interrupted Cuffe and advised him to "spare a discourse, which however rational, was not very seasonable, when he was taking leave of the world." Merrick further cleared Lord Mountjoy from having any knowledge of the plot and requested those present to intercede with the queen in Mountjoy's favor. Blount talked so long that the sheriff stopped him, saying the hour was past, but Lord Grey and Sir Walter Raleigh, Captain of the Guard, told the sheriff not to interrupt him. This caused Blount to ask, "Is Sir Walter Raleigh there?" Those on the scaffold answered, "Yes," and Blount told Raleigh he was thankful he was present and that he wanted his forgiveness before dying, both for the wrong done Raleigh and Blount's particular ill-intent toward him. Raleigh replied that he forgave him willingly but added that Blount would do well to confess that he was largely responsible for persuading Essex to revolt. Blount then related the conversation with respect to the use of the English army in Ireland to help Essex overthrow the government and stated that although he had agreed to consider it, he had determined that it should not be undertaken. "After which, he prepared himself to the block, and so died very manfully and resolutely."

SIX

At his death Essex left a son, Walter, by one of his mistresses (Birch says Essex was much more eminent for his temperance and sobriety than his continency),[1] and by his wife, Countess Frances, two daughters and one son, Robert (Essex III). Secretary Cecil showed no animosity toward the Essex family and was active in assisting the widow in various difficulties. Essex, of course, had forfeited his estates and titles because of his treason.

Elizabeth outlived the man she had refused to save by only two unhappy, regretful years. Young Robert Devereux was barely twelve when James VI of Scotland became James I of England. Remembering with some gratitude Essex's offer to help assure his succession and feeling kindly toward the family, James obtained from Parliament in 1604 an act restoring to young Robert the title and estates previously forfeited by the dishonor of his father.

The character of James I was a complicated mixture of good and bad, and his Court was no place for a young, impressionable boy. Deceived by an exaggerated opinion of his own learning, which was not inconsiderable, of his general abilities, which were far from contemptible, and of his capacity for government, which was very small, and confirmed in this delusion by the disgraceful flattery of his courtiers and bishops, James faced real difficulties. He was a foreigner, only rather distantly connected with the English royal line, and had come from a hostile and hateful kingdom to succeed the most renowned of sovereigns and to grasp a scepter that deep policy and long experience had taught her admirably to handle.[2]

James drank very strong, sweet wines. Lord Coke's father managed to get a draught while hunting with James and said it was so strong as not only to spoil his day's sport but to upset him for three days afterward.[3] James drank his sweet wine to excess, allowing some Court festivities to end in general intoxication. His courtiers accepted substantial "gifts" to use their influence. The king did not work too hard at the business of governing — it was easier to turn those matters over to his Privy Council, composed of six Englishmen and six Scots, and to Robert Cecil, son of Queen Elizabeth's secretary, William Cecil. Robert unfortunately had a humped back and was small but possessed all of his father's ability and more. James referred to him as his "little beagle" but rewarded his ability by making him Earl of Salisbury.[4] Hallam credits Cecil and his ripe wisdom and influence with the Council for having prevented James's blind attachment to Spain from precipitating him into a ruinous connection.[5] James's attachment to Spain may have been less strong than Hallam thought. Gardiner says that by Spring of 1609 James had everywhere taken up a position of hostility to the Catholics.[6]

That James was neurotic and highly unstable is not to be doubted. His doublet, heavily quilted against assassination, and his constant unconscious fumbling with his codpiece were outward signs. His difficult earlier years do much to explain his neuroticism. His childhood was motherless (Mary was imprisoned in England) and unloved. When he was five, there was a rebellion, and the youngster saw his grandfather die of wounds received in his defense. He never forgot his loneliness and in later years said, "I was alone, without fader or moder, brither or sister, king of this realme, and heir apparand [apparent] of England. This my nakedness made me to be weak and my enemies stark [strong]. . . . "[7]

Knowledge of the morals and behavior of James's Court helps us understand the character and actions of the young Lady Frances Howard, who now comes on stage. John Harrington, the godson of Queen Elizabeth, was appalled at what happened to the Court after Elizabeth's death. He called it incomparably the most disgraceful scene of profligacy that England had ever witnessed in the laxity of female virtue and without any sort of parallel in some other respects. Gross drunkenness was imputed even to some of the ladies who acted in the Court pageants. This statement by Hallam is based on a letter in "Nugae Antiquae," written by John Harrington to Mr. Secretary Barlow in 1606, describing a Court pageant given for visiting King Christian IV of Denmark, at which Harrington was present. The letter is unpleasantly illuminating: The ladies participating in the pageant were said to "abandon their sobriety and are seen to roll about in intoxication." The pageant depicted the Queen of Sheba arriving to visit Solomon in his temple. The lady acting Sheba's part, in attempting to present gifts of pastry and wine to Christian, spilled them on him. Faith, Hope and Charity were then scheduled to appear, but Hope was too drunk to make her speech, Faith "left the Court in a staggering condition," and when Charity arrived Hope and Faith "were both sick and spewing in the lower hall." The lady impersonating Victory fared no better; she was led away and laid to sleep on the outer steps. When Peace entered she was opposed and "most rudely made war with her olive branch and laid on the pates of those who did oppose her coming." Fortunately, in the meantime Christian had been put to bed. Harrington concluded: "I ne'er did see such lack of good order, discretion and sobriety as I have now done." A footnote by the editor of this edition of "Nugae Antiquae" says that, according to Sir Edward Peyton, on one occasion James got so drunk with Christian that he had to be carried to bed and that at another entertainment, this time given by Christian, the king, after giving thirty-five toasts, was carried away in his chair, and most of the officers of the Court were so drunk that they could not arise till late the next day.[8]

Weldon, James's clerk of the kitchen, said that at James's Court and in the London of his day the holy state of matrimony was made but a May game, brothels were much frequented and even great persons prostituted their bodies to satisfy their lusts, consuming themselves "in lascivious appetites . . . alehouses, dicing houses, taverns and places of vice and iniquity that beyond measure abounded in most places, . . . and evil intentions and counsels prospered rather than those that were profitable to the Commonwealth."[9]

Isaac D'Israeli, writing of James and his Court, said that young women, driven to necessity by the fashionable ostentation of their parents, were brought to the metropolis as if to a market, where they obtained pensions or sometimes marriages by their beauty, and that the same grossness of manners was seen among the higher females of the age. Sir Dudley Carleton, narrating the adventures of a bridal night, spoke of the romping of the "great ladies, who were made shorter by the skirts," thus displaying their coarse tastes. But worse, at a wedding celebration, the king was found going to the bride's bed in his nightgown to give a reveille-matin and remaining a good time in or upon the bed, "choose which you will believe."[10]

Since the center of the stage is now to be taken by Robert Carr, a man who was one of James's two great favorites, James's intense and unusual love for attractive young men must be briefly noticed. This passion was so notorious that a poem, obviously referring to Robert Carr's rapid advancement and the circumstances of its beginning, was written (probably by Ben Jonson) and widely circulated:

> Let any poor lad that is handsome and young,
> With parlevous France and voice for a song,
> But once get a horse and seek out good James,
> He'll soon find the house, 'tis great near the Thames.
> It was built by a priest, a butcher by calling,
> But neither priesthood nor trade could keep him from falling.
> As soon as you ken the pitiful loon,
> Fall down from your nag as if in a swoon;
> If he doth nothing more, he'll open his purse;
> If he likes you ('tis known he's a very good nurse)
> Your fortune is made, he'll dress you in satin,
> And if you're unlearn'd he'll teach you dog Latin.
> On good pious James male beauty prevaileth,
> And other men's fortune on such he entaileth.[11]

When Buckingham eventually succeeded Carr as the favorite, a contemporary gave this description of the relationship between James and the two men:

> He [the Earl of Carlisle] lay always under the comfortable aspect of King James his favor, though I never found him in his bosom, a place reserved for younger men and of more endearing countenance. . . . Now, as no other reason appeared in favor of their choice but handsomeness, so the love the King showed was as amorously conveyed, as if he had mistaken their sex, and thought them ladies. . . . Nor was his love, or what else posterity will please to call it . . . carried on with discretion sufficient to cover a less scandalous behavior; for the King's kissing them [Carr and Buckingham] after so lascivious a mode in public . . . prompted many to imagine some things done in the tiring-house [dressing-room], that exceed my expression no less than they do my experience.[12]

A letter written by James in 1625, evidently to young Villiers, whom he had made Duke of Buckingham, is interesting:

My only sweet and dear child, notwithstanding of your desiring me not to write yesterday, yet had I written in the evening if at my coming in out of the park such a drowsiness had not come upon me as I was forced to sit and sleep in my chair half an hour; and yet I cannot content myself without sending you this pullet, praying God that I may have a joyful and comfortable meeting with you, and that we may make at this Christenmass a new marriage, ever to be kept hereafter; for God so love me as I desire only to live in this world for your sake, and that I had rather live banished in any part of the earth with you, than live a sorrowful widow's life without you; and so God bless you, my sweet child and wife, and grant that you may ever be a comfort to your dear dad and husband. James R.[13]

The rapid rise of Robert Carr and the circumstances satirized by Ben Jonson in the doggerel printed above are recounted by a contemporary writer:

Amongst other accidents that happened about these times, the rising of one Mr. Carr was most remarkable, a man of mean parentage, inhabiting in a village near Edinburgh in Scotland, and there through the favor of friends, was preferred to be one of his Majesty's pages, for he kept twelve so long as he was in Scotland (according to the custom of the French). Afterwards at his coming into England, the Council thought it much more honorable to have [only] so many footmen to run with his Majesty, as the Queen had [had], before him. Whereupon those youths had clothes put to their backs, according to their places, and £50 apiece in their purses, and so were dismissed [from the] Court. This youth amongst the rest having thus lost his fortunes, to repair them again makes haste into France, and there continued until he had spent all his means and money: so that now being bare in a strange country, without friends, or hopes to obtain his expectation, returns back for England, bringing nothing with him but the language, and a few French fashions. Nevertheless, by the help of some of his countrymen, and ancient acquaintance, he was preferred unto the Lord Hayes (a Scotch man, and a favorite of the King's) to wait upon him as his page. Not long after amongst many others, this Lord was appointed to perform a tilting [take part in a tournament], who, bearing an affection to this young man, as well in respect he was his countryman, as that he found him to be of a bold disposition, comely visage, and proportionable personage, mixed with a courtly presence, he prefers [chooses] him to carry his device [Hayes's heraldic bearing] to the King, according to the custom of those past times used: Now when he should come to light from his horse to perform his office, his horse starts back, throws him down, and breaks his leg: This accident being no less strange than sudden, in such a place, causes the King to demand who it was, answer was made him, his name was Carr, he taking notice of his name, and calling to remembrance that such an one was his page, caused him to be had into the Court, and there provides for him, until such time as he was recovered of his hurt: After in process of time, the young man is called for, and made one of his Majesty's bedchamber, where he had not long continued in that place before (by his good endeavors, and diligent service in that office) the King showed extraordinary favor unto him, doubling the value of every action in estimation, so that many were obscured that he might be graced and dignified: Thus the hand of the diligent maketh rich, and the dutiful servant cometh to honor, and so he of all others (either without fraud to obtain it, or desert to continue it) is made the King's favorite. No suit, no petition, no grant, no letter, but Mr. Carr must have a hand in it; so that great rewards are bestowed upon him by suitors, and large sums of money by his Majesty, by which means his wealth increased with his favor, and with both honor, for worth and riches dignify their owners, being from a page raised to the dignity of knighthood. Afterwards his favor still increasing with his honor, there was no demand but he had it, no suit but was granted, whether it were Crown lands, lands forfeited or confiscated, nothing so dear but the King bestowed it upon him, whereby his revenues were enlarged, and his glory so resplendent, that he drowned the dignity of the best of the nobility, and the eminency of such as were much more excellent, by which means envy (the common companion of greatness) procures him much discontent: But yet passing through all disadventures, continues his favor; and men (being drawn to applaud that which is either strange or new) begin to sue to him, and most to purchase him to be their friend and assistant in Court, so great and eminent was his favor.[14]

Henry, James's brilliant heir, was about the age of young Essex, and the two boys were together a good deal. On one occasion when they were playing tennis, Henry, becoming provoked, taunted Essex with being the son of a traitor. Essex lost his temper and struck

Henry over the head with his racket. When Henry complained to James, the king upheld Essex. Henry thoroughly disliked the handsome young men his father gathered around him, especially Robert Carr, whom he distrusted as favoring the group that wanted Henry to marry a girl from the Spanish Court. Henry died in 1612, "a prince as eminent in nobleness as in blood, and having a spirit too full of life and splendor to be long shrouded in a cloud of flesh."[15] There was the usual rumor of poisoning; James had rather disliked his son, and the enmity between Carr and Henry was well known. The preacher who had been Henry's chaplain clearly hinted in a sermon that Carr had caused the young man to be poisoned. Later Chief Justice Coke hinted in court at the same thing, and the possibility became a factor in the criminal trial to which Carr was eventually subjected.[16]

The Howards were the most powerful family in the kingdom. The Saxon form of the family name, Hereward, was already eminent in tenth-century England. Under James, Lord Thomas Howard had acquired the highest of all offices in the Court, that of lord chamberlain, was made Earl of suffolk and later became lord high treasurer. In the meantime, his uncle, Lord Henry Howard, had been made a Privy Councillor and Earl of Northampton. Charles Howard was made Earl of Nottingham and as lord high admiral commanded the fleet that defeated the Spanish Armada. Northampton never married. He was not a wise man but achieved his status through flattery and shrewdness. A contemporary called him a man of great talents but one who dishonored those talents and his illustrious birth.

On January 15, 1606, young Essex was married to Frances Howard, a younger daughter of Lord Thomas Howard. The king, still kindly inclined toward the Essex family, had arranged the marriage; Robert Cecil, the power behind the throne, approved, "being mindfull of the asperity and sharpness that was betwixt him [Cecil] and the late Earl of Essex . . . [and thinking] it to be a good act of policy and piety not to suffer malice to become hereditary." Cecil had married his oldest son to Howard's oldest daughter and hoped "that the fathers' enmity might be closed up by the sons' nuptial fraternity."[17] James entered avidly into the marriage festivities, which lasted almost a week.

A contemporary who frequented the Court wrote of the marriage:

The Earl of Essex was 14 years of age, and she 13 when they married; too young to consider, but old enough to consent: Yet by the advice of friends separated after marriage, she under her mother's wing, and he visiting France and Germany till time should mature and ripen a happy co-union. [The parents thought it best to postpone consummation of the marriage until the children had become more mature.] The Court was her nest, her father being Lord Chamberlain; and she was hatched up by her mother, whom the sour breath of that age (how justly I know not) had already tainted; from whom the young lady might take such a tincture, that ease, greatness, and Court glories, would more stain and impress on her, than any way wear out and diminish. And growing to be a beauty of the greatest magnitude in that horizon, was an object fit for admirers, and every tongue grew an orator at that shrine.[18]

When Essex returned to England after his more than three years abroad, he found his wife a different person from the girl he had married. She had been living in an atmosphere where every person was given to self-indulgence and where intrigues of all kinds were the accepted thing. Her mother was "a lady whose indifferent morals rendered her totally unfit to look after Frances while her boy-groom was away."[19] A daughter of the leading family of England, young, beautiful and the toast of the Court, it is no wonder that Frances had become badly spoiled. Nevertheless, her protrait in the National Gallery in London gives no hint of the selfish disregard for everyone but herself of which she was later accused, and Sir Simonds D'Ewes, writing in his diary, wondered at the misdeeds alleged in her trial, "for I have heard one Captain Field, a faithful votary of the Earl of Suffolk, her father, protest, that having known her from her infancy, he had ever observed her to be of the best nature, and the sweetest disposition of all her father's children; ... execrating also, by his bitter expressions, my Lord of Northampton's wicked practices, by which she was first drawn to become the Earl of Somerset's adulteress."[20]

It seemed to have been popularly believed around the Court that Prince Henry was the first to enjoy Frances's favors. It is said in the "Aulicus Coquinariae" to be a notorious truth that Prince Henry made love to the Countess of Essex before doing so to any other lady. D'Ewes wrote in his diary that Northampton had incited Frances to win Henry's affection and that he was the first on whom she bestowed her favors. D'Ewes, about twenty-five at the time, thoroughly knowledgeable about everything going on at Court and encouraged by Selden and Cotton to keep elaborate diaries, was very positive in his opinion that "notwithstanding the inestimable Prince Henry's martial desires and initiation into the ways of godliness, the Countess, being set on by the Earl of Northampton, her father's uncle, first taught his eye and heart, and afterwards prostituted herself to him, who reaped the first fruits [of her virginity]."[21] However, there comes from several sources the anecdote that a courtier once picked up a glove dropped by Frances, handed it to Henry to please him but that Henry refused it with the scornful remark, "It has been stretched by another." There was already gossip around the Court that Carr was enjoying the favors of Frances.

It was obvious to everyone soon after the accident which first brought Carr to his attention that James was in love with his new protégé. One courtier wrote: "The Prince leaneth upon his arm, pinches his cheeks, smooths his rustled garments . . . the King teacheth him Latin every morning, and I think someone should teach him English too for he is a Scotch lad."[22] His honors followed fast: knight, Viscount Rochester, Privy Councillor, acting secretary of state, Earl of Somerset, treasurer of Scotland and lord chamberlain. He was the first Scot to sit in the House of Lords. Cecil's death, soon after Carr's rise began, freed Carr of an opponent and hastened his progress. Carr wanted Cecil's job, but no appointment was made at once; James acted as his own secretary but had the seal delivered to Carr. When eventually Winwood was made secretary, Carr retained the seal — which, since no state paper was valid without it, made Winwood rather a figurehead. When Suffolk (Frances's father) was made lord treasurer and Somerset succeeded him as lord chamberlain, the king declared that no man should marvel that he bestowed a place so near him upon his friend, whom he loved above all men living.[23]

Carr seems to have been personally honest. In a letter he wrote to Northampton in 1612, he boasted that he was the courtier whose hand never took bribes.[24] Since the king gave him all the money he could use, it could be true. Carr was smart enough always to tell James of the various "gifts" given to him by persons wishing favors. Although James was almost always in financial straits, and his officials and attendants were often unpaid, nevertheless, he made liberal gifts to his favorites. At one time he gave jewels to Frances valued at £ 10,000. By the end of 1613 his debts amounted to £ 680,000. Carr knew well how to cast his bread upon the waters. In 1613, when the treasury was empty, he sent for some of its officials and, delivering them the key of a chest, told them to take what they found there (probably £ 25,000 in gold) for the king's use.[25] The gesture paid off; before the year was out, Carr had grants of money and land making him one of the richest men in England.

One of the properties given to Carr was Sir Walter Raleigh's estate of Sherborne. When his lands were forfeited for his treason, Raleigh persuaded James to deed Sherborne to trustees for his wife and son. In now giving it to Carr, James relied on a clerical defect in the trust instrument. When Lady Raleigh begged at his feet, James's answer was "I maun [must] have the land, I maun have it for Carr." Raleigh, in the Tower, wrote a touching letter to Carr on January 2, 1608, beseeching him, "seeing your day is but now in the dawn and mine come to the evening . . . not to begin your first building upon the ruin of the innocent. . . . "[26] We do not know whether Carr answered, but James settled an annuity on Lady Raleigh and her son as compensation for loss of the land.

When the young Essex returned from overseas to claim his bride, he "found that beauty, which he had left innocent, so farded [covered with cosmetics] and sophisticated with some Court drug which had wrought upon her, that he became the greatest stranger at home. His patience made way for him for a while, and he bore up with a gentle gale against the stream of this woman's affections, which ran altogether (unknown to him) into another channel. . . . till surfeited . . . he went to the Earl of Suffolk (her father) and demanded his wife, thinking himself capable to enjoy both her and her love. The father, that thought there had been an intimacy betwixt them suitable to their conjugal knot, made use of his paternal power to reduce his daughter to the obedience of a wife."[27]

Suffolk's command failed to do much good. Codrington wrote in 1646 that Essex and Frances lived apart until about 1610, "at which time they enjoyed the society of one bed, and so continued until about the year 1613,"[28] but apparently nothing happened in that bed. "From the time he [Essex] was 18, he lay with her constantly in the same bed for three years, together, endeavoring, but in vain, to know her carnally. It was no advantage to a young lady's virtue to be teased and tempted to inclinations which could not be gratified: and her condition was really deplorable. She bore it, however, for about three years with great patience, till the Earl spoke of his own inability to several of his friends and relations, which soon made it to be the common talk about Court, and occasioned various private disputes between divines and civilians about the validity of the marriage. It was not to be expected in such a case, that the parties should live together in any great harmony: and rumors were raised to the Countess's disadvantage, as if she was unkind or disobedient to her husband."[29]

In writing the above passage, Carte was kinder to Frances than most historians have been. It seems quite possible that the marriage was never consummated, but contemporary accounts tend to indicate that Frances's passion for Carr and distaste for her husband made her so cold and unresponsive to him (she would sometimes shut herself in her room for weeks at a time) that the desire which he would normally have had for her was killed. It is also possible that drugs which she had administered to him may have deadened his natural virility. D'Ewes wrote in his diary: "Whether the Earl of Essex were in any way disabled by the sorceries practiced against him, I cannot determine."[30]

Whether at first Frances was sincerely in love with Carr, or whether she had given up hope of seducing Prince Henry and decided Carr was her best chance for a supreme position at Court, there is no doubt that she soon had an unreasoning passion for Carr. Consequently, she "had a double task to undergo for accomplishing her ends: One was, to hinder her husband from enjoying her; the other was to make the Viscount sure unto her: For dishonest love is most full of jealousy. Her husband she looked upon as a private person, and to be carried by him into the country, out of her element (being ambitious of glory, and a beauty covetous of applause), . . . [would be] an insufferable torment; though he was a man . . . that loved her with an extraordinary affection, . . ."[31]

Northampton did his best to promote the liaison between his niece and Carr. As Anthony Weldon put it in his contrived style: "Northampton, finding himself neglected by so mean a fellow [Carr], cast about another way, and followed Balaam's counsel, by sending a Moabitish woman [Frances] unto him."[32] Much information about the intrigue and its results is to be found in Weldon's "Court and Character of King James," but he was not unprejudiced. Clerk of the kitchen to James in 1604 and clerk of green cloth in 1609, Weldon accompanied James on a trip to Scotland in 1617. Sanderson refers to Weldon's book as a manuscript "which with some regret of what he had maliciously writ, [he] intended to the fire, and died repentant, though since stolen to the press out of a lady's closet."[33]

Akrigg calls Weldon an "anti-royalist," and it is true that his history was published under the Commonwealth. D'Israeli said Weldon "has been reproached for gaining much of his scandalous chronicle from the purlieus of the court" and mentions that for his zealous services to the Parliament during the Commonwealth he was voted a grant of £500 .[34] Nevertheless, Ribault, in editing the works of Overbury in 1856, said that Weldon's book is worthy of much more credit than is commonly assigned to it and that recent discoveries fully confirm the truth of his statements. Weldon's facts do seem accurate, and if we read him with the same expectation of slanted interpretation that we read newspaper articles, we can learn much of what went on at the Court of James.

Essex, at last deciding that he could never gain the affection of his wife as long as she was exposed to the distractions of the Court in which she so much delighted, again carried his problem to his father-in-law. "The old man being troubled with his daughter's disobedience, embittered her, being near him, with wearisome and continual chidings, to wean her from the sweets she doted on, and with much ado forced her into the country."[35] She now again resorted to her friend Mrs. Turner, whose advice and more tangible help through Dr. Forman's pills and spells she had been using to heighten the flame in Carr and dampen it in Essex. Mrs. Turner enjoyed some social standing and reputation, which perhaps explains Frances's trust in her. She was a pretty blonde of good birth and had been a companion of Frances before Frances left the Howards to live with Essex. After Turner's early death, the widow set up as a dressmaker but soon found it more profitable to assist the licentious members of the Court in their affairs. She procured love philters and other alleged aphrodisiacs and made her home available for illicit meetings. Frances and Carr often found release for their passions under her hospitable roof. Mrs. Turner had children by Sir

Arthur Mainwaring and in spite of her means of livelihood enjoyed a reasonably good reputation.

Mrs. Turner had introduced Frances to Dr. Forman, who from a start as an apothecary's apprentice had moved on to astrology, fortune-telling and, finally, necromancy. In spite of four imprisonments for practicing medicine without a license, he had received a degree of Doctor of Physics and Astronomy at Cambridge and had acquired a great reputation in London for his aid in matters of this sort. At Forman's house Frances had taken part in black magic rituals; some of the writings and incantations used were later produced in court, along with various obscene paintings, metal and wax figures of naked women, a copulating man and woman and "hex" figures. It was Forman who had given Frances these things and the philters to inflame Carr and to quench any desire Essex might still have. Roger Coke, grandson of Sir Edward Coke, wrote that "how cold soever the affections of the Countess were to the Earl, they were not less on fire to Carr; and that these flames might soar in an equal height, she, by the help of Mrs. Turner, procures one Dr. Forman to bewitch Rochester [Carr] into equal desires of mutual love with her, and the familiarity between them became publicly scandalous."[36]

We have only to look at a few entries in Forman's diary to size the man up:

> 1585 . . . the first of March I began to distil aqua vitae . . . the 31st day [of July] I was imprisoned again. . . . 1586. This year I had much trouble and suits in law . . . I got much and spent much. . . . 1587 . . . the 6 of March I was imprisoned . . . The 11 of May I begun to distil many waters . . . This year I had much trouble . . . I practiced magic . . . I thrived reasonable well. 1589 . . . I practiced then again necromancy and magic and physic, and my enemies prevailed against me, and I was like to have run into many mischiefs. 1592 . . . This year I did many notable cures, and began to be known, and come to credit.[37]

John Strype, in his "Life of Whitgift" (Archbishop of Canterbury), sheds more light on Forman: "The Archbishop in the month of July sent a letter to the College of Physicians in London; the occasion was this: One Simon Forman, a pretender to skill in physic and astrology, but a great imposter, was, by a warrant of the Censors of that College committed to prison. But getting out by some means or other, he fled to Lambeth, as a place of protection from the College officers. Whereupon the College addressed their letter to the Archbishop [describing Forman's practices] . . . ; miserably deceiving the innocency of simple-minded people." The letter asked the archbishop to frustrate Forman's expectations and to permit the college to use such lawful ordinary course as their laws provided to suppress Forman and similar offenders. The archbishop replied that he would not tolerate Forman, that he had heard not a very little of him and that he would call him up for misdemeanors if anyone would prosecute.[38]

Seeking aid and comfort from Mrs. Turner and Dr. Forman, Frances wrote from the country to "Sweet Turner" and "Sweet Father" letters which were placed in evidence at her trial and which complained of the fact that her husband was as lusty as ever, in spite of the medicines. She appealed to Mrs. Turner, "as you have taken pains all this while for me, so now do all you can, for never so unhappy as now; for I am not able to endure the miseries that are coming on me, but I cannot be happy so long as this man liveth: therefore pray for me, for I have need, but I should be better if I had your company to ease my mind."

"These instigations," wrote Camden, made [Forman] active, and the man being skillful in natural magic, did use all the artifice his subtlety could devise really to imbecilitate the Earl; for no linen came near his body that was not rinsed with their camphor compositions and other faint and wasting ingredients; and all inward applications were foisted on him by corrupted servants, to lessen and debilitate the seminal operations: Which veneficum [use of poisons] is one great part of witchcraft. . . . And this in time wrought such effects upon his person, that he found himself unable with her, though she permitted him; yet when he had been from her some reasonable time, to renovate his spirits, by shaking off those artificial applications, then his abilities made her unwilling and refractory. Though some are of opinion that he was not much debilitated, but that she got (by her virtuous agents) an artifice too immodest to be expressed, to hinder penetration. And thus she tormented him, till he was contented to let her steer her own course, which after run her on ground."[39]

Frances and Essex now returned to London. Essex had had enough of country life with his hateful spouse, and Frances was anxious to get back to London and into Carr's arms. "Coming to London next winter with this full sail, laden with lust, she found the Viscount much prepared for her, ... all those little artifices that mischievous women and cunning impostures could devise, had advanced him as much in his desires as they had hindered the other [Essex].... With an unbridled appetite, [they met at first] closely in corners (sin being at first shamefaced) but afterwards they grew more bold; and every hour that the Viscount could steal from his Royal Master, he dedicated it to his disloyal mistress."[40]

Carr, now Viscount Rochester, was almost omnipotent, in full possession of the king's favors, executing the place of principal secretary (Cecil had died), receiving all packets and dispatching answers without the knowledge of the king or Council.[41] This was James's wish and was not necessarily bad for the kingdom. Carr was shrewd, honest, intelligent, conversant with domestic and foreign affairs and had an able assistant in his secretary, Overbury. Many persons in the government had wanted to see him succeed Cecil as secretary. Sir Edward Peyton may have been correct when he said that Carr furnished his library only with twenty play-books and wanton romances, having no other type of book in his study, [42] but Weldon credits Carr with spending his time on serious study and associating with men who might better him intellectually. Bishop Goodman said, "Truly he was a wise, discreet gentleman; and as Sir Robert Cotton, the great antiquary, told me, he did very often send unto him for precedents, when ... things were to be done in the State which he doubted whether they were lawful and expedient and therefore did desire to have the example of former times for his warrant."[43] The good bishop, however, was always looking for the best in everybody.

Frances was now determined to marry Carr and share his glory. There was a family council of the Howards at which Essex's murder may have been seriously considered. It is known that later Frances sent a servant to a certain Mary Woods to reclaim a ring and some money. In explanation, Frances said she had left it with Mary to keep for her one day when she was in a great hurry to get to Court. Mary Woods differed; she said the ring and money were given her as part payment of £1,000 she was to receive for procuring delayed-action poison to be administered to Essex, but that she repented, decided not to become implicated and left London. A suit against her was brought and was being heard in Suffolk when, apparently on the word from higher authority, the case was dropped.[44]

That attempt, if made, having failed, the Howards determined that an annulment of the marriage would be the best solution. As a matter of fact, their marriage was so obviously hopeless that both Frances and Essex seem to have wanted the annulment. Goodman said that about a year or two before the marriage was questioned, he heard from a servant of the Earl of Essex that the earl was fully resolved to question the marriage and to prove a nullity and that he was confident that if the countess had not at that instant done it, the earl would himself have been the plaintiff.[45] Sanderson suggests that, in the light of Essex's words and his later life with a second wife, he probably was impotent; he was always observed to avoid the company of ladies and so much to neglect his own that to wish a maid into a mischief (vexation) was to commend her to "grumbling Essex," as he was called.

At this point Sir Thomas Overbury becomes a leading character in the drama. He was born a squire's son in 1581. His father was a barrister, a judge, recorder of the city of Gloucester and a member of Parliament. A brilliant scholar, Thomas received an Oxford degree and made the customary grand tour of Europe before settling down.[47]

Thomas's father later said of his son's meeting with Carr: "When Sir Thomas Overbury was a little past 20 years old he and John Guilbey, his father's chief clerk, were sent (upon a voyage of pleasure) to Edinburgh with £60 between them. There Thomas met with Sir William Cornwallis, one who knew him in Queen's College at Oxford. Sir William commended him to diverse, and amongst the rest to Robert Carr, then page to the Earl of Dunbar. So they came along to England together and were great friends."[48] The two had first met in Scotland when Carr was twelve; Overbury already had graduated from Oxford and had begun at Middle Temple to prepare himself for a legal career. Hero worship had developed, and Carr was happy to renew the friendship after a seven-year lapse.

A contemporary said of the relationship between the two men:

Sir Thomas Overbury for a time was known to have great interest and straight friendship with the Earl of Somerset [Carr], both in his meaner fortunes, and after; in so much, that he was ... a kind of oracle of direction unto him, and if you will believe his own vaunt (being indeed of an insolent and Thrasonical disposition), he took upon him, that the fortunes, reputation and understanding of this gentleman ... proceeded from his company and counsel: and this friendship rested not only in conversation and business at Court, but likewise in communication of business of State; for my Lord of Somerset [Carr had received the earldom at the time this was written] exercising at that time, by his Majesty's special favor and trust, the office of Secretary, did not forbear to acquaint Overbury with the King's packets and dispatches from all parts of Spain, France, and the Low Countries; ... packets were sent, sometimes opened by my Lord, sometimes unbroken, unto Overbury, who perused them, copied them, registered them, made table-talk of them, as he thought good: so, the time was, when Overbury knew more of the secrets of state, than the Council-table did. . . . [49]

It was a popular quip that while Carr ruled the king, Overbury ruled Carr. This remark eventually reached the ears of the king and did neither man any good. Overbury incurred the dislike of the queen by what she considered his insolence in walking in her garden with his hat on while she was looking out the window.[50] James's dislike of Overbury may have grown from jealousy aroused by the close friendship between him and Carr, and it is possible that either James or Carr, or both, may have been conscious that Overbury had information that if revealed might ruin Carr and implicate James. There was a rumor in Scotland that Carr and Overbury had attempted to poison Prince Henry; this rumor will crop up again later in the book.

Beyond question, Overbury was clever, but his arrogance earned him enemies. He was a friend of Ben Jonson, and Whibley says Overbury approved Jonson's quip that it is better to lose a friend than a jest; many people at Court were scarred by his biting tongue. Jonson composed a quatrain to Overbury: "I think, the fate of Court thy coming craved,/ That the wit there and manners might be saved:/ For since what ignorance, what pride is fled!/ And letters, and humanity in the stead!"[51]

Overbury's opposition to Carr's marrying Frances resulted in their falling out. Sanderson gives this account; his colloquial but forceful language lends a flavor worth retaining:

> It happened, that the Earl of Somerset fell into an unlawful
> love, towards that unfortunate lady the Countess of Essex, and to
> proceed to a marriage with her; this marriage and purpose did
> Overbury mainly impugn, under pretense to do the true part of
> a friend, for that he accounted her an unworthy woman; but the
> truth is, Overbury (who to speak plainly had little that was solid
> for religion or moral virtue, but was wholly possessed with ambi-
> tion and vainglory), was loath to have any partners in the favor of
> my Lord of Somerset, and especially not any of the House of
> Howards, against whom he had professed hatred and opposition.
> And that this is no sinister construction, will appear when you
> shall hear that Overbury made his brags that he had won him
> [Carr] the love of the lady by his letters [letters composed by him
> for Carr to send to Frances] and industry; . . . When Overbury
> saw that he was like to be dispossessed by my Lord's grace, which
> he had possessed so long, and by whose greatness he had prom-
> ised himself to do wonders; and being a man of an unbounded
> and impudent spirit, he began, not only to dissuade but to deter
> him from the love of that lady; and finding him fixed, thought to
> find a strong remedy; and supposing that he had my Lord's head
> under his girdle, in respect of communication of secrets of
> state, . . . [and] secrets of nature [the implication here is clear] and
> therefore dealt violently with him to make him desist, with men-
> aces of discovery and the like: Hereupon grew two streams of
> hatred upon Overbury; the one from the lady, in respect that he
> crossed her love and abused her name (which are furies in
> women), the other of a more deep nature, from my Lord of
> Somerset himself, who was afraid of Overbury's nature, and
> [that] if he did break from him and fly out, he would wind into
> him, and trouble his whole fortunes; so as certainly it was re-
> solved that Overbury must die."[52]

It is true that Overbury, thinking it only a passing indulgence,
had originally encouraged Carr's illicit affair with Frances and had
written for Carr some of the love letters which so affected her. But
Overbury never trusted her, and when he found Carr seriously
thinking of marriage, he warned him that Frances would ruin him.
Some of Overbury's language was pretty rough; Frances was a
"strumpet" and her mother and father "bawds." He wrote scurrilous

poems about Frances; one very long poem entitled "The Wife" has run through many editions. Weldon commented that against the marriage "did Overbury bellow louder, and in it showed himself more like an affectionate than a discreet and moderate friend: Had he compounded but one dram of discretion with an ounce of affection, he might with such a receipt have preserved his own life and their fortunes and honors."[53]

Overbury's advice to Carr was excellent but unlikely to be accepted in the words he used—that it was not the nature of a wise man to make a woman his wife whom he had made his whore. Carr should expect no better requital from her, Overbury told him, than such as she had showed to her former husband. Furthermore, he added, "honor is not attended by voluptuousness, nor the ruins of a rotten branch to be cherished upon a new planted tree," and if he wanted to become famous and to continue the friendship which he now freely enjoyed, Carr "should utterly leave and forsake the Countess's company, and hold her both hurtful and hateful."[54] Overbury may also have been influenced by his fear that since his fortunes were bound up with Carr's, Carr's fall from grace, due to such public injustice as marrying another man's wife with her husband still living, would result in his ruin as well.

Carr, thoroughly bewitched by Frances, was incapable of listening to this counsel and not only became incensed at Overbury but repeated Overbury's statements about her to Frances, who, as Camden said, "mustering up all her passions, with the greatest acrimony that a feminine malice could devise, she never left, till she had discharged all the volleys of her rage upon him."[55] Pretty strong language, but the adage that hell hath no fury like a woman scorned has seldom been disputed. Frustrated ambition to achieve a position in the Court which she could have only as Carr's wife may have actuated Frances more than her love for him. Robert Chambers, about 1800, carefully examining all the pertinent documents he could find, reached that conclusion.

There is available some inconclusive evidence that Frances may at first have hoped to eliminate Overbury through assassination. Sanderson says she "dealt with one Sir David Wood (an ill-looked, red-headed Scot), whom Overbury had prevented of a suit, valued £2,000. But his [Wood's] cowardice, not conscience, fearing to engage, she and they plotted the poisoning of . . . [Overbury] in prison."[56] There is some confirmation of this in D'Ewes's journal: "At first she broke the matter to Sir David Wood, a servant of Queen Anne's, whom she knew to have a particular quarrel with Sir Thomas, promising that if he would, by way of duel or otherwise, kill him, she would give him a thousand pounds." But Sir David was "loath to be carried to Tyburn for the lady's pleasure."[57]

By now almost everyone was anxious to see Overbury leave the Court. He had been insolent to Carr, the queen's animosity was well known, the king was jealous and perhaps afraid and the Howards regarded him as an enemy. Even worse, if Overbury were to tell what he knew of the relationship between Carr and Frances, chances for the divorce would probably be gone. Perhaps Overbury could be sent abroad for an indefinite period; a plot was hatched.

As Camden tells about it, the king having decided to send an ambassador abroad, the viscount (Carr) recommended Overbury to the king, extolling his abilities and fitness for the position publicly so that more notice might be taken of the affront if refused, and James chose him for the ambassadorship. The viscount (under a pretense of friendship) advised Overbury what intentions the king had toward him but told him he thought it would not be convenient for him to accept it, because he (Carr) should not only lose his conversation and company (which he highly valued) by such an alienation but many opportunities to advance him. Overbury was not so little a courtier or man of reason as not to realize the displeasure he would incur by refusing the king's commands. Therefore, he told the viscount that although wanting to retain both the king's favors and Carr's friendship, he didn't know how he could safely refuse the king's commands. But the viscount, promising to prevent the king's anger and smooth the way to his better advantage, prevailed on Overbury to stay at home, using his ambition as bait. When he had persuaded Overbury, Carr went to the king and incensed him with all the accusations against Overbury he could.[58]

John Chamberlain, writing to Carleton on April 29, 1613, analyzed Overbury's excuses and the replies of the representatives sent by James on April 21 to persuade him to accept the embassy. After much argument, he wrote, Overbury at last gave them a peremptory answer that he would not go and that he hoped that the king in neither law nor justice could compel him to leave his country. The answer so incensed the king that he asked the Council to

consider what punishment the refusal deserved; the Council pronounced Overbury guilty of contempt and ordered him sent to the
Tower. At that period it was almost compulsory to accept any office
offered by the Crown, by which means "the greatest oppression was
frequently masked as kindness and unwanted subjects exiled without
the necessity of proving any cause."[59] Some took Overbury's imprisonment as a diminution of Carr's credit and favor, but the king told
the Council the next day that it should not be construed in that
manner, "for that he had, and still did take more delight in his
company and conversation than in any man's living."[60]

Some people wondered why a member of the Howard family did
not pick a quarrel with Overbury on the grounds of his defamation
of Frances and kill him honorably in a duel, in which case the world
would have justified the action, but Weldon remarked that Buchan-
on's character of the Howard family would bar all expectation of so
much bravery of spirit. After mentioning the plot to get Overbury
imprisoned for refusing the embassy, he says, "and thus far I do
believe the Earl of Somerset (for so was he now created) was consenting," but he criticizes Overbury severely for not having had good
enough judgment to accept the mission.[61] Obviously, however, Overbury did not suspect Carr of any treachery and, not wanting to give
up his favorable position at Court, relied on some assurance, the
details of which we do not know, that Carr would protect him from
any bad consequences of his refusal. It, nevertheless, seems that
Overbury might well have become a little suspicious of Carr's sudden return to friendship after the open hostility that had grown out
of Overbury's attacks on Frances. "How harsh soever Rochester was
to Sir Thomas, when he . . . [attempted to dissuade] Rochester from
marrying the Countess, yet now he becomes in an instant kind to Sir
Thomas, and tells him how much he relied upon his integrity and
parts, which in his absence he should not only want, but that thereby
Sir Thomas would give occasion to his enemies, which were
many, . . . to ruin him . . . but if Sir Thomas would refuse to undertake the embassy, Rochester would, in a short time, undertake to
reconcile him to the King."[62]

We cannot be certain that Carr persuaded Overbury to refuse
the mission. Sir Henry Wotton, writing to Sir Edmund Bacon on
April 22, 1613, telling him of Overbury's having been sent to the
Tower and of the surprise, surmised that separating Overbury

from Carr was the reason that James had made the appointment and that in addition to Overbury's refusal, his imprisonment may have been influenced by the queen's dislike. Then he adds, "Now in this whole matter there is one main and principal doubt, which doth trouble all understandings; that is, *whether this were done without the participation of my Lord Rochester* ... For if it were done without his knowledge, we must expect of himself either a decadence or a ruin; if not, we must then expect a reparation by some other great public satisfaction whereof the world may take as much notice. These clouds a few days will clear. In the mean while, I dare pronounce of Sir Thomas Overbury, that he shall return no more to this stage...."[63] — an astutely prophetic remark!

Question must arise as to what extent James and his name were merely being used, whether he acted only as a favor to Carr or whether he was motivated by jealousy or some other dislike of Overbury. There is no certain answer. Ewald thinks that James had never liked Overbury and was glad to help get rid of him as soon as he found Carr to be willing.[64] Gardiner also suspects jealousy and displeasure over the statement that "while Rochester rules the King, Overbury rules Rochester." There was mentioned earlier Camden's suggestion that James may have feared Overbury's ability to disclose some guilty secret which would discredit him, and there is always the possibility that James was not expecting Overbury's refusal and was made genuinely angry by what he could well have considered a contemptuous act.

Shortly after Overbury was imprisoned, a change was made in the lieutenancy of the Tower. Sir William Wade, a man of known integrity, was replaced on May 6, 1613, by Sir Gervaise Elwes. Elwes paid £2,000 for the post, but no unfavorable implication can be drawn from this, as it was customary for someone obtaining a lucrative appointment to give a gift of money to the person at Court who obtained the position for him. Elwes, at Northampton's request, named a stranger to him, Richard Weston, as underkeeper and put him in charge of Overbury. Later the Crown tried to prove that the change was made at the instigation of Frances and Carr in order to clear the way for the poisoning of Overbury, but it might have been only to assure his being held incommunicado; the Howards were deathly afraid that, as already has been suggested, if Overbury told what he knew about the relationship between Frances and Carr and perhaps disclosed other secrets, an annulment of her marriage to Essex would not be granted.

It is just possible there may have been reasons for the change not connected with Overbury's imprisonment. Wade had been out of favor ever since the time, during his lieutenancy, that Arabella Stuart, a possible heir to the throne, had escaped the Tower and married. D'Ewes, however, had no doubt on the subject: "But the Countess's revenge brooking no delay . . . and finding Sir William Wade's integrity to be corruption-proof, so as there remained no hope of making him an instrument of murder, she used means at Court to remove him out of his place; and settled Sir Jarvis Elvis, Knt. [Elwes], in his room . . . His sad prisoner never saw a good day after his attaining that Lieutenantship."[65] Sir Henry Wotton (once a highly trusted Essex secretary, later diplomat and then provost of Eton College) disagreed with D'Ewes. In a letter written to Francis Bacon on May 14, he made plain his doubt whether Carr, (now Rochester) could have wanted Wade to have the appointment: "Sir Gervis Elvis (before one of the Pensioners) is now sworn Lieutenant of the Tower, by the mediation of the House of Suffolk [Howard], notwithstanding that my Lord of Rochester was the commender of Sir John Keys to that charge; which the said Keys had for a good while (and this maketh the case the more strange) always supplied even by patent, in the absence of Sir William Wade. Upon which circumstances (though they seem to bend another way) the logicians of the Court do make this conclusion: That his Majesty, satisfying the Suffolks with petty things, intendeth to repair the Viscount Rochester in the main and gross."[66]

Evidence of the Howard's insistence that Overbury be denied communication with anyone except by letters to acceptable recipients is offered in an incident involving Sir Robert Killigrew. Although a knight and member of Parliament, he was confined in Fleet Prison in 1613 for some cause not now known. When released early in May, he paid a visit to Raleigh, at that time imprisoned in the Tower, and on leaving was hailed from a window by Overbury, with whom he had been friendly. They conversed for a few minutes, for which offense Killigrew was put back in the Fleet,[67] but he was soon released to be made captain of Pendennis Castle. That he permitted the conversation between Overbury and Killigrew was one of the charges brought against Wade prior to his dismissal.

Sanderson has no question as to why the Howards had to control the Tower: "First, they should [otherwise] meet with many impediments in the giving . . . of the poison; secondly, they would be exposed to note and observation that might discover them; and thirdly, Overbury in the meantime might write clamorous and furious letters to his friends, and so all might be disappointed; and therefore the next link of the chain was to displace the then Lieutenant Wade, and to place Yelvis [Elwes], a principal abettor in the poisoning; to displace Carew, that was underkeeper in Wade's time, and to place Weston that was the actor in the poisoning."[68]

SEVEN

THE suit for divorce, or, more properly stated, for an annulment of Essex's and Frances's marriage, had already been decided upon before Overbury was sent to the Tower. Northampton, resenting his niece's grievances, had, as Camden put it, acquainted the king with her maiden bashfulness, how loath she was to divulge her husband's infirmities and that in spite of the long time since her marriage, she had not enjoyed the happiness of a wife, since her husband's inability resulted in an unnatural conjunction such as neither law nor reason could permit. Northampton added that there was a great affection between Carr and Frances, so that there seemed to be an excellent sympathy and union of souls in them more suitable to reason and nature than in the state she was in. Northampton's request for an annulment action was seconded by Carr, humbly submitted himself to the king's great wisdom and acknowledging that the king had not only raised him to what he was but might make him still happier by uniting him to a lady of so much honor and virtue. James, who always took delight in completing the happiness of those he loved, commanded the bishops to hear and determine a divorce proceeding between the Earl of Essex and his lady so that the viscount could marry her.[1]

Much as he undoubtedly wanted to get rid of Frances, Essex understandably was not willing to agree to a divorce based on the ground that he was impotent. On June 10 Chamberlain wrote to Carleton:

The divorcement between the Earl of Essex and his lady is on foot, and I think will shortly come to a conclusion. It hath been heard at Lambeth before certain commissioners, twice or thrice, but *à huis clos;* all the difficulty is, that though he be willing to

115

confess his insufficiency toward her, yet he will be left at liberty to marry any other, and stands upon it that he is *malefactus* only *ad illam* [incapable only toward her]. Now some lawyers are of the opinion that if she will swear that he is impotent toward her, there is sufficient cause of divorce, which it is thought she will make no bones of, being, as she presumes, provided of a second; which I should never have suspected, but that I know he [Carr] was with her three hours together within these two days, which makes me somewhat to stagger, and to think that great folks will have their ends, without respect of friends or followers.

The Hargrave report of the divorce trial is complete and needs no further introduction:

Proceedings between the Lady Frances Howard, Countess of Essex, and Robert, Earl of Essex, her husband, before the King's Delegates, in a Cause of Divorce: 11 James I. A.D. 1613.

Upon the petition of Frances, Countess of Essex [filed May 16, 1613], complaining that the Earl, her husband, was incapable of consummating their marriage, and praying a commission to examine if her complaint was well founded, the King granted her request, and appointed the following persons Commissioners: George, Archbishop of Canterbury, John, Bishop of London, Lancelot, Bishop of Ely, Richard, Bishop of Litchfield and Coventry, John, Bishop of Rochester, Sir Julius Caesar, LL.D., Sir Thomas Parry, LL.D., Sir Daniel Donne, LL.D., Sir John Bennet, LL.D., Dr. Francis James, and Dr. Thomas Edwards.

Gibbs and other commentators have said that there was no precedent in English law for the procedure used in this divorce. This is probably true, but it does not follow that the trial and the judgment rendered were technically invalid. The right of the Crown to innovate judicial procedure had been long recognized. As heretofore noted, Bracton had affirmed that the king is the proper judge for all temporal causes and that it is only the great mass of business that has compelled him to delegate judicial power to his courts and ministers. Fleta later made the unequivocal statement that all judicial power is derived from the Crown.[2] In earlier times the king's officers dealt only with civil or criminal causes concerning the king or affecting the king's peace and public order, but almost any kind of action might in some way have that effect. Certainly that is true of this divorce action and its effect as a precedent.

The Libel contained the following allegations:

I. That she, at the time of the marriage, was 13 years old, and is at this time 22 or 23. II. That she and Robert, Earl of Essex, were married by the public rites and ceremonies of the church in January, 1603. III. That the aforesaid Robert, at the time of the pretended marriage, was about 14, and is about 22 or 23 at this time; and ever since, and at this present, is a man (as far forth as a man may judge), and hath been in good health, and perfect state of body, nor any way hindered by any ague or sickness, but that he might have carnal copulation with a woman. IV. That since the pretended marriage, at least by the space of whole and continuous three years after the said Robert had fully attained the age of 18 years, as time and place did serve, after the fashion of other married folks, the said Frances Howard in hope of lawful issue, and desirous to be made a mother, lived together with the said Robert at bed and board, and lay both naked and alone in the same bed, as married folks use: and desirous to be made a mother, from time to time, again and again yielded herself to his power, and as much as lay in her offered herself and her body to be known, and earnestly desired conjunction and copulation. V. And also the said Earl, in the same time very often, again and again, did try to have copulation, as with his lawful wife, which she refused not, but used the best means she could: Notwithstanding all this, the said Earl could never carnally know her, nor have that copulation in any sort which the married bed alloweth. VI. Yet before the said pretended marriage, and since the said Earl hath had, and hath power and ability of body to deal with other women, and to know them carnally, and sometimes has felt the motion and pricks of the flesh carnally, and tending to carnal copulation, as he saith and believeth; and peradventure, by a perpetual and natural impediment hath been hindered all the former time, and is at this present, that he can have no copulation with the said Lady Frances. VII. Furthermore, the said Lady Frances hath been, and is fit and able to have copulation with a man, and [is] such a one as may be carnally known; neither hath in this regard any impediment. VIII. Moreover, the said Lady Frances remaineth, and is at this present a virgin. Also at the time of the pretended marriage, the said Lady Frances was unacquainted with the Earl's want of ability and

impediment, formerly mentioned. IX. And furthermore the said
Earl, long before this suit commenced, hath very often, and at
sundry times, confessed in good earnest, before witnesses of
good credit, and his friends and kinfolks, that although he did
his best endeavor, yet he never could, nor at this time can, have
copulation with the said Lady Frances, no not once. X. And
lastly, in regard of womanish modesty, the Lady Frances hath
concealed all the former matters, and had a purpose ever to
conceal them, if she had not been forced, through false rumors
of disobedience to the said Earl, to reveal them. She requireth,
since this pretended matrimony is but in fact, and not in right, it
may be pronounced, declared and adjudged as none, and of no
effect; and she may be quiet and free from all knots and bonds of
the same, by your sentence and authority.

The Earl of Essex put in his Answer the fifth of July, 1614.

The 1st and 2nd he answereth affirmatively. To the 3rd, he
thinketh that at the time of his marriage, he was full 14 years,
and is now 22 and upwards; neither since hath had or hath any
sickness or impediment to hinder him, but that he might have
had copulation with a woman, saving in the time of his sickness
of the smallpox, for two or three years after his marriage, which
continued for a month or six weeks, and at another time, when
he had a few fits of an ague. To the 4th, he affirmeth, that for
one year he divers times attempted; that the two other years,
when he was willing, she showed herself sometimes willing, but
other times refused, and he lay in bed most commonly with her,
but felt no motions or provocations. To the 5th, he answereth,
that he never carnally knew her, but found not any defect in
himself, yet was not able to penetrate into her womb, nor enjoy
her. To the 6th, he believeth, that before and after the marriage,
he hath found an ability of body to know any other woman, and
hath oftentimes felt motions and provocations of the flesh, tending to carnal copulation, but for perpetual and natural impediments, he knoweth not what the words mean; but that he hath
lain by the Lady Frances two or three years last past, and had
no motion to know her, and he believes never shall. To the 7th,
he believeth not that the said Lady Frances is a woman able and
fit for carnal copulation, because he hath not found it. To the 8th
and 9th, he believeth them both to be true, and thinketh that
once before some witnesses of credit, he did speak to this purpose, "That he oftentimes had endeavored carnally to know her,
but that he did not, nor could not." . . .

Essex's answer seems more honest than expected, but he was an honest and religious man. Carte believed that Essex could not, when under oath, avoid making this confession.[3] In addition, it should be remembered that he, too, wanted the marriage annulled, and the basis for the action had been agreed upon between the parties.

DEPOSITIONS taken in the case of the Earl of Essex and the Lady Howard.

The Oath taken by the Lady Frances Howard:

That since the Earl of Essex was 18 years of age, he and I have for the space of three years divers and sundry times lain together in naked bed all night. And at sundry of the said times the said Earl hath purposely endeavored and attempted to consummate marriage with me, and to have carnal copulation with me for procreation of children; and I have at such times, as the said Earl hath attempted so to do, yielded myself willing to the same purpose. All which notwithstanding, I say and affirm upon my oath, that the said Earl never had carnal copulation with me. FRANCES HOWARD. . . .

It is apparent from Canterbury's account that Frances appeared in person, was duly sworn, and that after she had taken the oath she signed the statement. Following her statement, the trial transcript contains a list of eight interrogatories requiring an answer by each witness except the Earl and Countess of Suffolk. These questions were designed to evidence any relationship or partiality of the witness to either party, to ascertain whether he had conferred with anyone about his testimony and whether there had been any coercion, to determine when Essex became eighteen, to elicit information regarding Essex's ability to know other women carnally and to prove any statements made by Essex to others about his marriage problems. I have omitted the list of interrogatories and the reply of each witness, since in each instance the replies were routine. There then follow the "depositions" of the witnesses pertinent to the facts actually at issue.

DEPOSITIONS upon the Articles of the Libel put in by the Lady Frances Howard, taken June 2, 1613.

Katharine Fines, daughter of Thomas, Lord Clinton, aged

about 18 years, deposeth, that ... from Midsummer last to All Saints' Day, the Earl of Essex and Lady Frances remained and kept company together as man and wife; ... And that for two of the nights they lodged at Drayton, being on a Sunday at night, and on a Monday at night, they to her knowledge lay together in one chamber; she seeing the Earl go into the said chamber undressed and ready for bed; and she verily believes they did lie together in the same bed those two nights, for that she knows there was but one bed in the said chamber. That before Christmas last the said Lady Frances, lying at Salisbury House in the Strand, the Earl came thither and went into the chamber where Lady Frances was in bed, and went to bed to her, and there was no other bed in that chamber; and this deponent heard the Earl and Lady Frances talking together a good part of that night. ...

The depositions of Raye, Dandenell, Jaconim, Bamforde, Powell, Power and Orwell, who were domestic servants or other persons familiar with the family life of Essex and Frances, were much alike and are omitted. The tenor of the testimony was that the couple lived together as husband and wife, "lay in naked bed together" and often talked far into the night. These facts were well known and undisputed. However, since the law was that impotency as a cause for divorce had to exist for a period of three years after the husband was eighteen, evidence to that effect was necessary and was given.

The DEPOSITION of Frances Britten, Widow, taken to the Libel.

That ... this deponent coming to Lady Frances's lodging at Hampton Court early in the morning, she was brought into the bedchamber, where she did see them [Frances and Essex] in naked bed together, as likewise she did at Lady Frances's lodging at Whitehall; that perceiving them in bed together, this deponent stepped back, but the Lady Katherine Howard, her sister, being there, called the deponent in, and then Lady Frances stepped out of her bed, and left the Earl there; that this was on St. Valentine's Day, for that Lady Katherine told the Earl, that there was a valentine for him; ... that when this deponent was at Hampton Court, as is before mentioned, after the Earl and Lady Frances were risen, the lady missing a pendant ruby that usually hung at the ring in her ear, desired this deponent to look for it in the bed; that thereupon she and the lady's chambermaid turned down the bedclothes, and there they saw the places where the

Earl and Lady had lain, but that there was such a distance between the two places, and such a hill between them, that this deponent is persuaded they did not touch one another that night. . . .

The DEPOSITION of the Right Honorable Thomas, Earl of Suffolk, Lord High Chamberlain of the Household, taken the 10th of June, 1613, aged about 57 years.

. . . Says, . . . that to that time and since, the Earl was, in the judgment of men, of good health and strength of body, except at two several times, when he was sick of the smallpox and an ague; and was likely to be able to have the carnal knowledge of a woman, for anything this deponent could judge. 4th Article: Knows that after the Earl was come to the age of 18 years, he and Lady Frances kept company, and lay together as man and wife, for three whole years; hath seen them in bed together sometimes. 5th and 6th Articles: That notwithstanding the premises, the Earl never had any carnal knowledge of Lady Frances, nor never could, as the Earl hath confessed to the deponent. 7th, 8th and 9th Articles: Believes these Articles to be true. 10th Article: That the Earl, in this deponent's hearing, confessed divers times, in several companies, that he had done his endeavor to have carnal knowledge of Lady Frances, and yet never could. . . .

The DEPOSITION of the Right Honorable Katherine, Countess of Suffolk; aged about 47 years.

To 1st, 2d, 3d Articles: Deposes they are true. 4th, 5th, 6th, 7th Articles: Believes to be true. 8th Article: Deposes to be true of her knowledge. 9th Article: Believes to be true. 10th Article: Hath heard it reported, and believes it to be true. 11th Article: Believes the same to be true. 14th Article, etc.: Concludes as the Earl of Suffolk. . . .

George Abbot, Archbishop of Canterbury, had been named by James to preside over the trial but had agreed most unwillingly. He was an exceedingly honest and courageous man, was famous for his theological studies and was well liked at Court. Although the king's most responsible officers were glad to see him appointed, Carr, knowing his stern integrity, and Northampton, a Papist, did not like the appointment. Frances's loose character and her relationship with Carr were well known; Abbot and some of the other commissioners viewed the whole proceeding with suspicion as a put-up job designed to free Frances for marriage to Carr and consented to by Essex only in order to relieve him of a burden which had become intolerable. This may have been the reason that the commissioners demanded proof of Frances's virginity.

At one time during the proceedings, Abbot fell down on his knees and entreated the king to release him from his duties on the commission, "which he would esteem a greater favor than all that he had received from James in being raised from a private position and in so short a time to the highest dignity." James refused, whereupon Abbot wrote him a letter pointing out his reasons for opposing the granting of the divorce. The letter was long and rambling, full of irrelevant quotations from theologians, and omitted mention of any of the points upon which the strength of his case rested (for instance, the deficiency of evidence and the danger of setting a precedent).[4] The letter served only to exasperate the king, who replied in part, "I must freely confess to you that I find the grounds of your opposition so weak as I have reason to apprehend that the prejudices you have of the persons is the greatest motive in breeding these doubts in you,"[5] and in rebuttal he presented a much better reasoned argument. Their adversary positions made Canterbury popular with the people[6] and perhaps did more to widen the breach between James and his subjects than did his rupture with Parliament.

Following the depositions, Howell's edition of the divorce proceedings sets out "The Lord Archbishop of Canterbury's Reasons against the Nullity" and "The King's Answer." Abbot argued that "we firmly believe that the Scripture doth directly, or by consequence, contain in it sufficient matter to decide all controversies," that he could find nothing in the Scriptures supporting the argument here presented for an annulment, that it was quite possible that whatever ailed Essex might be cured—possibly through alms, fasting and prayer or exorcism—that the Fathers and (Church) Councils do not recognize impotency unless it is complete and not just with one partner, that if the impotency grew out of some power of the devil exercised in this world the devil might be overcome and that other remedies might be available.

James in his reply effectively answered each of Abbot's arguments, except, perhaps, the implied but not clearly stated contention that to accept impotency toward one woman as a valid excuse for divorce would merely open the way to fraudulent and unjustified separations. As to Abbot's failure to find justification in the rulings of the Fathers and the Councils, James said, "You know much better than I, divers and many points betwixt the Papists and us are never mentioned by the Fathers, because they could never have dreamed that such questions would arise." As for the argument about possible cures, James said that in the first place there was nothing to show that the cures had not been attempted, and secondly that it was not an argument but a hope, and as for the justice of the thing, both Essex and Frances by the declaration of the nullity would "be capable to accomplish marriage with others, which they could never do between themselves; wherein they may have the satisfaction of their hearts, and enjoy the blessing of procreation of children . . . and for legal doubts, they concern none of your calling; if your conscience be resolved in points of divinity, that is your part to give your consent to the nullity, and let the lawyers take the burden of making that firm."

Notwithstanding the confessions in the Earl's answer, the . . . [commissioners] thought it necessary to satisfy themselves of the truth by the inspection of [Frances by] midwives and matrons. Whereupon it was decreed by the court that six midwives of the best note, and ten other noble matrons, out of which they themselves would choose two midwives and four matrons, should inspect the Countess. . . .

Accordingly between the hours of that day aforesaid, were presented before the delegates [commissioners] the said ladies, and sworn *ad inquirend et inspiciend:* 1. Whether the Lady Frances were a woman fit and apt for carnal copulation, without any defect which might disable her for that purpose. 2. Whether she were a virgin carnally unknown by any man. Whereupon they went from the presence of the commissioners into the next room where the Countess was, who was left alone with the said ladies. After some convenient time they returned, and delivered in their report under their hands; all persons being removed except the Register, that so the ladies and midwives might more freely deliver their secret reasons, etc. which were not fit to be inserted into the record; and this is in sum their report:

1. That they believe the Lady Frances fitted with abilities to have carnal copulation, and apt to have children. 2. That she is a **virgin uncorrupted**. . . .

John Chamberlain wrote to Carleton on June 23 that he considered a divorce decree would be a dangerous precedent and that the finding of Frances to be a virgin . . . "some doctors think a strange asseveration. . . . The world speaks liberally that my Lord of Rochester and she be in love one with another, which breeds a double question."[7] The disbelief that Frances could have been found to be a virgin was so widespread that it was generally believed and was asserted by several recorders of current events that the jury of matrons and midwives had been hoaxed. Howell so states, and Weldon says,

> Yet forsooth to make up the full measure of bawdry, . . . a search must be made, to find whether there had been a penetration, and a jury of grave matrons were found fit for that purpose, who with their spectacles ground to lessen, not to make the letter larger, after their inspection gave verdict, she was *intact virgo* [a virgin intact], which was thought very strange, for the world took notice that her way was very near beaten so plain as if *regia via* [a king's highway] and in truth, was a common way before Somerset did ever travel that way; besides, the world took notice they two long had lived in adultery, yet had old Kettle a trick for that also: The Lady of Essex, for modesty sake, makes humble suit to the reverend bawdy bishops (who were also plotters in this stratagem), that she might not appear barefaced, for blushing; but desired to come veiled, with a taffeta over her face; this by all means was thought so reasonable, for a pretty modest lady, that the bawdy bishops, and purblind ladies, who had forgotten modesty themselves, could not think it worthy the denial; one Mistress Fines, near kinswoman to old Kettle, was dressed up in the countess's clothes, at that time too young to be other than *virgo intacto* (though within two years after, had the old ladies made their inspection, the orifice would not have appeared so small), to have delivered such a verdict as they did, and a just one upon their view; tho upon some of their knowledges it was not that lady they were to give verdict upon. If any make doubt of the truth of this story, the author delivers upon the reputation of a gentleman, he had it verbatim from a knight, otherwise of much honor, . . . which did usher the lady into the place of inspection, and hath told it often to his friends in mirth.[8]

Camden also affirms the hoax: "The Countess being ashamed, and bashful, to come to such a trial, would not expose her face to the light; but being to appear before the matrons under a veil, another young gentlewoman, that had less offended, was fobbed into the place; and she passed, in the opinion both of jury and judges, to be a virgin."[9]

And to corroborate all this, the Countess in open court produced seven women of her consanguinity, that inasmuch as the truth was best known to herself, she might by virtue of her oath discover the same, and her oath should be no farther regarded than as it was confirmed by the oath of her kinswomen. In order hereto the Countess took an oath, that since the Earl was 18 years old, for three years he and she had lain in bed, etc. as in the Libel. . . .

This was an interesting variation of the ancient practice of trial by compurgation. In the early days of criminal law, if the Grand Jury or its forerunner found sufficient evidence of guilt to bring a defendant to trial, he had a choice of trial by battle or by ordeal or, if he was considered of good character, trial by compurgation, in which a number of his relatives and adherents, known as compurgators, the number varying with the offense, would swear under oath that his defense was true.

And then the seven noble women, viz. Katherine Countess of Suffolk, Frances Countess of Kildare, Elizabeth Lady Walden, Elizabeth Lady Knevet, Lady Katherine Thynne, Mrs. Katherine Fiennes, Mrs. Dorothy Neale, being sworn, deposed that they believed the same was true; and in particular because: 1. That after they were both grown to years of puberty, they both endeavored copulation. 2. That notwithstanding, on her part, as appeared by the inspectors, she remained a virgin uncorrupted. 3. That the Earl had judicially sworn, that he never had, nor could, nor should, ever know her carnally.

THE SENTENCE

Whereupon the delegates declared the law to be that *impotentia coëundi in viro* whatsoever, whether by natural defect, or accidental means, whether absolute toward all, or respective to his wife only, if it precede matrimony, and be perpetual (as by law is presumed, when after three years trial, after the man is of the age of 18 years, there has been *nil ad copulam,* and the marriage not consummated) is a just cause of divorce *a vinculo matrimonii;*

and that the proofs produced in this case were abundantly sufficient to convince them of the Earl's impotency; and therefore pronounced sentence that they should be divorced from each other, and be at liberty to marry again; which sentence was as follows:

That Robert Earl of Essex and the Lady Frances Howard, contracted by show of marriage, did cohabit in one house and lie together in one bed, *nudus cum nuda, et soles cum sola;* and that the said Lady Frances did show herself prompt and ready to be known of him, and that the said Earl neither did nor could have knowledge of her, although he did think himself able to have knowledge of other women; and that the said Lady Frances by inspection of her body by midwives, expert in matter of marriage, was proved to be apt for carnal copulation with man, and yet a virgin: Therefore we the said judges deputed in the cause, first invoking the name of Christ and setting God before our eyes, do pronounce, decree, and declare, that the Earl of Essex, for some secret, incurable, binding impediment, did never carnally know, or was or is able carnally to know the Lady Frances Howard: And therefore we do pronounce, have decreed, and do declare, the pretended marriage so contracted and solemnized *de facto* between them, to have been, and to be utterly void and to no effect, and that it did want, and ought to want the strength of the law: And that the Lady Frances was, and is, and so ought to be, free and at liberty from any bond of such pretended marriage, *de facto,* contracted and solemnized. And we do pronounce, that she ought to be divorced, and so we do free and divorce her, leaving them as touching other marriages to their consciences in the Lord.

Which our definitive Sentence and Decree ratify and publish. Thomas Wint.; Lancel. Ely; Rich. Coven. and Lichf.; John Rossen, Bishops.—Julius Caesar, Thomas Parry, Daniel Donne, Doctors." ["Doctors" were of course not doctors of medicine but Doctors of Law: LL.D's.]

The following Commissioners could not agree to this sentence, and therefore absented themselves: George Cant.; John London, Bishops.—John Bennet, Francis James, Thomas Edwards, Doctors.

It will be noticed that seven commissioners signed the sentence and five refused, although only ten had been originally placed on the commission. This happened because of the stalemate which had developed. Five commissioners were willing to vote yes, and the other five refused. James solved the impasse very simply. He asked the commissioners to make one more effort to come to a decision; if they were unable, Canterbury was to so advise the king. The king postponed the next hearing until September 18, at which time there appeared two additional bishops whom he had added to the commission. There was then no difficulty in getting the seven to five affirmative vote.

One of the two men added to the commission was Bishop Bilson of Winchester. Shortly after the annulment, his son was knighted, and it became a Court joke to call him "Sir Nullity Bilson." The Bishop of Rochester was a protégé of the House of Suffolk. Others were doubtless suitably rewarded. However, Carte is somewhat critical of Canterbury, saying that his "dissertation" may have been written to curry favor with the Puritans, whom Carte blamed for maligning the proceeding, alleging Crown influence, spreading black falsehoods about the countess and starting the improbable rumor about the substitution of a virgin.[10]

The other ecclesiastical dissenter was the Bishop of London. Goodman asked Dr. Overall, a highly regarded bishop and scholar, his opinion concerning the nullity. Overall replied that he himself had attempted to persuade the Bishop of London not to oppose the nullity but received the reply that his only reason of dissent was that he couldn't satisfy his own conscience as to the truth of the sworn statements that were made. Overall's opinion was that, under those circumstances, the bishop should have taken further time to examine the oaths and then to have either accepted them or considered secondary evidence. Goodman adds that the minister of Chiswick, who was with Frances "in her last sickness, when she was past hope of life, and speaking with her of this business, she did then protest upon her soul and salvation that the Earl of Essex was never her husband."[11]

The morning that the judges were to render their decision, the king sent an express command that the judges were not to argue or state any reasons but merely to vote yes or no, and in the sentence there was no cause stated except a reference to "some secret, incurable, binding impediment" of the earl. James, knowing that he was assured of his seven to five decision, wanted no argument from the dissenters which might cause others to criticize the judgment.[12]

The power of the Crown to influence an action of this kind was well recognized. Southampton wrote to Winwood on August 6, "Of the Nullity I see you have heard as much as I can write; by which you may discern the power of a king with judges, for of those which are now for it, I knew some of them when I was in England were vehemently against it, as the Bishops of Ely and of Coventry."[13] Another person in discussing the decision felt impelled to say, "But kings will never want fit ministers in corrupted times, both in church and commonwealth, as long as there are degrees, and places of ascent to climb to." Hallam, writing 200 years later, expressed about the same thought: "The courts of justice, it is hardly necessary to say, did not consist of men conscientiously impartial between the King and the subject; some corrupt with hope of promotion, many more fearful of removal, or awestruck by the frowns of power."[14]

We will note one final comment on the trial. Salmon, in his discussion, suggests that the subsequent trial of Frances for murder produced evidence indicating that the granting of the divorce may have been proved wrong and both king and commission egregiously imposed upon. He had in mind the disclosure that Frances had administered drugs to Essex to render him impotent, "which was the reason of his lying so quietly by the Countess the two last years." John Castle, writing toward the end of 1615, was of the same opinion: "I have sent you two letters of the Countess, urged at Turner's arraignment; you will see by them how abusively her lust wronged those great judgments that spoke for her separation from that noble Essex, upon whom they practiced *magiam maleficam,* to restrain him, *impotens esset ad coëundum.*"[15]

Salmon would have been interested in a piece of evidence not known to him in his analysis of the case. It is reported by one present at the proceedings that prior to the conclusion of the trial several of Essex's friends and attendants were in his room one morning when he got out of bed in his nightgown. There was an imposingly noticeable bulge in its fabric which could have had only one cause. When one of the men called attention to this cause as Essex removed the nightgown, there was much merry comment about what the commissioners would say if they could see this indisputable evidence of Essex's virile ability.

The foregoing account of the proceedings between the Earl of Essex and Lady Frances Howard, being but short and very imperfect, wanting the arguments of the civilians, etc., the following account, written by Dr. George Abbot, Archbishop of Canterbury, with the speech he intended to have made, and King James's letter to him, will throw much light upon this affair and help greatly to explain it. . . .

The papers mentioned are well written and do throw considerable light on the trial and those initiating and participating in it. They are too long to print here but, being full of interest, appear in the Appendix.

EIGHT

Poor Overbury had been having a very bad time of it in the Tower while the divorce was dragging on. He had been miserably ill almost from the time he was imprisoned. His father, hearing of it, asked the king that a doctor be sent to minister to him; James readily agreed and asked Carr to take care of it. Overbury's father later said, "Upon this, I only addressed myself to the Lord of Somerset [Carr's new title] and none else; who said my son should be presently delivered, but dissuaded me from preferring any more petitions to the King, which notwithstanding, I (seeing his freedom still delayed) did deliver a petition to the King to that purpose; who said he should have a present answer."[1]

Overbury himself was requesting medical aid. In a letter (probably to Carr) he wrote, "I have now sent to the Lieutenant to desire you (Mayerne being absent) to send young Craig hither and Nessmith. . . . I find great heat continues in all my body; and the same desire of drink and loathing of meat, and my water is strangely high, which I keep till Mayerne come." Dr. Mayerne appears to have attended him previously, for after complaining about scouring and vomiting Overbury added, "Yesternight about eight o'clock, after Mr. Mayerne was gone, I fainted."[2]

Certain documents and the testimony produced later at Carr's trial show that Overbury was attended in prison by at least Mayerne, Lobell and, by express authorization of both Carr and Northampton, Dr. Craig. Lobell, a French apothecary, was placed in attendance on Overbury by Mayerne, Lobell's brother-in-law. Mayerne was a Swiss nobleman and the king's personal physician, had an M.D. from Oxford and had been physician to Henry IV of France. Question has been repeatedly asked why, when the cause of Overbury's death was later being investigated, Mayerne was neither ex-

131

amined before the trials nor made a trial witness, the supposition
being that had he testified he either would have stated that the death
was not caused by poisoning or would have implicated persons in
high places. Documents in the State Paper Office indicate that Overbury was being treated by Mayerne for consumption, and after his
death Lobell testified that consumption had been its cause. Another
French apothecary, John Pomler, testified that Mayerne recommended Lobell to administer his prescriptions to Overbury because
Lobell lived handily near the Tower, and we have no positive reason
to attribute the recommendation to Lobell's relationship to Mayerne.[3]

The evidence that Overbury was poisoned is contained in the
testimony given in the trials set forth in Chapters Nine, Ten and
Eleven and can be evaluated as those chapters are read. Suffice it to
say here that it was generally believed at the time that the accusation
of poisoning was well founded. Weldon thought so and thought
further that James at least knew what was going on, but Weldon
wrote under the Commonwealth, when kings were not popular.
Carr, he said, constantly assured Overbury that he had not forgotten
his release and that it should not be long deferred, "wherein most
men did verily believe he meant both nobly, and truly, though
others [apparently including Weldon] conjectured his meaning was a
dissolution [release through death]."[4]

Camden believed that there was a poison plot, and that to assure
Elwes's cooperation in the plot, Northampton promised him large
rewards and told him that it would be an acceptable service to the
king to have Overbury removed. He says also that Northampton
advised Elwes not to permit visitors to see Overbury and that Elwes
was smart enough to know he had to make a dangerous choice
between two extremes (Northampton's anger or unlawful acts) but
elected to go along, hoping that Northampton had higher authority
for what he was doing.[5]

At this point in his history Camden makes a statement that casts
some doubt on the accuracy of his memory, even though he was at
Court while these things were going on. Apparently having forgotten that Carr and Frances were not married until after Overbury's
death, he says Overbury was made so unhappy at news of the
marriage and merry-making that he wrote a letter to Carr emphasizing his sad condition and his impaired health, which he imputed

to his close confinement, and imploring Carr's assistance. Such a letter was written, but in June, before the divorce was granted. Carr is said to have replied that the king was then very busy but that he would take the first opportunity to request Overbury's release, although James was highly incensed against Overbury. Carr said that in order that he might give Overbury's indisposition as grounds for the king's mercy, he was enclosing in the letter a white powder that he wanted Overbury to take, assuring him that though it would make him a little sick at first, it would do him much good in the end.[6] Much was said about this white powder at Carr's trial, where it was alleged that the powder was poisonous. However, Sir Robert Killigrew, a man of scientific attainments who had quite a reputation at the Court as a concocter of drugs and cordials, stated that Carr had in May sent to him requests on three separate occasions for one of his white powders. Carr told him the first was to be given to Overbury pursuant to his own request for an emetic, and the other two also were accounted for.[7]

Carr kept on diverting Overbury with "continual letters, partly with hopes and protestations for his delivery, and partly with other fables and negotiations."[8] Overbury can hardly have helped losing patience and being suspicious of Carr's good faith, but he had the poor judgment to send him several menacing letters. The Winwood papers contain one such long letter, sent to Carr under seal with a copy to a close friend, the copy under eight seals, threatening to expose shameful secrets unless Carr secured his release. The letter is in the Cotton Library (Titus B. VIII); a somewhat abridged copy was read at Carr's trial (see Chapter Eleven). The letter is not signed or dated, but since Overbury refers in it to five months imprisonment, it must have been written shortly before his death, and it may very well have hastened that death.

During the night of September 14 (according to the indictment, but some say September 13), the unfortunate Overbury gave up his struggle and died. It was later charged that his death was directly caused by a poisoned clyster (enema) given him on the previous day by an apothecary's boy whom Lobell sent, but at the time the official government story was that he had died of the French pox. Word of his death was at once sent by Elwes to Northampton, and they were in a big hurry to bury the body. A short note came back to Elwes posthaste:

Noble Lieutenant,

If the knave's body be foul, bury it presently; I'll stand between you and harm: but if it will abide the view, *send for Lidcote* [Overbury's brother-in-law], and let him see it to satisfy the damned crew. When you come to me, bring me this letter again yourself with you, or else burn it,

Northampton.[9]

Two more letters by Northampton appear in Winwood's Memorials (the first letter does not). They were sent within hours of each other and make evident a curious uncertainty and sequence of second thoughts on his part:

Worthy Mr. Lieutenant,

Let me entreat you to call Lidcote and three or four friends, if so many come, to view the body, if they have not already done it; and so soon as it is viewed, without staying the coming of a messenger from the Court, in any case see him interred in the body of the chapel within the Tower instantly.

If they have viewed, then bury it by and by; for it is time, considering the humors of that damned crew, that only desire means to move pity and raise scandals. Let no man's instance move you to make stay in any case, and bring me these letters when I next see you.

Fail not a job herein as you love your friends; nor after Lidcote and his friends have viewed, stay one minute, but let the priest be ready; and if Lidcote be not there, send for him speedily, pretending that the body will not tarry.

Yours ever.

In post haste at 12.[10]

A third letter was made necessary by Carr's request, just received by Northampton, that his friend be given a decent funeral. This letter and the postscript seem intended to suggest to Elwes that it would be nice if he could say that the body had been buried before he received the letter, but that, in any event, if he could use as an excuse for not complying a lack of precedent for giving up the body, that also would serve Northampton's purpose. The letter:

Worthy Mr. Lieutenant,

My Lord of Rochester desiring to do the last honor to his deceased friend, requires me to desire you to deliver the body of

Sir T. Overbury to any friend of his that desires it, to do him honor at his funeral. Herein my Lord declares the constancy of his affection to the dead, and the meaning that he had in my knowledge, to have given his strongest strain at this time of the King's being at Tiballes, for his delivery. I fear no impediment to this honorable desire of my Lord's but the unsweetness of the body, because it was reported that he had some issues [discharges] and, in that case the keeping of him above must needs give more offense than it can do honor. My fear is also, that the body is already buried upon that cause whereof I write; which being so, it is too late to set out solemnity.

This with my kindest commendations I end, and rest

> Your affectionate and assured friend,
> H. Northampton.

P.S. — You see my Lord's earnest desire, with my concurring care, that all respect be had to him that may be for the credit of his memory. But yet I wish withal, that you do very discreetly inform yourself whether this grace hath been afforded formerly to close prisoners, or whether you may grant my request in this case, who speak out of the sense of my Lord's affection, though I be a Councillor, without offense or prejudice. For I would be loath to draw either you or myself into censure, now I have well thought of the matter, though it be a work of charity.

Upon the back of this letter are the following words in Elwes's handwriting:

So soon as Sir Thomas Overbury was departed I writ unto my Lord of Northampton; and because my experience could not direct me, I desired to know what I should do with the body, acquainting his Lordship with his issues, as Weston has informed me, and other foulness of his body, which then was accounted the pox. My Lord writ unto me that I should first have his body viewed by a jury and I well remember his Lordship advised me to send for Sir John Lidcote to see the body, and to suffer as many else of his friends to see it as would, and presently to bury it in the body of the choir, for the body could not keep. Notwithstanding Sir T. Overbury dying about five in the morning, I kept his body unburied until three or four of the clock in the afternoon. The next day Sir John Lidcote came thither; I could not get him to bestow a coffin nor a winding-sheet upon him. The coffin I bestowed; but who did wind him I know not. For indeed the body was very noisome [smelling offensively], so that notwith-

standing my Lord's direction, by reason of the danger of keeping
the body, I kept it over long, as we all felt.
                    Ger. Elwes.[11]

In a "normal" murder trial where death was alleged to have been
caused by poisoning, the procedure would have been to introduce at
the trial all available statements by competent persons who examined
the body and the result of the coroner's inquest. This was not the
case at these trials—Coke did not dare. So far as these trials are
concerned, there was nothing introduced to show that persons *had*
examined the body, that there *had* been a coroner's inquest and that
the death had been certified to have been natural. However, Lobell
did examine the body, a coroner's inquest was held, and John Lidcote and possibly other friends or relatives viewed the body prior to
burial.

Robert Bright, a Middlesex County coroner, when examined on
October 1, 1615, testified that he was summoned by Elwes on the
morning Overbury died, that he asked for a jury of six warders and
six others to be summoned, that the coroner and the jury found the
body so thin as in effect to have been *consumed* away, having nothing
but skin and bones, and that there was a black ulcer between the
shoulder blades, in the left arm an "issue" kept open with a little
bullet of gold and on the belly blisters as yellow as amber. Bright
further testified that the inquest rendered its verdict in the afternoon but that he had not returned the verdict to the King's Bench,
as he should have, because he did not want the City of London,
which claimed jurisdiction, to take action against him – not too plausible an excuse.[12]

Overbury died in the part of the Tower that was in London. At
the hearing by the Grand Jury which returned the indictment on
which Weston's trial was predicated, the coroner giving evidence was
not Bright, who had conducted the inquest, but Fenshaw, "his Majesty's" coroner, presumably for London, and Weston was in the
custody of the sheriff of London, who had jurisdiction. Query: Was
Elwes instructed to call the Middlesex County coroner for the inquest so that its verdict of natural death (which must have been the
verdict, although not expressly so stated) would not have to be
placed in evidence at the trial for murder held in London, the situs
of jurisdiction?

It was no secret that there had been a coroner's inquest. D'Ewes wrote in his diary that Overbury's persecutors had it reported that he had died of the French pox (probably because of the condition of the body) and that the coroner's jury certified that he had died a natural death, after which the body was suddenly and obscurely buried, neither his father nor any of his friends being permitted even to see it.[13] The statements as to when the burial occurred are contradictory. Elwes wrote on the back of the third Northampton letter appearing above that he buried Overbury at 3:00 or 4:00 P.M. the day he died, and yet when Lidcote called the next day, a coffin and a winding-sheet were discussed. Probably the most accurate statement is that of Anthony Wood in his "History of Writers and Bishops Educated at Oxford": "He yielded up his last breath, occasioned by poison, as I have before told you, on the [night of the] 13th of September in 1613, and was buried, as some authors say, presently and very unreverently in a pit dug in an obscure and mean place. But the Register of the Tower Chapel, dedicated to St. Peter ad Vincula, says he was buried in the said chapel September 15, 1613.... Over his grave, though no memory by writing was ever put, yet Ben Jonson's epigram written to him, will eternize it."[14]

Once the divorce was granted, Frances became even more wanton in her prosperity. Essex was required to repay her marriage portion; to do so, he had to sell his fine estate of Benington but was said to have considered it a bargain. Frances was now the accepted queen of the Court—her beauty and graces were admired everywhere. She and her husband were the king's favorites, and James could now bestow her hand on Somerset; "he that took her away from one husband, can give her to another, who must be of equal rank to her, that she may not descend, therefore he is created Earl of Somerset; and all the splendid equipage, and magnificent preparation that can either fill a court with delight or people with admiration are not wanting for the marriage."[15] As they waited in the chapel on December 5, the wedding guests wondered how Frances would wear her hair; it was accepted that only a virgin bride might wear her hair down over her shoulders. They soon had their answer, when she appeared, as one guest wrote, "with her hair pendant almost to her feet; which ornament of her body (though a fair one) could not cover the deformities of her soul: But ... her indeed lovely cheeks did not betray themselves to blushes. These glorious days are seconded with as glorious nights, where masks and dancings had a continuous motion."[16]

A new favorite, George Villiers, was now rising to contest Carr's supremacy. He was the son of a knight of an ancient family and a woman described by Weldon as a waiting gentlewoman, with whom the old man fell in love and married and by whom he had three sons. In 1614 Lord Suffolk entertained the Court. Villiers was there and caught James's eye; the king was much impressed with his good looks and fine manners. Others observed James's sudden attachment, and those opposed to the Howards deliberately set out to build him up as a rival to Carr. One courtier gave Villiers his own place of cupbearer so that he might be constantly in the king's eye, another sent his own tailor to make him fine clothes and others took upon themselves the defense of his quarrels growing out of insults offered him by Somerset's faction.[17]

George Villiers must have been almost irresistible. Goodman thought that his beauty and grace of person had not been overrated; "they justly excited the warmest admiration of his contemporaries, . . . and truly his intellect was very great." Canterbury, a member of the anti-Howard faction, persuaded the queen to have James make Villiers a gentleman of the bedchamber despite Carr's opposition. Three years later, Gardiner tells us, James vouchsafed his love for Villiers in astonishing language: "I am neither a god nor an angel, but a man like any other, . . . and confess to loving those dear to me more than other men. You may be sure that I love the Earl of Buckingham [Villiers] more than anyone else. . . . Christ had his John, and I have my George." Even while Villiers was having his military troubles in Spain, the king still loved him, made him Duke of Buckingham and his younger brother Earl of Anglesey, "and the King did usually send for the nurse and the Duke's children into his own bedchamber and there play with them many hours together."[18]

Carr's conduct in the face of this threat of competition did nothing to help him maintain his position. He had alienated Winwood, the secretary of state, by treating him as an underling and taking all public work into his own hands. Camden, an observant onlooker, said that Carr cared not "whom he disobliged, or what malice he pulled upon himself; for, like a colossus, he stood the brunt of all the tempests of envy, making those that carried the greatest sail to strike and come under him. Nor would he suffer any place in Court or dignity in State to be bestowed, which was not sweetened with his smile that gave it, or their bounty that enjoyed it; so that (it was thought) he engrossed a mass of coin. . . . This pride and covetousness added to his other miscarriages such a number of underminers that he stood upon a tottering foundation, having no support but the King's favor."[19] Villiers, on the contrary, was at first "affable and courteous, seemed to court all men as they courted him, promoted men's suits to the King gratis, which Somerset would not do, . . . and stole all the hearts of the courtiers and petitioners to the King from Somerset, who was now wholly forsaken by God and all men."[20]

Carr now panicked a bit and began to act foolishly and to attempt to browbeat James. James had not lost his affection for Carr and was still weak where he was concerned, but he still had his dignity. He sent Somerset a long and unique letter, in which he denied any lessening of his affection for Carr or of Carr's standing at Court but warned him that he could not continue indefinitely to put up with Carr's recent sullen, irrational and overbearing behavior. The remedy was, James wrote him:

> Be kind. . . . in all the words and actions of your life . . . make it appear to me that you never think to hold grip of me but out of my mere love, and not one hair by force. . . . I told you twice or thrice, you might lead by the heart and not by the nose. . . . If ever I find that you think to retain me by one sparkle of fear, all the violence of my love will in that instant be changed into as violent a hatred. . . my love hath been infinite towards you; and only the strength of my affection towards you hath made me bear with these things in you, and bridle my passions to the uttermost of my ability. Let me be met, then, with your entire heart, but softened by humility. . . . Hold me thus by the heart; you may build upon my favor, as upon a rock that never shall fail you, that . . . shall never suffer any to arise in any degree of my favor, except they may acknowledge and thank you as a furtherer of it, and that I may be persuaded in my heart, that they love and honor you for my sake; not that any living shall come to the twentieth degree of *your* favor. . . . To make an end, then, of this unpleasing discourse, think not to value yourself so much upon other merits, as by love and heartily humble obedience. . . . it lies in your hands to make of me what you please — either the best master and truest friend, or if you force me once to call you ingrate, which the God of Heaven forbid, no so great earthly

plague can light upon you. In a word, you may procure me to delight to give daily more and more demonstrations of my favors towards you if the fault be not in yourself.[21]

These excerpts give only a hint of the style and flavor of this truly remarkable letter, which is printed in full in the Appendix.

James had no desire to referee a contest for his favor between Carr and Villiers. True to the promise in his letter to Carr, James sent Sir Humphrey May, a man who was in Carr's service but friendly with Villiers, to tell Carr that Villiers would come to him to offer his services and to desire to be his creature, that it was James's desire that Carr not refuse him but embrace him and that Carr would still stand a great man, though not the sole favorite. Carr was averse to the whole idea, and May then told him plainly that he was sent by the king to advise it and that Villiers would come to him to cast himself into his protection and to take his rise under the shadow of his wings. May had not been gone more than half an hour when Villiers came to Carr and said (perhaps in an arrogant or sarcastic voice—we do not know), "My Lord, I desire to be your servant, and your creature, and shall desire to take my Court preferment under your favor, and your Lordship shall find me as faithful a servant unto you as ever did serve you." Carr returned a quick and short answer: "I will none of your service, and you shall none of my favor; I will, if I can, break your neck, and of that be confident."[22]

By now, Carr must have felt pretty shaky about his future. Rumors had perhaps reached him that charges were to be brought against him by his enemies, although the only thing definite was a possible accusation involving the embezzling of some of the crown jewels. Camden says Carr was sufficiently frightened to throw himself at the king's feet, acknowledging that the great trust his Majesty had given to him and the weight of business lying on him might make him guilty of some miscarriages through youth and ignorance, adding that great employment often meets with envy. He therefore asked James to grant him a "general pardon for what was past, that he might not be exposed to the malice of those that would wrest all his actions to the worst meaning." The king ordered the drawing up of a general pardon in so ample and full a manner that it exceeded rather than stemmed from any former precedent. The king signed the pardon and sent it to the Great Seal, but the queen having noticed it, and using her power with the lord chancellor, prevented the seal from being affixed until the king's return to town from a journey through the West. By the time he returned, the rumors of the poisoning were numerous and loud, Winwood related the facts to the king, and James did not insist that the pardon be sealed.[23]

In the summer of 1615, William Trumbull, King James's ambassador at Brussels, advised the government that he would bring news which he dared not entrust to ordinary channels. Arriving in London, he went to Secretary of State Winwood and told his story. Shortly before he left Brussels, a young Englishman, thinking himself to be on his deathbed, had sent for Trumbull's servants to unburden himself of a secret without the telling of which he could not die in peace. The man was William Reeve, formerly an apprentice to Lobell. He said that in September, 1613, having been sent by Lobell to administer a clyster to Overbury in the Tower, he had mixed in it a poison (mercury sublimate) which resulted in Overbury's death the next day. Reeve claimed that Frances had paid him £20 for his misdeed.

The Countess of Shrewsbury was at that time imprisoned in the Tower and had already heard rumors of the poisoned clyster. She related them to Winwood, who then asked Elwes to meet him at the home of the Earl of Shrewsbury. Elwes confirmed the story without implicating himself, and Winwood went to the king with his information. Weldon has Winwood hear the story first from the Countess of Shrewsbury, alleging that she had it from Elwes, and Spedding says that Winwood mentioned the rumor casually to the Earl of Shrewsbury as a blot on Elwes's reputation and that Elwes then volunteered the statement to Winwood,[24] but it makes little difference how Winwood got the information. He told the story to James, believing he would gladly have been rid of Somerset, "yet the King dared not bring it in question, nor any question ever would have been, had not Somerset sought to cross him in his passion of love for his new favorite, in which the King was more impatient than any woman to enjoy her love."[25] D'Ewes, in agreement, wrote in his diary that James, "having at that time fixed his eyes upon the delicate personage and features of Mr. George Villiers, . . . was the more easily induced to suffer the Earl of Somerset, then his potent servant, . . . to be removed from his Court and presence to the Tower of London." D'Ewes said further that the murder had been long suspected but that, in view of the Somerset and Howard influence, none at first dared to call the matter into question.[26]

The evidence of Lobell's involvement was strong. His father, a distinguished botanist, had told a man named Edward Rider that there was no poisoning and that Overbury had died of consumption, but when a few days later Rider, the elder Lobell and their wives met on the street, Rider told Lobell that there was now no doubt but that it had been poison and that, "I heard it was done by an apothecary's boy in Lime Street near to Mr. Garret's, speaking as if I knew not that it was his son's boy, although I knew that it was his son's boy that did the deed; and Mrs. Lobell, standing by, hearing me say that he dwelt by Mr. Garret's and that he was run away, she, looking upon her husband, said in French, 'O, mon mari,' etc., that is, 'Oh, husband, that was William you sent into France' (or to that effect)." Lobell trembled and his teeth chattered, and when Rider asked him if he had sent the boy away, Lobell replied that he had sent him by letter to a friend in Paris but that he didn't know the cause of the boy's departing from his master unless perhaps of harsh usage.[27]

After Winwood's report to the king, James ordered Elwes to set down his declaration in writing. In his declaration of September 10, Elwes admitted that he had discovered Weston's intention to poison Overbury, that he had since heard from Weston that Overbury was really murdered and that it was done with a clyster administered by an apothecary's boy, who had been bribed. The only other person he implicated was Mrs. Turner, but he hinted that although he had set down the truth, it was perhaps not the whole truth, and it appears that in his first communication to Winwood he had used words understood to mean that the Somersets were implicated. On reading the declaration, the king, who seems not to have heard before the rumors involving the Somersets, referred the matter to some Councillors, with directions to inquire first whether there were any grounds for the imputation on the Somersets and, if not, to find out who was its author. When upon inquiry the facts appeared grave, Sir Edward Coke, as the highest officer of justice and the man most practiced in such investigations, was instructed to make a thorough examination.[28]

Not a moment was wasted. Coke's grandson, Sir Roger Coke, saying that he spoke with confidence because he had the account from one of Sir Edward's sons, wrote, "Sir Edward lay then at the

Temple [the center in London of lodgings for lawyers and jurists], and measured out his time at regular hours, two whereof were to go to bed at nine, and in the morning to rise at three. [This is confirmed by Campbell, who says that Coke worked hard from 3:00 A.M., entering in his "Commonplace Book" in late evening all he had learned during the day, then going to bed at 9:00P.M. At this time,] Sir Edward's son and some others were in Sir Edward's lodging but not in bed, when the messenger about one in the morning knocked at the door, where the son met him, and knew him: Says he, 'I come from the King, and must immediately speak with your father.' 'If you come from ten Kings,' he answered, 'you shall not, for I know my father's disposition to be such that if he be disturbed in his sleep, he will not be fit for any business; but if you will do as we do, you shall be welcome, and about two hours hence my father will rise, and you then may do as you please' — to which he assented." When Coke reached James, James told him of the murder, and saying, "They have made me a pimp to carry on their bawdry and murder," he instructed Coke to investigate and to spare no man.[29]

Coke began his work on September 27, 1615. After a week's daily examinations, he had found enough evidence against the Somersets to make it prudent to protect himself with the help of persons of higher rank. He broached this to the king at Royston; James then appointed as commissioners with Coke, Lord Chancellor Ellesmere, the Duke of Lenox and Lord Zouch. This was probably done on October 13.

On the morning of the day James had left Whitehall for Royston, he had sent for the judges, and with his lords and servants around him he knelt down and said: "My Lords the judges, it is lately come to my hearing, that you have now in examination a business of poisoning. Lord, in what a most miserable condition shall this kingdom be (the only famous nation for hospitality in the world), if our tables should become such a snare, as none could eat without danger of life, and that Italian custom should be introduced amongst us! Therefore, my Lords, I charge you, as you will answer it at that great and dreadful day of judgment, that you examine it strictly without favor, affection, or partiality; and if you shall spare any guilty of this crime, God's curse light on you and your posterity: and if I spare any that are found guilty, God's curse light on me and my posterity, forever!"[30] One writer added, "He did, and God did."

There are in Volume 41 of "Archaelogia" a letter written by James to Coke outlining in great detail the investigation he was to make and a letter written by James to Carr after Carr had complained about the appointment of the commission, in which James seems completely sincere in denying any ulterior motive for ordering the investigation and in which he promises to reward Carr if he is found innocent. When Coke sent for Carr at Royston to return to London for questioning, Carr complained to the king, taking it to be a great presumption, but the king replied, "You must go then; for if Coke sent for me, I must go too."[31]

A rather revolting scene took place at Royston when Carr left to go to London. As Weldon, who was present, described it, Carr never parted from James with more seeming affection between them than at this time, when James knew Somerset would never see him again. "Had you seen that seeming affection (as the author himself did)," Weldon wrote, "you would rather have believed he was in his rising than setting. The Earl, when he kissed his hand, the King hung about his neck, slobbering his cheeks, saying 'For God's sake, when shall I see thee again? On my soul, I shall neither eat nor sleep until you come again.' The Earl told him, 'On Monday' (this being on the Friday), 'For God's sake, let me,' said the King—'Shall I, shall I?' then lolled about his neck. 'Then for God's sake, give thy lady this kiss for me.' In the same manner at the stairs' head, at the middle of the stairs, and at the stairs' foot. The Earl was not in his coach when the King used these very words (in the hearing of four servants, of whom one . . . reported it instantly to the author of this history), 'I shall never see his face more.' "[32]

Carr was now sufficiently alarmed to attempt to get rid of any letters which might, justly or not, throw suspicion on either Frances or him. When Northampton had died, Carr had sent to Sir Robert Cotton, who had charge of Northampton's papers, for those letters he had written Northampton regarding Overbury's imprisonment. He seems to have burned those and to have altered certain letters of Overbury's that had been turned over to Cotton. He also sent one of his servants to find Lawrence Davis, who had been a servant of Overbury, and to obtain from him all the originals and copies Davis had of letters which Somerset had written to Overbury. He paid Davis £30 for these and destroyed them. Frances apparently had told Carr about Mrs. Turner's part in the affair; letters Mrs. Turner had written to Weston and others were stored at the home of

Weston's son. Carr, using his seal as lord chamberlain, now sent a pursuivant to seize some of those letters.

The commissioners held their first meeting on October 15. By the seventeenth they had heard of the raid on Mrs. Turner's letters which Carr had made on the sixteenth and were sufficiently convinced of the guilt of the Somersets to put them in confinement. A letter to Carr informed him that "by force of his Majesty's letters under his gracious signature to us directed (we having had due consultation of certain examinations and testimonies concerning your Lordship and thereupon having occasion to examine you), in his Majesty's name to will and require you to keep your chamber near the Cockpit at Whitehall without suffering of the access of any to you other than your own necessary servants until his Majesty's pleasure be further known." A similar letter required Frances to keep her chamber either at her house in the Blackfriars or at the house of the Lord Knollys near the Tiltyard. Both letters were signed, "Your very loving friends"! On the same day the commissioners reported to the king that they believed there was vehement suspicion, that the examinations were pregnant against Somerset as being an accessory before the fact in the poisoning and that they had resolved to have the earl committed to the Tower before the king's return.[33]

The next day the commissioners wrote the king a full report from York House. In it they told him that on the advice of the judges they had committed the earl and countess to their own chambers, had turned Mrs. Turner and Weston over to the custody of the sheriffs of London, would bring Weston to speedy trial and proposed to examine the earl and countess. They told James further that they had been informed by the chief justice of a great contempt committed by the earl and described the taking of Mrs. Turner's papers. This act the commissioners held to be a very great contempt of the king, intended to suppress the truth and frustrate their examinations; furthermore, one of Somerset's servants had attempted to deliver to Mrs. Turner a message from the Somersets to be of good comfort and not dejected, which the sheriff had refused to permit, and that in view of these things, the commissioners had committed the earl to the house of the Dean of Westminster under the custody of Sir Oliver St. John.[34]

Coke spared no effort to come up with as airtight a case as possible against all the suspected persons. He was not interested particularly in finding out who was really guilty or of what cause Overbury had died and did not (or possibly may not have been permitted to) examine the physicians who had attended him. He believed that James wanted to get rid of Carr and that it was his job to handle the evidence and trials in order to assure that end. Too, his rivalry with Bacon was intense. Bacon had acquired the attorney general's post which both men had wanted, and Coke had had to be content with the much less lucrative office of chief justice. The lord chancellor's post was even more important and lucrative. Lord Ellesmere was old, and the conduct of both Bacon and Coke was influenced by the desire to obtain the appointment to the vacancy which ought shortly to occur. The conviction of Somerset would be a substantial step in that direction. (Bacon eventually acquired the office.)

Coke in all made between two hundred and three hundred examinations of persons who might throw light on the affair. He carefully fitted together the pieces and did not hesitate to doctor the testimony and confessions where advantageous to his case. Records in his own handwriting of more than one hundred of the examinations still exist, many of which show his erasures and substitutions. He was now ready to try Richard Weston.

NINE

COKE had chosen to try Weston as the principal in the case and the others as accessories before the fact (persons who, though not actually present, aid and abet the one actually committing a felony). This made it necessary for him to secure Weston's conviction in order to clear the way for trying the others. If Overbury's death was actually caused by a poisoned clyster, and if Lobell's boy who administered the clyster knew it contained poison, which would appear to be the case from his having been sent out of the country and his subsequent confession in Brussels, then the boy was the principal. If the boy was not guilty or for any reason could not be prosecuted (it is not certain he was still alive), Lobell, who presumably had prepared the clyster, unless the boy did so without Lobell's knowledge, and had himself poisoned the clyster and sent the boy to inject it, was next in line of direct responsibility. For murky reasons we can suspect but not prove, Lobell was not even charged as an accessory. Weston was the only person other than Lobell's boy who could be charged with actually administering poison. He did not administer the clyster, nor was it proved that any poison given Overbury prior to the clyster was fatal or even that he had died from poison. However, since Weston admitted having accepted money to poison Overbury, he was preferred as the principal, and the times being what they were, no question of legality appears to have been raised by any of the defendants.

To a reader with even passing knowledge of the safeguards to assure defendants a fair trial that are commonplace today, questions about the disregard of these rules are bound to occur as the murder trials are read. Some of these should be discussed before we take up the trials themselves. To some extent these variations from present procedure have been mentioned in connection with the trials we have already covered.

Sir James Stephen, in his valuable "General View of the Criminal Law of England," makes the overall statement that prior to 1640, although the general procedure in criminal trials was much like that of today, there were some important differences, which were disadvantageous to the accused. He mentions eight:

1. The first step in the procedure was to lock up the accused, making it difficult for him to provide for his defense.

2. He was kept in ignorance of the evidence against him.

3. His examination was rigorous, sometimes including torture (and even where torture was not used, the threat was always there).

4. The accused had no affirmative right to witnesses, and if as a matter of grace one was permitted, the witness could not be examined under oath.

5. The jury had little more than a veto on his conviction; unusual intestinal fortitude was required to exercise the veto.

6. There were no rules of evidence; written depositions and "confessions" taken in secret were often used, and heresay evidence was not barred.

7. The accused had no right of cross-examination.

8. The accused was not entitled to counsel, and if counsel was permitted, he was permitted to do nothing but discuss questions of law.[1]

Plucknett, in referring to Stephen's discussion of the subject, adds that the confessions of accomplices were not only admitted against each other but were regarded as specially cogent evidence, but that, however, bail was freely granted, offering some opportunity for preparing a defense. However, in cases with political implications, bail was not often permitted.

Lack of the defendant's right to summon witnesses or to require that the state's witnesses be sworn and be present to confront him probably evolved from the way in which the jury system originated and developed. Originally, jurors were chosen because of their first-hand knowledge of the facts at issue. They were really themselves the official witnesses and after hearing each other's evidence gave their verdict; the use of other witnesses to give evidence was not considered necessary to a correct verdict. Only later were they assisted in arriving at their verdict by the testimony of witnesses in the modern sense of the word. Even as late as 1571, the Duke of

Norfolk, on trial for treason, asked to be confronted with the witnesses but was refused, and into the seventeenth century jurors could still decide cases from their own knowledge. By Statute in 1562-63 witnesses could be compelled to attend, but it was not until the 1600's that the accused could call witnesses (and then not in treason or felony trials), and only near the end of the century could they be required to be sworn in.[2]

An additional factor may lie in the ancient institution of inquests and the feeling that accusation by the Grand Inquest was almost equivalent to conviction, its consequences only to be averted by trial by ordeal or compurgation. The same reasoning explains fining the jury if it did not give the verdict the king's advisers wished, a practice which, although criticized, continued into the time of Elizabeth.[3]

Similar reasoning was used to justify the depriving a defendant both of counsel and of the right to call witnesses. Blackstone said, "It was an ancient and commonly received practice, that, as counsel was not allowed to any prisoner accused of a capital crime, so neither should he be suffered to exculpate himself by the testimony of any witness."[4]

As to counsel, he wrote, "But it is a settled rule at common law, that no counsel shall be allowed a prisoner upon his trial upon the general issue in any capital crime, unless some point of law shall arise proper to be debated. [The rule] . . . (however it may be palliated under cover of that noble declaration of the law, when rightly understood, that the judge shall be counsel for the prisoner; that is, shall see that the proceedings against him are legal and strictly regular) seems to be not at all of a piece with the rest of the humane treatment of prisoners by the English law."[5]

A lawyer writing only eight years after these trials were held has an interesting and different explanation, albeit naive and not very flattering to the legal profession: "Upon this plea of only Not Guilty, the party indicted shall not have counsel learned in the law to plead for him, or to say anything in his behalf in the same plea . . . for when the offender is put to answer to an indictment of treason or felony, he must answer it in proper person, and not by attorney, or counsel learned: for the plea of Not Guilty doth tend to the fact, the which the party himself doth best know, and therefore he can best make answer unto it. And if his counsel learned should plead his plea for him, and defend him, it may be that they would be so covert in their speeches, and so shadow the matter with words, and so extenuate the proofs and evidence, that it would be hard or long to have the truth appear. Also if the party himself defend it, peradventure his conscience will prick him to utter the truth, or his countenance, or gesture will show some tokens thereof, or by his simple speeches somewhat may be drawn from him to bolt out the verity of the cause, which would not be won of men learned in the law, who endeavor to speak providently, and artificially, which be the causes that the offender shall answer in his own person, and not by counselor learned."[6]

Short shrift can be made of the theory that the chief justice (or the lord high steward in the trial of peers) could be relied upon to protect the interests of the defendant and to see that he received a fair trial. Amos gives many contrary examples, and it is necessary only to read the trials appearing in this book to realize that in practice, at least, the presiding judge or the lord high steward was there only to convict if conviction was deemed profitable for the Crown or to acquit for one sufficiently enjoying the favors of the Crown.

The influence of the Crown, when it desired to exercise it, can hardly be overestimated. Judges in those times held office at the pleasure of the sovereign and, unless falling into disfavor or given a promotion, were apt to hold the office permanently. True, no judge was dismissed for political reasons under either Elizabeth or James, but at least one was kicked upstairs to get rid of him, and the threat of dismissal was always there.

As noted above, the Crown, if supported by the Council, could exercise great influence on jury verdicts through the right of the Star Chamber to fine the jury if it did not give the verdict the king's advisers wished. Such control was exercised through an action of attaint against the jury for having brought in a wrong verdict. The attaint had to be tried by a jury of twenty-four members, and in theory at least there had to be prima facie evidence of error before an attaint action could be started, but again Crown influence could well control the results. Even before Elizabeth's time, the Star Chamber used the attaint action usually, but not always, in the interests of justice rather than for political reasons. After 1670 the action could be brought only where the verdict was corrupt rather than merely wrong.[7]

Weston came to trial on October 19, 1615.

The Trial of RICHARD WESTON, at the Guild Hall of London, for the Murder of SIR THOMAS OVERBURY, 19 Oct. 13 JAMES I A.D. 1615.

The Commissioners were the Lord Mayor, Hayes; the Lord Chief Justice of England, Coke; Justice Crook; Justice Doderidge; Justice Haughton; Serjeant Crew; and Sir Henry Montague, Recorder.

This trial could and normally would have been held before judges of the King's Bench, but, possibly in order to obtain maximum control over the proceeding, Coke chose to use a specialized form of proceeding before commissioners of Oyer and Terminer. Normally a criminal trial would be predicated upon an indictment returned by a Grand Jury that had investigated the probability of guilt. However, rather early in the development of English law a procedure was devised under which the Crown would appoint several commissioners to "hear and determine" the case. Such a commission could have jurisdiction over the indictment as well as the pleading, trial, judgment and sentence.[8] We can safely assume that the men here commissioned to serve with Coke could be relied upon to go along with his suggestions. Only the importance of obtaining Weston's conviction in order to clear the way to try the others as accessories can explain the use of this procedure and these blue-ribbon commissioners to try a common felon.

Coke ran into an interesting question of jurisdiction, which he discusses in his "Institutes." The ancient wall of London had extended through the middle of the Tower; the part west of the wall was in London and the east part was in Middlesex County. Overbury's chamber was west of the wall, wherefore his accused murderer was properly tried in London, but the use of a Middlesex County coroner gave Coke the jurisdictional problem mentioned before in our discussion of the inquest. In order to try any of the accessories before the King's Bench, Coke had to put up to the justices of the bench the question whether, since the King's Bench sat in Middlesex, accessories to a murder committed in London and the principal having been tried and convicted in London could be tried before the King's Bench. The justices held that they could. The Somersets were, of course, to be tried by their peers before the lord steward , so no such question arose regarding them.[9]

The Court being set, and the King's special commission read, the Lord Chief Justice gave the Charge, the effect whereof was:

First, to express the King's pious inclinations and command unto just proceedings against all such as should be any way proved to be guilty of the murdering and poisoning of Sir Thomas Overbury, his Majesty's prisoner in the Tower.

Secondly, to aggravate the manner and quality of the murdering, in showing the baseness of poisoning above all other kinds of murder, declaring the vengeance of God, and his justness in punishing offenders. He alleged 9 Gen. 6. ["Whoso sheddeth man's blood, by man shall his blood be shed: for in the image of God made he man."] He also took the example of Uriah by David; he therein observed how adultery is most often the begetter of that sin.

Then he declared, that of all felonies, murder is the most horrible; of all murders, poisoning the most detestable; and of all poisoning, the lingering poisoning.

He showed how that by an Act of Parliament, 22 H. 8, cap. 9, it was made treason, and that willful poisoners should be boiled to death; rehearsing the example of one Richard Rowse, that had poisoned a man and woman, and was therefore scalded to death.

Then he laid open to the jury the baseness and cowardliness of poisoners, who attempt that secretly against which there is no means of preservation or defense for a man's life; and how rare it was to hear of poisoning in England, so detestable it was to our nation. . . .

He finished his charge with serious exhortations to the jury to do justice in presenting the truth, notwithstanding the greatness of any that upon their evidence should appear to be guilty of the same offense [observe throughout these trials how Coke improperly constantly hints that the Somersets are also guilty, although they had not yet even been indicted], comforting both judges and jury with the scripture, Psal. 5, v. ultimo, "For thou, Lord, wilt bless the righteous; with favor wilt thou compass them as with a shield."

The charge being ended, the jury, consisting of 14 persons, did for the space of an hour depart the court into a private room, where they received their evidence from Mr. Fenshaw, his Majesty's Coroner, and his Highness's counsel prepared and instructed for that purpose, with the examinations and confessions as well of the prisoner himself, as of divers other witnesses, before that time taken by the Lord Chief Justice of England, and others the Lords of his Majesty's Council.

In the meantime, Mr. William Goare, Sheriff of London, was commanded to fetch his prisoner, remaining at his house, to be ready in court for his arraignment.

So a certain space after, the Grand Jury returned to the Bar, and delivered in their bill of indictment, signed *Billa Vera* [True Bill]. Whereupon the prisoner was set up to the Bar, and the indictment read by Mr. Fenshaw, which contained in effect as followeth:

That Richard Weston, being about the age of 60 years, not having the fear of God before his eyes, but instigated and seduced by the devil, devised and contrived not only to bring upon the body of Sir Thomas Overbury, Knight, great sickness and diseases, but also to deprive him of his life; and to bring the same to pass, 9 May, 1613, 11 Jacobi, etc. at the Tower of London, in the parish of All Hallows Barking, did obtain and get into his hand certain poison of green and yellow color, called rosalgar [disulphide of arsenic], (knowing the same to be deadly poison) and the same did maliciously and feloniously mingle and compound in a kind of broth poured out into a certain dish, and the same broth so infected and poisoned, did give and deliver to the said Sir Thomas Overbury as wholesome and good broth, to the intent therewith to kill and poison the said Sir Thomas, which broth he took and did eat.

Also the said Weston upon the first of July, 11 Jacobi, as aforesaid, did in like manner get another poison or poisons compounded, called white arsenic and (knowing the same to be deadly poison) did give unto the said Sir Thomas Overbury, as good and wholesome to eat, who took and did eat.

Also that Weston, upon the said nineteenth of July following, did get another poison called mercury sublimate (knowing the same to be mortal poison), and put and mingled the same in tarts and jellies, and gave the same unto Sir Thomas Overbury, as good and wholesome to eat, which he in like manner took and did eat.

Also the said Weston, and another man being an apothecary, afterwards, upon the fourteenth of September, feloniously did get a poison, called mercury sublimate (knowing the same to be deadly poison), and put the same into a clyster mingled with the said poison; and the said clyster the said apothecary, for the reward of £20 promised unto him, did put and minister (as good and wholesome) into the guts of said Sir Thomas; and that Weston was present and aiding to the said apothecary in ministering and infusing the said clyster; and that immediately after, as well the taking of the said poisoned meats, and ministering the said clyster, the said Sir Thomas did languish, and fell into diseases and distempers; and from the aforesaid times of taking and eating the said poisoned meats, and ministering said clyster, he died: And so the jury gave their verdict, that Weston in this manner had killed, poisoned, and murdered the said Sir Thomas against the King's peace and dignity. [Note that the indictment charges Weston with actually putting the poison in all these foods and in the clyster. It will be interesting to see whether Coke's evidence proves this.]

Which indictment being read, he was demanded if he were guilty of the felony, murdering and poisoning, as aforesaid, yea or no. To which he answered, doubling his speech, "Lord have mercy upon me! Lord have mercy upon me!" But being again demanded, he answered, "Not Guilty." And being then demanded how he would be tried, he answered, he referred himself to God, and would be tried by God; refusing to put himself and his cause upon the jury or country, according to the law or custom.

Hereupon the Lord Chief Justice, and all others in their order, spent the space of an hour in persuading him to put himself upon the trial of the law; declaring unto him the danger and mischief he ran into by resisting his ordinary course of trial, being the means ordained by God for his deliverance, if he were innocent; and how by this means he would make himself the author of his own death, even as if he should with a knife or dagger kill or stab himself, exhorting him very earnestly either with repentance to confess his fault, or else with humility and duty to submit himself to his ordinary trial. Whereupon he subbornly answered, "Welcome by the grace of God," and he referred himself to God. And so when no persuasions could prevail, the Lord Chief Justice plainly delivered his opinion, that he was persuaded that Weston had been dealt withal by some great ones, guilty of the same fact, as accessory, to stand mute, whereby they might escape their punishment [the Somersets again!]; and therefore he commanded (for satisfaction of the world) that the Queen's Attorney there present should declare, and set forth the whole evidence, without any fear or partiality; and yet notwithstanding, he once more used such persuasion to the prisoner to consider what destruction he brought upon himself by his contempt; and declaring unto him how his offense of contempt was, in refusing his trial, and how the laws of the land had provided a sharper and more severe punishment to such offenders than unto those that were guilty of high treason, and so he repeated the form of judgment given against such, the extremity and rigor whereof was expressed in these words, *onere frigore et fame.* For the first, [that] he was to receive his punishment by the law to be extended and then to have weights laid upon him, no more than he was able to bear, which were by little and little to be increased.

For the second, that he was to be exposed in an open place, near to the prison, in the open air, being naked.

And lastly, that he was to be preserved with the coarsest bread that could be got, and water out of the next sink or puddle to the place of execution, and that day he had water he should have no bread, and that day he had bread he should have no water; and in this torment he was to linger as long as nature could linger out, so that oftentimes men lived in that extremity eight or nine days; adding further, that as life left him, so judgment should find him. And therefore he required him, upon consideration of these reasons, to advise himself to plead to the country, who notwithstanding absolutely refused.

Salmon says that Weston stood mute because "practiced upon by a certain great man."[10] Howell, in a footnote to the trial, says that Coke had intelligence underhand that Yelverton, who was under obligation to the Howards, had persuaded Weston to stand mute in order to prevent his trial and conviction and hence to prevent the prosecution of the accessories, who could be tried only if Weston, the principal, were tried and found guilty. It is significant that although Yelverton was the solicitor general, he took no part in any of the Overbury murder trials, although he would normally have participated. Coke, apparently balked, was understandably furious. We can imagine the tone of voice in which he explained to Weston the penalty for standing mute.

The situation facing Coke grew out of a highly technical procedural provision in the English law of that period. After a plea of not guilty, the prisoner was asked how he wanted to be tried, and the prescribed response was "By God and my country." Without this response the trial could not proceed. In order to force the prisoner to give the proper response, the court was authorized, if he insisted on standing mute, to subject the prisoner to *"peine forte et dure."* Coke's explanation of this to Weston was accurate. Ordinarily a defendant who stood mute and accepted this torture did so because, if he died in this manner rather than by execution pursuant to a

verdict, his property was not forfeited to the Crown and could be
preserved for his wife and children. Weston had no such reason
here; we do not know what promises had been made him by the
Howards, but they were insufficient to hold him in line against the
threats which were doubtless made to him during the trial recess.
This strange rule was not abolished for another one hundred and
fifty years.

Hereupon the Lord Chief Justice willed Sir Lawrence Hyde,
the Queen's Attorney, and there of counsel for the King, to
manifest unto the audience the guiltiness of the said Weston by
his own confession, signed with his own hand; and if in the
declaration thereof they may meet with any great persons whatsoever, as certainly there were great ones confederate in that fact,
he should boldly and faithfully open whatsoever was necessary,
and he could prove against them. Whereupon Mr. Attorney
began his accusation:

First, he charged the Countess of Somerset and the Earl to be
principal movers unto this unhappy conclusion, Mrs. Turner to
be of the confederacy and the pay mistress of the prisoner's
reward; in which the Attorney's boldness was very observable, in
terming the Countess a dead and rotten branch, which being
lopped off, the noble tree, meaning that noble family, would
prosper the better.

Secondly, he proceeded to the cause, which he affirmed to be
the malice of the Countess, and the ground of this malice he
alleged, and by many inducements he evidently affirmed, that Sir
Thomas Overbury had dissuaded [meaning *attempted* to dissuade]
the Viscount Rochester from that adulterate marriage with the
Countess of Somerset, then Countess of Essex. And for this he
alleged as followeth:

Sir T. Overbury having divers times dissuaded the Earl, then
Viscount Rochester, from seeking by any means to procure marriage with the Countess of Essex, to which he saw the Earl too
much inclined; and having very earnest conference with the Earl
one night in private in the gallery at Whitehall concerning his
intention, perceiving the Earl too much at that time to desire that
unlawful communication; in the ardency of his fervent affection
unto the Earl, and great prescience of the future misery it would
inevitably bring unto him (his well-beloved lord and friend), used
speeches to this effect:

"Well, my Lord, if you do marry that filthy base woman, you

will utterly ruin your honor and yourself; you shall never do it by my advice or consent; and if you do, you had best look to stand fast."

My Lord, bewitched with the love of the said Countess, moved with Sir T. Overbury for so slighting her, answered, "My own legs are straight and strong enough to bear me up; but, in faith, I will be even with you for this," and so parted from him in a great rage.

This conference was overheard by some in an adjoining room, and their depositions for the truth thereof were read in court.

Although this conference moved the Earl to such a sudden choler, yet it seemed Sir T. Overbury conceived it no otherwise than a sudden extreme distemperature or passion, and not a final conclusion of their bosom friend[ship] as before, in which the Earl seemed reciprocal: howsoever, in his double-dealing it seemed to be clearly otherwise.

For upon this the Earl moved the King to appoint Sir T. Overbury Ambassador for Russia. The King, willing to prefer Sir T. Overbury, as one whose worth and valor was not unknown to his Majesty, accordingly adjoined him that service; the which Sir T. was most willing to accept of, as a gracious aspect of the King towards him, which willingness of his was proved by the depositions of two or three several witnesses read in court, and by the oath of Sir Dudley Diggs, who voluntarily, at the arraignment in open court, upon his oath, witnessed how Sir Thomas had imparted to him his readiness to be employed on an embassage.

The Earl as well abusing the King's favors, in moving to show favor where he meant the party should take no benefit, as bearing dishonest friendship, in conference with Sir Thomas concerning that employment, persuaded him to refuse to serve ambassador, "Where," quoth he, "I shall not be able to perform such kindness to your advantage, as having you with me, and . . . if you be blamed or committed for it, care not; I will quickly free you from all harm." Sir Thomas, thus betrayed by a friend, refused to serve in that nature, whereupon he was committed to the Tower.

Being thus committed, he was presently committed close prisoner, and a keeper he must have; and who must that be but this Weston, who was commended by the Countess of Essex to Sir T. Monson, to be by him recommended over unto the Lieutenant of the Tower, to be keeper to Sir T. Overbury. Sir T. Monson, according to the Countess's request, commended the said Weston to Sir Jervis Elwes; whereupon the said Lieutenant entertained the said Weston, and appointed him to keep Sir T. Overbury. The said Weston, upon his own confession read in court, signed with his mark, had during the time that she was Countess of Essex, been a procurer and pander to the said Earl, then Viscount Rochester, and the Countess of Essex, for the conveying and effecting of their adulterate desires, which they did divers times consummate, meeting in Mrs. Turner's house once between the hours of eleven and twelve, and at Hammersmith, and at divers times elsewhere, for that purpose; that now, by the procurement of the Countess (who hated Sir T. Overbury for being a good means to keep them from contaminating themselves with such lustful embracements, and from the purposed marriage they mutually labored to compass) her pander was become his keeper, a fit agent for lust and murder.

Weston now being become Sir T. Overbury's keeper, kept him so close that he scarce had the comfort of the day's brightness; neither suffered he anyone to visit him; father, brother, his best friends, his nearest kindred were strangers to him from the beginning of his imprisonment unto the end.

Mrs. Turner, upon the first day's keeping, promised to give him a contenting reward, if he should administer such things to Sir T. Overbury as should be sent unto him, thinking him a fit instrument to compass black murder, that was so well acquainted with foul lust; and so indeed they found him, for he agreed and did promise to administer whatsoever she would send him. Mrs. Turner, upon this murderous promise, the very same day that Weston became Sir T. Overbury's keeper, being the sixth day of May, 1613, sent unto him the said Weston certain yellow poison, called rosalgar, in a vial.

Weston having received that poison, the aforesaid sixth of May at night, bringing Sir T. Overbury's supper in one hand, and the vial of poison in the other, meets with the Lieutenant, and asks him in these terms, "Sir, shall I give it him now?" Upon this word "now," the Lord Chief Justice demurs, to aggravate the maliciousness; affirming that this particle "now," showed a resolution to poison him. "What shall you give him?" replies the Lieutenant. Weston replies, "As if you did not know, Sir." The Lieutenant blaming him, he carries the poison into an inner room, which Weston, the ninth of May did administer to Sir T. Overbury in broth. This was proved both by Weston and the Lieutenant's confession.

Weston having given this poison, which wrought very vehemently with him by vomits and extreme purging, he presently demands his reward of Mrs. Turner, who replies, "The man is not yet dead: perfect your work, and you shall have your hire." This was also confessed by Weston under his marks.

Sir T. Overbury, by his close imprisonment, growing sick and daily languishing, after three or four weeks space (considering he had not got his freedom and release, having no friends suffered to come unto him, but only such as the Earl sent to comfort him, of his own followers), wrote to the Earl to remember his imprisonment; and received answer, "The time would not suffer, but so soon as possible might be, he would hasten his delivery." So indeed it seems he intended to do, but not so as Sir. T. Overbury conceived, whose true affection would not admit his judgment to debate the strangeness of his imprisonment, which he might well think the Earl might easily have relieved.

The fifth of June, Viscount Rochester sent a letter to Sir T. Overbury. In the letter he sent him a white powder, willing Sir T. to take it: "It will," quoth he, "make you more sick; but fear not, I will make this a means for your delivery, and for the recovery of your health." Sir T. Overbury never dreaming of base treachery, but conceiving it as a friendly policy, received the said powder, which wrought upon him more vehemently; whereupon his sickness grew more vehement or violent, and his languishment increased; which white powder, upon Weston's confession, was poison.

Sir T. Overbury's sickness increasing, and with it his wondering that he could not in two months space be released, after his physic taking, he thus writes to the Earl, lamenting his own estate; for his faith being thus shaken with the Earl's unkindness, gave way for his judgment to scan those actions, rather like an understanding man than like a loving friend, as appeareth by his letter sent to Viscount Rochester, the effect whereof was thus, as it is averred by the deposition of Sir T. Overbury's servants, who saw the letter: "Sir I wonder you have not yet found means to effect my delivery; but I remember you said, you would be even with me [Here Hyde commented, "not suspecting, as it seemeth, any poisoning, but an unkind forgetfulness of my Lord of Rochester"] and so indeed you are; but assure yourself, my Lord, if you do not release me, but suffer me thus to die, my blood will be required at your hands."

My Lord comforts him, and excuses, that it cannot yet be compassed; Sir Thomas, after the powder taken, languisheth deadly; and to comfort him, some followers of my Lord of Rochester's are sent to him daily, in the name of my Lord by the appointment and procurement too of the Lady of Essex (as Weston confessed) to visit and comfort him, and to entreat him if he desired any meat, that he should speak, and it might be better perhaps provided for him, than he should have in the Tower: This was about three months after his imprisonment. He, as men sick desire luscious meats, desired tarts and jellies, which were provided by Mrs. Turner, with the knowledge of the said Countess and sent unto him, of which he did eat; the which tarts were poisoned with mercury sublimate, not being so well colored as other tarts are, and Weston confessed that he was strictly charged not to taste thereof.

Sir T. thus continuing languishing with the extremity of sickness, until the sixth of September, when the aforesaid Mrs. Turner did procure an apothecary's boy for £20 to poison a clyster, which was by the boy and Weston afterwards administered as good physic, upon the seventh day of October [sic]; after the receipt of the clyster, he fell into a great extremity of vomiting and other purging, which left him not, till it caused his soul to leave his poisoned body: this Weston confessed and signed. Being thus dead, he was presently and very unreverently buried in a pit, dug in a very mean place; on his body thus venomously infected, appeared divers blains and blisters, whereupon they, to take away as well his good name as his life, did slanderously report that he died of the French pox; but this report was cleared in court, by the depositions of his servants and other men of worth there read, that before his imprisonment he had a clean and sound body, only he had an issue in his left arm, purposely made for the benefit of his nature, for the voiding of rheum and ill humors, which, with continual sitting at his study, he had subjected himself unto. He further observed the confession of the Lieutenant to be, that if any prisoner died there, his body was to be viewed, and inquisition to be taken by the coroner.

But Sir T. Overbury's friends and others by no means might be suffered to see his body; and although it was reported that there was an inquisition taken, yet it could by no means be found.

Coke's action in having the evidence read in court even though the trial could not proceed was indefensible. It would have been bad enough had all the evidence read been pertinent to Weston's guilt, but the documents read and the comments made were intended primarily to evidence the guilt of the Somersets, who had not yet been indicted. Coke was simply not able to resist the center of the stage. He had a large audience in court that day, including "some of the nobility and many gentlemen of great quality," whom he was not willing to disappoint. The commissioners (amenable to Coke as anticipated) thought it proper, he said, "to have openly and at large read the confessions of the said Richard Weston, and the testimonies of others, as well concerning the fact of the said Richard Weston as the Earl and Countess of Somerset, and Mrs. Turner, without sparing any of them, or omitting anything material against them." Feeling obliged to give some sort of reason, Coke offered as an excuse "the necessity and course of the evidence," because "it appeared thereby that the said Richard Weston was procured and wagered by some of them." The whole thing was, of course, ridiculous. As Spedding says, if the story could not be told without what amounted to a declaration from the bench of the guilt of parties who had. not yet been so much as accused, it would surely have been better to leave it untold.[11]

> . . . Then, by the commandment of the court, were read by Mr. Fenshaw the examinations of divers witnesses taken before my Lord Chief Justice and others, which in effect were as follows:
> Laurence Davies, servant to Sir T. Overbury, examined the 15th of October, before the Lord Chief Justice.
> He saith, that he had served Sir T. Overbury eight or nine years, in all which time he was very healthful, and never kept his bed for any sickness, only he was sometimes troubled with the spleen, for ease whereof he had by the advice of his physician an issue made in his left arm; but before his imprisonment, he had no, sores, blisters, or other defects in all his body. Also he saith, Sir T. would have gone over upon the embassage, but was dissuaded by Somerset, who promised to bear him out; he complained, he needed not to be prisoner if Somerset would [unless Somerset wished] and that if he died, his blood would be required at his hands, that Somerset was as good as his word, who told him at Newmarket, he would be even with Sir T. Overbury.
> Henry Payton, another servant of Sir T. Overbury's, examined the 15th of October, 1615.
> He affirmeth, that Sir T. was of a very good constitution of body; that he used sometimes to run, to play at foils, and such like; that he was of a moderate diet, never had any sores, saving the issue in his arm. That Sir T. wrote letters to Somerset, signifying that he needed not to lie in prison if Somerset would, and if he died, his blood should be required at his hands. That

Sir T. at one of the clock at night, meeting Somerset in the gallery at Whitehall, had speech with him touching the Countess, whom he called base woman, and told Somerset he would over-throw all the King's favors and honors; and upon displeasure between them at his conference, Sir T. Overbury desired Somer-set that he might have his portion due, and he would shift for himself. Whereunto Somerset answered: "And my legs are straight enough to carry me," and so flung away in anger. All which this examinee heard, being in a chamber next to the gallery.

Sir Dudley Diggs being present in court, and sworn, declared *viva voce,* that he was sent by a Privy Councillor, a great man, to Sir T. Overbury to bring him to this great man, which he did; and coming back together over the water in a boat, Sir T. was much discontented; the reason whereof he said was, that he was persuaded by the great man to withdraw himself from the Court for some reasons which he disclosed not: And Sir Dudley after-ward being sent by the Lords, to know the resolution of Sir T. touching the embassage, he found him to rely upon the Lord of Somerset, saying, "My precious chief knows the King's mind better than any, and I the mind of my precious chief."

Richard Weston, the prisoner, examined the 6th of October, 1615, coram [before] Coke and Crew.

He affirmeth, that before Sir T. Overbury was in the Tower, he, this examinee, carried three letters to Somerset from the Lady Essex, to Royston, Newmarket, and Hampton Court, and he delivered answer to Mrs. Turner; and that upon the letter to Hampton Court, he had answer only by word of mouth, that his Lordship would come: and that coming back, he met with the Countess and Mrs. Turner half way, in the coach, whom he told, that the Lord only answered so; whereupon the Countess struck out of the way into a farmer's house hard by, whither within a little space Somerset came, and that afterwards they met in the night at Mrs. Turner's house in Paternoster Row. And he con-fesseth, that for a year before Sir T.'s imprisonment, no man carried letters between them but he.

Sir Thomas Monson examined the 5th of October, coram Coke and Crew.

He saith, that he never knew Weston until Sir T. Overbury was prisoner in the Tower, and that he preferred [recommended] him to the Lieutenant to be keeper of Sir T. Overbury at the request of the Countess.

Anne Turner, widow, examined the 11th of October, 1615, coram Coke and Crew.

She saith, that Weston was an ancient servant, and her husband's bailiff in the country. She denieth to have anything to do in placing him in the Tower; but saith, that the Countess of Essex did effect it, and used the help of Sir Thomas Monson therein.

Sir Jervis [Gervaise] Elwes examined the 3rd day of October, 1615, coram Coke and Crew.

He saith, he had a letter from Sir T. Monson, requesting him that Weston might be keeper of Sir T. Overbury, and that he did perform it; and afterwards having conference with Sir T. Monson, he told him that his keeper was not to suffer any letters or tokens, or any things to be delivered to him.

Richard Weston the prisoner examined again.

He confesseth, he showed ... the glass that was delivered him by his son from the Countess to the Lieutenant and told him that it came from the Countess of Essex, and that he [the Lieutenant] persuaded him not to give it to Sir Thomas.

He saith, that he had divers tarts from the Countess to give to Sir T., with caveats [warnings] that he himself should not taste them; and confesseth that he thought they were poisoned.

He saith, Mrs. Turner appointed him to come to Whitehall, and that she dealt with him to give Sir T. Overbury the water, and told him he should not drink thereof; and was promised a great reward, and he suspected it was poison. His son afterwards delivered him the glass, which he showed to the Lieutenant, who rebuked him, and so he set the glass in a study near to Sir T.'s chamber, but gave it him not; although he told Mrs. Turner the next day, he had given [him] the water, which made Sir T. to vomit often and to be exceeding sick.

He saith, Mr. James and Mrs. Rawlins, servants to the Countess, came often to know of the examinee how Sir T. Overbury did, and what he would eat; and they delivered him jellies and tarts which he gave Sir T., who did eat thereof.

He saith, he demanded of Mrs. Turner his reward, who answered, he was to have no reward until Sir T. was dead, and he was promised a pursuivant's place; but confesseth, that afterwards, at two several times, he received secretly after the death of Sir T. for a reward of Mrs. Turner from the Countess, £ 180.

Wm. Weston, son to the prisoner, examined.

He confesseth, he received a glass from the Countess by her servant, two inches long, being wrapped in paper, which he delivered to his father in the Tower.

Then was read the Confession of the Lieutenant to the King.

He saith, that Weston met him, carrying Sir T.'s supper in the one hand and the glass in the other, and demanded of the Lieutenant this, "Sir, shall I give it him now?" Whereat the Lieutenant stepped to him and asked him, "What?" To which Weston said, "Why, sir, know you not what is to be done?" And so the Lieutenant having made him to confess the matter, dissuaded him, and he seemed to be resolved not to do it; and afterwards this Weston confessed, that an apothecary had £20 for administering a clyster to Sir T. Overbury.

Weston, the prisoner, examined before the Lord Zouch and others.

Confesseth, that Sir T. had a clyster which gave him 60 stools and a vomit; also being confronted with the writings of Sir Jervis Elwes, and charged therewith, he confesseth the same to be true.

Simon Marson, musician, examined.

Saith, he served Sir T. Monson six years, and is preferred by him to the King's service, but waiteth sometimes upon Sir T. Monson; he saith, that he received divers tarts and jellies from the Countess of Essex, to be carried to the Lieutenant of the Tower for Sir T. Overbury.

Paul de la Bell [Lobell], examined.

Saith, that on the 3rd of July, he made Sir T. Overbury a bath by Dr. Micham's advice, to cool his body, and that he saw his body very exceeding fair and clear; and again, he saw his body, being dead, full of blisters, and so consumed away as he never saw the like body.

George Rawlins, a kinsman to Sir T. Overbury, examined.

Saith, that upon the bruit [rumor] of the murder of Sir T. he was taxed by some, why he made no prosecution; he thereupon made a petition, and delivered it to the King, that the examination of the cause might be referred to law, and denieth that he was persuaded by any to the contrary: he saith, that he coming often to the Tower to see Sir T. could not be suffered to see him so much as out at the windows; and Weston told him, it was the commandment of the Council and of the Lieutenant.

The Lieutenant of the Tower examined, coram Coke and Crew.

He saith, that after the death of Sir T., Weston came to him and told him he was much neglected and slighted by the Countess, and could receive no reward; but afterwards he confessed he had received £100, and should receive more; and the Lieutenant also saith, that Sir T. Overbury was very angry with his apothecary at certain vomits which he had, and also at the tarts and jellies he had, which would be found within a day or two standing, ill-colored, and that nobody did eat thereof but Sir T.; and Weston confessed unto him, that the apothecary had £ 20 for administering the clyster.

These examinations being read, and applied to the purpose, the Lord Chief Justice said, he would discharge his duty, first to God, in giving all glory for the bringing to light of so horrible and wicked a fact; and next to the King, his great master, who as in cases of the like nature, as in the case of Sanquer and Turner, so especially in this, hath given straight charge of just and due examination to be had without any manner of partiality or fear in the world; to the intent, that as well the innocent might be freed, as the . . . guilty severally punished.

And for this purpose, his Majesty hath with his own hand written two sheets of paper on both sides, concerning justice to be administered to all parties which were to be examined; which writing the Lord Chief Justice showed to the Lord Mayor and the rest of the commissioners; and then he declared the King's justice, who, albeit the many favors and honors which his Majesty had bestowed on the Lord Somerset, and his nearness to his person, by reason of his office, yet he had committed him prisoner to the house of the Dean of Westminster, under the custody of Sir Oliver St. John, and also had committed his lady. So having last of all, again demanded of the prisoner, if he would put himself to be tried by the country, which he refused.

The court was adjourned until Monday following, at two of the clock in the afternoon.

During the four-day recess everyone got busy. When James first heard of the adjournment, he wanted Weston to be confronted in the interval with Frances, with Mrs. Turner and, if needful, with the earl himself. If Weston were not to be convicted but were to die through the application of *peine forte et dure,* James wanted to obtain whatever information concerning the guilt of the Somersets might arise from a confrontation. Such a confrontation might have cleared up several doubts, but Coke told the king that a reexamination or confrontation, after a public conviction of the party delinquent, would not be legal. The fact that Weston had not been convicted seems to have escaped both Coke and James. As a result, Carr was not examined until after Weston had been executed.[12]

James now told the commissioners that if Weston stayed obstinate, judgment should be prosecuted against him and he should be executed, but not until both Weston and the Somersets had been examined to see whether it was they who had persuaded him to stand mute. On October 22 Coke wrote Winwood that he would proceed against Weston the next day, "as his standing mute was equal to a confession; and to go to court and do nothing would be so ridiculous that he could not do it without express command from the King."[13] In reply, Winwood told Coke that the king would think it Coke's masterpiece if he could discover who persuaded Weston to stand mute. Seeing that he was beaten, Weston decided to stand trial, making the remark, however, "But I hope they will not make a net to catch the little fishes and let the great go."[14]

> On Monday the 23rd of October, 1615, to which day the court was adjourned by the said commissioners, after proclamation made, the jury of life and death called, the prisoner Weston was set to the Bar, and Mr. Fenshaw, Clerk of the Crown, declared unto him that he had been formerly arraigned and had pleaded Not Guilty; so he demanded of him, how he would be tried, whereupon the prisoner answered, "By God and my country." And thereupon, the jury being sworn and the indictment being read as before, Sir Lawrence Hyde, the Queen's Attorney, being of counsel with the King, having briefly rehearsed the effect of the indictment, showed how that he must necessarily mention others that were guilty of the same fact, wherein if any other man or woman were touched, the cause it was, and not he that touched them.
>
> And therefore Weston being but a stranger to Sir T. Overbury, and one who by himself could reap no benefit by his death, it was against all reason that he would do it of himself, therefore, said he, "I must needs open the whole plot"; ... [The rest of Hyde's speech is omitted; it was largely the same as the one he had given on the nineteenth.]
>
> And to all this opened and set forth by Mr. Attorney, Mr. Warr only added this much, which he desired the jury to consider: That Weston was servant to Mrs. Turner when Sir T. was committed, and then he was entertained and made keeper to Sir T. Overbury; and having dispatched his business (Sir T. being dead and poisoned), he stayed no longer at the Tower, but returns again to Mrs. Turner.
>
> Then the Lord Chief Justice exhorted the jury to take God before their eyes, and with equal balance to weigh as well the answer of the prisoner, as the proofs and examinations against him; declaring unto them how quietly and freely he had exam-

ined him from time to time, without menacing or rough usage, which the prisoner confessed; and my Lord, for matter of law, satisfied the jury that albeit the poisoning in the indictment be said to be with rosalgar, white arsenic and mercury sublimate, yet the jury were not to expect precise proof in that point, showing how impossible it were to convict a poisoner, who useth not to take any witnesses to the composing of his sibber sauces; wherefore he declared the law in the like case, as if a man be indicted for murdering a man with a dagger and it fall out upon evidence to have been done with a sword or with a rapier, or with neither, but with a staff; in this case the instrument matters not, so that the jury find the murderer. And so in this prisoner's case, if they be satisfied of the poisoning, it matters not with what; therefore he requireth them to attend the proof.

Coke now realized that it might be difficult to prove Overbury's poisoning by any of the poisons specifically mentioned in the indictment or to prove that Weston actually put the poisons in Overbury's food. He needed support for the position that proof of Overbury's death by any poison administered by Weston would be sufficient to support the indictment. The justices of the King's Bench obligingly expressed that opinion. Coke explained in his "Institutes": "For the substance of the indictment was, whether he was poisoned or no, by the said Richard Weston. And upon this indictment he was arraigned, pleaded not guilty, and had judgment given against him. . . . and it fell out in evidence, that Franklin had prepared divers other poisons than were contained in the indictment, as the powder of diamonds, the powder of spiders, lapis causticus, and cantharides, over and besides the poisons in the indictment. And it was resolved, that any of these was sufficient to prove [support] the indictment; for the substance of the indictment was poisoning. . . . "[15]

Then were read first the Examinations of Laurence Davies, as at the first arraignment; then of Henry Payton, both servants to Sir T. Overbury; then of Weston himself formerly read.

The Examination of Sir David Wood, taken the 21st of October, 1615, since the first arraignment.

He saith, he had obtained the King's consent to a suit for which he was a petitioner and that he was crossed by the Lord Rochester and Sir T. Overbury, that for certain words he had received from Sir T. Overbury, he intended to bastinado him; that his suit would have been worth £2,200, and that Rochester would not let it pass unless he might have £1,200.

That the Lady Essex sent for this examinee upon the day that the King and Queen went to Rochester with the Lady Elizabeth, and told him, she understood that he had received much wrong from Sir T. Overbury, and that he was a gentleman that could revenge himself, and that Sir T. had much wronged her; and Sir David answered that Sir T. had refused him the field; she persuaded him to kill him, and promised him £1,000 for his reward, and protection from his enemies; which he refused, saying he would be loath to hazard going to Tyburn upon a woman's word; but she still persuaded him he might easily do it, as he returned late home from Sir Charles Wilmot's in his coach.

Then were read the Examinations of Sir T. Monson and Mrs. Turner, as at the first arraignment.

Next, the Examination of Weston before the Lord Zouch and Sir Ralph Winwood, Sir T. Parry, and Sir Foulke Greville, at the Duchy House, the twenty-ninth of September, 1615, where Weston did confess that he was preferred [recommended] to the keeping of Sir T. Overbury by Mrs. Turner, upon the means and request of Sir T. Monson to the Lieutenant; and that she told him, if he would give Sir T. Overbury a water which the Countess would send him, he should be well rewarded; and being confronted with a relation in writing which Sir J. [Gervaise] Elwes had made to the King, as touching Sir T. Overbury, he confessed the same to be all true.

The Examination of the Lieutenant, taken the 5th of October, 1615.

He saith, that having conferred with his servants about the time of Weston's coming to the Tower, he found it to be the very next day after himself was made Lieutenant and had the possession of the Tower; and that he had letters from Sir Thomas Monson, that Weston might be keeper to Sir T. Overbury, which letters he had lost. Sir Thomas Monson told him the chief purpose of Weston's keeping of Sir T. Overbury, was to suffer no letters or other messengers to pass to or from him, and to that purpose he advised the Lieutenant.

Weston's Examination the 5th of October, 1615.

He confesseth, that the next day [after] he was preferred to the Tower, he had the keeping of Sir T. Overbury, and soon after he received the glass by his son secretly from the Countess; and that the Lieutenant told him, all the tarts came likewise from her; and he confesseth, the Countess willed him to give them to Sir T. but not to taste of them himself.

Weston's Examination the 1st of October, 1615.

Confesseth, that Mrs. Turner appointed him to come to White-hall to the Countess, the next day that he was at the Tower; and that he went, and the Countess did request him to give to Sir T. Overbury a water, which she would deliver him, but not to drink of it himself; she promised to give him a good reward, and he suspected it was poison; he received the glass by his son, and told the Lieutenant of it, who did rebuke him, and he set the glass into a little study. He confesseth, he told Mrs. Turner he had given it him, and demanded his reward; that Mr. James and Mr. Rawlins, my Lord of Somerset's men, came often to know of him what tarts, jellies, or wine Sir T. would have, and that they brought divers times tarts and jellies, whereof he did eat.

He confesseth to have received of the Countess in rewards, after Sir T. Overbury's death, by Mrs. Turner secretly, in all £ 180.

The Confession of the Lieutenant to His Majesty.

[Omitted, since substantially identical with that read on the nineteenth.]

Here the Lord Chief Justice observed by this question of Weston to the Lieutenant, "Shall I give it him now?" that it was certainly agreed and plotted before what should be done, and that nothing more was doubted on but the time when it should be done.

The Testimony of Laurence Davies, taken upon Oath before Coke and Crew.

He affirmeth, that . . . bringing a letter from Rochester to Sir T. Overbury, he delivered it to Weston, and a paper of white powder fell out which Rochester persuaded Sir T. to eat, and not to fear though it made him sick, for that should be a means for his enlargement [gain of his freedom]; so they put the powder into the letter again. He saith, that he saw some part of the powder in Weston's hands after the death of Sir T. Overbury.

Then were read the Examinations of William Weston and Paul de la Bell [Lobell], as at the first arraignment.

The Examination of George Rawlins.

[Omitted, since substantially identical with that read on the nineteenth.]

And here the Lord Chief Justice declared what a scandal they put upon his Majesty and the State, that a gentleman and a freeman, being only committed upon contempt, should be more straightly and closely kept than a traitor or a bondslave, so that neither his father, brother, nor friend might possibly see him.

And to that point, Mr. Overbury, father to Sir T., swore, being present in court; who said, that his son being prisoner in the Tower, and himself not being suffered to have access unto him, found at last that Rochester was the man that withstood it.

The Lieutenant examined on the 5th of October.

Saith, that after the death of Sir T. Overbury, Weston told him that he was neglected by the Countess, and demanded his reward; Mrs. Turner told him the Countess had not money; but afterwards he confessed he had received some and should have more; and that Mr. James told him, my Lord of Somerset would reward him for the pains he took with Sir T. Overbury. He saith, that the tarts were sent from the Countess to Sir T. which looked ill-favored, and that the jellies with a little standing would be furred, and thinketh they were poisoned; also Weston told him, that the apothecary had £ 20 for giving the clyster, and that he was poisoned with that clyster.

Here was well observed by the court, as by the Queen's Attorney, that Weston was not single in his confession, but whensoever he had confessed anything in any of his examinations, it was likewise confirmed by the examinations of others, as the Lieutenant, his son, etc.

The Examination of William Goare, one of the Sheriffs of London.

Saith, Weston being in his custody, he often persuaded him to put himself to be tried by his country, telling him he would first kill himself and ask God forgiveness afterwards; and Weston answered, he hoped he would not make a net to catch little birds, and let the great ones go.

Then Mr. Warr craving leave of the court to speak, protested, in his experience he never found a business [the murder] so prosecuted with degrees of malice [effected so maliciously], which was the ground of Sir T. Overbury's overthrow; he urged the evidence in the examination of Sir David Wood, and showed the reasons for the malice against him to be that he was so great an impediment to affections. Then he made the dependency Mrs. Turner had to the lady, and Weston to Mrs. Turner, and how they all concluded to kill Sir T. Overbury, the like whereof he said our fathers never saw before us; and he lamented the place from whence the poison came should be from the Court, the place (said he) from whence all men expect their safeties and protection.

Lastly, he observed the finger of God even in this, that the poison had been scarcely suspected at all, or inquired after, had it not been for the extraordinary strange things appearing after his death, which was the first only cause of suspicion and muttering.

The evidence being given, Weston was demanded what he could say for himself. Who, although he had before confessed all his examinations to be true, yet he seemed to excuse himself in a kind of ignorance or unawares; he said, he received the said glass and thought it was not good, but desired the giving of it to Sir Thomas; being demanded why he had formerly accused one Franklin for delivering him the said glass from the Countess (from whom indeed it was sent), he confessed it was to save his child, and finally could say nothing that had any color of material or substantial point to excuse or argue innocency in him. So the court referred him to the jury, who went together and within a short space returned, being agreed upon their verdict, and there at the Bar gave in, that Weston was guilty of the felonious murdering and poisoning of Sir T. Overbury. And then the Clerk of the Crown demanded of Weston what he could say for himself, why judgment should not be pronounced against him according to law. To which he answered, he referred himself to my Lord, and to the country. And then the Lord Chief Justice, before he pronounced sentence of death, spoke to this effect, that for the duty of the place, he must say somewhat, and that to two several persons: First, to the auditory, and secondly, to the prisoner.

And that which he spoke to the auditory he divided into four parts: First, the manifestation of the glory of God, and honor of the King; Second, the preventing of other damned crimes of poisoning; Third, an answer to certain objections; Fourth, that there is no practice of conspiracy in prosecuting . . . the business. . . .

Coke's discussion (here omitted) of his four points was typically bombastic, with much said about the finger of God at work, the providence of God, the contrite repentance of Weston, the horrid nature of poisoning, the necessity for making an example of those here guilty, the unjust criticism of his having the evidence read on the nineteenth and the baseness of those slandering the course of justice. He ended by exhorting Weston to make a complete, contrite confession and reminding him of the good he could do to bring to light the guiltiness of the "great ones." He then somehow identified this poisoning as a Popish trick and gave examples of similar tricks in the past.

He then proceeded to give judgment, which was,

That the prisoner should be carried from thence to the place from whence he came, and from thence to Tyburn, and there to be hanged by the neck till he was dead.

Judgment being given, the Lord Chief Justice commanded that the prisoner might have convenient respite and the company of some godly learned men to instruct him for his soul's health.

He was afterwards executed at Tyburn, pursuant to the sentence. At the time of his execution, Sir John Hollis (afterwards Earl of Clare) and Sir John Wentworth, out of friendship to the Earl of Somerset, rode to Tyburn and urged Weston to deny all that he had before confessed, but Weston being prepared for death, resisted their temptations, sealing penitently the truth of his confessions with his last gasp; and Sir John Hollis, Sir John Wentworth, together with Mr. Lumsden, who had published a relation of the proceedings against Weston at his arraignment, were afterwards prosecuted in the Star Chamber for traducing the King's justice in those proceedings.

The Hollis-Wentworth incident, in which Overbury's brother-in-law Lidcote was also involved, was curious. There is no evidence that the government was right in stating in its official version that the men urged Weston at the execution to deny all that he had before confessed. What they had really asked him was whether he had actually poisoned Overbury. In addition, Hollis had said at the time the jury gave its verdict that if he had been on the jury, he would have been in doubt what to do. For this the two men were tried in the Star Chamber "for traducing public justice" in casting a doubt on Weston's guilt, and Coke sentenced each to a heavy fine and a year in the Tower, quoting Ovid to prove the bad taste the men had shown in going to a public execution! Camden thought that the men were in fact activated by the hope that Weston, being beyond the reach of restraint, might deny his guilt and thus aid Somerset. Weston's actual answer to their question seems to have been that he had "left his mind behind with the Lord Chief Justice," a reply which might well be construed to discredit Coke and which may have been responsible for the severity of the punishment meted out to the two men.[16]

The Trial of ANNE TURNER, Widow, at the King's Bench, the 7th of November, for the Murder of Sir Thomas Overbury, Mich. 13 James I. A.D. 1615.

The indictment whereupon Richard Weston took his trial being repeated verbatim, she was indicted for comforting, aiding and assisting the said Weston, in the poisoning to death Sir T. Overbury; to which she pleaded Not Guilty, putting herself upon God and the country. Whereupon a sufficient jury of two knights, and the rest esquires and freeholders of Middlesex, were sworn and impanelled for the trial, whereof Sir T. Fowler was foreman.

Sir Ed. Coke, Lord Chief Justice, told her that women must be covered in the church, but not when they are arraigned, and so caused her to put off her hat; which done, she covered her hair with her handkerchief, being before dressed in her hair, and her hat over it.

Sir Laurence Hyde, the Queen's Attorney, opened the matter much to the effect as he did at Weston's arraignment, showing the wickedness and heinousness of poisoning; he showed further that there was one Dr. Forman, dwelling in Lambeth, who died very suddenly, and a little before his death, desired that he might be buried very deep in the ground, or else (saith he) I shall fear you all. To him, in his lifetime, often resorted the Countess of Essex and Mrs. Turner, calling him father: Their cause of com-·ing to him was, that by force of magic, he should procure the now Earl of Somerset, then Viscount Rochester, to love her, and Sir Arthur Mainwaring to love Mrs. Turner, by whom, as it was there related, she had three children. About this business, the Countess of Essex wrote two letters, one to Mrs. Turner, another to Dr. Forman, as followeth:

The Countess's Letter to Mrs. Turner.
(Burn this Letter.)

"Sweet Turner: I am out of all hope of any good in this world, for my father, my mother, and my brother said, I should lie with him [her husband Essex]: and my brother Howard was here, and said, he would not come from this place all winter; so that all comfort is gone; and which is worst of all, my Lord [Essex] hath complained that he hath not lain with me, and [that] I would not suffer him to use me. My father and mother are angry, but I had rather die a thousand times over; for besides the sufferings, I shall lose his [Rochester's] love if I lie with him [Essex]. I will never desire to see his [Rochester's] face, if my Lord do that unto me. My Lord is very well as ever he was, so . . . you may see in what a miserable case I am. You may send the party [Rochester] word of all; he sent me word all should be well, but I shall not be so happy as the Lord [Rochester] to love me. As you have taken pains all this while for me, so now do all you can, for never so unhappy as now; for I am not able to endure the miseries that are coming on me, but I cannot be happy so long as this man [Essex] liveth: Therefore pray for me, for I have need, but I should be better if I had your company to ease my mind. Let him know this ill news; if I can get this done, you shall have as much money as you can demand; this is fair play. – Your sister, FRANCES ESSEX."

A Letter from the Countess to Dr. Forman.

"Sweet Father: I must still crave your love, although I hope I have it, and shall deserve it better hereafter: Remember the galls, for I fear though I have yet no cause but to be confident in you, yet I desire to have it as it is yet remaining well; so continue it still, if it be possible, and if you can you must send me some good fortune; alas! I have need of it. Keep the Lord [Rochester] still to me, for that I desire; and be careful you name me not to anybody, for we have so many spies that you must use all your wits, and all little enough, for the world is against me, and the heavens favor me not, only happy in your love; I hope you will do me good, and if I be ungrateful, let all mischief come unto me. My Lord is lusty and merry, and drinketh with his men; and all the content he gives me, is to abuse me, and use me as doggedly as before: I think I shall never be happy in this world, because he hinders my good, and will ever, I think so; remember, I beg for God's sake, and get me from this vile place. - Your affectionate, loving daughter, FRANCES ESSEX. - Give Turner warning of all things, but not the Lord [Rochester]: I would not have anything come out for fear of the Lord Treasurer, for so they may tell my father and mother, and fill their ears full of toys [an obsolete use of the word toy is "amorous dallying"]."

There were also showed in court certain pictures of a man and woman in copulation, made in lead, as also the mold of brass, wherein they were cast, a black scarf ... full of white crosses, which Mrs. Turner had in her custody. At the showing of these and enchanted papers and other pictures in court, there was heard a crack from the scaffolds, which caused great fear, tumult and confusion among the spectators and throughout the hall, everyone fearing hurt, as if the devil had been present and grown angry to have his workmanship showed by such as were not his own scholars; and this terror continuing about a quarter of an hour, after silence proclaimed, the rest of the cunning tricks were likewise showed.

Dr. Forman's wife being administratrix of her husband, found letters in packets, by which much was discovered; she was in court, and deposed that Mrs. Turner came to her house immediately after her husband's death, and did demand certain pictures which were in her husband's study; namely, one picture in wax, very sumptuously apparelled in silks and satins, as also one other sitting in form of a naked woman, spreading and laying forth her hair in a looking-glass, which Mrs. Turner did confidently affirm to be in a box, and that she knew in what part or room of the study they were. Mrs. Forman further deposeth, that Mrs. Turner and her husband would be sometimes three or four hours locked up in his study together. She did depose further, that her husband had a ring would open like a watch.

There was also a note showed in the court, made by Dr. Forman, and written in parchment, signifying what ladies loved what lords in the Court; but the Lord Chief Justice would not suffer it to be read openly in the court. [D.N.B. says the paper listed Forman's female clients and gave accounts of their intrigues. One potent reason for Coke's unusual discretion: He saw the paper for the first time when it was presented in court; in looking at it he saw that the first name on the list was that of his wife.][17]

Mr[s]. Turner sent Margaret, her maid, to Mrs. Forman, and wished that all such letters and papers as concerned the Earl of Somerset, or the Countess of Essex, or any other great personages, should be burned; telling her, that the Council's warrant should come to search the study, and that all his goods might be seized: Whereupon she and her maid Margaret, with the consent of Mrs. Forman, burned divers letters and papers; but yet she kept some without their privity. There were also enchantments showed in court, written in parchment, wherein were contained all the names of the blessed Trinity mentioned in the Scriptures; and in another parchment, "+B.+C.+D.+E." and in a third, likewise in parchment, were written all the names of the Holy Trinity, as also a figure, in which was written this word "Corpus"; and upon the parchment was fastened a little piece of the skin of a man. In some of these parchments were the devil's particular names, who were conjured to torment the Lord Somerset and Sir Arthur Mainwaring, if their loves should not continue, the one to the Countess, the other to Mrs. Turner.

Mrs. Turner also confessed, that Dr. Savories was used in succession after Forman, and practiced many sorceries upon the

Earl of Essex's person. Mrs. Turner being in a manner kept close prisoner in one of the sheriff's houses in London, before she was brought to the Bar, knew not that Weston was executed; but by the proceedings, having understanding thereof, and hearing divers examinations read, it so much dejected her that in a manner she spoke nothing for herself. Also examinations and witnesses, *viva voce,* that were produced at Weston's arraignment, and divers others, were now read again, as the examinations of one Edward Payne, John Wright, and Robert Freeman.

Symcots, Rawlins, Payte, and Williams, at one of these examinations, gave evidence that one Franklin, being an apothecary and druggist, was the provider of all the poisons given to Sir Thomas Overbury. A chirurgeon [doctor] there deposed that he cured Franklin of the pox, and that at several times he demanded of this chirurgeon, what was the strongest poison? The chirurgeon demanding of him what he would do with it, Franklin replies,"Nothing but for his experience, and to try conclusions." Another examination of one Mercer, who had conference with the said Franklin, calling him cousin, who demanded of this examinee, "What news?" he answered, "I hear ill news, I am sorry that my old lord and master's son is found insufficient, and not able to content the lady." Franklin replies, "I have a hand in that business; I have a great friend of my Lady of Essex, she allows me 2s. 6d. a day for my boat hire, and 10s. a week for my diet; I could have any money I would." Mercer replies, "But, cousin, how can God bless you in this business?" Franklin answers, "Let them talk of God that have to do with him, my Lord of Somerset and the Countess will bear me out in any thing I do; if you have any suit, wherein you may do yourself any good, and I may gain by it, I will warrant you I will get it." . . .

The Lord Chief Justice made a speech upon divers examinations there read: That the Earl of Somerset gave directions, that of the powder he sent to Overbury, that which should be left should be brought back again; his pretext was that it should make him sick, which should be the ground to make the King grant his liberty, saying further, it would do Overbury good; and he had tarts and jellies likewise sent him by the Countess, with express commandment that none must eat of them but Sir Thomas, saying, "They will do him no harm." At another time, the Countess sent tarts, jellies and wine, with directions that those which had been formerly sent should be brought back again, and those last brought, should be given him at supper, and then all should be well; but directions given that neither the Lieutenant nor his wife might eat of them, but they might drink of the wine, for in the tarts and jellies there might be *letters*, but in the wine there might be none. And afterwards it was openly related, and proved by divers witnesses, that that word "letters" was a private token between the Countess and Lieutenant and Weston, to give notice what things were poisoned, and what not. In the examinations that were of Weston, it was related that Mr. James told him that the Earl, his master, would pay him for his pains about Sir T. Overbury.

Then the Lord Chief Justice gave in charge to the jury, concerning the evidence they had formerly heard, and told them that Weston at his examination had confessed that all he had said formerly was true. He further related what a great vexation and grief it was to the King that Somerset only by making use of his favor and love, so foul a fact was done as First, to be the occasion to put Sir T. Overbury to employment for the embassage at Russia; Second, to make him refuse the same and to give right cause for his commitment; Third, to bear him in hand that he would work his liberty, but still aggravated and labored the contrary, and gave directions to the Lieutenant of the Tower, to look surely to him and to keep him close prisoner, and that he should send to none of his friends, or they to him, urging great matters against him. Sir Thomas Monson was often employed to give directions to the Lieutenant therein, which was a most barbarous course to be so dealt withal, only for a contempt; concluding, that Overbury was a close prisoner to all his friends, but open to all his enemies, such as Somerset would have or send unto him.

Mrs. Turner is seen to have been convicted in large part on the basis of the confession of a man who had already been executed and was not available for questioning by her as part of her defense. Even in that day, this was a decided breach of accepted procedure. It might also be said that most of the charges referred to by Coke were not really pertinent to her guilt and were obviously made for use in the forthcoming trial of the Somersets. However, there can be no doubt as to Mrs. Turner's actual guilt, if Overbury's death was due to poison.

Then the Lord Chief Justice told Mrs. Turner that she had seven deadly sins, viz. a whore, a bawd, a sorcerer, a witch, a papist, a felon, and a murderer, the daughter of the devil Forman; wishing her to repent and to become a servant of Jesus

Christ, and to pray to him to cast out of her those seven devils. [And this was the man on whom she was expected to rely to see that she had a fair and impartial trial, and whose presence was supposed to eliminate the necessity for her having counsel to represent her!]

She desired the Lord Chief Justice to be good unto her, saying, she was ever brought up with the Countess of Somerset, and had been of a long time her servant, and knew not that there was poison in any of those things sent to Sir T. Overbury.

Then the jury went forth, and not long after returned, finding her Guilty. . . . being asked, what she had to say for herself why judgment should not be pronounced against her, she only desired favor, but could not speak anything for weeping.

Then Judge Crook [another judge of the King's Bench] made another grave speech exhorting her to repentance, and to prepare herself ready for death, and that the little time which should be assigned her to live, she should not spend it either in hope or in imagination to get life, for that hope was but a witch. Upon conclusion of which speech, he gave judgment, and told her she had had a very honorable trial, by such men as he had not seen for one of her rank and quality; and so [she] was delivered to the sheriffs.

Upon the Wednesday following, she was brought from the sheriff's in a coach to Newgate, and was there put into a cart; and casting money often among the people as she went she was carried to Tyburn, where she was executed, and whither many men and women of fashion came in coaches to see her die, to whom she made a speech, desiring them not to rejoice at her fall, but to take example by her, she exhorting them to serve God, and abandon pride and all other sins; relating her breeding with the Countess of Somerset, having had no other means to maintain her and her children, but what came from the Countess; and said further, that when her hand was once in this business, she knew the revealing of it would be her overthrow. The which, with other like speeches, and great penitency there showed, moved the spectators to great pity and grief for her.

There are in the State Paper Office several papers in Coke's handwriting having to do with the efforts made to obtain a post-conviction confession from Mrs. Turner which would substantiate the verdict and possibly aid in the trials of the others. On November 10 and November 11 Dr. Whiting, a cleric, visited her to administer communion. Mrs. Turner confessed her guilt, acknowledged herself to be a monstrous sinner, "after many exhortations and pressings of her" confessed she knew Overbury was being poisoned and kept it secret but denied it upon her examination, professed her great affection for Frances and "meaned" (complained of) Northampton. At their second meeting she said that Franklin was a villain and "desired much that she might not die that day he died, he is so foul." Asked if Monson did not have a hand in the poisoning, she replied, "if you will have me say so I will" — a rather illuminating remark. She lamented that the lieutenant might have "saved all this," adding, "if any were in it that I know, it was the Lord Privy Seal [Northampton]." Asked about Somerset, she said he spoke such broad Scottish that she could not understand him and asked if they did not have enough against the Somersets already. She did admit that she had seen the jellies in Frances's chamber to go to Overbury but neither knew who made them nor who carried them. As to Weston, she said he had told her that he was "set on work to poison Overbury."

Mrs. Turner's opinion of James's Court verified the criticisms appearing some chapters back: "O the Court, the Court! God bless the King and send him better servants about him, for there is no religion in the most of them, but malice, pride, whoredom, swearing, and rejoicing in the fall of others; it is so wicked a place, as I wonder the earth did not open and swallow it up. Mr. Sheriff, put none of your children thither." On reading all of Whiting's notes on the two confessions, one cannot help but feel sorry for Mrs. Turner. The original papers indicate Coke's anxiety to phrase Whiting's memorandum in such manner as best to justify the proceedings against her. There are many interlineations, in some instances written over erasures.

The third paper gives a more complete account of Mrs. Turner's execution than that in the State Trials. She told the people present that she had deserved death and had had a just trial, asked forgiveness from all the world and in turn forgave all the world. She asked their prayers, for she had been a grievous sinner and wished all people to take example by her. After praying God to bless the king and the Council, she asked if she could pray for Frances. Whiting assented. Coke says in his account that the sheriff said that when she named Frances, she likewise named the earl but that he (Coke) heard no such thing. At Mrs. Turner's request, the executioner bound her hands with a black silk ribbon and pulled over her face a black veil which she wore on her head, before the cart was driven away, "and she left hanging, in whom there was no motion at all perceived."[18]

Among her pursuits, Mrs. Turner was a dress designer and had become famous for her use of a yellow starch in ruffs and other lawn and lace fashionable in the clothing of the day. Camden says the custom had originally come from France and had been invented to make the sallow faces of the time look better.[19] So well-known was her yellow starch that Shakespeare in "All's Well that Ends Well" (Act IV, Scene 5) wrote: "Whose villainous saffron would have made all the unbaked and doughy youth of a nation in his color," and Ben Jonson in his "Devil's an Ass" said that even "car-men and chimney-sweepers are got into the yellow starch." (It was common to refer to the yellow starched items as saffroned linen.) The women at the execution were excited to see that Mrs. Turner was wearing her yellow starch.

She did not die unpitied. John Castle wrote to a friend: "Since I saw you, I saw Mrs. Turner die. If detestation of painted pride, lust, malice, powdered hair, yellow bands, and the rest of the wardrobe of Court vanities; if deep sighs, tears, confessions, ejaculations of the soul, admonitions of all sorts of people to make God and an unspotted conscience always our friends; if the protestation of faith and hope to be washed by the same Savior and by the like mercies that Mary Magdalene was, be signs and demonstrations of a blessed penitent, then I will tell you that this poor broken woman went *a cruce ad gloriam,* and now enjoys the presence of her and our Redeemer. Her body being taken down by her brother, one Norton, servant to the Prince, was in a coach conveyed to St. Martin's of the Fields, where in the evening of the same day she had an honest and a decent burial."[20]

TEN

The Trial of Sir JERVIS [Gervaise] ELWES, knt., Lieutenant of the Tower, at the Guildhall of London, the 16th of November, for the Murder of Sir Thomas Overbury: 13 JAMES I. A.D. 1615.

The form of the Indictment was the malicious aiding, comforting, and abetting of Weston in the poisoning and murdering of Overbury, whereupon it was laid against him as follows:

First, when Weston received the vial of poison of two inches long, to give Sir T., he having the glass in one hand and broth for Sir T. in the other hand, meeting the Lieutenant, asked him thus, "Sir, shall I give it him now?" the Lieutenant reproved him; yet that night he gave it him in his broth: Ergo, the Lieutenant knew of the practice and poisoning of Sir T. Overbury, . . . After this was known to be poison, yet he kept Weston still; he favored, countenanced and graced him, and one time sent him a cup of sack, and bid his man tell him, that he loved him as well as ever he did; all this while he paid him no wages, and as soon as Overbury died, Weston was removed. The Countess wrote a letter to the Lieutenant; with the letter she sent poisoned tarts to Overbury, and wine to the Lieutenant's wife, and bade him give the tarts to Overbury, for there were letters in them, but his wife and children might drink the wine, for she was sure there were no letters in it. The Earl of Northampton wrote a letter to the Lieutenant concerning the imprisonment of Overbury; the said Earl wrote two [three] letters to Rochester containing these words:

The Earl of Northampton's letter to Rochester.

"Sweet lord: [Most of the letter was only an effusive declaration of Northampton's love for Carr; only the last sentence is pertinent.] . . . I spent two hours yesterday, prompting the Lieutenant with cautions and considerations; observing with whom he is to deal, that he might the better act his part, for the adventure in which he dealeth. H. NORTHAMPTON."

Another Letter to Rochester.

"Sweet lord: I cannot deliver unto you with what caution and consideration, etc. . . . [is] the Lieutenant looking to his business, which concerns no more than text affords, that marched in his affairs; I shall hold him discreet, and love him better whilst I live, for this his conclusion, for this negro can no more change his skin than a leopard his spots. HENRY NORTHAMPTON."

Another Letter to Rochester.

"Sweet lord: [Northampton first told of the condition of Overbury's body and mentioned his speedy burial.] . . . God is gracious in cutting off ill instruments from off the factious crew: [Northampton several times used this phrase in referring to the anti-Howard faction]. If he had come forth, they would have made use of him. Thus, sweet Lord, wishing you all increase of happiness and honor, I end, Your Lordship's more than any man, HENRY NORTHAMPTON."

The Lieutenant wrote a letter to the Earl of Northampton, certifying him, that he undertook Sir T. Overbury according to his instructions; that as soon as he came to the place, Sir T. protested his innocency upon the Bible; and then (quoth he) he asked me what they meant to do with him. I answered, "They mean to refine you, that your pureness may appear a little better." After[wards] I walked with him in his chamber, and advised him to give way to the match between Rochester and the Countess . . . he grew hot against your Lordship and the Countess of Suffolk [Frances's mother], saying, If he were the Countess of Suffolk's prisoner (as he thought he was), "then . . . let her know that I care as little to die as she to be cruel." The Countess of Suffolk I find to be joined with you in this plot, though the Chamberlain knows not of it, nor any one else. But Rochester's part I shall much fear, until I see the event to be clearly conveyed. And so he concluded his letter.

JERVIS ELWES."

The Answer of Sir Jervis Elwes to the Points Proposed.

"My lord: Before I answer to the matter of charge against me, let me remember your Lordship of one speech which I learned from your mouth: I have heard you speak it at the Council Table, and you have delivered it at the assizes in the country: That when a prisoner stands at the bar for his life, comfortless,

A 17th-century English trial in Westminster Hall attended by both Houses of Parliament. *From a contemporary print.*

Coronation portrait of Queen Elizabeth I. *Portrait by Guillim Stretes.*

Robert Carr, Earl of Somerset, and Lady Frances Howard. *From a contemporary print.*

Robert Devereux, Earl of Essex. *Artist unknown.*

Robert Carr, Earl of Somerset. *Portrait attributed to John Hoskins.*

Lady Frances Howard, Countess of Somerset. *Artist unknown.*

Sir Edward Coke. *From a contemporary print.*

Sir Thomas Overbury. *Artist unknown.*

The death of Queen Elizabeth I. *Painting by Delaroche.*

Queen Elizabeth I while still a princess. *Artist unknown.*

Francis Bacon. *Engraving by William Marshall.*

Robert Cecil, Earl of Salisbury. *From an engraving by Elstrake.*

William Cecil, Lord Burghley. *From an engraving by W. H. Mote after a painting by Mark Gerard.*

King James I. *Portrait by Daniel Mytens.*

allowed no counsel, but strong counsel against him, perchance affrighted with the fear of death, his wife and children to be cast forth out of doors, and made to seek their bread, you have always pitied the cause of such a one; you have protested you had rather hang in hell for mercy to such a one, than for judgment. My Lord, you have not observed your own rule in my case; you have paraphrased upon every examination, you have aggravated every evidence, and applied it to me, so that I stand clearly condemned before I be found guilty: If I be so vile a man as your Lordship conceives me, I were unworthy of any favor; but I hope your Lordship shall not find it. So I will deny nothing that hath evidence of truth against me, I will not tell a lie to save my life, and I beseech your Lordship so to conceive of me, move your charity towards me."

Then desired he the court, that the heads of the accusations might be collected by the counsel for the King, which were the same which were mentioned before; to which he severally answered:

To the first, "Shall I give it him now?" he answered, that when Weston asked him the question, he saw no poison in his hand, "and therefore," said he, "in Weston's and my examination, the question was, 'Shall I give it him now?' not, 'Shall I give him this now?' for there is a great difference between *hoc* and *id* in matter of prevention. But further, when Weston had told me that it was poison which he meant to give, I reproved and beat him down with God's judgment; nay, I humbled him so, that upon his knees he thanked God and me, and told me, that he and his had cause to bless God for me, for that I withheld him from doing that act; and if you call this comforting and abetting, to terrify a man for his sins, and to make him so confess his faults to God, and to abhor and detest the act, then was I an abettor and comforter of Weston.

To the second, after I had thus terrified Weston with God's judgments, and saw him cast down for his offense; I could do him no better office than of charity, to raise him up, who was thus down, and therefore favored him; I showed him kindness, I drank to him, to the intent I might encourage the intentions of his mind, which I found then resolved in abhorring the fact; and that I gave him no wages, it is true; I took him from the commendations of my Lord of Northampton and Sir Thomas Monson, whom I took to be my friends, and thought they would commend no man to be a keeper, which might any way endanger me.

To the third, I never knew any other meaning to the Countess's words in her letters, but the bare literal meaning; and sure ... after I had received the tarts, and they had stood awhile in my kitchen, I saw them so black and foul, and of such strange colors, that I did cause my cook to throw them away, and to make other tarts and jellies for him.

To the fourth, ... the Earl of Northampton's letter to me, was not anything touching the poisoning of Overbury, but for a close restraint; to the end, that Overbury might agree to their purposes concerning the marriage to be had between Rochester and the Countess; if the Earl of Northampton had any other plot to take away his life, I was not anything of his counsel, or had knowledge therein.

To the fifth, whereas it is said, I received him according to my instructions, I meant none other thing than I have delivered before, which was concerning the closeness of his imprisonment.

But being asked what he meant by these words, "Rochester's part I shall greatly fear, until I see the event to be clearly carried," in this, he staggered and wavered much, and gave his answer: "It was long since I wrote this letter, and for the particular circumstances that induced me to this speech, I cannot now call to memory; but sure I am, that at that time, knowing myself to be innocent, I could the better have satisfied my remembrance, so that I meant nothing the taking away of his life; but because I was a stranger to Rochester, and had heard and known of that great league that was between them, I might well think, suspect, and fear, whether he would always countenance these projects for his restraint."

The lieutenant's confusion was quite understandable. It is probable that the words Coke quoted had not been in the letter Elwes wrote. Northampton's letters were read in full, but Elwes's letter was merely summarized in words Coke chose to use. In "Truth Brought to Light by Time," the letter is set out in full; there the sentence in question is said to have read, "At my next coming to him (Overbury), I found him, not in sense, but in fury, he let fly at you, but was respectful to my lord of Rochester, whose part he took altogether."[1] The language Elwes had thus actually used (and which naturally he could no longer recall two years later) did not at all lend itself to the interpretation Coke put on the language he said Elwes had used. It's dismal to think that a man's life could have been made to depend on outwitting this kind of trickery.

These were the answers he made to his accusations, and after he had made many protestations between God and his soul, of his innocency of this malicious plotting and abetting of Over-bury's death, he applied himself to the jury, and told them thus:

"I will prove unto you by many infallible and unanswerable reasons, that I could not be aider and complotter with Weston in this poisoning. First, I made a free and voluntary discovery of it myself, I was not compelled: will any man imagine that I would discover a thing, whereof I could not clear myself? Nature is more kind than to be its own accuser. Besides, that my clearness might more appear, and remain in the world without any suspicion, I proceeded and accused the murderer Weston: it had been a senseless thing, and absurd in me, if I had not thought myself clear, to have accused him, who might have done as much for me. Nay, Weston himself proved me to be an honest man before the Chancellor of the Exchequer; for he confessed to him and others being present, that he thought that the Lieutenant knew not of the poison; and in his examination before the Lord Chief Justice and Serjeant Crew, being asked the meaning of these words, 'Shall I give it him now?' he answers, that he thought that those which had set him on work, had acquainted the Lieutenant with their plot. Also I was confident in my own innocency, that I told my Lord Chief Justice and my Lord Zouch, the way to make Weston confess and to discover all; which was by fair and gentle entreaty of him, and so by this means they might search the bottom of his heart: In this the Lord Chief Justice witnessed with him. And after Sir T. Overbury was dead, Weston and Mrs. Turner were sent to know of me whether I had any inkling of the death of Sir Thomas. What need they have made this question, if I had known anything thereof? Also that which I do know concerning the poisoning of Sir T. was after his death, by relation of Weston; and here I am, indicted as accessory before the fact, when I knew nothing till after the fact."

After that he had confirmed these reasons by sundry proofs and witnesses, he went further in his own defense: "If I be in the plot, the Lord Treasurer [Suffolk] is; I have his letter to show; in it, he called me to his lodging, and said, 'The plots you know them as well as I, the plots were only to repair her honor'; my wife hath the letters from my Lord Treasurer and Monson; for these plots I will run willingly to my death, if circumstances be knit with any matter of fact."

He proceeded further and told the Lord Chief Justice, that he spoke not this to justify himself, so that no blemish or stain might cleave unto him, "for," said he, "this visitation is sent me from God; and whether I live or die, it is the happiest affliction to my soul that I ever received; I have laid open my whole heart for blood-guiltiness; I have not repented me other than of errors of my judgment, in not detecting what I suspected, and yet I do ask God [for] forgiveness daily for lesser sins; but of this I know no other, but the gross error of my judgment in not preventing it, when I saw such intendment and imagination against him."

Then he put to my Lord Chief Justice this case: "If one that knoweth not of any plot to poison a man, but only suspecteth, is no actor or contriver himself, only imagineth such a thing, whether such a one be accessory to the murder; for the words of the indictment are, abetting and comforting with malice: Now if there be any man that charges me expressly or in direct terms, that I was an abettor, or if the court shall think in this case which I have put that such a concealing without malice is an abetting, I refuse not to die, I am guilty." This was the sum of his speech.

Then the Lord Chief Justice replied, that to his knowledge, he spoke no more concerning the evidence than he could in conscience justify, which was only to express the evidence of things, and not wresting anything in prejudice of his life. But further he told him . . . , "two days before Sir T. Overbury died, you wished his man to bring his best suit of hangings to hang his chamber, which you knew were your fees."

Another of Coke's unfair tactics was not making his accusation or not introducing the hitherto unknown confession of Franklin that he next brought forth, until Elwes had concluded his defense. Up to this point, Elwes's honest account of himself and of what he had done, the fact that he had voluntarily told Winwood the complete story and the fact, as Elwes pointed out, that since the government itself had sent Weston to him to sound him out as to what he knew, it could hardly have regarded him as one of the conspirators, had visibly impressed the jury. Coke's unfair cross-examination, this allegation about the hangings (tapestries and draperies) and the sudden production of Franklin's confession were designed to confuse Elwes regardless of his guilt and did have that effect. As a matter of fact, there was no necessary implication of guilt in Elwes's suggestion to Overbury that he have the hangings brought. Overbury was obviously an exceedingly sick man and apt to die any day. The suggestion may have been mercenary but was not evidence of guilty participation in the poisoning.

And . . . he told him that his accusation of the Lord Treasurer was very malicious; for in the examinations he had taken, and in all the exact speech he could work for the finding out of the truth, he saw not that honorable gentleman any way touched. In conclusion he told him, "It is not your deep protestations, nor your appealing to God, that can sway a jury from their evidence, which is not yet answered unto. But to leave you without excuse, and to make the matter as clear as may be, here is the confession of Franklin," (which he then drew out of his bosom) saying, "This poor man, not knowing Sir Jervis should come to his trial, this morning he came unto me at five o'clock, and told me that he was much troubled in his conscience, and could not rest all that night until he had made his confession; and it is such a one (these were his words) as the eye of England never saw, nor the ear of Christendom never heard."

The Confession of JAMES FRANKLIN,
the sixteenth of November, 1615.

Mrs. Turner came to me from the Countess and wished me from her to get the strongest poison I could for Sir T. Overbury. Accordingly, I bought seven, viz. aquafortes, white arsenic, mercury, powder of diamonds, lapis costitus, great spiders, and cantharides: All these were given to Sir T. Overbury at several times. And further confesseth, that the Lieutenant knew of these poisons, for that appeared . . . by many letters which he [the Lieutenant] wrote to the Countess of Essex, which I saw, and thereby knew that he knew of this matter: One of these letters I read for the Countess, because she could not read it herself, in which the Lieutenant used this speech, "Madam, the scab is like the fox, the more he is cursed, the better he fareth," and many other speeches. . . .

Only one sentence in Franklin's "confession" pertains to Elwes; the one set out above. Almost everything Franklin stated in his several examinations was what he thought Coke wanted to hear. His excuse here, that he had read the letter to Frances because she could not read it herself, is wide open to suspicion. Letters in her handwriting had been used in the Turner trial; she could read and write very well. John Castle suggested that she could not read the letter because of the poor handwriting, but Frances should have been more familiar with Elwes's handwriting than Franklin.

J. F. Stephen was one of the most astute students of English criminal law. He commented on Elwes's defense, saying, "He defended himself with so much energy and skill that he might perhaps have escaped had not Coke, the presiding judge, cross-examined him as to some expressions in his letters he was unable to explain, and (which is even more at variance with our modern views) produced against him, after his defense had been made, a 'confession' by one Franklin, who had made the confession privately and not even upon oath, before Coke himself, at five o'clock that morning before the court sat. Elwes had no chance to think or to cross-examine, and was so surprised that 'he knew not what to answer.' "[2]

Amos quotes a statement that when Elwes heard Franklin attribute to him the remark about the scab, he was amazed and, striking his hand on his breast, said to himself, "Lord have mercy on me," and that one of the jury standing next to him saw his behavior, heard the words he spoke and reported it to the rest of the jury. The implication is that the jury regarded his action as evidence of guilt, although it is hard to see why. After his conviction, Elwes was submitted to the usual clerical pressure to confess and at that time said that it had been agreed between Northampton, Frances, Monson and him to use the word "scab" as the by-word for Overbury in their correspondence.[3]

> Those were all the materials in Franklin's confession. To this Sir Jervis Elwes knew not what to answer, or to make of his own letters.
> Then presently the jury departed from the Bar, and shortly after returned, and found him guilty; and the Lord Chief Justice gave judgment of death against him.

John Castle was present at the trial and execution and described them in a long letter written to James Milles. He said that Elwes "entered into his answer with so great art to move affections, and laid his groundwork with so much show of soundness and confidence, binding himself by protestation to God that he would not in the course of his defense speak a lie to save his life, that all men that had brought thither indifferent ears, hath wished him innocent, and expected the conclusion should have been as they wished. But, . . . (when the line from Franklin's confession referring to the 'scab' was read) he was stricken as with a thunderbolt, having nothing to reply further, either in denial or interpretation."[4] Camden, apparently also present, wrote that Elwes was much pitied and thought that he was drawn in "by the allurements of Northampton to be a spectator rather than an actor in the bloody tragedy, but this connivance cost him his life."[5]

On Monday the twentieth of November, 1615, he was executed at Tower Hill, upon a gibbet there set of purpose, about six o'clock in the morning. He came on foot to the gibbet from Sheriff Goare's house, between Dr. Whiting and Dr. Felton, two of his Majesty's chaplains; and coming to the ladder's foot, he talked a word or two to the executioner. Then he went up the ladder four or five steps, the executioner sitting over his head, upon the top of the gibbet; Sir Jervis finding the ladder to stand too upright for his ease, spoke to have it amended, which forthwith, he coming down, was done, being fastened in the ground; and then he went up again six steps, where after a while, sitting easily, he said: . . .

There are available at least three versions of what Elwes said on the scaffold. Hargrave uses the official government version; John Castle wrote his impressions as a spectator; and the State Paper Office contains an account in Coke's handwriting. That account has Coke's usual erasures and interlineations. Dr. Whiting and another cleric had been sent to Elwes "for ghostly comfort" after his conviction, and "they pressing his conscience" obtained the usual "confession" of guilt on the plea of its necessity to open his way to heaven. Elwes repeated that confession on the scaffold. Coke has him say that "the State had dealt honorably, justly, and round with him, in punishing of him for that bloody murder, which he knew, gave way unto, and might so easily have prevented." This passage does not appear in Hargrave, and Castle has him say only that justness and roundness had been used toward him. Castle says further that Elwes said that if any of his friends had been ill-satisfied at the confidence and protestation he used on the day of his trial, they would be pleased to excuse him, as being encouraged thereunto out of a persuasion of his innocence. Needless to say, nothing in either the government or the Coke version contained this statement.

Elwes's speech was too long to reproduce in full here. He said that the clerics had made him see his fearful error in believing that the concealment of a sin was not in itself a sin. He accounted it a special favor to be permitted to die on Tower Hill rather than at

Tyburn, which was associated in the public mind with common criminals. He said very openly that he would not have fallen into his trouble if he had not trusted a man who was a most perfidious wretch (Northampton), that by various tricks he was drawn into the action, which he received from Northampton, Monson and none other, about which tricks and all other circumstances he had given a full and true confession to Coke, taken under "the seals of the precious body and blood of Christ," which would now be sealed with his own blood. He was very thankful for his death in this manner since it had given him time to prepare his soul for entry into heaven through the confession of his sins, which might not have been true had he met sudden death in some other manner. He said, "I protest before you all, I never came over this hill, in the chiefest of all my prosperity, with more joy than now I have at this present, for I now know that presently I shall behold the glorious face and sight of my Creator." Elwes thought that two judgments had been brought by God upon him. One had to do with his gambling, which he confessed had been long and costly. Concerning this fact he called for confirmation from a friend standing by with whom he had often gambled the night away; he had frequently tried to reform and had vowed seriously to God, "Lord, let me be hanged if ever I play any more." That his request had been taken literally was now obvious. God's other judgment against him was for his "excessive pride in the faculty of his pen," resulting in his now finding that his own handwriting proved a snare to take his life, for he thought, on his conscience, if it had not been for that letter mentioned in Franklin's confession, he would not now have lost his life. And he protested that he could not yet bring to mind why he wrote any such letter to the countess (he still didn't realize that perhaps he had not).[6]

His speech ended with a fervent wish for others to profit by his example, regret that he had not revealed the plot immediately upon his discovery of it so that lives would have been saved, sorrow for his wife and soon-to-be eight fatherless children and a vehement denial that he was an Anabaptist or his wife a Papist. This was a favorite accusation of Coke, intended to raise popular antagonism against the defendant. It is too bad that Elwes could not have known that when, after his death and the forfeiture of his estate, the king gave the estate to Lord Pembroke, Pembroke freely bestowed it on Elwes's widow and eight children.

His prayer being ended, he asked if he might pray privately; the doctor said, "Yes, sir." Then made he a short prayer to himself, with his face covered, and after he uncovered it, . . . [he] said, "Now I have prayed, now I must pay, I mean, do the last office to justice." With that Dr. Whiting said, "Sir Jervis, you may stand one step lower on the ladder." To whom the sheriff answered, "It is better for him, Mr. Doctor, to be where he is." "Stay," quoth the doctor to the executioner, "for he hath given a watchword, he is in private prayer again." "Yea," quoth he, "I know that, for he hath given me a watchword, when I shall perform my office to him." He uncovered his face after his second short prayer, and first took his leave of all the assembly, saying, with a cheerful voice and countenance, "I pray you pray for me, who shall never more behold your faces." Then he said with a great fervency of spirit, "Lord, I desire at thy hands this bitter cup of death, as the patient receiveth a bitter potion, not once demanding what is in the cup, but takes and drinks it off, be it never so bitter." As soon then as he had audibly said, "Lord Jesus, receive my soul," which, it seems, was the executioner's watchword, he presently turned him off the ladder; and being off, the executioner's man caught hold of one of his feet, his own man on the other foot, whereby they suddenly weighed his life; where hanging a small distance of time, his body not once stirred, only his hands a little stirred and moved, being tied with a little black ribbon, which a little before he had reached to the executioner, putting up his hands to him for that purpose. All which being ended, both corpse and high gibbet were from thence removed.

The Trial of JAMES FRANKLIN, at the King's Bench, 27th of November, for the Murder of Sir Thomas Overbury: Mich. 13 JAMES I. A.D. 1615.

After he had put himself for his trial upon the country, a jury of esquires and gentlemen was impanelled to pass upon his life. Then Weston's indictment was read, and Franklin accused as accessory to the poisoning of Sir T. Overbury, and in his examination formerly taken were these words:

James Franklin's Confession

He confesseth, that in a house near to Doctors Commons, Mrs. Turner did first come unto him about the poisoning of Sir T. Overbury, and prayed him to provide that which should not kill a man presently, but lie in his body for a certain time, wherewith

he might languish away by little and little; at the same time she
gave him four angels [a gold coin worth at that time nine or ten
shillings], wherewith he bought a water called aqua fortis, and
sent it to Mrs. Turner, who, to try the operation thereof, gave it
to a cat, wherewith the cat languished and pitifully cried for the
space of two days and then died.

Afterwards Mrs. Turner sent for Franklin to come to the
Countess, who told him that aqua fortis was too violent a water;
"but what think you," quoth she, "of white arsenic?" He told her
it was too violent. "What say you," quoth she, "to powder of
diamonds?" He answers, "I know not the nature of that." She
said, then he was a fool; and gave him pieces of gold and bade
him buy some of that powder for her. Franklin demands of the
Countess, what was the reason she would poison Sir T. Overbury? She told him, he would pry so far into their state that he
would overthrow them all.

A little before Sir T. Overbury's death, the Countess sent for
Franklin and showed him a letter written from the Lord of
Rochester, wherein he read these words: "I marvel at these de-
lays, that the business is not yet dispatched." Whereby Franklin
thinketh in his conscience, was meant the poisoning of Sir T.
Overbury. And in another letter from the Lord of Rochester was
written, that Sir Thomas was to come out of the Tower within
two days, and they all should be undone: Whereupon the
Countess sent for Weston, and was very angry with him that he
had not dispatched Sir T. Overbury. Weston told her, that he
had given him a thing that would have killed twenty men.

Also, a fortnight after Weston's apprehension, the Countess
sent for Franklin to her house at St. James's Park, where he
found the Earl and Countess walking together, and as soon as he
came, the Earl went apart into a chamber. Then she told him,
Weston had been sent for by a pursuivant, and had confessed all,
and we shall all be hanged: "But on your life," quoth she, "do not
you confess that you brought any poison to me or to Mrs. Turner, for if you do you shall be hanged, for I will not hang for you,
and, says Mrs. Turner, 'I will not hang for you both.'" The
Countess told him that the lord who was to examine him would
promise him a pardon to confess, "but believe him not, for they
will hang thee when all is done." Weston comes to Franklin's
house, and told him, now the Countess's turn is served, she used
him unkindly, and they should be poisoned, and that two were
set of purpose to poison him.

Franklin having confessed his former Examinations under his own hand, being permitted to speak for himself, said that at the entreaty of the Countess and Mrs. Turner, he did buy these poisons, but protested his ignorance what they meant to do with them; and for the rest, he referred himself to the conscience of the jury: Who went from the Bar, and within a quarter of an hour, did return, and pronounced him Guilty.

Then Judge Crook, after a brief exhortation, gave the sentence of death upon him.

The Lord Chief Justice made a short exhortation also, with addition of these words: That knowing as much as he knew, if this had not been found out, neither the Court, city, nor any particular family had escaped the malice of this wicked cruelty.

He was afterwards executed according to the sentence.

Although Franklin had thus pleaded Not Guilty, he did not deny the truth of his confession; he preferred to rely on the slender hope that his complete cooperation with Coke might win him clemency, and the verdict of guilty was based on his confession. Almost a book could be written on the small value of everything he said in his various examinations and on the many contradictions and discrepancies in them. As has been suggested, he was willing to say whatever he thought Coke wanted him to say. His statement that Overbury ate hardly anything that didn't contain poison was obviously ridiculous since he lived five months under such a regime, although the precautions Elwes claimed to have taken in throwing out poisoned food and substituting similar articles prepared in his own kitchen, if true, might be a partial explanation.

Franklin claimed to have prepared for Overbury seven deadly poisons, in spite of which Frances found it necessary to scold him for lack of diligence and to require him to continue his ministrations.

His confessions were used in three trials, but each confession was different each time used. He is alleged to have had three pretrial examinations (November 12, 16 and 17), but no record of any examination can be found in the State Paper Office or other public repository of such papers. Amos says it would be a remarkable circumstance if such important documentary evidence used in early state trials had been lost, whereas evidence of minor importance read at the same trials is to be found in abundance. Only his alleged

confessions after conviction as written in Coke's notes are now preserved.

These "confessions," obtained by Dr. Whiting under promise of
eternal salvation, contain Coke's usual erasures and interlineations.
Coke's account quoted Franklin as saying, "Wheresoever I dine
today, I doubt not but to sup with the Lord Jesus," and says that
when Whiting spoke of his bloody and sanguinary sin, Franklin
replied, "O Lord forgive that for thy mercy's sake." Coke also quotes
him as saying that there were three other great lords in the foul act
not yet named, to which when Whiting replied that the lord chief
justice would find them out, Franklin replied, "I think so, too."
(Carr, Northampton and Suffolk were probably meant.) Coke says
that on the scaffold Franklin declared that everything set down in
any of his examinations or declarations under his hand "which my
Lord Chief Justice hath, are true upon my soul" and that he repeated on the gallows that there were three greater birds and lords
than yet discovered. He is then pictured as praying to himself as the
cart was driven away from under him. Other papers in Coke's
handwriting allege Franklin to have told Dr. Whiting that Somerset
"neither loved the Prince nor the Lady Elizabeth" (the King's son
and wife) and that he could say more but would not. Coke was
supporting his hinted accusation that Carr had helped cause Prince
Henry to be poisoned. Coke also notes that upon being asked whether the king had used an outlandish physician and an outlandish
apothecary about him and about the late prince, Franklin
replied, "Therein lyeth a long tale. . . . there was never such a plot as
this. I could discover knights, great men, and others. I am almost
ashamed to speak what I know."[7] As we shall see, James did not take
kindly to this hinting at the poisoning of Prince Henry.

We have only Coke's worked-over notes to support these aver-
ments about what Franklin confessed. The Egerton papers contain a
letter which gives quite a different picture of Franklin's repentance.
"This morning, about half an hour after ten, Franklin was hanged at
St. Thomas of Watering. As soon as he came out of the prison, he
went to the cart and leaped up into it with a great show of resolution. The hangman came to him and offered to put the rope around
his neck, but he took it out of his hand and strove to put it about the
hangman's neck, and laughed in doing it: then he stood upright and
stretched himself, and gave money to everyone that begged of him,

and all this in so strange fashion, which he continued till his death, that all men thought him either mad or drunk. As soon as he came to the gallows he kissed it, and made a cross upon it, and putting his hat before his eyes crossed himself. . . . [He failed to make the expected speech even when asked to, but he replied that] he was come thither to die . . . that he died justly, and was willing to die, and had long desired this hour, and that was all he had to say. . . . [Upon further questioning, he said that all his confessions were true. He hinted at knowledge he had of the guilt of others:] 'There are some yet left behind, and great ones too, with which — (and then he clapped his hands twice or thrice upon the coffin that lay upon the cart before him) — but let that pass.' . . . [He was urged to speak more clearly but refused to do more than hint about "greater heads abroad than they are aware of." Upon his saying,] 'Come, pray let me be dispatched,' the cart was driven forward and he died, never heard to pray one word except to say that 'he hoped to sup with Christ tonight." A postscript to the letter said, "My Lady . . . commands me to tell that Franklin did give the hangman a box on the ear before he was hanged."[8]

It was now Sir Thomas Monson's turn. Here was a defendant of a different stamp from those previously convicted. Monson had been knighted for services to the kingdom, had an excellent reputation for integrity and was well known and well liked. On the surface at least, his only connection with the poisonings was his naming Elwes lieutenant of the Tower for a monetary consideration and at Northampton's request. This may have been mercenary, although the practice was common and was not looked down upon, but it certainly bore no implication of felonious intent. In spite of the scanty evidence he had, Coke called Monson guilty and insisted on trying him. James felt that Monson was of too high rank and too popular to be convicted lightly; after checking the evidence himself, he ordered Coke not to bring him to trial, but Coke replied that it was then too late to call off the trial.[9]

The Arraignment of Sir THOMAS MONSON, knt. at the Guildhall of London, 4th December, for the Murder of Sir THOMAS OVERBURY: 12 JAMES I. A.D. 1615.

When he came to the Bar, he made a motion to the Lord Chief Justice, That, whereas he had written unto his Lordship to ask the Lord Treasurer two questions, which my Lord would do; he desired then an answer, and that Sir Robert Cotton might be present.

After the questions were read, he was indicted for conspiring with Weston to poison Sir T. Overbury; to which he pleaded, Not Guilty, and would be tried by God and his country.

The Lord Chief Justice broke up the proceedings, and made a speech to this effect, viz. . . . [Here Coke thanked God for delivering the city from what he chose to portray as a plot against the entire kingdom, and to praise the king for his justice and for his mildness "in so great an affair" in not causing the Somersets' and Monson's houses to be searched (a criticism?) and in committing Monson not to the sheriff but to an alderman to whom he was related. He continued:] I never knew the like favor, nor do I like it so well, but do declare it as a gentle proceeding from the King. For other things, I dare not discover secrets; but though there was no house searched, yet such letters were produced which make our deliverance as great as any that happened to the children of Israel. . . . But for this present, . . . he [Monson] must be conveyed to the Tower as a safer place, till further order be taken.

On the night before the trial the king, while playing cards with some of his gentlemen, had remarked casually, "Tomorrow comes Thomas Monson to his trial." His cardholder replied, "Yes, where if he not play his master's prize, your Majesty shall never trust me." This hint that Monson had a trump card to use in his defense so disturbed the king that at the conclusion of the round he said he was sleepy and would finish the set the next night. His gentlemen then departed to their lodgings, but the king immediately sent word for his cardholder to return. It is not known what the man told James, but James sent a message to London posthaste to tell Coke he wanted to see Monson's examination and confession to determine if it were worthy to take his life for so small a matter. This fear of James — that something could be revealed in these trials that would unfavorably affect his reputation or honor — is continuously evident.

Coke was very angry when he received the message but had no choice at the end of the arraignment than to postpone the trial. The speech he made before doing so was construed as another hint that there was a connection between Overbury's poisoning and the death of Prince Henry. What prompted him we do not know. Possibly he believed Northampton's assurance to Elwes that the killing of Overbury would be acceptable to the king, or he may have had some other secret hint intimating that Overbury was poisoned in retaliation for his having, in league with Carr, poisoned Prince Henry.

Then the Lord Chief Justice addressed his speech to Sir Thomas Monson, saying, "Whereas you name my Lord Treasurer, every man's fame is dear unto him, and he hath ever been honorable, you shall hear what he hath answered to my letter: 'After my hearty commendations, I have heard that Sir Thomas Monson thinks I can clear him, but I know nothing of him to accuse or excuse him; but I hope he is not guilty of so foul a crime.' You hear . . . that he will neither accuse you, nor excuse you."

Monson. I do not accuse the Lord Treasurer, nor calumniate him, for I know he is very honorable, but I desire to have an answer to my two questions.

L.C.J. You shall hear more of that when the time serveth; do you as a Christian, and as Joshua bade Achan, "My son, acknowledge thy sin, and give glory to God."

Monson. If I be guilty, I renounce the King's mercy and God's; I am innocent.

L.C.J. There is more against you than you know of.

Monson. If I be guilty, it is of that I know not.

L.C.J. You are popish, that pulpit was the pulpit where Garnet died, and the Lieutenant [Elwes] as firmly; I am not superstitious, but we will have another pulpit.

Doderidge. It is an atheist's word to renounce God's mercy; you must think the change of your lodging means somewhat.

Hyde. I have looked into this business, and I protest, my Lord, he is as guilty as the guiltiest.

Monson. There was never man more innocent than I; in this I will die innocent.

After this speech, certain yeomen of his Majesty's guard, attending for that purpose, conducted him to the Tower, where between the yeomen and the warders, there was some contention about his entertainment.

According to Weldon, Coke was so malicious that after saying, "Take him away; we have other matters against him of a higher nature," he made Monson go on foot from the Guildhall to the Tower. It was raining heavily, Monson was not well and the walk almost cost him his life.[10] Weldon may have been wrong about the walk in the rain. The writer of Monson's brief biography in D.N.B.

credits an eyewitness with having said he saw Monson enter Sir George More's coach. This writer also questions whether James interfered with the trial, but it seems well established that he did.

Arthur Wilson, in his history of James, wrote: "It was rumored that the King (heightened to so much passion by this eruption of Sir Edward Coke's) [his statement from the bench hinting at Prince Henry's poisoning], went to the Council Table, and kneeling down there, desired God to lay a curse upon him and his posterity forever, if he were consenting to Overbury's death. . . . So the sudden stopping of Monson's trial put strange imaginations into men's heads, and those seconded by reports too high for private discovery. . . . But the Lord Chief Justice was blamed for flying out of his way; that having enough to prosecute the business, he would grasp after more till he lost all."[11]

Coke's conduct made the prosecution even more difficult to handle. Unless such announcements made by the chief justice from the bench could be sufficiently supported by the evidence when produced, the people would naturally conclude that something had been hushed up. Should Somerset be acquitted after what Coke had said more than once about the adequacy of the evidence to convict him, the people must suppose that Weston's fear had been realized and the great fish broken through the net. Even worse, the people might assume that somebody was implicated with whom justice dare not meddle. Unfortunately, if Coke wanted to believe something, a very little amount of evidence satisfied him. As a matter of fact, in Monson's case Coke may well have had no evidence of any kind except the uncorroborated statement of a man under sentence of death (Franklin) who was pretending to know secrets in hope of prolonging his life.[12]

Monson was kept in the Tower for some months and was finally let out on bail until the trial could be resumed. The situation became more and more embarrassing. James asked Bacon and Yelverton what to do; on December 7, 1616, they recommended a pardon, since, "It is altogether unfit to have a proceeding to a trial, both because the evidence itself (for as much as we know of it) is conjectural . . . secondly, to do nothing in it is neither safe for the gentleman nor honorable (as we conceive) for your Majesty, whose care of justice useth not to become faint or weary in the latter end. Therefore we are of the opinion that it is a case fit for your Majesty's pardon, as upon doubtful evidence, and that Sir Thomas Monson plead the same publicly, with such protestations of his innocency as he thinks good, and so the matter may come to a regular and just period." The king followed their advice; on February 12, 1617, Monson deliverd up his pardon at the King's Bench and made his speech declaring his innocence; both were approved by the chief justice and the case was ended.[13] The king had given Coke a stinging rebuke; as Camden said, "The lord chief justice's wings were clipped for it ever after."[14] When the Somersets came to trial, it was Bacon who prosecuted them; Coke sat only with the other justices as an adviser on points of law, and he was soon dismissed from his post.

Coke's behavior at Monson's arraignment was not the sole cause for his dismissal — it was merely the last straw. James had for some time been dissatisfied with Coke's conduct of the prosecution and had begun to realize that he was overly zealous and more interested in furthering his own career than in ascertaining the true facts. Chamberlain had written to Carleton on April 20, 1616, that although the arraignment of the Somersets was set for April 29, he had heard that it was to be postponed "till the sixth of May or God knows when," since a new commission had been appointed to examine and proceed in the case, from which Coke was excluded, and that Lord Chancellor Ellesmere, the Duke of Lennox and Attorney General Bacon had been at the Tower to examine Carr, not relying on what Coke had done before.[15]

Coke now leaves our stage but not public life. A skunk he may have been, but he was a brilliant one. His disposition was selfish, overbearing and arrogant, but even Bacon said that without Coke, "the law by this time had been like a ship without ballast." Hallam called him a man of strong though narrow intellect, confessedly the greatest master of English law that had ever appeared, a flatterer and tool of the Court till he had obtained his ends, yet after his promotion to chief justice, a steerer of a more independent course.[16] Plucknett gives Coke credit for sincerity in changing his outlook upon the attainment of high office, saying, "Just as the soldier and courtier, Thomas Becket, became transformed into a churchman of the sternest school on becoming Archbishop of Canterbury, so Coke, once the upholder of prerogative, discovered a new point of view.... As a Crown Lawyer he magnified the prerogative; as the head of the common law system he exalted law to almost mystical heights. This meant a complete revision of his attitude towards the Crown, and there can be no doubt that many capable minds besides

Coke, who were content to trust the Crown under Elizabeth, were equally likely to distrust it under James. . . . "[17]

Coke's argument in Shelley's Case, known to every student of the law, made him famous and the recognized leader of the bar. With his huge fees he bought up estate after estate, until he became one of the wealthiest men in England. During his earlier career he was speaker of the House, where he curried favor with Queen Elizabeth. After twelve years as attorney general, he became chief justice of the Court of Common Pleas, in 1606, and he then insisted on the independence of the judiciary. In 1613 Bacon manipulated him into the chief justiceship of the King's Bench, a less lucrative job, so that Bacon could get the attorney generalship, the present holder of which being willing to switch to the Common Pleas but not to the King's Bench. A different kind of rivalry between the two men ended when Coke took as his second wife Lady Hatton, a wealthy widow high in Court circles, who had already refused Bacon. Aubrey tells us that Lady Hatton was with child when Coke married her and that Coke, laying his hand on her belly (when he came to bed) and feeling a child stirring, asked, "What, flesh in the pot?" to which she replied, "Yes, or else I would not have married a Cook." Coke's name was, of course, pronounced "Cook" and was in fact at that time sometimes so spelled.[18]

Although dismissed from office by James in 1616, Coke later regained a place in the Privy Council and still later went back into the House of Commons, where he used his influence to get Bacon investigated on the charge of accepting bribes. Coke guided the work of the investigating committee and got Bacon impeached in the Commons, but Bacon pleaded guilty in order to avoid trial by the House of Lords. He was sentenced to a large fine, confinement in the Tower and ineligibility to hold public office. Coke now fronted for the Commons in its quarrels with James. This resulted in his temporary confinement in the Tower, during which his house and chambers were sealed and his papers seized. Prince Charles obtained his release, but he was put off the Privy Council. When Charles became king, Coke served as sheriff of Buckinghamshire, was elected to Parliament from two different districts and while in Parliament framed and engineered the enactment of the Petition of Rights, which was the basis for the settlement of the Revolution of 1688 and guaranteed the liberties of Englishmen. After his death "such as could be found" of Coke's papers were restored to his family, but in what condition we do not know.[19]

The Somersets had been under arrest since October and all others indicted in the Overbury case, except for Monson, had been found guilty and executed, but it was well into 1616 before Frances and Carr were brought to trial. There were several causes for the delay. Frances, pregnant and in poor health, was not delivered until December 9, 1615. More delay was caused by the appointment of the new commissioners and the time expended in their investigations. When their evidence became available, still more time was spent in an attempt to persuade Carr to plead guilty. James was afraid that extended hearings and investigations might further tarnish his reputation and that of his Court. Also, pleas of guilty by the two would give James a reasonable excuse for reducing their punishment. If they were to be tried, the government had to step warily and be sure of a strong case, as Coke had publicly announced that there was sufficient evidence to convict both. A "not guilty" verdict might have dangerous consequences; the people were already construing the delay to mean that Weston was right in fearing that the great fish would not be netted.

Frances was in private custody until March 27, but since the Grand Jury had returned true bills against both her and Carr on January 10, it was thought advisable to move her to the Tower on March 27. The final postponement of her trial was caused by a severe illness, perhaps induced by drugs in an attempt at suicide. Chamberlain wrote Carleton on May 18 that the stage in Westminster Hall was completed, the lords assembled and everything ready for trial on Wednesday when the order for postponement came on Tuesday, disappointing many people who had stayed in town for the trial and now had to leave with loss of the payments they had made for places in Westminster Hall.[20] The average price for a seat in the Hall appears to have been about £51 — in those days a very large sum of money.

When Frances finally came to trial on May 24, Westminster Hall was jammed. The lord high steward [Chancellor Ellesmere] sat under a high canopy at one end. Close by were the garter king at arms, the seal bearer and black rod and the sergeant at arms. The peers summoned as a jury sat on either side of the high steward, and the red-robed judges a row lower. Elsewhere were the lawyers, separated by a bar from the prisoner's platform, in front of which stood the gentleman-porter with the axe.[21] The trial proved to be so short that the spectators hardly got their money's worth. However, although this does not appear in the official report, they did enjoy a vicarious thrill when, as Camden tells it, all of the letters that passed between Forman and Frances were read in open court, and the waxen and brazen puppets were made visible, dancing up and down from hand to hand, revealing the folly of her actions.[22]

The Trial of the LADY FRANCES COUNTESS OF SOMERSET, the 24th of May, for the Murder of Sir THOMAS OVERBURY: 14 JAMES I. A.D. 1616.

The Summons of the Peers to the Trial.

After our hearty commendations to your Lordship; whereas the King's Majesty has resolved that the Earl of Somerset and the Countess his wife, lately indicted of felony for the murder and poisoning of Sir Thomas Overbury, then his Majesty's prisoner in the Tower, shall now receive their lawful and public trial, by their peers, immediately after the end of this present Easter term; at the trial of which noble personages your Lordship's presence, as being a peer of the realm and one of approved wisdom and integrity, is requisite to pass upon them: These are to let your Lordship understand that his Majesty's pleasure is, and commandeth by these our letters, that your Lordship make your repair to the City of London, by the eleventh day of the month of May following, being some few days before the intended trial; at which time your Lordship shall understand more of his Majesty's pleasure. So not doubting of your Lordship's care to observe his Majesty's directions we commit you to God. - Your Lordship's very loving friend, G. Cant.; T. Ellesmere, Canc.; Fenton; E. Watton; Tho. Lake; Lord Darcy of the South; C. Edmunds; E. Worcester; Lenox; P. Herbert; Ralph Winwood; Fulke Greville; Jul. Caesar.

From Whitehall this 24th April, 1616.

The names of the Peers:

Earl of Worcester, Lord Privy Seal. - Earl of Pembroke, Lord Chamberlain. - The Earls of Rutland, Sussex, Montgomery, and Hertford. - Lord Visc. Lisle. - Lord Zouch, Warden of the Cinque Ports. - Lord Willoughby of Eresby. - Lord Delaware. - Lord Dacres of the South. - Lord Mounteagle who being sick went away before judgment. - Lord Wentworth. - Lord Rich. - Lord Willoughby of Parham. - Lord Hunsdon. - Lord Russell the second day was not there. - Lord Compton. - Lord Norris. - Lord Gerrard. - Lord Cavendish. - Lord Dormer.

Thomas Lord Ellesmere, Chancellor of England, Lord High Steward *hac vice*. His assistants in the Commision there present:

Sir Edw. Coke, L. C. Justice of England. - Sir H. Hubbart, L. C. Justice of the Common Pleas. - Sir L. Tanfield, L. C. Baron of the Exchequer. - Judge Altham, one of the Barons of the Exchequer. - Judge Crook, one of the judges of the King's Bench. - Judge Doderidge, one of the judges of the King's Bench. - Judge Houghton, one of the judges of the King's Bench. - Judge Nicholls, one of the judges of the Common Pleas.

The Counsel that were there the first day:

Sir F. Bacon, the King's Attorney General; Serj. Montague; Serj. Crew; Sir Henry Yelverton, the King's Solicitor; Francis Moor, the Queen's Serjeant; Sir Lawrence Hyde, the Queen's attorney; Mosley, attorney of the Duchy; Sir John Davis, the King's Serjeant; Mr. Walter, the Prince's attorney; Mr. Finch, Keeper of the Records of Attainders. More the second day. - Serj. Tho. Moor; Serj. Finch.

The peers named above were all that appeared at any time at the trial, though there were six others summoned, but why they absented themselves is not known; and those were, the Duke of Lennox, Lord Steward of the Household; Earl of Huntingdon; Lord Darcy of Meuell; Lord Eure; Lord Hunsdon; Lord Darcy of Chiche;

The Form of their Sitting, and their Ceremonies.

When my Lord Chancellor, who for this time was High Steward of England, came into the court, there came before him six Sergeants at Arms, with their maces; Sir Geo. Coppin with his patent; Sir Rd. Coningsby with his white staff; Mr. Mainwaring with the great seal, he himself, at the upper end of the court, sitting under a canopy of state; on both hands of him the peers, under them the judges; at the farther end the King's counsel, below the judges; on one side Finch, Keeper of the Records of Attainders; the Clerk of the Crown and his deputy, in the middle of the court, the Sergeant Crier standing by him; Sir Rd. Coningsby, Sir Geo. Coppin, the Seal Bearer, at my Lord Steward's feet; the prisoner at the Bar behind the King's counsel; the Lieutenant of the Tower in a little place adjoining to the Bar.

All being silent, Sir Geo. Coppin rises and delivers the patent to the Lord High Steward, upon his knee; he receives it and kisses it, then redelivers it to Mr. Fenshaw, who takes it kneeling. Then the Sergeant Crier makes a proclamation in the Lord High Steward's name, to keep silence; then Mr. Fenshaw reads the commission, which bears date the tenth of May; then there is another Oyes, to certify [to] my Lord Steward, whether Weston

were convicted as principal for the murder of Sir T. Overbury.
Then the Lord Chief Justice delivers a schedule endorsed with a
certificate of four judges of the King's Bench, and others the
Commissioners. This Fenshaw, turning to my Lord Steward,
reads. [It will be remembered that none of the accessories to the
crime could be tried unless the person tried as principal had been
convicted.] A third Oyes, for certifying of other indictments: my
Lord Coke delivers another schedule endorsed with the certificate of my Lady Somerset's indictment, which Fenshaw, as
before, read. A fourth Oyes, for Walter Lee, Sergeant at Arms,
to return the precépt for the peers of Frances Countess of Somerset; which accordingly, after his three reverences to the Lord
High Steward, he delivered to Mr. Fenshaw: he reads the endorsement. A fifth Oyes, to call the Lords summoned by the
command of the Lord High Steward, to answer to their names,
which they accordingly did, beginning at the first; and as every
one was named they put off their hats, and stood till the next was
named. A sixth Oyes to the Lieutenant of the Tower, to return
his precept, and bring the prisoner to the Bar; which he did, and
gave his precept to the Sergeant, who gave it to Mr. Fenshaw,
and he, as before, read the endorsement. The prisoner made
three reverences to his grace and the peers; she was in black
tammel, a cypress chaperon, a cobweb lawn ruff and cuffs.
[Frances had been shrewd enough to dress as a penitent. Her
gown was black, the "cypress chaperon" was a black hood of
crepe or lawn commonly used for mourning and her ruff and
cuffs were plain white.]

L.H.S. My Lords, the reason why you be called hither this day,
is to sit as peers of Frances Countess of Somerset.

Mr. Fenshaw, Clerk of the Crown. Frances Countess of Somerset, hold up thy hand.

She does so, and held it up till Mr. Lieutenant told her she
might put it down; and then he read the indictment, containing
Weston's accounts in the poisoning of Sir T. Overbury, and her
abetting of him, the eighth of May, 1613. The Countess of
Somerset, all the while the indictment was reading, stood, looking
pale, trembled, and shed some few tears; and at the first naming
of Weston in the indictment, put her fan before her face, and
there held it half covered till the indictment was read.

Mr. Fenshaw. Frances Countess of Somerset, what sayest thou?
Art thou guilty of this felony and murder or not guilty?

The Lady Somerset, making an obeisance to the Lord High
Steward, answered Guilty, with a low voice, but wonderful fearful.

My Lady, upon her arraignment, having pleaded guilty, the proceeding after was thus:

Mr. Attorney. May it please your grace, my Lord High Steward of England, I am glad to hear this lady's so free acknowledgment, for confession is noble. Those that have been formerly indicted, at their arraignment persisted in denial, as Weston, Elwes, Franklin and Turner; but you see this lady's humility and repentance by so pleading; and certainly she cannot but be a spectacle of much commiseration, if you either respect the sex, a woman, or her parentage, honorable; but this day and tomorrow are to crown justice; the mercy seat is the inner part of the temple, the throne public, and therefore I shall now only pray a record of the confession and judgment; but since the peers are met, for honor's sake it is good to declare the King's justice. This is the second time since the King's coming, these 13 years, that any peers have been arraigned, and both these times your grace had the place of High Steward; the first were Grey and Cobham, and though they were convicted, yet execution followed not. No noble blood hath yet been spilled since his Majesty's reign. The first was revenge of treason amongst malcontents; and this of a particular offense to a private subject, against those that have been so high in the King's grace and favor, and therefore deserve to be written in a sunbeam. But his being the best master in the world, hinders him not from being the best king; for he can as well plane a hill, as raise a valley: a good lesson to put to my Lords the peers; he is lieutenant to him that is no respecter of persons. This that I should now speak of, may be reduced to that which was acted in the vault, and since upon the stage: the first I will not now enter into, because I will neither grieve a lady that is present, nor touch a lord that is absent; my duty requires it not, and my humanity forbids it. For that which hath been upon the stage, which is the theatre of God's justice, you shall understand that which hath been worthily acted by the King, in this noble work of justice, and right well by his ministers. Overbury died poisoned the 15th of September, 1613, in the Tower of London; he was no sooner dead, but there was a certain rumor and muttering, that was *vox populi*, that Overbury came strangely to his death; and in that time, on the contrary hand, there was another rumor, but that was *vox diaboli*, that he died of a foul disease, so foul a one as is not fit for me to name, But for two years after this, though Overbury's blood cried for revenge, *vox Dei* was not heard. "*Gloria Dei celare, regis perscrutare rem*": It is the glory of God to conceal a thing, of a king to find it out; yet all the while God so dazzled the eyes of these two great procurers and their instruments, that the first looked not about them, the other fled not. About the beginning of the last progress it first broke forth; and as all murders are strange in their discovery, so this was miraculous, for it came out in a compliment thus: my Lord of Shrewsbury, who is now with God, commended Sir J. Elwes to a Councillor of State; and it was by him that Sir J. in respect of the good report he had heard made of his honor and worth, desired to be made known unto him. That Councillor answered that he took it for a favor from him, but withal added, "There lies a kind of heavy imputation on him about Overbury's death: I could wish he would clear himself, and give some satisfaction on the point." This my Lord Shrewsbury related back, and presently Elwes was struck with it, and makes a kind of discovery, that some attempts were undertaken against Overbury but took no effect, as checked by him. Though the truth be, he lacked rather fortitude in the repulse, than honesty. This Councillor, weighing well this narration from Elwes, acquainted the King with the adventure; who commanded presently that Elwes should set down his knowledge in writing, which accordingly he did, but still reserving himself within his own compass, not to touch himself, endeavoring rather to discover others than any else should undertake that office, and so accuse him. The King still endeavors to search the truth of this business, gives direction for the examination of the truth of it, commits it to certain Councillors; they pick something out of Weston; then the further inquiry is delivered over to my Lord Coke, who in this cause was very painful, took two or three hundred examinations, but when he found it might touch upon greater persons, then he desired some others might be joined with him, which was accordingly granted; namely, the Lord Chancellor, Lord Steward, the Lord Zouch. But then there were no practices left untried for the suppression of the discovery. Weston was solicited to stand mute, but at last this dumb devil was cast out. Then follows Elwes, Turner, Franklin, all of which were actors in this tragedy, without malice, but no authors. Now when this lady comes to her part, she meets justice in the way, by confession, which is the cornerstone either of mercy or judgment; yet it is said, that mercy and truth be met together. Truth you have in her confession, and that may be a degree to mercy, which we must leave to him in whose power it resides; in the meantime this day must be reserved for judgment. Now to conclude, and give you an account of the often procrastinations in this business [trial postponements]; the first was due to humanity, her childbirth; the second was for reasons of state;

and the last had a grave and weighty cause. Those directions the King at the first gave written with his own hand, for the examination of his business, I desire may be read.

The King's Instructions read.

There be two things in this cause to be tried, and the verity can be but in one of them; first, whether my Lord of Somerset and my Lady were the procurers of Overbury's death; or, that this imputation hath been by some practiced to cast an aspersion upon them. I would first have you diligently inquire of the first; and if you find them clear, then I would have you as carefully look after the other, to the intent such practices may be discovered, and not suffered to pass with impunity.

Mr. Attorney. There be other directions in these instructions, by way of interrogatories, that are not now necessary to be read.

L.H.S. Let the Lords the Peers view these directions from the King.

Lord Coke. None of these interrogatories, which the King desired there should be examinations upon, came away empty; and whatsoever whisperings there be abroad of the death of Weston, they all (some before the hour of their death) confessed the fact, and died penitent; and if need should require, I have brought their confessor along (namely, Dr. Whiting).

L.H.S. My Lords, you see, and have heard those directions under the King's hand; give the glory to God, and honor to the King.

[Ellesmere made this comment to stop what might have become an interchange between Bacon and Coke, Bacon belittling the interrogatories and Coke explaining how valuable they had been.]

Mr. Attorney. May it please your grace, etc., whereas Frances Countess of Somerset hath been indicted as accessory before the fact, of the willful poisoning and murder of Sir T. Overbury; upon her indictment, she hath been arraigned; upon her arraignment, pleaded guilty: I desire that her confession may be recorded, and judgment given against the prisoner.

Fenshaw. Frances Countess of Somerset, hold up thine hand: Whereas thou hast been indicted, arraigned, and pleaded Guilty, as accessory before the fact, of the willful poisoning and murder of Sir T. Overbury; what canst thou now say for thyself, why judgment of death should not be pronounced against thee?

C. of Som. I can much aggravate, but nothing extenuate my fault; I desire mercy, and that the Lords will intercede for me to the King (This she spoke humbly, fearfully, and so low, the Lord Steward could not hear it, but Mr. Attorney related it.)

Mr. Attorney. The lady is so touched with remorse and sense of her fault, that grief surprises her from expressing of herself; but that which she hath confusedly said, is to this effect, that she cannot excuse herself, but desires mercy.

Sir R. Coningsby, sitting before the Lord High Steward, rises, and upon his knee delivers him the white staff.

L.H.S. Frances Countess of Somerset, whereas thou hast been indicted, arraigned, pleaded Guilty, and that thou hast nothing to say for thyself, it is now my part to pronounce judgment; only thus much before, since my Lords have heard with what humility and grief you have confessed the fact, I do not doubt they will signify so much to the King, and mediate for his grace towards you: But in the meantime, according to the law, the sentence must be this, That thou shalt be carried from hence to the Tower of London, and from thence to the place of execution, where you are to be hanged by the neck till you be dead; and the Lord have mercy upon your soul.

The speech made by Bacon was too long and was unnecessary in view of Frances's plea of guilty. However, Bacon was astute and realized not only that he had the limelight but that the spectators deserved something for the exorbitant prices they had paid for their seats. He had ready a much longer and more carefully prepared speech to use had Frances pleaded not guilty. Too much of it was flattery of the king and some of the more powerful peers. It was, of course, colored by Bacon's intense desire to see Frances convicted in order to clear the way for the conviction of her husband.

All commentators have noted Frances's extreme nervousness. Surely there was ample cause. As a headstrong, spoiled darling she had been denied nothing from the time of her birth; she had grown to feel that whatever she wanted to do she could do with impunity; her baby had been taken away from her when she was sent to the Tower; she had lost the support of her closest friend (Mrs. Turner), who had been hanged; her powerful great-uncle, Northampton, who might have been able to protect her, was dead; and her husband was in no position to give her any help. She was a completely broken woman.[23] Sanderson says that at her trial, "She seemed drowned in a deluge of grief, being therein beholden to nature, that she could vent herself in tears; seeing that sorrow which cannot bleed in the eyes does often fester in the heart, and so it appeared in her excess; women can hardly do anything without overdoing; feminine passions must either not be full, or overflow, and indeed, she could not utter one word in her own defense, which begat relenting, even in the counsel that pleaded against her. . . . But her sorrowful silence needed the less rhetoric in them to urge her guilt."[24]

ELEVEN

Robert Carr, Earl of Somerset, king's prisoner in the Tower, was not given much peace during the last weeks before his trial. James had made his confidant, Sir George More, Carr's keeper. Hoping to catch some slip that would be an admission of guilt, More kept Carr engaged in conversation, and Carr charged More with many long messages to the king; James cautiously refused to receive any direct communications from Carr. The new commissioners put him through many examinations; James's anxiety to avoid a trial, with its possible exposure of secrets, caused him to pull out all the stops.

Bacon and the commissioners reported their progress to James in an undated letter, the tenor of which was that they had done their best to carry out James's instruction to examine Carr, that they had impressed on Carr how serious his situation was and that his trial was not far off, that while in his conversations with the commissioners there was little he could say which would affect his guilt, there was much he could say which would be helpful to him in procuring James's mercy, and that they had told him the opinion of the best judges of the kingdom was that the evidence was sufficient to convict him and that accordingly a confession was not needed. In addition, they advised him that although James could not be expected to make any promises, he could, nonetheless, be compassionate toward Carr if Carr would give him some basis for it. But as long as Carr stood upon his innocency and trial James could in honor do nothing but proceed according to justice. They had also warned Carr that since he was a close prisoner he could not understand how much the world, knowing of James's love for justice, expected James to insist on justice in this case but that, nevertheless, a frank and clear confession might give James an excuse for mercy without sacrificing

211

honor. Further, the report continued, the commissioners had impressed on Carr that Frances, as he knew, after many oaths to the
contrary, had in the end become remorseful and confessed, that she
who had led Carr to offend might lead him likewise to repent, that
the confession of only one of the couple could not do much good
but that the confession of both might well help both. Also the
commissioners wished Carr not to shut the gate of James's mercy by
being longer obdurate, hinting that Carr might well discern for
whom they were speaking, since commissioners for examination
themselves could not talk of any possible mercy. Finally, the commissioners advised James that they found Carr no closer to confession
and that his behavior was very sober, modest and mild, different
in earlier examinations but that he still seemingly was insistent on
trial. It was suggested in a postscript that some preacher, "well
chosen," be given access to Carr for preparing and comforting him
even before the trial. There is real irony in the words "well chosen"
and that the purpose was for Carr's "preparing and comforting."
The preacher was, of course, intended to endeavor to extort a
confession from Carr under threats of eternal damnation if he
persisted in his obstinacy.

Spedding thinks that Carr did not yet believe that he would be
arraigned at all or that he had yet exhausted the resources which he
thought he possessed in the well-known weaknesses of the king. He
first tried vehement upbraiding, against which he knew James's soft
and sensitive nature was seldom unyielding. He then sought to instill
in him distrust of the commissioners, hinting at the secrets he could
reveal but refusing to tell to James through the commissioners what
they were. This frightened the king and increased his anxiety for a
confession, but not sufficiently to save Carr from trial. Nevertheless,
James and Bacon did draw up plans for what to do under various
circumstances if Carr made good his threat.

In preparing for the trial Bacon worked closely with James on
every step, including plans of procedure if Carr should confess or if
he should be found not guilty. Bacon would submit outlines through
Villiers; these would be returned to him with James's "postils" (comments and approval or disapproval) noted in the margins. Also
considered was what to do if Frances in her trial sought to clear Carr
of knowledge of the plot and what to do at Carr's trial if he broke
out into any accusation against the king. This last problem was
solved by stationing on each side of Carr at the trial a guard with a

cloak, with which at the first words he was to be muffled and dragged away to the Tower.[2]

One of these annotated outlines appears as an appendage to Frances's trial as set forth in Howell, and there are several more in Spedding. The first is dated April 28. Bacon's first question was what to do if Carr confessed before trial — whether to call off the trial or let it go to a judgment that would then be reprieved — which would save both his lands from forteiture and "the blood from corruption." The third possibility, to pardon Carr after judgment, would save only his life. James opted for the first or last, with the choice to be made after he had heard the confession. Bacon then pointed out that if the first suggestion were adopted, there were three considerations: The Somersets must plead for mercy, prostrate at the king's feet; James must decide whether to take away all hope of restoring any of their fortunes or favors, "whereof if there should be the least conceit, it will leave in men a great deal of envy and discontent"; finally, it might be well to let the people think that there was cause for further examination of Carr regarding matters of state, thus making politics a reason for the stay, as well as clemency. As to these James commented, "This Article cannot be mendit [bettered] in any point thereof."

If Frances should confess but Carr should stand trial and be found guilty, Bacon suggested that since the case against Carr "resteth chiefly upon presumptions" (quite an admission!), he might handle it so that the balance between guilt and innocence seemed fairly even as far as malice was concerned, thus leaving more ground for clemency, and "it shall be my care so to moderate the manner of charging him, as it make him not odious beyond the extent of mercy." Bacon added that this kindness should be dependent on Carr's not "by his contemptuous and insolent behavior at the bar, make himself incapable and unworthy" of it; James said amen.

Another possibility was that Carr might stand mute and not plead. If this happened the Weston procedure could be followed, and the trial would be adjourned until James could decide what he wanted done. The fourth case, Bacon wrote, "is that which I would be very sorry should happen; but it is a future contingent [possibility]: That is, if the peers should acquit him and find him not guilty." In this unfortunate event, Bacon recognized the impossibility of their doing anything about it, but the lord high steward could be instructed to remand Carr to the Tower as a close prisoner for questioning, in the Star Chamber or otherwise, about many other "high and heinous offenses (though not capital)." James's marginal comment on this proposal was, "This is so also."[3]

All concerned seemed satisfied that Carr was guilty; the only question was whether it could be proved. On May 2 Bacon wrote to Villiers, "Yesterday being Wednesday, I spent four or five hours with the judges, whom his Majesty designed to take consideration with the four judges of the King's Bench, of the evidence against Somerset. They all concur in opinion, that the questioning him, and drawing him on to trial is most honorable and just, and that the evidence is fair and good."[4]

When Bacon sent James his proposed trial procedure and outline of the evidence, James wrote in the margin, "You will do well to remember likewise in your preamble, that insigne [meaning here, perhaps, "basic premise"] that only the zeal to justice makes me take this course. I have commended you not to expatiate nor digress upon any other points, that may not serve clearly for . . . [proof] of that point whereof he is accused."[5] Bacon's entire outline and discussion of the evidence is illuminating and interesting but too long to set forth here. The problem of how to prevent unwanted statements by Carr came up in several other letters. In one, under the caption, "A particular remembrance for His M., " Bacon wrote, "It were good that after he is come into the Hall (so that he may perceive he must go to trial), and shall be retired into the place appointed until the court call for him, then the Lieutenant should tell him roundly that if in his speeches he shall tax the King, that the justice of England is that he shall be taken away, and the evidence shall go on without him, and all the people will cry, 'Away with him,' and then it shall not be in the King's will to save his life, the people will be so set on fire."[6]

The trial opened at 10:00 on May 25, 1616, in Westminster Hall. The scene was the same as described for the trial of Frances the day before, and the room was equally crowded. There was little sympathy for Carr on the part of those in the audience or the common people who eagerly awaited the result. A silly bit of doggerel which was being circulated gave popular expression to the prevailing sentiment: "I.C.U.R. (I see you are), /Good Monsieur Carr, about to fall,/U.R.A.K. (You are a knave), /As most men say; but that's not all./ U.O.Q.P. (You occupy), /With your annullity That naughty pack,/ S.X.Y.F. (Essex's wife), /Whose wicked life, hath broke your back."[7]

There are several reports of the trial, agreeing remarkably well under the circumstances but having a few material differences that will be mentioned. We shall use the Hargrave account, with occasional reference to an account in the State Paper Office designated the "manuscript copy" and to an account in the library of Cambridge University. There is still a fourth version of Bacon's speech. The Hargrave (official government) version contains fewer than usual distortions and omissions of evidence. Usually the government was prone to doctor the material in such way as to help convince the people that a popular hero was justly convicted. Here Carr's conviction was demanded by the people, and doctoring was not necessary but was indulged in a few times. Substantial variations in the accounts begin to appear near the end, when the reporters were worn out. Thirteen hours in that hot, crowded, airless hall must have been quite an ordeal for everyone.

The Trial of ROBERT CARR Earl of Somerset, May 25, for the Murder of Sir THOMAS OVERBURY: 14 JAMES I. A.D. 1616.

Ser. Crier. Oyes, My Lord High Steward of England purposes this day to proceed to the trial of Robert Earl of Somerset. Oyes, Whosoever have any indictments touching this cause, publicly give them in.

My Lord Coke delivers in the indictment of my Lord of Somerset to Mr. Fenshaw, endorsed.

Ser. Crier. Oyes, Walter Lee, Sergeant at Arms, return the precept for the Lords, which thou hast warned to be here this day. Oyes (He calls every Lord by his name, and they stand up as they are called). My Lord High Steward excuses the Lords Mounteagle and Russell of their absence, in respect of their sickness.

Ser. Crier. Oyes, Lieutenant of the Tower, return thy precept, and bring the prisoner to the Bar. Which he did, and my Lord makes three reverences to the Lord High Steward and the Lords.

Mr. Fenshaw. Rob. Earl of Somerset, hold up thy hand.

He holds it up so long, until Mr. Lieutenant bade him hold it down. The indictment is read, containing Weston's actions in the poisoning of Sir T. Overbury, and his abetting of him, the eighth of May, 1613. My Lord of Somerset was apparelled in a plain black satin suit, laid with two satin laces in a seam; a gown of unent velvet lined with unshorn, all the sleeves laid with satin lace; a pair of gloves with satin tops, his George about his neck, his hair curled, his visage pale, his beard long, his eyes sunk in his head. Whilst his indictment was reading, he three or four times whispered to the Lieutenant.

Mr. Fenshaw. Robert Earl of Somerset, What sayest thou, art thou Guilty of this felony and murder whereof thou standest indicted, or Not Guilty?

My Lord of Somerset, making an obeisance to the Lord High Steward, answered, Not Guilty.

Mr. Fenshaw. How wilt thou be tried?

Ld. Som. By God and the country; but presently recalling himself, said By God and my peers.

Ser. Crier. Oyes, all you that be to give in evidence against Robert Earl of Somerset, who stands now at the Bar upon his deliverance, make your appearance, and you shall be heard what you have to say against him.

My Lord of Somerset, upon his arraignment, having pleaded Not Guilty, the proceeding after was thus:

Lord High Steward (Ellesmere, Lord Chancellor). Robert Earl of Somerset, you have been arraigned, and pleaded Not Guilty; now I must tell you, whatsoever you have to say in your own defense, say it boldly, without fear; and though it be not the ordinary custom, you shall have pen and ink to help your memory; but remember that God is the God of truth; a fault defended is a double crime; hide not the verity, nor affirm an untruth; for, to deny that which is true, increases the offense; take heed lest your willfulness cause the gates of mercy to be shut upon you. Now for you, my Lords the Peers, you are to give diligent attention to that which shall be said; and you must not rest alone upon one piece of evidence, but ground your judgment upon the whole. This moreover I would have you remember, that though you be not sworn as common juries, upon a book, yet that you are tied in as great a bond, your own honor and fidelity, and allegiance to the King; and thus I leave the whole proceeding to your censures. And for you that be of the King's counsel, free your discourse from all partiality, but let truth prevail, and endeavor to make it appear.

Serj. Montague. My Lord High Steward of England, and you my Lords, this cannot but be a heavy spectacle unto you, to see what that man that not long since in great place, [who] with a white staff went before the King, now at this Bar hold up his hand for blood; but this is the change of fortune, nay, I might better say, the hand of God, and work of justice, which is the King's honor. But now to the fact; Robert Earl of Somerset stands indicted as accessory before the fact, of the willful murder and poisoning of Sir T. Overbury, done by Weston, but procured by him; this, my Lord, is your charge. The indictment hath been found by men of good quality, seventeen knights and esquires of the best rank and reputation, some of whose names I will be bold to read unto you: Sir T. Fowler, Sir W. Slingsby, and fifteen more; these have returned *billa vera*. Now ... [the] indictment is but an accusation of record in form thus: Weston, at four several times, gave Overbury four several poisons, the first May ninth, 1613: that was rosalgar; carrying this poison in one hand and his broth in the other; the second was June following, and that was arsenic; the third was July tenth following, and that was mercury sublimate in tarts; the fourth was September fourteenth following, and that was mercury sublimate in a clyster, given by Weston and an apothecary yet unknown, and that killed him. [Weston had nothing to do with the giving of the clyster, and the government *did* know who the apothecary was.] Of these four several poisons ministered by Weston, and procured by you, the fifteenth of September, 1615, Overbury died, and the author is ever worse than the actor. The first poison laid in the indictment that Weston gave Sir T. Overbury, was the ninth of May; and therefore we say, that the Lord Somerset, the eighth of May, hired, counseled and abetted Weston to this fact; and as this day, my Lord, I do charge you for a king, so heretofore King David was charged in the like case, for the murder of Uriah; and though David was under his pavilion, and Uriah in the army, yet David was the cause of his murder: so though you were in the King's chamber and Overbury in the Tower, yet it was you that killed him. [Since David had Uriah killed in order that he might get Uriah's wife, Montague here selected an apt comparison.] It was a stronger hand than Weston's that wrought this. The proof, Mr. Attorney, will follow; and I will now conclude with two desires to the peers: first, that they will not expect visible proofs in the work of darkness. The second is that whereas in an indictment there be many things laid only for form, you are not to look that the proof should follow that, but only that which is substantial; and the substance must be this, whether my Lord of Somerset procured or caused the poisoning of Sir T. Overbury, or no.

L.H.S. That indeed, my Lords, is that which you are to look after, whether my Lord of Somerset was the cause of his poisoning, or not.

Lord Coke. This was very well moved by Mr. Recorder, and the law is clear in this point, that the proof must follow the substance, not the form.

The judges all rising, affirmed this to be true.

This indictment—which, since read in Latin, Carr was doubtless unable to understand, despite the earlier Latin lessons given him by James—simply accused Carr of having procured Weston to administer certain poisons to Overbury, of which Overbury died. The law required that specific dates and places be named, which was done, but this apparent compliance was nullified by a ruling from the judges (based on earlier decisions in Sir Harry Vane's and other cases) that the indictment could be proved if the evidence produced on trial showed that Carr caused Overbury's death from any poison at any time in any place! The ruling was essential to conviction, since only three of the four specific acts of poisoning named in the indictment with which Weston had any connection occurred more than two months before Overbury's death. These Overbury cases are now the leading authority for holding that the outward certainty of an indictment is totally unsubstantial.[8]

Att. Gen. (Sir Francis Bacon). May it please your grace, my Lord High Steward of England, and you my Lords the Peers, you have here before you Robert Earl of Somerset to be tried for his life, concerning the procuring and consenting to the poisoning of Sir T. Overbury, then the King's prisoner in the Tower of London, as an accessory before the fact. I know your honors cannot behold this noble man, but you must remember the great favors which the King hath conferred on him, and must be sensible, that he is yet a member of your body, and a peer, as you are; so that you cannot cut him off from your body, but with grief: and therefore you will expect from us that give in the King's evidence, sound and sufficient matter of proof to satisfy your honors' consciences. As for the manner of the evidence, the King our master, who amongst his virtues, excelleth in that virtue of the imperial throne which is justice, hath given us command that we should not expatiate nor make invectives, but materially pursue the evidence, as it conduceth to the point in question. . . . First, my Lords, the course that I will hold in delivering of that which I shall say, for I love order, is this: 1st, I will speak somewhat of the nature and greatness of the offense, which is now to be tried, not to weigh down my Lord with the greatness of it, but rather contrarywise to show, that a great offense needs a good proof. And that the King, howsoever he might esteem this gentleman heretofore as the signet upon his finger (to use the scriptural phrase), yet in such a case as this, he was to put it off. 2nd, I will use some few words touching the nature of the proofs, which in such a case are competent. 3rd, I will state the proofs. And, lastly, I will produce the proofs, either out of examination and matters of writing, or witnesses *viva voce*.

For the offense itself, it is of crimes, next unto High Treason, the greatest; it is the foulest of felonies. It hath three degrees: First, it is murder by poisoning; Secondly, it is murder committed upon the King's prisoner in the Tower; Thirdly, I might say that it is murder under the color of friendship; but that is a circumstance moral, and therefore I leave that to the evidence itself.... [In the omitted portion Bacon indulged in Biblical and historical parallels and elaborated on the evils and horrors of poisoning, pointedly impressing on the jurors that no man can think himself safe from being poisoned.] Now for the third degree of this particular offense, which is that it is committed upon the King's prisoner, who was out of his own defense and merely in the King's protection, and for whom the King and the State were a kind of respondent, it is a thing that aggravates the fault much, for certainly (my Lord of Somerset) let me tell you this, that Sir T. Overbury is the first man that was murdered in the Tower of London, save the murder of the two young princes, by the appointment of Richard III.

This much of the offense; now to the proofs.... [The omitted passage dwelt on the invidious and secret nature of poisoning and the difficulty of proof] but yet we are not at our cause, for that which your Lordships are to try is not the act of poisoning, for that is done to your hands; all the world, by law, is concluded [compelled] to say, that Overbury was poisoned by Weston ... [This and Montague's later assertion—that the finding by four separate juries that the white powder sent Overbury by Carr was poison which caused Overbury's death was conclusive and not subject to contradiction by anyone—were simply not true. Such presumptions have since been specifically repudiated by law. If the death of Overbury by poisoning as determined by the jury in Weston's trial were now to be conclusive on Carr, he could be convicted on the basis of a trial in which he took no part and had no chance of showing that it was not so. Had Carr been permitted to participate in the Weston trial, he might have been able to persuade the jury that Overbury did not die from poison-

ing. Should Carr suffer the penalty for Weston's poor defending
of himself, or should the peers now trying Carr be bound by the
decision of a common jury in another action?[9]]: but the question
before you is of the procurement only, and as the law termeth it,
as accessory before the fact; which abetting is no more, but to do
or use any act or means which may aid or conduce to the poisoning. So that it is not the buying, nor the making of the poison,
nor the preparing, nor confecting, nor commixing of it, nor the
giving or sending, or laying of the poison, that are the only acts
that do amount unto the abetment; but if there be any other act
or means done, or used to give opportunity of poisoning, or to
facilitate the execution of it, or to stop or divert any impediments
that might hinder it, and that it be with an intention to accomplish and achieve the poisoning; all these are abetments and
accessories before the fact. As for example, if there be a conspiracy to murder a man as he journeyeth on the way, by in-
vitation or by color of some business, and another taketh upon
him to dissuade some friend of his company, that he is not strong
enough to make his defense, and another hath a part to hold him
in talk till the first blow be given: all these, my Lords, without
scruple, are accessories to the murder, although none of them
give the blow, nor assist to give the blow. My Lords, he is not the
hunter alone that lets slip the dog upon the deer, but he that
lodgeth him and hunts him out, or sets a train or trap for him
that he cannot escape, or the like. But this, my Lords, little
needeth in this case; for such a chain of acts of poisoning as this,
I think, was never heard nor seen. And thus much of the nature
of the proofs.

To descend to the proofs themselves, I shall keep this course:
First, I will make a narration of the fact itself. Secondly, I will
break and distribute the proofs, as they concern the prisoner.
And thirdly, according to the distribution, I will produce them
and read them, to use them. [One spectator wrote that at this
point Carr told the lord high steward that his memory was short
and that so he could answer every point he would like to deal
with each as it was raised, but Carr was told that the entire
evidence must be in before he could reply, relying on his pen and
ink, after which Bacon addressed the following sentence to
him:[10] "So that there is nothing that I shall say, but your Lordship shall have three thoughts or cogitations to answer it. First,
when I open it, you may take your aim; second, when I distribute
it, you may prepare your answers without confusion; and third,
when I produce the witnesses, or the examinations themselves,

you may again ruminate, and readvise to make your defense. And this I do, because your memory and understanding may not be oppressed or overloaded with length of evidence, or with confusion of order; nay more, when your Lordship shall make your answer in your time, I will put you in mind, .where cause shall be of your omission."...

The next part of Bacon's speech is omitted here. It merely narrated the story as we already know it, emphasizing the phases he thought would help his case most. There were emphasized the close friendship of the two men, their cooperation and their sharing of state secrets, the knowledge dangerous both to Carr and the king thus acquired by Overbury, Overbury's opposition to Carr's proposed marriage, which resulted in Overbury's incurring the hatred of both Carr and Lady Frances, the enmity between Overbury and the Howards, the decision of Frances, Carr and Northampton to put Overbury out of the way, the choice of poisoning after failure of their effort to procure his murder, the plot to get him into the Tower by persuading him to refuse an ambassador's mission, the putting of Elwes into the lieutenancy of the Tower and the making Weston Overbury's jailer in order to cut him off from the outside world and to make possible his poisoning. Bacon then related the kinds of poison alleged to have been used, the methods used in administering the poisons and the trickery used by Carr to persuade Overbury up to the time of his death that efforts were being made to procure his release.

The evidence as then produced followed Bacon's narrative very closely, except for a few discrepancies. For example, where Bacon accused Overbury and Carr of making "table-talk" of the king's packets which they opened, a more accurate account of what they actually did says they made "tables" of their contents. Some obvious errors, probably typographical, making the meaning difficult to interpret, appear in the omitted passage. Both the manuscript and Cambridge versions are better for this speech. Bacon next addressed himself to Carr.

Now, for the distribution of the proofs, there are four heads to prove you guilty, whereof two are precedent to the poisoning, the third is present, and the fourth is following or subsequent.... The first head or proof is, that there was a root of bitterness, a mortal malice or hatred, mixed with a deep and bottomless mischief, that you had to Sir T. Overbury. The second is, that you were the principal actor, and had your hand in all those acts, which did conduce to the poisoning and gave opportunity to effect it, without which the poisoning could never have been, and which could seem to tend to no other end but to the poisoning. The third is, that your hand was in the very poisoning itself, that you did direct poison, and that you did deliver poison, and that you did continually hearken to the success of the poisoning, and that you spurred it on and called for dispatch when you thought it lingered. And lastly, that you did all things after the poisoning which may . . . [evidence] a guilty conscience, for the smothering of it, and the avoiding of punishment for it; which can be but of three kinds: That you suppressed, as much as in you was testimony; that you did deface, destroy, clip and misdate all writings that might give light to the poisoning; and you did fly to the altar of guiltiness, which is a pardon of murder, and a pardon for yourself, and not for yourself [the meaning of this clause is obscure].

In this, my Lord, I convert my speech unto you, because I would have you alter the points of your charge, and so make your defense the better. And two of these heads I have taken to myself, and left the other to the King's two serjeants. . . . [First] is the mortal malice coupled with fear, that was in you to Sir T. Overbury, although you did palliate it with a great deal of hypocrisy and dissimulation, even to the very end. I will prove it, my Lord Steward, the root of his hate was that which cost many a man's life, that is, fear of . . . [disclosing] secrets; I say, of secrets of a dangerous and high nature, wherein the course that I will hold, shall be this: I will show that a breach and malice was betwixt my Lord and Overbury, and that it burst forth into violent threats and menaces on both sides; Secondly, that these secrets were not of a light, but of a high nature . . . ; they were such as my Lord of Somerset had made a vow that Overbury should neither live in Court nor country; that he had likewise opened himself so far, that "either he or himself must die for it"; and of Overbury's part, he had threatened my Lord, "that whether he did live or die, my Lord's shame shall never die," but that, "he would leave him the most odious man in the world." . . . Thirdly, I will show you that all the King's business was, by my Lord, put into Overbury's hands, so as there is work enough for secrets whatsoever, they write them, and like princes they had confederates, their ciphers and their jargons. And lastly, I will show you that it was but a toy, to say the malice was only in respect he spoke dishonorably of the lady, or for doubt of breaking the marriage, for that Overbury was coadjutor to that love, and the Lord of Somerset was as deep in speaking ill of the lady as Overbury; and again, it was too late for that matter, for the bargain of the match was then made and past; and if it had been no more than to remove Overbury for disturbing the match, it had been an easy matter to have landed [handed?] over Overbury, for which they had a fair way, but that would not serve. . . .

For the next general head or proof, which consists in the acts preparatory, or middle acts, they are in eight several points of the compass, as I may term them. . . . [The matter to be covered by each of his eight compass points, or "links" as he sometimes called them, are omitted here, as they are stated again as each piece of pertinent evidence is introduced.]

And now for producing of my proofs, I will use this course: Those examinations that have been taken upon oath, shall be here read; and the witnesses also I have caused to be here, that they may be sworn, and to justify or deny what they hear read, and to diminish or add to their examinations; and besides that, my Lord of Somerset, and you my Lords the Peers, may ask them what further questions you please. [Bacon's first "link," now to be proved, held that there had been plotting by Frances, Carr and Northampton to get rid of Overbury before the poisoning conspiracy was entered upon.]

H. Payton, servant of Sir T. Overbury, now of his father, examined before the Lord Chief Justice.

He saw a letter of his master's, whose hand he knew, to my Lord of Somerset, wherein were these words, "If I die, my blood lie upon you." And in that or another letter there was this clause, "My Lord, you are now as good as your word, you have kept your vow to me." Moreover, that in the privy gallery at Whitehall, my Lord of Somerset coming late to his chamber, met there Sir T. Overbury; "How now," said my Lord, "are you up yet?" "Nay," answered Sir T. Overbury, "what do you here at this time of night? Will you never leave the company of that base woman? And seeing you do so neglect my advice, I desire that tomorrow morning we may part; and that you will let me have that portion you know is due to me; and then I will leave you free to yourself, to stand on your own legs." My Lord of Somerset answered, that his legs were strong enough to bear himself, and so departed in great displeasure. And to his certain knowledge, they were never perfectly reconciled again. And being asked how he heard this discourse, he said it was in the dead of the night and he, being in a room within the gallery, heard all that passed. [This remarkable occurrence seems not to appear in any other account of Payton's testimony — significant, perhaps, because it hardly seems likely that any spectator would have overlooked or forgotten such a startling story.]

H. Payton. I acknowledge every part of this examination to be true: And more, that my master being in the Tower, he sent a letter by Weston to me, to carry to my Lord; and withal, to deliver my Lord this message, that that powder he had sent him had made him very sick, and given him in one night 60 stools, besides vomits. This letter I carried to the Court, and delivered to Mr. Rawlins to carry in to my Lord, who was then in his chamber. My Lord presently came out; asked me how my master did. I told him very sick; and withal, this message how the physic had wrought with him. My Lord smiled, and cried, "Pish"; and so turned away. [Carr's nonchalant reception of this message would seem to bear out his claim that the only white powder he sent Overbury was the one he had obtained from Killigrew and which was intended to induce "scouring and vomiting," as the purgative either requested by Overbury, or sent him, as Carr had told him, to bring on temporary symptoms which might help Carr to persuade James to relase him.]

L. Davies, sometime servant of Sir T. Overbury now of Sir H. May, his Examination before the Lord Coke.

Saith, that he hath heard his master say that he would have gone ambassador, but that my Lord of Rochester [Carr] dissuaded him. He hath seen some letters of Sir T. Overbury's, wherein he wrote that the Lord of Rochester was even with him; but he thinks he (i.e. the Lord Rochester) never saw those passages.

Davies's testimony as to what he had heard Overbury say about what Carr had said to him was, like most of the testimony given, pure hearsay. A modern definition of hearsay is: Hearsay is evidence of a statement which is made by other than a witness who is testifying, which is offered to prove the truth of the matter stated. If, for example, Smith was being tried for murdering Brown, and Black testified that Jones had told him that Smith had murdered Brown, that would be hearsay evidence and would be inadmissible. If, however, Jones were being sued for criminal libel because he had made the statement about Smith to Black, then one question at issue would be whether the statement had actually been made by Jones (as distinguished from whether Smith had really murdered Brown), and on that issue Black's testimony would be admissible. An example of such admissible evidence as used in this trial was the testimony given later by Sir D. Wood. Frances had asked him to assassinate Overbury, which was in the nature of an *act* done by her.[11]

Lord of Som. I pray you, my Lords, note he says I never saw those passages.

Mr. Att. It is true: For those letters were lost; but after found by him, who knew them to be his master Sir T. Overbury's hand.

Sir Thomas Overbury's first Letter to my Lord Somerset.

"Is this the fruit of my care and love to you? Be these the fruits of common secrets, common dangers? As a man, you cannot suffer me to lie in this misery; yet your behavior betrays you. All I entreat of you is, that you will free me from this place, and that we may part friends. Drive me not to extremities, lest I should say something that you and I both repent. And I pray God that you may not repent the omission of this my counsel, in this place, whence I now write this letter."

L. Wentworth. How did you know these letters were sent from him to my Lord of Somerset?

L. Coke. They were found in a cabinet, among some other things, left in trust by my Lord of Somerset with Sir R. Cotton, and thus they were discovered. Sir R. Cotton, fearing searches, delivers them to a friend of his in Holborn, one Mrs. Farneforth; she, to the intent they might be safely kept, sent them to a merchant's house in Cheapside, where some nine months before she had lodged, and desired that they might safely be kept for her, pretending they were some writings that concerned her jointure. On St. Thomas's day she herself comes to have them again, saying, she must carry them to her counsel to peruse. He said, "If you will suffer me to open it before you, and that there be nothing else, you shall have them." But she by no means would consent to the breaking of it open. Then he answered, "It is a troublesome time; I will go to my Lord Chief Justice, and if he find no other writings than such as concern you, you shall have them again." So coming to my chamber, and not finding me within (for I was gone to St. Paul's to the sermon), he went to my Lord Zouch, one of the appointed commissioners for this cause, who himself alone would not break it up, but came to St. Paul's to me; where in a by-room we broke it up, and in it found these letters, and divers from my Lord of Northampton, besides many other papers.

L. Zouch. I affirm this relation of my Lord Coke's to be true. [Even in that time of little regard for the rights of defendants in political trials, it could hardly have been proper for one who was, in effect, a juror to give testimony].

Sir Thomas Overbury's second letter to my Lord of Somerset.

"This comes under seal; and therefore shall be bold. You told my brother Lidcote, that unreverend style might make you neglect me. With what face could you do this, who know you owe me for all the fortune, wit, and understanding that you have?" (Here were inserted some borrowed names.)

Mr. Att. Under these false names they meant great persons; Julius, the King; Dominic, my Lord of Northampton; Unclius [Ductius?], my Lord of Canterbury.

The rest of the Letter.

"And yet pretend the reason why you seek not my liberty, to be my unreverend style; whilst, in the meantime, you sacrifice me to your woman, still holding friendship with those that brought me hither. You bade my brother Lidcote keep my desire of liberty secret: Yet this shall not serve your turn; for you and I, ere it be long, will come to a public trial of another nature. I upon the rack, and you at your ease: And yet I must say nothing! When I heard (notwithstanding my misery) how you went to your woman, curled your hair, preferred Gibbe into the bedchamber, and in the meantime send me nineteen projects, how I should cast about for my liberty; and give me a long account of the pains you have taken, and then go out of town. I wonder to see how you should neglect him, to whom such secrets of all kinds have passed: And suffer my mother and sisters to lie here in town, expecting my liberty; my brother Lidcote to be in a manner quite overthrown, in respect of my imprisonment; and yet you stand stupid: Nor have neither servant nor friend suffered to come to me. Well, all this vacation I have written the story betwixt you and me: How I have lost my friends for your sake; what hazard I have run; what secrets have passed betwixt us; how after you had won that woman by my letters, and then you concealed all your after-proceedings from me; and how upon this there came many breaches betwixt us; of the vow you made to be even with me, and sending for me twice that day that I was caught in the trap, persuading me that it was a plot of my enemies to send me beyond sea; and urging me not to accept it, assuring me to free me from any long trouble. On Tuesday I made an end of this, and on Friday sent it to a friend of mine under eight seals; and if you persist still to use me thus, assure yourself it shall be published. Whether I live or die, your shame shall never die, but ever remain to the world, to make you the most odious man living."

H. Payton and L. Davies. We both, upon our oaths, know this to be Sir T. Overbury's hand.

Simcocks's Examination before my Lord Coke, written with his own hand.

He says that Weston many times, when Sir T. Overbury was in the Tower, told him that my Lord of Somerset charged him to look to Overbury well; for if ever he came out, one of us two must die.

L. Som. I would fain know whether Weston were examined, or no.

L. Wentworth. How long is it since this familiar acquaintance betwixt Simcocks and Weston?

Simcocks. He and I were of ancient and familiar acquaintance long since.

Mr. Attorney. Weston had continually access to my Lord, had rewards from him: My Lord charged him to look to Overbury well. It could not be his marriage that made him so much fear; but what the secrets were that caused it, it is not the work of this day. Now to show that the greatest matters of state were communicated to him, read Davies.

L. Davies examined. There was a packet of letters, and sealed, which as he takes, came from Sir. J. Digby, directed to the King; and his master Sir T. Overbury opened it, took brief notes for my Lord of Somerset, and sealing it again, sent both the notes and packets to him. Another of this he saw his master had at Newmarket from Sir Thomas Edmunds to the King, out of which, after he had taken extracts, he sealed it up again, and sent back by this examinee to my Lord Somerset.

Mr. Attorney. I will not now, my Lords, endeavor to press the greatness of this offense: But I urge it thus, that you may see there were no mean secrets betwixt my Lord and Sir T. Overbury, that might rather cause him to fear him, than the hindrance of his marriage. If that had been it alone, his going beyond sea would have served the turn.

These comments by Bacon on the evidence were not intended to clarify it but were argumentative or inflamatory. Today such comments would not be permitted during the taking of evidence. Many remarks of the same nature will be noticeable if they are watched for as the trial continues.

L. of Som. exam. says, That amongst many other characters for names, that passed between Sir T. Overbury and him, Simonist was for Sir H. Neville, Wolfy for the now Lord Treasurer, Ductius for my Lord of Canterbury.

Mr. Attorney. In good faith, these two made plays of all the world besides themselves; but though it were a play then, it hath proved tragical since.

A Letter of My Lord of Northampton to my
Lord of Somerset.

"Now all is concluded about the form of the . . . [nullity], I doubt not but God will bless the next bargain. I hope hereafter to find better pen and ink in this lady's chamber. [Any double entendre here?] Be still happy." Underneath subscribed, "H. Northampton," and "I am witness to this bargain. Fra. Howard."

This letter was showed my Lord of Somerset, and he confessed the hand.

Mr. Attorney. For the second branch that I mean to follow; and that is, that you used the means to expose him to the Tower, and there to keep him close prisoner. It is a chain of eight links, and shall be showed you upon eight points of the compass. But before we come to these, it is to be considered, that as no consultation is ripe in an hour, so no more was theirs: For they purposed at first to have taken away his life by assault. And Franklin tells you the cause of this malice.

Franklin examined before my Lord Coke, but not upon oath.

He saith, that my Lady Somerset said the cause of this hatred of Sir T. Overbury was, that he would pry so far into my Lord of Somerset, that he would put him down. [In effect, Franklin said Frances said that Carr said he hated Overbury for this reason. The statement was not only hearsay but was not made under oath. It was made by a person since dead, convicted for the same offense now being tried. It would be totally inadmissible in today's trials. So much of the evidence was in this category that it is unnecessary to point out other individual instances.]

Sir D. Wood examined before Lord Coke.

He saith, my Lady Somerset, knowing there was some discontent betwixt Overbury and him, in respect of a suit that he crossed him in, told him, that if he would kill Sir T. Overbury he should have £ 1,000 and besides, she would make his greatest enemy to become his greatest friend, and he knew no enemy he had in Court but my Lord of Rochester. He answered that if my Lord of Rochester would give him his hand, or but pass his word, if he did it, that he should escape and have his pardon, he would do it. Upon this she paused, and desired some time to give her answer; and when he came again to her, she told him that could not be, but promised all favor possible unto him, and warranted him to go on upon her life. [Wood's testimony concerning Frances's last words to him as it appears in the manuscript copy was much less favorable to Bacon's case than the words appearing above. That copy states only that Wood said merely that the assurance by Somerset that he would be pardoned "being denied him, . . . he refused to undertake it, and so the enterprise was quashed."]

L. of Som. examined saith, it was once resolved somebody in Court should fall out with Overbury, and offer him some affront; but that was not followed.

Mr. Attorney. Note, my Lords, he does not say it was disliked. And now to the puddle of blood, the first link of which is, that the means to entrap Overbury for the Tower, was by the means of my Lord of Somerset.

Sir Dudley Diggs sworn.

Sir T. Overbury once told me, that he went to undertake the employment offered him to go beyond sea; but afterwards he sent me word by Sir R. Maunsel, that he had changed his mind. And Sir R. Maunsel told me further, that he saw a letter from the Lord of Somerset to Overbury, that dissuaded him from that course. Seeing Mr. Attorney hath called me so far out of the country for this small testimony, I wish Sir R. Maunsel were here to justify it.

My Lord of Somerset's Declaration in writing to the King.

Being told by my Lord Chief Justice that I was indicted, and was shortly to expect my arraignment, I did not then believe him; for I did not look for that way. Your Majesty hath three kingdoms, wherein to exercise the prerogative of your power, and but few that taste of the first of your favors; in which number I did think myself, if not the first, yet inferior to very few. And having committed no offense against your person, nor the State, I hope your Majesty will not for this bring me to a public trial, which for my reputation's cause, I humbly desire to avoid. Grace truly given may be a benefit; for it is not enough to give life, and not to save reputation. But if I must come to my trial, knowing the presumptions may be strong against me, in respect I consented to, and endeavored the imprisonment of Sir T. Overbury (though I designed it for his reformation, not his ruin), I therefore desire your Majesty's mercy, and that you will be pleased to give me leave to dispose of my lands and goods to my wife and child, and graciously to pardon her, having confessed the fact. For myself, being uncertain how I shall be judged upon presumptions, I humbly desire that in the meantime you will be pleased to give my Lord Hays and Sir Robert Carr leave to come to me.

Mr. Attorney. The second link is, how that Elwes came to be Lieutenant of the Tower by your means; and yet that must have a color; my Lord of Shrewsbury and Lord Chamberlain must prefer him to you as their friend, though it was resolved before he should have the place.

Sir J. Elwes examined, but not on oath. He saith, Sir T. Monson told him that Wade was to be removed; and that if he succeeded Sir W. Wade, he must bleed, that is, give £ 2,000. And ten days after Wade was removed he came into the place and paid £1,400 of the money at his uncle Alderman Elwes's house to Dr. Campian.

Mr. Attorney. You may see they had ciphers for money. He must bleed; a strange presage! And as it is impossible to serve God and mammon, so in that kind it is hard to serve a king.

Sir Thomas Monson examined, but not on oath, saith, my Lord of Northampton, upon the displacing of Wade, moved the King for Sir J. Elwes; and that he directed Sir J. Elwes to go to the Lords of Shrewsbury and Pembroke, to move my Lord of Somerset to speak for him to the King.

Sir Jervis Elwes examined. When it was resolved Wade should be removed, and he to succeed him, then he was advised to desire my Lord of Somerset to move for him; which he did accordingly, but took that only to be but for a color, because it was resolved before.

Mr. Attorney. Now the third link concerns the placing of Weston for his keeper.

Sir Thomas Monson examined. Saith, he recommended Weston to the service of Sir J. Elwes, and to keep Sir T. Overbury, upon the Countess of Somerset's entreaty; and further saith, that my Lord of Northampton was acquainted with the placing of him.

R. Weston examined. My Lord and Lady Somerset gave good words of him to the Lieutenant.

This is a good example of the improper use made at all these trials of scraps from Weston's various examinations and confessions, which if read in context with the remainder of the documents would have had a much different meaning—again, improper procedure today and very unfair even then. Had all Weston's examinations been read, they would have showed that if Overbury was poisoned, it was not done by Weston (the clyster having been the probable cause of death), would have discredited most of Simcocks's testimony, would have contradicted Davis about the white arsenic alleged to have been sent Overbury by Carr and would have contained much to discredit Weston's statements in their entirety.[12]

L. of Som. examined. He denies the knowledge of Weston, either before his coming into the Tower, or since.

Simcocks examined. Weston, during the time Sir T. Overbury was in his keeping, came often to my Lord, had much money of him, and wondered Sir T. Overbury had so good an opinion of my Lord; and thought he had not so much wit as the world esteemed, for there was no man hindered his liberty but he; and whenever he came to my Lord, he might use such means as Rawlins his man must not know.

(In this interim a scaffold broke, and there was a great noise and confusion; but after silence was proclaimed, all hushed and quiet.)

Mr. Attorney. All the confessions of Weston were taken before conviction, and these last two witnesses are merely to his denying the knowledge of Weston. Now for the fourth link, which is the placing and displacing officers.

Sir Jervis Elwes examined. Saith, that Overbury was committed April 30th, and May 6th himself came to be Lieutenant of the Tower; and that Weston was preferred to be Sir T. Overbury's keeper May 7th; and that all this time he served, he never had wages from him.

Mr. Attorney. Now the fifth link or point of the compass I promised to show you, was, that this must not be done suddenly, but by degrees; and so he must be poisoned leisurely, to avoid suspicion. And in the mean space you entertained his father and mother with frivolous hopes; and yet indeed hindered and made opposition (but underhand) to all the means that were used for his delivery.

Mr. Overbury, the father, sworn. After my son was committed, I heard that he was very sick; I went to the Court and delivered a petition to the King: The effect whereof was, that in respect of my son's sickness some physicians might have access unto him. The King answered, that his own physician should go to him, and then instantly sent him word by Sir W. Button, that his physician should presently go. Upon this I only addressed myself to my Lord of Somerset, and none else; who said my son should be presently delivered, but dissuaded me from preferring any more petitions to the King; which notwithstanding, I (seeing his freedom still delayed) did deliver a petition to the King to that purpose; who said I should have a present answer. And my Lord of Somerset told me, he should be suddenly relieved; but with this, that neither I nor my wife must press to see him, because that might protract his delivery; nor deliver any more petitions to the King, because that might stir his enemies up against him. And then he wrote a letter to my wife, to dissuade her from any longer stay in London.

My Lord of Somerset's letter to Mrs. Overbury.

"Mrs. Overbury: Your stay here in town can nothing avail your son's delivery; therefore I would advise you to retire into the country, and doubt not before your coming home you shall hear he is a free man."

Mr. Overbury. Then after my son's death, he wrote another letter to me.

My Lord of Somerset's letter to Mr. Overbury.

"Sir: Your son's love to me got him the malice of many, and they cast those knots on his fortune that have cost him his life; so, in a kind, there is none guilty of his death but I, and you can have no more cause to commiserate the death of a son, than I of a friend. But though he be dead, you shall find me as ready as ever I was to do all the courtesies that possibly I can to you and your wife, or your children. In the meantime, I desire your pardon from you and your wife for your lost son, though I esteem my loss the greater. And for his brother that is in France, I desire his return, that he may succeed his brother in my love." [In the manuscript copy the advice to retire to the country said above to be in the first letter does not appear, and the second letter is addressed to Mrs. Overbury, containing a promise by

Carr, omitted above, to defray the expenses of another son, at that time in France.]

Mr. Attorney. By this you see my Lord's dissimulation. And I think he was a piece of a lawyer, by his insinuating with his next kindred, for fear of appeals. Now to come to the sixth link, which shows how light my Lord of Somerset made both of Sir T. Overbury's fortunes and sickness, read Simcocks.

Simcocks examined. Saith, that Weston told him he wondered Sir T. Overbury should have so great confidence in my Lord of Somerset, and think that he loved him so well; for he knew that he could not abide him, and thought of nothing less than his liberty.

Sir John Lidcote sworn. Saith, he desired my Lord of Somerset that either he or Sir R. Killigrew might have leave to see Sir Thomas Overbury in his sickness, which my Lord obtained from the King. And so they had a warrant from my Lord of Northampton, and some other Councillors, to see him; and found him very sick in his bed, his hand dry, his speech hollow. And at this time he desired me to write his will; I proposed to come to him again the next day. Now being ready to depart, the Lieutenant going out before, Overbury asked me softly this question, whether Somerset juggled with him, or not? But I then told him, as I believed, that I thought not. But the Lieutenant looking back, and perceiving that some whispering had passed, swore that I had done more than I could justify. But afterwards, coming to press my Lord of Somerset about Sir T. Overbury, I perceived he dealt not plainly with him. And once speaking with my Lord about him, he gave a counterfeit sigh (as this deponent conceived), for at that instant he smiled in my face.

Mr. Attorney. The seventh link is to show you the manner of his keeping; which was close prisoner in the Tower, his offense being only a contempt: And [as to] who was the author of this, read Sir Thomas Monson.

Sir Thomas Monson examined, but not upon oath, saith, My Lord of Northampton and my Lord of Somerset gave directions to the Lieutenant of the Tower to keep him close prisoner.

L. Davies examined, Saith, That he was a suitor to my Lord of Somerset, that he might wait upon his master Sir T. Overbury in the Tower, though he were shut up with him. But my Lord answered, he shortly purposed to procure his total liberty, and this might hinder it.

Mr. Attorney. Now the eighth and last link is, in the interim that Overbury in the Tower was plied with poisons, my Lord thirsted after the news, to know what became of him, and continual posts went between him and my Lady; and all this while bore him in hand with other pretenses.

Franklin (but not upon oath) saith, that being with my Lady Essex, she told him that she had that day received a letter from my Lord of Rochester, wherein he wrote that if Weston did not presently dispatch [him], Sir T. Overbury would be out.

Sir Jervis Elwes examined. Saith, he received divers letters from my Lady Essex, wherein she desired to know how Overbury did, that she might certify to the Court.

Lord of Som. examined. Saith, that there passed many letters betwixt my Lady and him, but not concerning Overbury. But then desired that this point might be altered; for it might be that some letters concerning Overbury might have then passed betwixt them.

Mr. Attorney. My Lord knew not whether any of these letters were extant, and therefore desired that this might be altered.

Lobell, an apothecary, a Frenchman, saith, that coming to my Lord of Somerset, he asked him of Overbury and how he did, and he said, ill. Another time also he sent for him to inquire about Overbury, and then he answered him, that he was ill, but hoped he might recover. "What," says my Lord, "do you think he would recover if he were at liberty?" And he answered, "Yes." Again, my Lord sent for him a third time, and carrying him into the gallery at Whitehall, asked him how Overbury did. He answered, he was very sick, and further added, he found him ill before the twenty-fifth of June, that he came to him. [According to the manuscript copy, Lobell also said in his testimony that Carr asked him to write to Dr. Maiot (Mayerne?) concerning a physic to be given to Overbury. Perhaps because it might have gained Carr a little public favor, it was omitted by Bacon.]

L. of Som. examined. Denies that ever he saw Lobell but once, at Theobalds.

Mr. Attorney. Here again you see my Lord falsified; but it seems, imagining or not knowing that Lobell could say more against him than he hath done, he denied the knowledge of him, as he did of Weston.

L. Coke. It was doubted [suspected] Lobell might be a delinquent, and therefore I dared not examine him upon oath, no more than I did Franklin. But when in their testimony they accuse themselves, it is as strong as if upon oath.

Mr. Attorney. Now in respect Overbury had a working brain, my Lord of Northampton must in show negotiate about his delivery, and the terms of his coming out, whilst they intended his poisoning: That was real, and the other but in pretense.

My Lord of Northampton's first letter to my
Lord of Somerset.

"In this business concerning Overbury there must be a main drift, and a real charge: You may imagine the meaning."

My Lord of Northampton's second letter to my
Lord of Somerset.

"I yesterday spent two hours in prompting the Lieutenant, with as great caution as I could, and find him to be very perfect in his part. And I long exceedingly to hear his report of this adventure."

My Lord of Northampton's third letter to my
Lord of Somerset.

"You need not use many instruments, so long as I am in town, with the Lieutenant."

My Lord of Northampton's fourth letter to my
Lord of Somerset.

"I cannot deliver with what caution and discretion the Lieutenant hath undertaken Overbury. But for his conclusion, I do and ever will love him the better; which was this, that either Overbury shall recover and do good offices betwixt my Lord of Suffolk and you, which if he do not, you shall have reason to count him a knave; or else, that he shall not recover at all, which he thinks the most sure and happy change of all; for he finds sometimes from Overbury many flashes of a strong affection to some enemies of his." [These letters could well have referred only to the keeping of Overbury completely isolated from outside contacts — there is no necessary implication that they referred to a poison plot.]

L. of Som. I acknowledge these letters to be my Lord of Northampton's and all those that I sent to him were delivered me after his death by Sir R. Cotton, all which, the evening before my commitment to the Dean of Westminster's, I burned.

Mr. Attorney. These letters of Northampton were found in the box Sir R. Cotton gave Mrs. Farneforth. And here my part ends, and that that rests behind, I leave to the two serjeants.

L.H.S. My Lord, you have heard what hath been urged against you, and may imagine that there rests much behind: And therefore you had best confess the truth; otherwise you will but more and more wind in yourself.

L. of Som. My Lord, I came with a resolution to defend myself. . . .

Serj. Montague. May it please your grace, my Lord High Steward of England, it falls to my part to uncover those secrets that were concurrent and present with the murder of Sir T. Overbury. And there be three things that make evident that my Lord of Somerset was the principal procurer: 1. A powder that was sent Sir T. from your own hand, which was poison, and taken by him. 2. Poison in tarts, which you occasioned to be sent. 3. That you thirsted after . . . success, and wondered that he was no sooner dispatched. . . . [As Bacon did in his speech introducing the evidence over which he was in charge, Montague here outlined the pertinent part of the story as we know it and as it appeared as the evidence was given; it is omitted.]

Franklin's examination. Mrs. Turner desired him to buy some of the strongest poisons he could get; which he did, and brought them to Mrs. Turner and my Lady, and at that time they both swore him to secrecy. And afterwards he perceived that these poisons were sent to the Tower; and amongst the rest a kind of white powder called arsenic, which she told him was sent Overbury in a letter; and after showed him, and told him of many more poisons that were sent and to be sent by Weston to Overbury. And those poisons which my Lady showed him were wrapped in a paper, written with a Roman hand. And they tried some of the poisons upon a cat, or a dog, which was wonderfully tormented and died.

Weston's examination. My Lady told him that he should be well rewarded; but before she could procure that, the fact must be done; and that he had already given him as many poisons as would poison twelve men.

L. of Som. examined. Saith, that he caused a vomit to be sent him at his own request, which was a white powder; and it was the same that he had had before of Sir R. Killigrew, and sent by Rawlins; and it may be that this second sent by Davies was in a letter.

L. Davies examined. Saith, that three weeks after Sir Jervis Elwes came to be Lieutenant of the Tower, my Lord sent, in a letter by him, a white powder to Sir T. Overbury; and [said] that it would make him a little sick, so he might have the better opportunity to speak for him to the King; and he saw this letter. Next day Weston told him how sick Overbury had been, and showed him what loathsome stuff he had vomited, which he would have had carried to the Lord Somerset; but Weston would not let him, saying that it was an unfit sight to show him.

H. Payton examined. Saith, that this powder gave Sir Thomas 50 or 60 stools and vomits for four or five days.

There was never any acceptable proof offered that Carr sent Overbury a poisonous white powder. Killigrew said he had sent only three powders to Carr; two of these were accounted for, one having been taken by Carr himself and one lost. A third went to Overbury and had the anticipated effect. Killigrew's statement is in the manuscript copy but not in Hargrave. The manuscript copy also contains reference to a letter written by Overbury to Carr that the powder which he had received from the earl had agreed with him but that, nevertheless, he did not intend to take any more powders of that kind, which letter was verified by Cotton. Query: Why does the official report refer neither to that letter nor to Cotton's testimony? The only real testimony that Carr sent any white powder to Overbury other than the one in question is that of Davis, Overbury's own servant (unlikely enough that Carr would choose him to take poison to his master), and that testimony is contradicted by Weston. Further, the letter to which Davis testified is, according to Amos, in exact agreement with a letter testified by Rawlins to have been given by Carr to him for delivery to Overbury, enclosing the wholesome powder supplied by Killigrew, and with the word from Carr that it was to aid in Overbury's release. The likeliest explanation for all this confusion is that of the three powders sent by Killigrew to Carr, one was lost, one was taken by Carr, the third was sent to Overbury either at his own request or to induce the symptoms of illness intended to make him seem sick enough to procure his release, that it was delivered by Rawlins and that there is no persuasive evidence that Carr sent him any other powder.

> Serj. Mont. Four several juries have found that this powder was poison, and of this poison Sir T. Overbury died; now for the proof of the poisoned tarts.
> La. of Som. examined. She saith, she knoweth of no tarts were sent Sir T. Overbury, but either from herself or my Lord.
> Sir Jervis Elwes examined. Saith, by "letters" my Lady meant poison, but the word was then used to clear his eyes.

> The Lady Somerset's letter to Sir Jervis Elwes.
> "I was bid to bid you say that these tarts came not from me; and again, I was bid to tell you that you must take heed of the tarts because there be 'letters' in them, and therefore neither give your wife nor children of them, but of the wine you may, for there are no 'letters' in it; Sir T. Monson will come from the Court this day, and then we shall have other news."

> La. of Som. examined. Saith, that by "letters" she meant poison.

This, too, was dishonest. Frances, when asked what she meant by "letters," had said "perhaps" she meant poison. She was, of course, badly confused by that time and was not thinking clearly. Moreover, we are told in the Domestic State Papers that examinations of Monson and Elwes on October 3 and 5, 1615, reveal that when Monson recommended Weston to Elwes, he warned him to search all tarts and jellies for *letters,* and, further, that numerous letters to and from Overbury went into and from the Tower in jellies and tarts.

> Serj. Mont. Now for my Lord's haste to spur this on (and here I end), read Franklin's Examination.
> Franklin's examination. Saith, in a letter which my Lady told him was sent her from my Lord, there were these words, that he wondered things were not yet dispatched, and that he thinks was meant about Overbury, by reason of her then speeches to him, and present sending for Weston.

This testimony was relied on heavily by Bacon and, if true, might indicate guilty knowledge. Carr's defense has been criticized as being weak on this point and not sufficiently emphasizing what was known to be true—that Franklin was a villain and a liar. Furthermore, as has been noted, since Franklin had been convicted of the same crime, his confession was inadmissible. The manuscript copy contains a paragraph from Carr's speech that was omitted from the Hargrave version and that nullifies the criticism. It reads: "The confession of Franklin, who said he dare not take his oath upon the Bible that I consented to Overbury's death, who further said that I was in an inner room, as he knew by my voice, at Whitehall last Michaelmas, when Frances sent ... for him to tell him that Weston was apprehended, who yet again affirmed that he had seen divers letters of mine unto Frances during the progress of Overbury's imprisonment, concerning plots, businesses, etc., I humbly move your Lordships to conceive that, being the most affectionate to Frances, ... I had much occasion to write to the Countess of secrets of moment, perhaps concerning Overbury, yet not coasted on the red sea of blood or death, which that perjured Franklin (by a letter of mine, which he avouched he did read) did prove without all contradiction. The letter was urged by you, Serjeant Mon-

tague—namely, that Overbury was likely to come out within these
few days, if Weston did not play his part, etc., whereupon the
Countess sent for this Franklin. If this letter is to be produced, if
Frances ever confessed that I did send such a letter unto her, I am
then guilty and convicted without excuse; but I call Heaven now to
witness I never wrote any such a letter, neither can any such be
produced. Let not you then, my noble Peers, rely upon the memo-
rative relation of such a villain as Franklin, neither think it a hard
request, when I humbly desire you to weigh my protestations, my
oath upon my honor and conscience, against the lewd information
of so bad a miscreant; for, my Lords, both in his life and death he
proved himself atheistical."

Serj. Crew. My part is now to discover those acts that succeeded the fact, and then my Lord begins to sew fig leaves: 1.
Practices to suppress all testimonies. 2. To surprise all letters. 3.
To get a pardon, and desires a pattern of the most large pardon. . . . [Crew outlined the facts he contended constituted an
effort by Carr to suppress the testimony of Franklin, contended
that Carr was in the next room while Frances was telling Franklin
what to say if he were examined, accused Carr of suppressing
and changing pertinent letters and documents, fraudulently obtaining some and instructing Cotton to alter others, told of Carr's
effort to obtain a pardon, supposedly to cover past errors in
matters of state but actually broad enough to cover the murder
and, finally, alleged that Carr had requested the king for leave to
dispose of his lands to his wife and child. For proof of all this, he
first had Franklin's testimony read.]

Franklin's examination. When my Lord of Somerset came to
town, after Weston's apprehension, he (Franklin) was sent for to
the Cock Pit, and there my Lady swore him again to secrecy, told
him Weston was taken and that it was likely he should be so
shortly, and that they should all be hanged. Then retiring into an
inner room, to speak with one (whom he verily believes to be my
Lord of Somerset), she came again and told him that the Lords,
if they examined him, would put him in hope of a pardon upon
confession, "But," said she, "believe them not; for when they
have got out of you what they would, we shall all be hanged."
"Nay," saith Mrs. Turner, "Madam, I will not be hanged for you
both."

Examination (not upon oath) of Mary Erwin, Mrs. Turner's
maid.

Mrs. Turner sent her for Franklin, to bring him to the Cock Pit, at ten o'clock at night; and is sure that night my Lord of Somerset came from Court, and was at the Cock Pit when she came.

Lady Som. examined. She confesseth all that Franklin said concerning her discourse with him, and that my Lord was with her that night at the Cock Pit.

Mr. Serj. Crew. Next follows the proof for surprising letters.

L. Davies [Overbury's servant] examined, Saith, that in summer last my Lord sent Rawlins to him, to desire that if he had any letters, either from my Lord to Sir T., or from him to my Lord, that he would send them by him, which he did; and for this my Lord did afterwards send him by Rawlins £30.

George Errat the Constable's Examination.

Saith, that Poulter, a messenger, brought him a warrant from my Lord of Somerset, to break open and search a house for certain writings, which were pretended to be one Mrs. Hide's, a sister of Mrs. Turner's; and that he showed him a part of the warrant only, but not all; so that for that cause he would not execute it. Whereupon, Poulter got smiths himself to break open the house and doors, and found in the cellar a box and bag of writings, where he saw the name of Mrs. Turner; and those were carried to my Lord.

L. of Som. For these letters, Sir R. Cotton delivered them me back after my Lord of Northampton's death; and concerning the dates, you need not trouble yourself, for it now grows late, and I shall have very little time to answer for myself. I confess, Sir R. Cotton delivered me back those letters I had sent my Lord of Northampton, and that I burned them, and that some parts were cut off as impertinent.

Sir R. Cotton examined. Saith, My Lord delivered into his hands many of Sir T. Overbury's letters, and that he cut and dated them by my Lord's direction, and that he put in dates the next day to some of the letters, after Weston's arraignment.

Mr. Serj. Crew. I desire my Lord will be pleased to look upon this book of Overbury's letters. And now for the copy of the largest pardon ["broadest" pardon. This was the second pardon requested — not the one that the Chancellor had refused to seal]:

Sir R. Cotton saith, that at my Lord of Somerset's entreaty, a little before Michaelmas last, he got him a draft of the largest pardon, and the precedent was of one that King Henry VIII granted to Cardinal Wolsey; and if he desired such a one, I told him the best way was to follow precedent. The pardon was read:

Wherein, amongst other offenses, before and after, of small account, treason and murder be foisted in. [This might be explained as merely a continued attempt to obtain a pardon, since the one James had signed before the apothecary's boy had confessed and the investigation commenced was ineffective for lack of the seal, although it was now requested in broader form.]

Mr. Serj. Crew. And this was it that made Weston fear that the net was for the little fishes, and that the great ones could break through.

Alderman Bowles examined. Saith, that after he had persuaded Weston from standing mute, he [Weston] told him that he feared the net was laid for the little fishes, and that the great ones would break through.

Mr. Serj. Crew. The last thing I urge, is my Lord's declaration to the King, which I desire should be read (the same that were noted before, after he understood by my Lord Coke that he was to be arraigned).

Mr. Attorney. You see, my Lords, in this declaration of my Lord Somerset there is a brink of confession; I would to God it had a bottom. He urges that in respect he hath formerly been so great in the King's favor, and had never committed any treason, neither against his person nor state, that he should never have been called to an account for this fault, though he had been guilty; that grace timely given is a benefit; and that it is not only enough to give life, but to save reputation; but if he must be urged, then he desires his wife might be pardoned, having confessed the fact; and that if he must be put upon the hazard of a trial, the King will before give him leave to dispose of his lands and goods to the use of his wife and child; and that in the meantime he will give my Lord Hay and Sir R. Carr leave to come to him. [The complete "declaration" was read earlier in the trial. Note how this summarization omits the parts which might help Carr's case.]

Mr. Serj. Crew. This declaration is an implicative confession.

Mr. Attorney. I think there is none here but wonders, seeing that all poisons be works of darkness, how this should so clearly appear: But it seems, his greatness in fortune caused this grossness in offending.

L.H.S. My Lord of Somerset hath behaved himself modestly in the hearing, and only this (before you speak for yourself), by way of advice, I will say unto you, in giving you two examples. Your wife, that yesterday confessed the fact, and there is great hope of the King's mercy, if you now mar not that which she made. On the contrary, Byron, who when the King of France used all the means he possibly could to bring him to the acknowledgment of his offense, which if he had done, there was no question to be made of the King's grace. And I think there never was, nor is, a more gracious and merciful king than our master. But Byron still persisting in the denial of his fact, you know his end.

Carr took up his defense under a heavy handicap. It was 7:00 P.M., dark enough for the lord high steward to halt the proceeding while candles were brought. Everyone was tired and hungry—probably Carr most of all—and many of the spectators left during the pause. Carr, not too bright at this sort of argument to begin with, was plainly confused by the mass of testimony and oratorical charges and accusations that had been fired at him for nine hours without relief. It is a wonder he did as well as he did.

> L. of Som. I am confident in my own cause and am come hither to defend it. And in respect the King's counsel have been so long in speaking against me, that neither my memory nor notes will give me leave to answer every particular in order, I will begin with some of the last things that they seemed most to urge against me, and so answer the rest that I think do anything at all touch me.
>
> For the powder that was sent Overbury to make him sick, that so I might have the better occasion to speak for him to the King for that purpose, he himself desired it, and upon his letter I sent it. And though it be true that I consented to his imprisonment, to the end he should make no impediment in my marriage; yet I had a care of his lodgings, that they should be where he might have the best air, and windows both to the water and within the Tower, so that he might have liberty to speak with whom he would. So you see it was against my intention to have him close prisoner. Whereas the breach of friendship betwixt Overbury and me is used for an aggravation against me; it is no great wonder for friends sometimes to fall out, and least of all with him; for I think he had never a friend in his life that he would not sometimes fall out with, and give offense unto, and this they termed insolence in him, but I give it a better name. For the great trust and communication of secrets between Overbury and me, and for the extracts that he took of ambassadors' letters, I confess this; I knew his ability, and what I did was by the King's commission. For other secrets, there were never any betwixt us.
>
> And for his fashion of braving both in words and writing, there was none that knew it better, nor feared it less than myself.

At that time he was in disgrace with the Queen, and for that cause was enforced for a time to absent himself from Court, and this was for some particular miscarriage of his towards her Majesty; and though I labored his reconcilement and return, yet he with main violent terms laid the cause of his disgrace upon me. And another time my Lord of Salisbury [Cecil] sent for him, and told him that if he would depend upon his favor, he would presently help him with a suit that should benefit him £2,000, which presently Overbury, coming to me, told me of: To which I answered, he did not need to rely upon anybody but me; and that, if he would, he might command my purse, and presently have more than that; and so he had. And yet afterwards, upon some causeless discontent, in a great passion he said that his love to me had put him out of my Lord of Salisbury's favor, and made him lose £2,000.

Whereas it was urged that I caused him to refuse the employment that was imposed upon him, it is not so, for I was very willing he should have undertaken it, but he not. My Lord of Canterbury moved him to it, but not without my privity; for I should have been glad to have removed him, both in respect of my marriage and his insolence. But Overbury came to me and said, "I will tell Sir Dudley Diggs I will undertake this embassage, that he may so return answer to my Lord of Canterbury, but then you must write to me not to do so, and so take it upon you."

Whereas it is pretended that I should cause poisoned tarts to be sent him to the Tower, my wife in her confession saith, that there were none sent but either by me or her, and some were wholesome and some not: Then it must needs follow, that the good ones were those which I sent and the bad hers.

L. Lisle. If you had sent him good tarts, you should have seen them conveyed by a trusty messenger.

L. Compton. My Lady, in her letter to the Lieutenant, writes, "I was bid to bid you do this." Who should bid her? [More probably Northampton than Carr.]

Mr. Serj. Montague. The continual letters between my Lord and her argue that [it was Carr].

L. of Som. If Franklin knew me so well, and that I was privy to the plot, why should then my wife and I (as he pretends) when he was there, speak so closely, and always out of his hearing and sight? But for Overbury, my furthest intent in his imprisonment was that he should be no impediment to my marriage; and this I communicated to my Lord of Northampton and Elwes.

Serj. Montague. You could not couple yourself worse than with them two.

L. of Som. Whereas Simcocks says, from the relation of Weston, that he so often came to me, I protest I never saw him till after Overbury's death, and then Rawlins brought him to me.

Serj. Crew. Sir Jervis Elwes in his examination saith that Weston many times told him that my Lord of Somerset many times sent for him: And for this purpose you shall have Weston's examination.

Weston's examination. Saith, that my Lord of Somerset many times sent him directions, before Overbury's going to the Tower, to appoint meetings betwixt him and my Lady.

L. of Som. This may hold, and yet that I never spoke to him: So for those messages he spoke of, he might receive directions from me by a third person. And for that which Payton alleges about the powder which I sent, and made Sir T. Overbury so sick, that powder I sent was one of them which I received from Sir R. Killigrew.

Serj. Crew. But this, my Lord, was none of the powders you received from Sir R. Killigrew, for you had three from him: The first was lost; the second you sent him by Rawlins; and the third yourself took at Buly. Now a fourth, which was sent by Davis, was that that made him so sick, and gave him so many stools; and that was poison, and sent three weeks after that that Rawlins carried.

Sir R. Killigrew saith, that my Lord desired him to give him powders, which he himself sometimes used to take for a vomit; but he thought it had been only for himself, not that he had had a purpose to send it to Sir T. Overbury; and that my Lord never had of this powder of him but thrice.

Mr. Rawlins, examined. Saith, that the first vomit Sir R. Killigrew gave my Lord, was laid upon a tester of a bed and lost; and that then upon that he got another, which my Lord sent to Sir T. Overbury by him; and afterwards a third, which my Lord took at Buly: But he never heard that Sir T. Overbury desired my Lord to send him any.

Franklin's examination. Saith, that he provided a white powder, which was poison, for my Lady called it arsenic; which, as my Lady did afterwards tell him, was sent to Sir T. Overbury in a letter.

L. of Som. I do not think you can take Franklin for a good witness. Now for the antedates which are used as a circumstance against me; Sir R. Cotton moved me to it, saying that the dates might prove useful to me at this time. Whereas my Lord of Northampton writes in one of his letters, that he had prompted the Lieutenant: I conceive his meaning to be, that he should endeavor to make Overbury be a good instrument betwixt my Lord of Suffolk and me; and to that end, those whom he thought to be his principal enemies should be the only causers of his freedom. And what I understand by Elwes's conclusion, which my Lord of Northampton relates in the end of one of his letters to me, that death is the best way, I wish that my answers to those letters were now to be seen; and if I had ever thought that those letters of my Lord of Northampton's would be dangerous to me, it is likely I would never have kept them. For the warrant I made, my wife desired me to do it for Mrs. Turner's sake; Packer formed it, and told me, I might do it as a Councillor alone, without other hands; for I would have had at that time my Lord Knollys to have joined with me, but that he was at Council. And when this warrant was sent, I was not commanded from Court, as is pretended.

L.H.S. All the Council together could not justify the making of such a warrant.

L. of Som. For my endeavoring to get a pardon: Having had many things of trust under the King, and the custody of both the seals without particular warrant, I desired by this means to be exonerated. And for all general words, the lawyers put them in without my privity, and for the precedent of the largest pardon, which I had from Sir. R. Cotton, it was upon this occasion: Sir R. Cotton said, "In respect you have received some disgrace in the opinion of the world, in having passed that pardon which the last summer you desired, especially seeing there be many precedents of larger, I would have you now get one after the largest precedent, that so by that addition you might recover your honor." And upon this I bade him search for the largest.

Serj. Mont. Sir R. Cotton says otherwise.

Sir R. Cotton's examination. Saith, my Lord desired to seek precedents of the largest pardons.

L. of Som. For the declaration which I lately sent to the King, and particularly the word (mercy), which is now so much urged against me, it was the Lieutenant's; for I would have used another, but he said it could be nothing prejudicial unto me; but when I wrote it, I did not think thus to be sifted in this declaration; for I in that, in all humility, did so far endeavor to humble and yield myself, that the King might the better express his grace. And for the words (that I did consent to and endeavor the imprisonment of Sir T. Overbury), it is true, for the reason there alleged.

Mr. Attorney. May it please your grace, my Lord here hath had a most gracious hearing, and hath behaved himself modestly and wittily.

L.H.S. If you have any more to say, my Lord, you shall be heard at length; we will not straiten you in time.

L. of Som. For Lobell, I never saw him but twice; he affirms the contrary, I deny it; and there is none else that proves it but himself. For Sir R. Cotton, I could wish that he were here to clear many things that now be obscure.

Mr. Attorney. If he were here he could not be sworn for reason of state, being held for a delinquent. [And yet the testimony on which Carr was convicted was not only that of "delinquents" but convicted delinquents. This statement of Bacon's also exposes the hollowness of his earlier offer to Carr to let him ask questions, since the witnesses he would wish to question were those who could not be sworn.]

Lord of Som. For Sir D. Wood, there was a suit wherein he might have benefited himself £1,200 which I was willing to further him in, conditionally that Overbury should have been a sharer; but for the not effecting of it, it seems, he took some dislike to Sir T. Overbury. The money that is said Sir J. Elwes gave for his place, I had no part of it. Whereas the shifting of offices is urged against me, to make the more easy way for Elwes's entrance, it is well known, the reason of Wade's displacing was in respect of his carelessness in suffering the Lady Arabella to have a key, by which she might have conveyed herself out of prison. [Carr would hardly have made this statement if it were not true, since the peers would have known the truth. Several state papers give this reason for Wade's dismissal. Chamberlain wrote to Carleton on May 13, 1613, that Wade had been removed on complaint of having stolen Arabella's jewels. This might have been merely the official excuse, but the accusation had been made before Overbury was commited.] More I cannot call to mind, but desire favor.

Mr. Attorney. It hath, my Lord, formerly at arraignments, been a custom, after the King's counsel and the prisoner's defense hath been heard, briefly to sum up what hath been said; but in this we have been so formal in the distribution, that I do not think it necessary, and therefore now there is no more to be done, but that the peers will be pleased to confer, and the prisoner to withdraw until the censures be passed. [Although Bacon thus relinquished his right to sum up his case, the manuscript copy contains a flowery speech of Montague addressed to Carr. Montague pretended to hear the ghost of Overbury heaping reproaches on Carr and addressing him with Caesar's "*Et tu, Brute.*" His purpose, of course, was to amass so much shame and charge of infamy on Carr as to prevent any feelings of sympathy for him on the part of the peers.]

L. of Som. My Lords, before you go together, I beseech you

give me leave to recommend myself and cause unto you. As the King hath raised me to your degree, so he hath now disposed me to your censures. This may be any of your own cases, and therefore I assure myself you will not take circumstances for evidence; for if you should, the condition of a man's life were nothing. In the meantime, you may see the excellence of the King's justice, which makes no distinction, putting me into your hands for a just and equal censure. For my part, I protest before God I was neither guilty of, nor privy to, any wrong that Overbury suffered in this kind. A man sensible of his own preservation, had need to express himself.

So he being withdrawn from the Bar, my Lord High Steward briefly reported to the Lords the proofs against my Lord of Somerset. Then the Lords by themselves (and my Lord Steward for his ease, but returning before the rest) stayed some time together; in which interim they sent for the two Chief Justices; being returned, the Sergeant Crier, Mr. Fenshaw, called every Lord by his name, Robert Lord Dormer, and so to the rest, before my Lord High Steward spoke.

L.H.S. Robert Lord Dormer, how say you? Whether is Robert Earl of Somerset guilty of the felony, as accessory before the fact, of the willful poisoning and murder of Sir T. Overbury, whereof he hath been indicted and arraigned, or not guilty? And so particularly to every Lord, one by one.

L. Dormer. Guilty, my Lord (standing up and bareheaded; then sitting again). My Lord Norris, when it came to him, said, "Guilty of Murder," but being told by my Lord High Steward, that he must say either Guilty, or Not Guilty, to the indictment, he said, Guilty. Then Mr. Lieutenant brought the prisoner again to the Bar. He had before taken off his George himself. [The "George" was a jewel suspended from the collar, emblematic of membership in the Order of the Garter.]

Mr. Attorney. My Lord High Steward, Robert Earl of Somerset hath been indicted and arraigned, and put himself upon his peers, who all, without the difference of one voice, have found him Guilty: I pray Judgment.

Mr. Fenshaw. Robert Earl of Somerset, hold up thy hand. Whereas thou hast been indicted, arraigned, and pleaded Not Guilty, as accessory before the fact to the willful poisoning and murder of Sir T. Overbury, and hast put thyself upon thy peers, who have found thee Guilty, what hast thou to say for thyself. why sentence of death should not be pronounced against thee?

L. of Som. The sentence that is passed upon me must be just: I only desire a death according to my degree. For that Simcocks said . . .

L.H.S. My Lord, you are not now to speak any more in your defense, but why judgment of death should not be pronounced.

L. of Som. Then I have no more to say; but humbly beseech you my Lord High Steward and the rest of the Lords to be intercessors to the King for his mercy towards me, if it be necessary.

My Lord High Steward, taking the white staff from Sir R. Coningsby, pronounced sentence.

L.H.S. Robert Earl of Somerset, whereas thou hast been indicted, arraigned, and found guilty as accessory before the fact of the willful poisoning and murder of Sir T. Overbury, you are therefore to be carried from hence to the Tower, and from thence to the place of execution, where you are to be hanged till you be dead: And the Lord have mercy upon you. [Although the evidence seems insufficient to convict Carr as an accessory *before* the fact, and he very possibly took no part in the poisoning, it is clear that he did conceal evidence and assist the guilty persons after the crime. In that this was done knowingly and for the purpose of thwarting justice and the punishment of the guilty, he could perhaps have been found to be an accessory *after* the fact.]

L. of Som. My Lords the Peers, I beseech you, as you have been the judges of this day, so you will be my intercessors.

Then my Lord Steward broke his staff, the court dissolved, and the prisoner was carried away.

No matter how we may feel about the justice of the verdict, it was the only one to have been expected. The rule that the accused is innocent until proved guilty beyond a reasonable doubt was not then fixed, least of all in a political trial. The burden of proof was supposedly on the prosecution, but the rule was differently applied. Gardiner says it was the duty of the court in those days to find the accused guilty unless there was positive reason to suppose him innocent,[13] but his conclusion does not seem to find much support elsewhere. Salmon, in commenting on the trial, said that every man is supposed to be innocent and ought to be dealt with as such until he is convicted, but he was writing over a hundred years after the trial and was primarily criticizing the solitary confinement and the deprivations suffered by a suspect pending his trial.[14] As we have seen, the theory at this time, at least in major trials, was that the relation between judges and king was so close that if the judges brought a person to trial and he was acquitted, the king himself was dishonored.

Coke, at least, was well satisfied with these trials. He wrote that he had given the Somerset trials so much attention in his "Institutes" for two causes: "First, for that we remember not any of the nobility of this realm to have been attainted in former times for poisoning of any; Secondly, for that it is the first case that fell out upon the said Act of 2 E. 6 in case of trials by peers of any that was noble, and the proceeding herein was by great advisement."[15]

TWELVE

Ever since Carr was tried there has been discussion, continuing even today, as to whether James wanted him to be convicted and whether James had a guilty secret he was afraid Carr might reveal. That the king was worried about accusations Carr might make is reasonably certain, but it does not follow that they would have been true. Disclosures Carr could make might have been of several kinds: state secrets learned while he was handling all dispatches; aid given by James in the divorce action against Essex; James's complicity in putting Overbury in the Tower; James's actual aid in or knowledge of the poisoning plot, as, for instance, his changing the lieutenantcy of the Tower; other actions of James of which Carr might be aware; or even an immoral relationship between James and Carr or Villiers or both. This last is not as unlikely as might be thought. Harris, a historian of the reign of James I, in discussing what the secret which so worried James may have been, conjectured that "it was the revealing of that (most unnatural) vice to which James seems to have been addicted, that was the object of his fear." Howell, in setting out his opinion as an adjunct to his editing of the trial, cites Weldon, Osborn and Peyton to the same effect.

Several evidences of James's guilty fear of disclosure have been suggested:

1. Four letters written by James in his own hand (as opposed to his normal practice of having his letters written by a secretary) and sent with great secrecy to his good friend Sir George More, whom he had made lieutenant of the Tower and put in charge of Carr. These letters show James to have been very anxious for a confession, but only a few sentences can be construed to mean anything more. (In the first letter): "I am extremely sorry that your unfortunate prisoner turns all the great care I have of him, not only against

himself, but against me also, as far as he can.... It is easy to be seen that he would threaten me with laying an aspersion upon me of being in some sort accessory to the crime." (In the second letter, after reminding More that he relied on his secrecy): "I have now, at last, sent the bearer hereof, an honest gentleman, and who once followed him [Carr], with such directions unto him, as if there were a spark of grace left in him, I hope they shall work a good effect. My only desire is that you would make his convoy unto him in such secrecy as none living may know it, and that after his speaking with him in private, he may be returned back again as secretly." (In the third letter, after telling More to assure Carr that if he would confess before trial James would not only perform what he had promised by the messenger but would enlarge upon it): "I mean not that he shall confess if he be innocent, but you know how unlikely that is.... You will do well likewise, of yourself, to cast out unto him, that he fear his wife shall plead weakly for his innocence, and that you find the commissioners have, you know not how, some secret assurance, that in the end she will confess of him; but this must only be as from yourself." This was not true — Frances had firmly refused to implicate Carr in any way. The fourth letter was to instruct More that if Carr, who had said he would refuse to go to the Hall to stand trial, appeared distracted at trial time, there should be a postponement. The letter ended with the request that he be advised at once if Carr had said anything momentous in a conversation he had had with Lord Hayes, who had been Carr's original sponsor at Court.[1]

2. "The insolence and menaces of Somerset in the Tower, the shrinking apprehensions of him which the King could not conceal, the pains taken by Bacon to prevent his becoming desperate, ... [all evidence that] he was master of some secret which it would have highly prejudiced the King's honor to divulge.... [these things all leading to the conclusion that] Overbury's death was occasioned, not merely by Lady Somerset's revenge, but by his possession of important secrets, which in his passion he had threatened Somerset to divulge; that Somerset conceived himself to have a hold over the King by the possession of the same or some other secrets...; that the King was in the utmost terror at hearing of these measures...; that Bacon was in the King's confidence, and employed by him so to manage Somerset's trial, as to prevent him from making any imprudent disclosure, or the judges from getting any insight into that which it was not meant to reveal."[2]

3. The possibility that Carr, with James's knowledge or perhaps even complicity, may have caused the poisoning of Prince Henry. James's dislike and jealousy of his son were well recognized, as was Henry's hatred of Carr. In the preface to Fox's history of the early part of the reign of James II, Fox is said to have written Lord Lauderdale, "I recollect that the impression upon my mind was, that there was more reason than is generally allowed for suspecting that Prince Henry was poisoned by Somerset, and that the King knew of it after the fact."

4. James's leniency after Carr's conviction (the reprieve, the grant of estates and income, the pardon, the request for Carr's help against Villiers and correspondence back and forth by letter almost weekly).[3] That the king consulted Carr (probably visiting him for the purpose) about how to deal with Villiers's insolence is indicated in papers found by Lord Sinclair when he acquired Nesbit House, an ancient seat once owned by Carr. The papers appear in "Archaeologia."[4]

5. The government's failure to question Mayerne, who was in charge of the treatment given Overbury for his illness while in the Tower. These facts about Mayerne given by Rimbault may have significance: He had been physician to Henry IV of France and was well experienced in secret state poisonings that went on in his Court; he was asked by James to come to England as his personal physician, possibly in part to handle English state poisonings; he compounded prescriptions containing raspings from human skulls, human bones and "balsam of bats" (a delightful mixture of adders, bats, sucking whelps, earthworms, hog's grease and stagmarrow);[5] and he was the brother-in-law of Lobell, who made and caused the clyster to be administered to Overbury, although if it contained poison, it is uncertain whether Lobell or his apprentice poisoned it. Mayerne enjoyed high standing in his profession (although this was partially earned later) and probably would not have poisoned a patient, but he was intensely loyal to James and might well have kept silent about what he knew had been done by others. The government's failure to question him is hard to explain on any grounds except its knowledge of what he could disclose.

6. James's liberation of Monson for fear of what he might reveal, and in this connection, the incident related in an earlier chapter about James's stopping his card game and sending for the return of the man who had hinted at Monson's having a trump card to play.

7. The fact that when Carr told More that the king *dare* not

bring him to trial because he could publicly tax him with something, the king did not disregard it as a harmless threat but was seriously alarmed. This threat and Carr's assertion that they would have to carry him to court in his bed to get him there were made about midnight, after Carr had been told that he was to be tried the next morning. More was so frightened that he hurried to Greenwich and insisted that the king be routed from bed to talk to him and give him instructions. James is said to have fallen into a passion of tears and to have said, "On my soul, More, I know not what to do, thou art a wise man, help me in this great strait and thou shall find thou does it for a thankful master." More got back to the Tower about three in the morning, went to Carr, told him he had just been with the king, had found him a most affectionate master to him and full of grace in his intentions toward him but that he had said that to satisfy justice Carr must appear, if only to return at once with no proceeding taken against him. With this trick More quieted Carr and got him to court about eight in the morning, but in fear of what Carr might do when he found he had been tricked, More put guards at his sides, as also mentioned in a previous chapter. Carr, however, finding he had been outwitted, went on calmly with the trial.[6]

8. The king's extreme worry and restlessness on the day of the trial. Weldon wrote, "But who had seen the king's restless motion all that day, sending to every boat he saw landing at the bridge [the Court was at Greenwich], cursing all that came without tidings, would have easily judged all was not right, and there had been some ground for his fear of Somerset's boldness; but at last one bringing him word he was condemned, and the passages, all was quiet. This is the very relation from More's own mouth, and this told to two gentlemen, of which the author was one, . . . [they] never speaking of it till the King's death."[7] James's conduct on that day is similarly described by several others; Sherburn, for instance, wrote Carleton on May 31 that James was "so extreme sad and discontented, as he did retire himself from all company, and did forbear both dinner and supper until he had heard what answer the said Earl had made."

It is unlikely we shall ever know the true facts. Spedding, who studied all material then available in preparation for his "Letters and Life of Francis Bacon," concluded that there was no sound basis for suspecting James. His explanation for the rumors and suspicions which have been so prevalent is simple; it all rests on Franklin's assertions. Franklin, Spedding said, was a great villain but no fool. In the course of the examinations to which Coke subjected him, he discovered the soft spot in Coke's head that caused him to believe anything he heard that pointed in the direction he wanted, that is, a heinous plot of which Overbury's murder was only one facet. Franklin took advantage of this, and when Coke announced publicly his belief, based on Franklin's lies, the people naturally assumed Coke must know what he was talking about. It was a very neat theory, and conveniently useful for Bacon, but hardly an answer to the many and diverse grounds for suspicion.

Weston proved right in his fear that only the little fishes would be caught in the net. At the conclusion of the trial the Somersets were returned to the Tower. Carr was given permission to write to the king but for a time was so sullen in his pride that he would not ask for mercy, but only, as Chamberlain wrote, that his judgment of hanging be changed to beheading and that his daughter could have whatever of his property the king did not resume and reserve in his own hands. Chamberlain added that the Lady Knollys [Frances's sister] and some other friends had seen her various times since her conviction, had carried her young daughter to her two or three times (this was written on June 8, two weeks after Carr's conviction) but that although much urged to confess the offense both before his arraignment and since, Carr stood firm in denial.[8]

Nevertheless, James reprieved their sentences; Carr remodeled and refurnished their apartments in the Tower, and he and Frances settled down for a long residency. Reports differ as to how they got along. Married life in the Tower as convicted felons was far different from married life as the spoiled darlings of the Court. There was some bickering, and as time went on this apparently grew into mutual hatred.

Only by comparison with their former state were the Somersets in poverty. Carr's attempt to save their jewels had been frustrated, but probably only in part; John Castle wrote to James Milles on November 28, 1615, that jewels of the Lord of Somerset, in the value of £60,000, committed by him to Cotton's trust, had been lately recovered.[9] Not all of Carr's estates were confiscated, and eventually James settled on him an income of about £4,000 a year. Although thus permitted to enjoy the greater part of his property, Carr, perhaps conscious of his innocence, felt he was entitled to restoration of the rest and feared that James might die before taking appropriate action; this proved true. There is on Page 1 of the Cabala a most peculiar letter written by Carr to James on this subject. Camden said the whole of the letter is couched in obscure terms and that some of the sentences require an interpreter, which is an understatement. There may be a relationship between this letter and a report current at the time that Carr had sent James by way of the lieutenant of the Tower a message threatening that if he did not receive his pardon, he would disclose an important secret which it was in James's interest to have concealed. The letter can hardly be condensed; it is printed in full in the Appendix. After James's death, Carr petitioned King Charles for the return of the remainder of his estates, pulling many strings to get the petition granted, but it was denied.

James had good reasons for pardoning Carr and none for pardoning Frances, except perhaps a feeling of responsibility for having had some part in causing her child-marriage. Too, her father was still one of the most powerful of James's nobles; in any event, her pardon was issued first. The government's official reasons for it were formulated by Bacon. He wrote James that there had been inserted in the pardon four motives: respect for her father and family; her voluntary confession; the promise made by the lord high steward and the peers to intercede for mercy for her; and her conviction not as a principal, but only as an accessory before the fact. The references to the request for mercy by the peers were inserted at James's request, as was a provision that imprisonment in the Tower or other confinement was not pardoned. The pardon, both in Latin and in English, is printed in Howell.

On January 18, 1621, the king had, by order of Council, granted the Somersets permission to retire to a country house of Lord Wallingford, but they were still in confinement and restricted to the house and the area not more than three miles from it. Carr's pardon was issued in 1624, about four months before the death of James. People were inclined to associate James's death so soon after the pardon with his vow made earlier that if he ever pardoned any proved guilty in connection with the murder, he merited the curse of God. Although it seems probable that James never lost his love for or dependence on Carr, Carte suggests that doubt as to Carr's guilt and fear that his punishment was more severe than his offense merited may have caused James to issue the pardon. The French ambassador wrote to the French Court that certainly the least country gentleman in England would not have suffered for what the Earl of Somerset was condemned, that if he had not had great enemies, the proof against him would not have been deemed convincing, only circumstantial, such as might serve in France for putting him to the question, which was not the custom of England, and that he was truly sorry to see a man disgraced into the hands of his enemies.[10]

There is some evidence that Carr and James continued in rather close contact until the time of James's death. Carr was never deprived of his place in the Order of the Garter, a thing so unheard of for a convicted felon that he had considered it proper to remove the George from his neck when he returned to court for sentencing. As already noted, papers printed in "Archaeologia" tell of James's calling on him for aid when James fell out of favor with Villiers. Hallam says as to this, "It is a remarkable fact ... that James in the last year of his reign, while dissatisfied with Buckingham [Villiers], privately renewed his correspondence with Somerset, on whom he bestowed at the same time a full pardon, and seems to have given him hopes of being restored to his former favor. A memorial drawn up by Somerset, evidently at the King's command, ... contains strong charges against Buckingham."[11] Weldon goes even further, saying the two corresponded almost weekly until James's dying day, and it appears fairly certain that James paid visits to Carr.

Anne, the couple's only child, would seem to have had two strikes against her from the start, but she grew up to be both good and beautiful, with all the fine qualities of character her parents lacked. Carr doted on her, and she was good for him. The truth about her parents was somehow kept from her until she was grown; she is said to have fainted when she accidentally found one of the broadsides about the trial that were circulated in London after the trial's conclusion, but she never reproached her parents. Anne and young Lord Russell, son of the Duke of Bedford who had helped plot Carr's downfall, fell in love. "Marry whom you like but a daughter of Somerset" was Bedford's edict to his son. Nevertheless, when King Charles, probably at Dr. Mayerne's instigation (guilty conscience?), intervened with Bedford, he agreed to the marriage if Carr would provide a dowry of £ 12,000. Like many others, Charles thought Carr had concealed wealth. This was not so, but Carr sold Chiswick and what remained of his plate and jewels to raise the amount, preferring impoverishment to the ruin of his daughter's chance for happiness. The man was far from all bad.

Wilson, perhaps influenced by his desire to please his patron, Essex, paints a very gloomy picture of Frances's last years, her mind failing as she lived amidst filth and squalor. Goodman discounts this picture as being prejudiced, but it has support from other writers. When it appeared that she was very ill, thought was given to calling Dr. Mayerne, and he may have seen her, but there was nothing he could do; she died at thirty-nine of cancer of the womb. Camden's description, although written with his usual pseudomoralizing and lack of restraint, is worth repeating for its vivid and contemporaneously observed picture of her last days: "She died before him [Carr]. Her death was infamous, his without fame, the obscurity of the rest of his life darkening the splendor of it. And though she died (as it were) in a corner (in so private a condition), the loathsomeness of her death made it as conspicuous as on the housetop: For that part of her body which had been the receptacle of most of her sin, grown rotten (though she never had but one child), the ligaments failing, it fell down, and was cut away in flakes, with a most nauseous and putrid savor; which to augment, she would roll herself in her own ordure in her bed, and took delight in it. Thus, her affections varied; for nothing could be found sweet enough to augment her beauties at first, and nothing stinking enough to decipher her loathsomeness at last: Pardon the sharpness of these expressions, for they are for the glory of God, who often makes his punishments (in the balance of his justice) of equal weight with our sins."[12]

Once relieved of his incubus, young Essex embarked on what became a long and rather distinguished service to his country. He was, of course, a member of the House of Lords. In addition to his parliamentary duties, he took part in several military expeditions, rising first to subordinate and then to full command. In 1631 he married Elizabeth, daughter of Sir William Paulet, but the marriage did not turn out well. Carte says that although Essex married her indeed in a hurry, they lived together in such manner as to convince the great world of his laboring under the defect imputed to him at the time of his divorce, and that at the time she was delivered of a son, who died in infancy, it was said in the letters of great men on that occasion that she had got her husband an heir for his estate, nobody imagining the child to be of the earl's begetting. A separation followed, but Elizabeth affirmed that the charge of adultery was the result of a conspiracy among Essex's attendants, who were jealous of her influence over him, and it is true that overconfidence in those about him was one of his chief weaknesses.

Essex sided with Parliament against Charles so far as he could do so without actual disloyalty. Charles tried to assure his allegiance by making him lord chamberlain, and he remained at Charles's side as long as his conscience would permit, but when the chips were down, he accepted appointment as general of the parliamentary army and was declared a traitor by Charles. During the ensuing wars he displayed great personal bravery and firmness of character, but his lack of experience handicapped him. He enjoyed several military successes, followed by partial failure. Part of his army was placed under separate command, at which he was greatly aggrieved, but another failure resulted in his having to surrender to the enemy his remaining troops. He died on September 14, 1646, while the strife was still going on, in poor health and unhappy in his resentment at his treatment by the government but was buried in great state at public expense. The earldom died with him.[13]

Perhaps our book can appropriately end with a quotation from the comments on the Overbury case made by that crusty old moralizer, Salmon, in his abridgment of the Howell Trials: "All this mischief proceeded from an unlawful amour, in which perhaps the parties at first thought there was very little hurt. Had they foreseen that train of evils that succeeded; that injustice, treachery, and ingratitude; the barbarous murder they must commit to conceal the first crime; the many persons there would be a necessity of drawing into the same guilt; the lives that must be lost, and the eternal infamy that must succeed, they would surely never have engaged in such an attempt: Which ought forever to caution others, how they deviate from the paths of virtue: We are insensibly led from one step to another, till we find ourselves involved in crimes which we could not at first have reflected on without horror. And thus we see, how changes are frequently brought about unexpectedly in Courts and Kingdoms: One is disgraced, another preferred, and the whole world sometimes put into confusion by a little piece of gallantry, as some term it."[14]

And so perhaps, although it ought not to have been, the first and second Earls of Essex were right in begging their sons to eschew public life and not to fall victim to the tinsel allure of life at the Court of England.

APPENDIX A

The Speech of Robert Devereux, Earl of Essex, on the Scaffold

I desire your Lordships and you my Christian brethren here present to see my just punishment, to bear witness that I confess to the glory of God and the beating down the pride of my own flesh, that I am a most wretched sinner, that the number of my sins are more than the hairs of my head, that I have spent my youth in wantonness, the lusts of the flesh and uncleanness, that I have been puffed up with pride and vanity and love of this world's pleasures, and that notwithstanding divers good motions inspired in me by the spirit of God, the good which I would do I have not done, and the evil which I would not, I have done, for all which I humbly beseech my Saviour Christ to be a mediator to the eternal Majesty for my pardon; especially I acknowledge this great sin, this bloody sin, this infectious sin against God's ordinance wherein I have offended God, my Sovereign and the world. I beseech God to forgive it us all and to forgive it me the most wretched of all; and I beseech Her Majesty to forgive it me, I beseech all men to forgive me; especially I crave pardon of those Lords and gentlemen that for love of me have fallen into this act, and are like to taste the same punishment. I entreat that all men would have a charitable opinion of me who never, I protest to God, intended violence or harm to her Majesty's person or dignity. I heartily forgive all the world, and so desire all men to forgive me. I pray God give her Majesty a religious and wise heart, a long reign (if it be his will) and a prosperous. I beseech God to bless her, the nobles, the ministers of the church and the people. And I desire you all to mark my protestation that I never was, I thank God, atheist, to deny God or the Scriptures, or to hold any heresy against the Godhead, nor papist to ascribe anything to my own works, but I hope only to be saved by the mercies of God in the merits of Christ Jesus, my only Saviour; and so forward I believe all the articles of that religion and faith in which I was baptised, in which I was brought up, wherein I hope to continue to my last gasp. I was never

261

(I take God to witness) in my heart guilty of any hypocrisy in religion, but I know myself subject to all the frailties and imperfections of the flesh. I am a most imperfect creature.

I desire your Lordships and you my Christian brethren to join your spirits with mine, for now will I give myself in prayer to God, which I will perform on my knees, so that all of you may hear that it will please God to give me an humble heart, and to assist me in this greatest temptation of my death, for I am not able to endure without his special grace, this last conflict.

[While kneeling in the straw before the block, he said:] Here, Lord, I submit myself in obedience and humility to thy commandment in obedience to thy ordinance, to thy will, O God, I submit myself to my deserved punishment. O God, creator of all things, and judge of all men, that hast taught me by warrant out of thy word that Satan is then most busy when our end is nearest, and that being resisted he will flee, I humbly beseech thee to assist me in this my last combat. O Lord, I acknowledge that through my own ignorance and dullness I cannot offer up my prayers as I ought, but I desire to do it, and thou (O God) will take that for the act. I desire, O Lord, that thou will give me power to pray, not with tongue and understanding only, but with faith, with zeal and with confidence. O Lord, I beseech thee to lift up my heart from all worldly thoughts and let thy mercies in Christ Jesus be the only object of the eye of my mind; perfect by thy grace what thou seest in my flesh to be frail and weak. Give me patience and strength to endure this last judgment inflicted upon me by so honorable a trial. Grant that my flesh may not tremble or show resistance at the stroke of death. Let thy spirit seal up my soul in the assurance of thy mercies and lift it up above all earthly cogitations, that in this dissolution of mine I may have thee only before my eyes, even to the last breath.

I prostrate myself here before thee [doing so] O Lord God, beseeching you that thy blessed angels may be ready to receive my soul up into Heaven as soon as it is departed from my body. And I pray you all here present to join with my spirit when my arms are stretched out, for I will only stretch them out when the executioner shall do his office.

APPENDIX B

Francis Bacon's "Declaration Touching the Treasons of the Late Earl of Essex and his Accomplices"

Though public justice passed upon capital offenders, according to the laws, and in course of an honourable and ordinary trial (where the case would have borne and required the severity of martial law to have been speedily used), do in itself carry a sufficient satisfaction towards all men, specially in a merciful government, such as her Majesty's is approved to be: yet because there do pass abroad in the hands of many men divers false and corrupt collections and relations of the proceedings at the arraignment of the late Earls of Essex and Southampton; and again, because it is requisite that the world do understand as well the precedent practices and inducements to the treasons, as the open and actual treasons themselves (though in a case of life it was not thought convenient to insist at the trial upon matter of inference or presumption, but chiefly upon matter of plain and direct proofs); therefore it hath been thought fit to publish to the world a brief Declaration of the practices and treasons attempted and committed by Robert late Earl of Essex and his complices against her Majesty and her kingdoms, and of the proceedings at the convictions of the said late Earl and his adherents upon the same treasons: and not so only, but therewithal, for the better warranting and verifying of the narration, to set down in the end the very confessions and testimonies themselves, word for word taken out of the originals, whereby it will be most manifest that nothing is obscured or disguised, though it do appear by divers most wicked and seditious libels thrown abroad, that the dregs of these treasons, which the late Earl of Essex himself, a little before his death, did term a Leprosy, that had infected far and near, do yet remain in the hearts and tongues of some misaffected persons.

The most partial will not deny, but that Robert late Earl of Essex was by her Majesty's manifold benefits and graces, besides oath and allegiance, as much tied to her Majesty as the subject could be to the sovereign; her Majesty having heaped upon him both dignities, offices, and gifts, in such measure, as within the circle of twelve years

263

or more there was scarcely a year of rest, in which he did not obtain at her Majesty's hands some notable addition either of honour or profit.

But he on the other side, making these her Majesty's favours nothing else but wings for his ambition, and looking upon them not as her benefits but as his advantages, supposing that to be his own metal which was but her mark and impression, was so given over by God (who often punisheth ingratitude by ambition, and ambition by treason, and treason by final ruin), as he had long ago plotted it in his heart to become a dangerous supplanter of that seat, whereof he ought to have been a principal supporter; in such sort as now every man of common sense may discern not only his last actual and open treasons, but also his former more secret practices and preparations towards those in treasons, and that without any gloss or interperter but himself and his own doings.

For first of all, the world can now expound why it was that he did aspire, and had almost attained, unto a greatness like unto the ancient greatness of the *Pro fectus Pro torio* under the Emperors of Rome, to have all men of war to make their sole and particular dependence upon him; that with such jealousy and watchfulness he sought to discountenance any one that might be a competitor to him in any part of that greatness; that with great violence and bitterness he sought to suppress and keep down all the worthiest martial men which did not appropriate their respects and acknowledgments only towards himself. All which did manifestly detect and distinguish, that it was not the reputation of a famous leader in the wars which he sought (as it was construed a great while), but only power and greatness to serve his own ends; considering he he never loved virtue nor valour in another, but where he thought he should be proprietary and commander of it, as referred to himself.

So likewise those points of popularity which every man took notice and note of, as his affable gestures, open doors, making his table and his bed so popularly places of audience to suitors, denying nothing when he did nothing, feeding many men in their discontentments against the Queen and the state, and the like, as they ever were since Absalon's time the forerunners of treasons following, so in him were they either the qualities of a nature disposed to disloyalty, or the beginnings and conceptions of that which afterwards grew to shape and form.

But as it were a vain thing to think to search the roots and first motions of treasons, which are known to none but God that discerns the heart, and the devil that gives the instigation; so it is more than to be presumed (being made apparent by the evidence of all the events following) that he carried into Ireland a heart corrupted in his allegiance, and pregnant of those or the like treasons which afterwards came to light.

For being a man by nature of an high imagination, and a great promiser to himself as well as to others, he was confident that if he were once the first person in a kingdom, and a sea between the Queen's seat and his, and Wales the nearest land from Ireland, and that he had got the flower of the English forces into his hands (which he thought so to intermix with his own followers, as the whole body should move by his spirit), and if he might have also absolutely into his hands *potestatem vito   et necis* and *arbitrium belli et pacis* over the rebels of Ireland, whereby he might entice and make them his own, first by pardons and conditions, and after by hopes to bring them in place where they should serve for hope of better booties than cows, he should be able to make that place of Lieutenancy of Ireland as a rise or step to ascend to his desired greatness in England.

And although many of these conceits were windy, yet neither were they the less like to his, neither are they now only probable conjectures or comments upon these his last treasons, but the very preludes of actions almost immediately subsequent, as shall be touched in due place.

But first, it was strange with what appetite and thirst he did affect and compass the government of Ireland, which he did obtain. For although he made some formal shows to put it from him; yet in this, as in most things else, his desires being too strong for his dissimulations, he did so far pass the bounds of *decorum*, as he did in effect name himself to the Queen by such description and such particularities as could not be applied to any other but himself; neither did he so only, but further he was still at hand to offer and urge vehemently and peremptorily exceptions to any other that was named.

Then after he once found that there was no man but himself (who had other matters in his head) so far in love with that charge as to make any competition or opposition to his pursuit, whereby he saw it would fall upon him, and especially after himself was resolved upon, he began to make propositions to her Majesty by way of taxation of the former course held in managing the actions of Ireland, especially upon three points; The first, that the proportions of forces which had been there maintained and continued by supplies, were not sufficient to bring the prosecutions there to period. The second, that the axe had not been put to the root of the tree, in regard there had not been made a main prosecution upon the arch-traitor Tyrone in his own strength, within the province of Ulster. The third, that the prosecutions before time had been intermixed and interrupted with too many temporizing treaties, whereby the rebel did ever gather strength and reputation to renew the war with advantage. All which goodly and well-sounding discourses, together with the great vaunts that he would make the earth tremble before him, tended but to this, that the Queen should increase the list of her army and all proportions of treasure and other furniture, to the end his commandment might be the greater. For that he never intended any such prosecution may appear by this, that even at the time before his going into Ireland he did open himself so far in speech to Blunt, his inwardest counsellor, *That he did assure himself that many of the rebels in Ireland would be advised by him:* so far was he from intending any prosecution towards those in whom he took himself to have interest. But his ends were two; The one, to get great forces into his hands; the other, to oblige the heads of the rebellion unto him, and to make them of his party. These two ends had in themselves a repugnancy; for the one imported prosecution, and the other treaty: but he, that meant to be too strong to be called to account for anything, and meant besides when he was once in Ireland to engage himself in other journeys that should hinder the prosecution in the North, took things in order as they made for him. And so first did nothing, as was said, but trumpet a final and utter prosecution against Tyrone in the North, to the end to have his forces augmented.

But yet he forgat not his other purpose of making himself strong by a party amongst the rebels, when it came to the scanning of the clauses of his commission. For then he did insist, and that with a kind of contestation, that the pardoning, no not of Tyrone himself, the capital rebel, should be excepted and reserved to her Majesty's immediate grace; being infinitely desirous that Tyrone should not look beyond him for his life or pardon, but should hold his fortune as of him, and account for it to him only.

So again, whereas in the commission of the Earl of Sussex, and of all other lieutenants or deputies, there was ever in that clause which giveth unto the lieutenant or deputy that high or regal point of authority to pardon treasons and traitors, an exception contained of such cases of treason as are committed against the person of the King; it was strange, and suspiciously strange even at that time, with what importunity and instance he did labour, and in the end prevailed, to have that exception also omitted; glosing then, that because he had heard that by strict exposition of law (a point in law that he would needs forget at his arraignment, but could take knowledge of it before, when it was to serve his own ambition,) all treasons of rebellion did tend to the destruction of the King's person, it might breed a buzz in the rebels' heads, and so discourage them from coming in; whereas he knew well that in all experience passed, there was never rebel made any doubt or scruple upon that point to accept of pardon from all former governors, who had their commissions penned with that limitation (their commissions being things not kept secretly in a box, but published and recorded): so as it appeared manifestly that it was a mere device of his own out of the secret reaches of his heart then not revealed; but it may be shrewdly expounded since, what his drift was, by those pardons which he granted to Blunt the marshal, and Thomas Lee, and others, that his care was no less to secure his own instruments than the rebels of Ireland.

Yet was there another point for which he did contend and contest, which was, that he might not be tied to any opinion of the Counsel of Ireland, as all others in certain points (as pardoning traitors, concluding war and peace, and some other principal articles) had been before him; to the end he might be absolute of himself, and be fully master of opportunities and occasions for the performing and executing of his own treasonable ends.

But after he had once by her Majesty's singular trust and favour toward him obtained his patent of commission as large, and his list of forces as full as he desired, there was an end in his course of the prosecution in the North. For being arrived into Ireland, the whole carriage of his actions there was nothing else but a cunning defeating of that journey, with an intent (as appeared) in the end of the year to pleasure and gratify the rebel with a dishonourable peace, and to contract with him for his own greatness.

Therefore not long after he had received the sword, he did voluntarily engage himself in an unseasonable and fruitless journey into Munster, a journey never propounded in the Counsel there, never advertised over hither while it was past: by which journey her Majesty's forces, which were to be preserved entire both in vigour and number for the great prosecution, were harassed and tired with long marches together, and the northern prosecution was indeed quite dashed and made impossible.

But yet still doubting he might receive from her Majesty some quick and express commandment to proceed; to be sure, he pursued his former device of wrapping himself in other actions, and so set himself on work anew in the county of Ophaley, being resolved, as is manifest, to dally out the season, and never to have gone that journey at all: that setting forward which he made in the very end of August being but a mere play and a mockery, and for the purposes which now shall be declared.

After he perceived that four months of the summer and three parts of the army were wasted, he thought now was a time to set on foot such a peace as might be for the rebels' advantage, and so to work a mutual obligation between Tyrone and himself; for which purpose he did but seek a commodity. He had there with him in his army one Thomas Lee, a man of a seditious and working spirit, and one that had been privately familiar and entirely beloved of Tyrone, and one that afterwards, immediately upon Essex open rebellion, was apprehended for a desperate attempt of violence against her Majesty's person; which he plainly confessed, and for which he suffered. Wherefore judging him to be a fit instrument, he made some signification to Lee of such an employment, which was no sooner signified than apprehended by Lee. He gave order also to Sir Christopher Blunt, marshal of his army, to license Lee to go to Tyrone, when he should require it. But Lee thought good to let slip first unto Tyrone (which was nevertheless by the marshal's warrant) one James Knowd, a person of wit and sufficiency, to sound in what terms and humours Tyrone then was. This Knowd returned a message from Tyrone to Lee, which was, *That if the Earl of Essex would follow Tyrone's plot, he would make the Earl of Essex the greatest man that ever was in England: and further, that if the Earl would have conference with him, Tyrone would deliver his eldest son in pledge for his assurance.* This message was delivered by Knowd to Lee and by Lee was imparted to the Earl of Essex, who after this message employed Lee himself to Tyrone, and by his negotiating, (whatsoever passed else) prepared and disposed Tyrone to the parley.

And this employment of Lee was a matter of that guiltiness in my Lord, as, being charged with it at my Lord Keeper's only in this nature (for the message of Knowd was not then known) that when he pretended to assail Tyrone he had before underhand agreed upon a parley, my Lord utterly denied it that he ever employed Lee to Tyrone at all, and turned it upon Blunt, whom he afterwards required to take it upon him, having before sufficiently provided for the security of all parts, for he had granted both to Blunt and Lee pardons of all treasons under the great seal of Ireland, and so, himself disclaiming it, and they being pardoned, all was safe.

But when that Tyrone was by these means (besides what others God knows) prepared to demand a parley, now was the time for Essex to acquit himself of all the Queen's commandments, and his own promises and undertakings for the northern journey; and not so alone, but to have the glory at the disadvantage of the year, being but 2500 strong of foot, and 300 of horse, after the fresh disaster of Sir Coniers Clifford, in the height of the rebels' pride, to set forth to assail, and then that the very terror and reputation of my Lord of Essex person was such as did daunt him and make him stoop to seek a parley; and this was the end he shot at in that September journey, being a mere abuse and bravery, and but inducements only to the treaty, which was the only matter he intended. For Essex drawing now towards the catastrophe or last part of that tragedy for which he came upon the stage in Ireland, his treasons grew to a further ripeness. For knowing how unfit it was for him to communicate with any English, even of those whom he trusted most and meant to use in other treasons, that he had an intention to grow to an agreement with Tyrone to have succours from him for the usurping upon the state here, (not because it was more dangerous than the rest of his treasons, but because it was more odious, and in a kind monstrous, that he should conspire with such a rebel against whom he was sent, and therefore might adventure to alienate men's affections from him,) he drave it to this, that there might be, and so there was, under colour of treaty, an interview and private conference between Tyrone and himself only, no third person admitted. A strange course, considering with whom he dealt, and especially considering what message Knowd had brought, which should have made him rather call witnesses to him than avoid witnesses. But he being only true to his own ends, easily dispensed with all such considerations. Nay there was such careful order taken that no person should overhear one word that passed between them two, as because the place appointed and used for the parley was such as there was the depth of a brook between them, which made them speak [with] some loudness, there were certain horsemen appointed by order from Essex to keep all men off a great distance from the place.

It is true that the secrecy of that parley, as it gave to him the more liberty of treason, so it may give any man the more liberty of surmise what was then handled between them; inasmuch as nothing can be known but by report from one of them two, either Essex or Tyrone.

But although there were no proceeding against Essex upon these treasons, and that it were a needless thing to load more treasons upon him then, whose burthen was so great after; yet for truth's sake, it is fit the world know what is testified touching the speeches, letters, and reports of Tyrone, immediately following this conference, and observe also what ensued likewise in the designs of Essex himself.

On Tyrone's part it fell out, that the very day after that Essex came to the Court of England, Tyrone having conference with Sir William Warren at Armagh, by way of discourse told him, and bound it with an oath, and iterated it two or three several times; *That within two or three months he should see the greatest alterations and strangest that ever he saw in his life, or could imagine: and that he the said Tyrone hoped ere long to have a good share in England.* With this concurred fully the report of Richard Bremingham, a gentleman of the Pale, having made his repair about the same time to Tyrone to right him in a cause of land; saving that Bremingham delivers the like speech of Tyrone to himself; but not what Tyrone hoped, but what Tyrone had promised in these words, *That he had promised* (it may be thought to whom) *ere long to show his face in England, little to the good of England.*

These generalities coming immediately from the report of Tyrone himself, are drawn to more particularity in a conference had between the Lord Fitz-Morrice, Baron of Liksnawe in Munster, and one Thomas Wood, a person well reputed of, immediately after Essex coming into England. In which conference Fitz-Morrice declared unto Wood, that Tyrone had written to the traitorous titulary Earl of Desmond, to inform him that the condition of that contract between Tyrone and Essex was, *That Essex should be King of England; and that Tyrone should hold of him the honour and state of Viceroy of Ireland; and that the proportion of soldiers which Tyrone should bring or send to Essex, were 8,000 Irish.* With which concurreth fully the testimony of the said James Knowd, who, being in credit with Owny Mac Roory, chief of the Omoores in Lemster, was used as a secretary for him, in the writing of a letter to Tyrone, immediately after Essex coming to England. The effect of which letter was, *To understand some light of the secret agreement between the Earl of Essex and Tyrone, that he the said Owny might frame his course accordingly.* Which letter, with further instructions to the same effect, was in the presence of Knowd delivered to Turlagh Macdavy, a man of trust with Owny, who brought an answer from Tyrone: the contents whereof were, *That the Earl of Essex had agreed to take his part, and that they should aid him towards the conquest of England.*

Besides, very certain it is, and testified by divers credible persons, that immediately upon this parley there did fly abroad as sparkles of this fire (which it did not concern Tyrone so much to keep secret, as it did Essex) a general and received opinion, that went up and down in the mouths both of the better and meaner sort of rebels, *That the Earl of Essex was theirs, and they his: and that he would never leave the one sword, meaning that of Ireland, till he had gotten the other in England; and that he would bring them to serve, where they should have other manner of booties than cows;* and the like speeches. And Thomas Lee himself, (who had been, as was before declared, with Tyrone two or three days, upon my Lord's sending, and had sounded him) hath left it confessed under his hand, *That he knew the Earl of Essex and Tyrone to be one, and to run the same courses.*

And certain it is also, that immediately upon that parley Tyrone grew into a strange and unwonted pride, and appointed his progresses and visitations to receive congratulations and homages from his confederates, and behaved himself in all things as one that had some new spirit of hope and courage put into him.

But on the Earl of Essex his part ensued immediately after this parley a strange motion and project, which thought no doubt he had harboured in his breast before, yet for anything yet appeareth, he did not utter and break with any in it, before he had been confirmed and fortified in his purpose by the combination and correspondence which he found in Tyrone upon their conference. Neither is this a matter gathered out of reports, but confessed directly by two of his principal friends and associates, being witnesses upon their own knowledge, and of that which was spoken to themselves: the substance of which confessions is this: *That a little before my Lord's coming over into England, at the castle of Dublin, where Sir Christopher Blunt lay hurt, having been lately removed thither from Reban, a castle of Thomas Lee's, and placed in a lodging that had been my Lord of Southampton's, the Earl of Essex took the Earl of Southampton with him to visit Blunt, and there being none present but they three, my Lord of Essex told them, he found it now necessary for him to go into England, and would advise with them of the manner of his going, since to go he was resolved. And thereupon propounded unto them, that he thought it fit to carry with him of the army in Ireland as much as he could conveniently transport, at least the choice of it, to the number of two or three thousand, to secure and make good his first descent on shore, purposing to land them at Milford Haven in Wales, or thereabouts; not doubting, but that his army would so increase within a small time by such as would come in to him, as he should be able to march with his power to London, and make his own conditions as he thought good. But both Southampton and Blunt dissuaded him from this enterprise; Blunt alleging the hazard of it, and that it would make him odious: and Southampton utterly disliking of that course, upon the same and many other reasons. Howbeit thereupon Blunt advised him rather to another course, which was to draw forth of the army some 200 resolute gentlemen, and with those to come over, and so to make sure of the Court, and so to make his own conditions.* Which confessions it is not amiss to deliver by what a good providence of God they came to light: for they could not be used at Essex arraignment to charge him, because they were uttered after his death.

But Sir Christopher Blunt at his arraignment, being charged that the Earl of Essex had set it down under his hand that he had been a principal instigator of him to his treasons, in passion brake forth into these speeches: *That then he must be forced to disclose what further matters he had held my Lord from, and desired for that purpose (because the present proceeding should not be interrupted) to speak with the Lord Admiral and Mr. Secretary after his arraignment;* and so fell most naturally and most voluntarily into this his confession, which if it had been thought fit to have required of him at that time publicly, he had delivered before his conviction. And the same confession he did after (at the time of his execution) constantly and fully confirm, discourse particularly, and take upon his death, where never any man showed less fear, nor a greater resolution to die.

And the same matter so by him confessed was likewise confessed with the same circumstances of time and place by Southampton, being severally examined thereupon.

So as now the world may see how long since my Lord put off his vizard, and disclosed the secrets of his heart to two of his most confident friends, falling upon that unnatural and detestable treason, whereunto all his former actions in his government in Ireland (and God knows how long before) were but introductions.

But finding that these two persons, which of all the rest he thought to have found forwardest, Southampton, whose displacing he had made his own discontentment (having placed him, no question, to that end, to find cause of discontentment), and Blunt, a man so enterprising and prodigal of his own life (as himself termed himself at the bar), did not applaud to this his purpose, and thereby doubting how coldly he should find others minded, that were not so near to him; and therefore condescending to Blunt's advice to surprise the Court, he did pursue that plot accordingly, and came over with a selected company of captains and voluntaries, and such as he thought were most affectionate unto himself and most resolute, though not knowing of his purpose. So as even at that time every man noted and wondered what the matter should be, that my Lord took his most particular friends and followers from their companies, which were countenance and means unto them, to bring them over. But his purpose (as in part was touched before) was this; that if he held his greatness in Court, and were not committed (which in regard of the miserable and deplored estate he left Ireland in, whereby he thought the opinion here would be that his service could not be spared, he made full account he should not be) then, at the first opportunity, he would execute the surprise of her Majesty's person. And if he were committed to the Tower or to prison for his contempts (for besides his other contempts, he came over expressly against the Queen's prohibition under her signet), it might be the care of some of his principal friends, by the help of that choice and resolute company which he brought over, to rescue him.

But the pretext of his coming over was by the efficacy of his own presence and persuasion to have moved and drawn her Majesty to accept of such conditions of peace as he had treated of with Tyrone in his private conference; which was indeed somewhat needful, the principal article of them being, *That there should be a general restitution*

*of rebels in Ireland to all their lands and possessions, that they could pretend
any right to before their going out into rebellion,* without reservation of
such lands as were by Act of Parliament passed to the Crown, and so
planted with English, both in the time of Queen Mary, and since;
and without difference either of time of their going forth, or nature
of their offence, or other circumstance: tending in effect to this,
That all the Queen's good subjects, in most of the provinces, should
have been displanted, and the country abandoned to the rebels.

When this man was come over, his heart thus fraughted with
treasons, and presented himself to her Majesty, it pleased God, in his
singular providence over her Majesty, to guide and hem in her
proceeding towards him in a narrow way of safety between two
perils. For neither did her Majesty leave him at liberty, wherby he
might have commodity to execute his purpose; nor restrain him in
any such nature, as might signify or betoken matter of despair of his
return to Court and favour. And so the means of present mischief
being taken away, and the humours not stirred, this matter fell
asleep, and the thread of his purposes was cut off. For coming over
about the end of September, and not denied access and conference
with her Majesty, and then being commanded to his chamber at
Court for some days, and from thence to the Lord Keeper's house, it
was conceived that these were no ill signs. At my Lord Keeper's
house he remained till some few days before Easter, and then was
removed to his own house, under the custody of Sir Richard Barkley, and in that sort continued till the end of Trinity Term following.

For her Majesty all this while looking into his faults with the eye
of her princely favour, and loath to take advantage of his great
offences in other nature than as contempts, resolved so to proceed
against him as might (to use her Majesty's own words) tend *ad
correctionem, et non ad ruinam.*

Nevertheless afterwards, about the end of Trinity Term following, for the better satisfaction of the world, and to repress seditious
bruits and libels which were dispersed in his justification, and to
observe a form of justice before he should be set at full liberty; her
Majesty was pleased to direct, that there should be associate unto her
Privy Counsel some chosen persons of her nobility, and of her
judges of the law; and before them his cause (concerning the breaking of his instructions for the northern prosecution, and the manner
of his treating with Tyrone, and his coming over and leaving the
kingdom of Ireland contrary to her Majesty's commandment, ex-

pressed as well by signification thereof made under her royal hand and signet as by a most binding and effectual letter written privately to himself) to receive a hearing; with limitation nevertheless that he should not be charged with any point of disloyalty; and with like favour directed that he should not be called in question in the open and ordinary place of offenders in the Star Chamber, from which he had likewise by a most penitent and humble letter desired to be spared, as that which would have wounded him for ever as he affirmed, but in a more private manner at my Lord Keeper's house. Neither was the effect of the sentence that there passed against him any more than a suspension of the exercise of some of his places: at which time also, Essex, that could vary himself into all shapes for a time, infinitely desirous (as by the sequel now appeareth) to be at liberty to practise and revive his former purposes, and hoping to set into them with better strength than ever, because he conceived the people's hearts were kindled to him by his troubles, and that they had made great demonstrations of as much; he did transform himself into such a strange and dejected humility, as if he had been no man of this world, with passionate protestations that he called God to witness *That he had made an utter divorce with the world; and he desired her Majesty's favour not for any wordly respect, but for a preparative for a* Nunc dimittis; *and that the tears of his heart had quenched in him all humours of ambition.* All this to make her Majesty secure, and to lull the world asleep, that he was not a man to be held any ways dangerous.

Not many days after, Sir Richard Barkley his keeper was removed from him, and he set at liberty; with this admonition only, *That he should not take himself to be altogether discharged, though he were left to the guard of none but his own discretion.* But he felt himself no sooner upon the wings of his liberty but (notwithstanding his former shows of a mortified estate of mind) he began to practise afresh, as busily as ever reviving his former resolution; which was the surprising and possessing the Queen's person and the Court. And that it may appear how early after his liberty he set his engines on work, having long before entertained into his service, and during his government in Ireland drawn near unto him in the place of his chief secretary, one Henry Cuffe, a base fellow by birth, but a great scholar, and indeed a notable traitor by the book, being otherwise of a turbulent and mutinous spirit against all superiors:

This fellow, in the beginning of August, which was not a month after Essex liberty granted, fell of practising with Sir Henry Nevill, that served her Majesty as leiger ambassador with the French King, then newly come over into England from Bulleyn; abusing him with a false lie and mere invention, that his service was blamed and misliked and that the imputation of the breach of the treaty of peace held at Bulleyn was like to light upon him (when there was no colour of any such matter), only to distaste him of others and fasten him to my Lord; though he did not acquaint him with any particulars of my Lord's designs till a good while after.

But my Lord having spent the end of the summer (being a private time, when everybody was out of town and dispersed) in digesting his own thoughts, with the help and conference of Master Cuffe, they had soon set down between them the ancient principle of traitors and conspirators, which was, *to prepare many, and to acquaint few;* and, after the manner of mines, to make ready their powder and place it, and then give fire but in the instant. Therefore the first consideration was of such persons as my Lord thought fit to draw to be of his party; singling out both of nobility and martial men and others such as were discontented or turbulent, and such as were weak of judgment and easy to be abused, or such as were wholly dependants and followers (for means or countenance) of himself, Southampton, or some other of his greatest associates.

And knowing there were no such strong and drawing cords of popularity as religion, he had not neglected, both at this time and long before, in a profane policy to serve his turn (for his own greatness) of both sorts and factions, both of Catholics and Puritans, as they term them; turning his outside to the one and his inside to the other, and making himself pleasing and gracious to the one sort by professing zeal and frequenting sermons and making much of preachers, and secretly underhand giving assurance to Blunt, Davies and divers others, that (if he might prevail in his desired greatness) he would bring in a toleration of the Catholic religion.

Then having passed the whole Michaelmas Term in making himself plausible, and in drawing concourse about him, and in affecting and alluring men by kind provocations and usage (wherein, because his liberty was qualified, he neither forgot exercise of mind nor body, neither sermon nor tennis-court, to give the occasion and freedom of access and concourse unto him) and much other practice and device; about the end of that term, towards Christmas, he grew to a more framed resolution of the time and manner, when and how he would put his purpose in execution. And first, about the end of Michaelmas Term, it passed as a kind of cipher and watchword amongst his friends and followers, *That my Lord would stand upon his guard:* which might receive construction in a good sense, as well guard of circumspection as guard of force: but to the more private and trusty persons he was content it should be expounded that he would be cooped up no more, nor hazard any more restraints or commandments.

But the next care was, how to bring such persons as he thought fit for his purpose into town together, without vent of suspicion, to be ready at the time when he should put his design in execution; which he had concluded should be some time in Hilary Term; wherein he found many devices to draw them up, some for suits in law, and some for suits in Court, and some for assurance of land: and one friend to draw up another, it not being perceived that all moved from one head. And it may be truly noted, that in the catalogue of those persons that were the eighth of February in the action of open rebellion, a man may find almost out of every county of England some; which could not be by chance or constellation: and in the particularity of examinations (too long to be rehearsed) it was easy to trace in what sort many of them were brought up to town, and held in town upon several pretences. But in Candlemas Term, when the time drew near, then was he content consultation should be had by certain choice persons, upon the whole matter and course which he should hold. And because he thought himself and his own house more observed, it was thought fit that the meeting and conference should be at Drury House, where Sir Charles Davers lodged. There met at this council, the Earl of Southampton, with whom in former times he had been at some emulations and differences in Court. But after, Southampton having married his kinswoman, and plunged himself wholly into his fortune, and being his continual associate in Ireland, he accounted of him as most assured unto him, and had long ago in Ireland acquainted him with his purpose, as was declared before. Sir Charles Davers, one exceedingly devoted to the Earl of Southampton, upon affection begun first upon the deserving of the same Earl towards him, when he was in trouble about the murther of one Long. Sir Ferdinando Gorge, one that the Earl of Essex had of purpose sent for up from his government at Plymouth by his letter, with particular assignation to be here before the second of February. Sir John Davis, one that had been his servant, and raised by him, and that bare office in the Tower, being Surveyor of the Ordnance, and one that he greatly trusted: and John Littleton, one they respected for his wit and valour.

The consultation and conference rested upon three parts: The perusal of a list of those persons, whom they took to be of their party: The consideration of the action itself which they should set afoot, and how they should proceed in it: And the distribution of the persons, according to the action concluded on, to their several employments.

The list contained the number of sixscore persons, noblemen and knights and principal gentlemen, and was (for the more credit's sake) of the Earl of Essex own handwriting.

For the action itself, there was proposition made of two principal articles: The one, of possessing the Tower of London: The other, of surprising her Majesty's person and the Court; in which also deliberation was had what course to hold with the City, either towards the effecting of the surprise or after it was effected.

For the Tower was alleged, the giving a reputation to the action, by getting into their hand the principal fort of the realm, with the stores and provisions thereunto appertaining, the bridling of the City by that piece, and commodity of entrance in and possessing it, by the means of Sir John Davis. But this was by opinion of all rejected, as that which would distract their attempt from the more principal, which was the Court, and as that which they made a judgment would follow incidently, if the Court were once possessed.

But the latter, which was the ancient plot (as was well known to Southampton), was in the end by the general opinion of them all insisted and rested upon.

And the manner how it should be ordered and disposed was this: That certain selected persons of their number, such as were well known in Court, and might have access without check or suspicion into the several rooms in Court, according to the several qualities of the persons and the differences of the rooms, should distribute themselves into the Presence, the Guardchamber, the Hall, and the utter Court and gate, and some one principal man undertaking every several room with the strength of some few to be joined with him, every man to make good his charge, according to the occasion. In which distribution, Sir Charles Davers was then named to the Presence and to the great chamber, where he was appointed, when time should be, to seize upon the halberds of the guard; Sir John Davis to the Hall; and Sir Christopher Blunt to the utter gate; these seeming to them the three principal wards of consideration. And that things being within the Court in a readiness, a signal should be given and sent to Essex to set forward from Essex House, being no great distance off. Whereupon Essex, accompanied with the noblemen of his party, and such as should be prepared and assembled at his house for that purpose, should march towards the Court; and that the former conspirators already entered should give correspondence to them without, as well by making themselves masters of the gates to give them entrance, as by attempting to get into their hand upon the sudden the halberds of the guard, thereby hoping to prevent any great resistance within, and by filling all full of tumult and confusion.

This being the platform of their enterprise, the second act of this tragedy was also resolved; which was, that my Lord should present himself to her Majesty as prostrating himself at her feet, and desire the remove of such persons as he called his enemies from about her. And after that my Lord had obtained possession of the Queen and the state, he should call his pretended enemies to a trial upon their lives, and summon a Parliament, and alter the government, and obtain to himself and his associates such conditions as seemed to him and them good.

There passed speech also in this conspiracy of possessing the City of London, which Essex himself, in his own particular and secret inclination, had ever a special mind unto: not at a departure or going from his purpose of possessing the Court, but as an inducement and preparative to perform it upon a surer ground. An opinion bred in him (as may be imagined) partly by the great overweening he had of the love of the citizens; but chiefly, in all likelihood, by a fear that although he should have prevailed in getting her Majesty's person into his hands for a time with his two or three hundred gentlemen, yet the very beams and graces of her Majesty's magnanimity and prudent carriage in such disaster working with the natural instinct of loyalty, which of course (when fury is over) doth ever revive in the hearts of subjects of any good blood or mind (such as his troop for the more part was compounded of, though by him seduced and bewitched) would quickly break the knot, and cause some disunion and separation amongst them;

whereby he might have been left destitute, except he should build upon some more popular number; according to the nature of all usurping rebels, which do ever trust more in the common people than in persons of sort or quality. And this may well appear by his own plot in Ireland, which was to have come with the choice of the army, from which he was diverted, as before is showed. So as his own courses inclined ever to rest upon the main strength of the multitude, and not upon surprises, or the combinations of a few.

But to return: These were the resolutions taken at that consultation, held by these five at Drury House some five or six days before the rebellion, to be reported to Essex, who ever kept in himself the binding and directing voice: which he did to prevent all differences that might grow by dissent or contradiction. And besides he had other persons (which were Cuffe and Blunt) of more inwardness and confidence with him than these (Southampton only excepted) which managed that consultation. And for the day of the enterprise, which is that must rise out of the knowledge of all the opportunities and difficulties, it was referred to Essex his own choice and appointment; it being nevertheless resolved that it should be some time before the end of Candlemas Term.

But this council and the resolutions thereof were in some points refined by Essex, and Cuffe, and Blunt: for first it was thought good, for the better making sure of the utter gate of the Court, and the greater celerity and suddenness, to have a troop at receipt to a competent number, to have come from the Mews, where they should have been assembled without suspicion in several companies, and from thence cast themselves in a moment upon the Court gate, and join with them which were within, while Essex with the main of his company were making forward.

It was also thought fit, that because they would be commonwealth's men and foresee that the business and service of the public state should not stand still, they should have ready at Court and at hand certain other persons to be offered to supply the offices and places of such her Majesty's counsellors and servants as they should demand to be removed and displaced.

But chiefly it was thought good, that the assembling of their companies together should be upon some plausible pretext: both to make divers of their company, that understood not the depth of the practices, the more willing to follow them and to engage themselves;

and to gather them together the better without peril of detecting or interrupting: and again, to take the Court the more unprovided, without any alram given. So as now there wanted nothing but the assignation of the day: which nevertheless was resolved indefinitely to be before the end of the term, as was said before, for the putting in execution of this most dangerous and execrable treason. But God, who had in his divine providence long ago cursed this action with the curse that the psalm speaketh of, *That it should be like the untimely fruit of a woman, brought forth before it came to perfection,* so disposed above, that her Majesty, understanding by a general churme[1] and muttering of the great and universal resort to Essex House, contrary to her princely admonition, and somewhat differing from his former manner (as there could not be so great fire without some smoke), upon the seventh of February, the afternoon before this rebellion, sent to Essex House Mr. Secretary Herbert, to require him to come before the Lords of her Majesty's Council, then sitting in counsel at Salisbury Court, being the Lord Treasurer's house: where it was only intended that he should have received some reprehension for exceeding the limitations of his liberty granted to him in a qualified manner, without any intention towards him of restraint; which he, under colour of not being well, excused to do: but his own guilty conscience applying it that his trains were discovered, doubting peril in any further delay, determined to hasten his enterprise, and to set it on foot the next day.

But then again, having some advertisement in the evening that the guards were doubled at Court, and laying that to the message he had received overnight, and so concluding that alarm was taken at Court, he thought it to be in vain to think of the enterprise of the Court by way of suprise: but that now his only way was to come thither in strength and to that end first to attempt the City. Wherein he did but fall back to his own former opinion, which he had in no sort neglected, but had formerly made some overtures to prepare the City to take his part; relying himself (besides his general conceit that himself was the darling and minion of the people and specially of the City) more particularly upon assurance given of Thomas Smith, then sheriff of London, a man well beloved amongst the citizens, and one that had some particular command of some of the trained forces of the City, to join with him. Having therefore con-

[1] *charme,* in the original.

cluded upon this determination, now was the time to execute in fact all that he had before in purpose digested.

First therefore he concluded of a pretext which was ever part of the plot, and which he had meditated upon and studied long before. For finding himself (thanks be to God) to seek, in her Majesty's government, of any just pretext in matter of state, either of innovation, oppression, or any unworthiness: as in all his former discontentments he had gone the beaten path of traitors, turning their imputation upon counsellors and persons of credit with their sovereign, so now he was forced to descend to the pretext of a private quarrel; giving out this speech, how that evening, when he should have been called before the Lords of the Council, there was an ambuscado of musketers placed upon the water by the device of my Lord Cobham and Sir Walter Raleigh, to have murdered him by the way as he passed. A matter of no probability; those persons having no such desperate estates or minds, as to ruin themselves and their posterity by committing so odious a crime.

But contrariwise, certain it is Sir Ferdinando Gorge accused Blunt to have persuaded him to kill, or at least apprehend, Sir Walter Raleigh; the latter whereof Blunt denieth not, and asked Sir Walter Raleigh forgiveness at the time of his death.

But this pretext, being the best he had, was taken; and then did messages and warnings fly thick up and down to every particular nobleman and gentleman, both that evening and the next morning, to draw them together in the forenoon to Essex House, dispersing the foresaid fable, That he should have been murdered; save that it was sometime on the water, sometime in his bed, varying according to the nature of a lie. He sent likewise the same night certain of his instruments, as namely one William Temple, his secretary, into the City, to disperse the same tale, having increased it some few days before by an addition, That he should have been likewise murdered by some Jesuits to the number of four: and to fortify this pretext, and to make the more buzz of the danger he stood in, he caused that night a watch to be kept all night long towards the street, in his house. The next morning, which was Sunday, they came unto him of all hands, according to his messages and warnings. Of the nobility the Earls of Rutland, Southampton, and the Lord Sands, and Sir Henry Parker, commonly called the Lord Mounteagle; besides divers knights and principal gentlemen and their followers, to the number of some three hundreth. And also it being Sunday and the hour when he had used to have a sermon at his house, it gave cause to some and colour to others to come upon that occasion. As they came, my Lord saluted and embraced, and to the generality of them gave to understand, in as plausible terms as he could, *That his life had been sought, and that he meant to go to the Court and declare his griefs to the Queen, because his enemies were mighty, and used her Majesty's name and commandment;* and desired their help to take his part; but unto the more special persons he spake high and in other terms, telling them *That he was sure of the City, and would put himself into that strength that her Majesty should not be able to stand against him, and that he would take revenge of his enemies.*

All the while after eight of the clock in the morning, the gates to the street and water were strongly guarded, and men taken in and let forth by discretion of those that held the charge, but with special caution of receiving in such as came from Court, but not suffering them to go back without my Lord's special direction, to the end no particularity of that which passed there might be known to her Majesty.

About ten of the clock, her Majesty having understanding of this strange and tumultuous assembly at Essex House, yet in her princely wisdom and moderation thought to cast water upon this fire before it brake forth to further inconvenience: and therefore using authority before she would use force, sent unto him four persons of great honour and place, and such as he ever pretended to reverence and love, to offer him justice for any griefs of his, but yet to lay her royal commandment upon him to disperse his company, and upon them to withdraw themselves.

These four honourable persons, being the Lord Keeper of the Great Seal of England, the Earl of Worcester, the Comptroller of her Majesty's household, and the Lord Chief Justice of England, came to the house, and found the gates shut upon them. But after a little stay, they were let in at the wicket; and as soon as they were within, the wicket was shut, and all their servants kept out, except the bearer of the seal. In the court they found the Earls with the rest of the company, the court in a manner full, and upon their coming towards Essex, they all flocked and thronged about them; whereupon the Lord Keeper in an audible voice delivered to the Earl the Queen's message, *That they were sent by her Majesty to understand the cause of this their assembly, and to let them know that if they had any particular cause of griefs against any persons whatsoever they should have hearing and justice.*

Whereupon the Earl of Essex in a very loud and furious voice declared, *That his life was sought,* and *that he should have been murdered in his bed,* and *that he had been perfidiously dealt withal;* and other speeches to the like effect. To which the Lord Chief Justice said, If any such matter were attempted or intended against him, it was fit for him to declare it, assuring him both a faithful relation on their part, and that they could not fail of a princely indifferency and justice on her Majesty's part.

To which the Earl of Southampton took occasion to object the assault made upon him by the Lord Gray: which my Lord Chief Justice returned upon him, and said, That in that case justice had been done, and the party was in prison for it.

Then the Lord Keeper required the Earl of Essex, that if he would not declare his griefs openly, yet that then he would impart them privately; and then they doubted not to give him or procure him satisfaction.

Upon this there arose a great clamour among the multitude: *Away, my Lord; they abuse you, they betray you; they undo you; you lose time.* Whereupon my Lord Keeper put on his hat, and said with a louder voice than before, *My Lord, let us speak with you privately, and understand your griefs; and I do command you all upon your allegiance to lay down your weapons and to depart.* Upon which words the Earl of Essex and all the rest, as disdaining commandment, put on their hats; and Essex somewhat abruptly went from him into the house, and the Counsellors followed him, thinking he would have private conference with them as was required.

And as they passed through the several rooms, they might hear many of the disordered company cry, *Kill them, kill them;* and others crying, *Nay, but shop them up, keep them as pledges, cast the great seal out at the window;* and other such audacious and traitorous speeches. But Essex took hold of the occasion and advantage to keep in deed such pledges if he were distressed, and to have the countenance to lead them with him to the Court, especially the two great magistrates of justice and the great seal of England, if he prevailed, and to deprive her Majesty of the use of their counsel in such a strait, and to engage his followers in the very beginning by such a capital act as the imprisonment of Counsellors carrying her Majesty's royal command-ment for the suppressing of a rebellious force.

And after that they were come up into his book-chamber, he gave order they should be kept fast, giving the charge of their custody principally to Sir John Davis, but adjoined unto him a warder, one Owen Salisbury, one of the most seditious and wicked persons of the number, having been a notorious robber, and one that served the enemy under Sir William Stanley, and that bare a special spleen unto my Lord Chief Justice; who guarded these honourable persons with muskets charged and matches ready fired at the chamber-door.

This done, the Earl (notwithstanding my Lord Keeper still re-quired to speak with him) left the charge of his house with Sir Gilly Mericke; and using these words to my Lord Keeper, *Have patience for awhile, I will go take order with the Mayor and Sheriffs for the City, and be with you again within half an hour,* issued with his troop into London, to the number of two hundreth, besides those that remained in the house; choice men for hardiness and valour; unto whom some gentlemen and one nobleman did after join themselves.

But from the time he went forth, it seems God did strike him with the spirit of amazement, and brought him round again to the place whence he first moved.

For after he had once by Ludgate entered into the City, he never had so much as the heart or assurance to speak any set or confident speech to the people, (but repeated only over and over his tale as he passed by, *that he should have been murthered,*) nor to do any act of foresight or courage; but he that had vowed he would never be cooped up more, cooped himself first within the walls of the City, and after within the walls of an house, as arrested by God's justice as an example of disloyalty. For passing through Cheapside, and so towards Smith's house, and finding, though some came about him, yet none joined or armed with him, he provoked them by speeches as he passed to arm, telling them, *They did him hurt and no good, to come about him with no weapons.*

But there was not in so populous a city, where he thought himself held so dear, one man, from the chiefest citizen to the meanest artificer or prentice, that armed with him: so as being extremely appalled, as divers that happened to see him then might visibly perceive in his face and countenance, and almost moulten with sweat, though without any cause of bodily labour but only by the perplexity and horror of his mind, he came to Smith's house the sheriff, where he refreshed himself a little and shifted him.

But the meanwhile it pleased God that her Majesty's directions at Court, though in a case so strange and sudden, were judicial and sound. For first there was commandment in the morning given unto the City, that every man should be in a readiness both in person and armour, but yet to keep within his own door, and to expect commandment; upon a reasonable and politic consideration, that had they armed suddenly on the streets, if there were any ill-disposed persons, they might arm on the one side and turn on the other, or at least if armed men had been seen to and fro, it would have bred a greater tumult, and more bloodshed; and the nakedness of Essex troop would not have so well appeared.

And soon after, direction was given that the Lord Burghley, taking with him the King of Heralds, should declare him traitor in the principal parts of the City; which was performed with good expedition and resolution, and the loss and hurt of some of his company. Besides that, the Earl of Cumberland, and Sir Thomas Gerard, Knight-marshal, rode into the City, and declared and notified to the people that he was a traitor: from which time divers of his troop withdrawing from him, and none other coming in to him, there was nothing but despair. For having stayed awhile, as is said, at Sheriff Smith's house, and there changing his pretext of a private quarrel, and publishing *That the realm should have been sold to the Infanta,* the better to spur on the people to rise and [having] called and given commandment to have brought arms and weapons of all sorts, and been soon after advertised of the proclamation, he came forth in a hurry.

So having made some stay in Gracious Street, and being dismayed upon knowledge given to him that forces were coming forwards against him under the conduct of the Lord Admiral, the Lieutenant of her Majesty's forces, and not knowing what course to take, he determined in the end to go back towards his own house, as well in hope to have found the Counsellors there, and by them to have served some turn, as upon trust that towards night his friends in the City would gather their spirits together and rescue him, as himself declared after to M. Lieutenant of the Tower.

But for the Counsellors, it had pleased God to make one of the principal offenders his instrument for their delivery; who seeing my

Lord's case desperate, and contriving how to redeem his fault and save himself, came to Sir John Davis and Sir Gilly Mericke, as sent from my Lord; and so procured them to be released.

But the Earl of Essex, with his company that was left, thinking to recover his house, made on by land towards Ludgate; where being resisted by a company of pikemen and other forces, gathered together by the wise and diligent care of the Bishop of London, and commanded by Sir John Luson, and yet attempting to clear the passage, he was with no great difficulty repulsed. At which encounter Sir Christopher Blunt was sore wounded, and young Tracy slain, on his part; and one Waits on the Queen's part, and some other. Upon which repulse he went back and fled towards the waterside, and took boat at Queenhive, and so was received into Essex House at the watergate, which he fortified and barricado'd; but instantly the Lord Lieutenant so disposed his companies, as all passage and issue forth was cut off from him both by land and water, and all succours that he might hope for were discouraged: and leaving the Earl of Cumberland, the Earl of Lincoln, the Lord Thomas Howard, the Lord Gray, the Lord Burghley, and the Lord Compton, Sir Walter Raleigh, Sir Thomas Gerrard, with divers others, before the house to landward, my Lord Lieutenant himself thought good, taking with him the Lord of Effingham, Lord Cobham, Sir John Stanhope, Sir Robert Sidney, M. Foulk Grevill, with divers others, to assail the garden and banquetting-house on the waterside, and presently forced the garden, and won to the walls of the house, and was ready to have assailed the house; but out of a Christian and honourable consideration, understanding that there were in the house the Countess of Essex, and the Lady Rich, with their gentlewomen, let the Earl of Essex know by Sir Robert Sidney, that he was content to suffer the ladies and gentlewomen to come forth. Whereupon Essex, returning the Lord Lieutenant thanks for the compassion and care he had of the ladies, desired only to have an hour's respite to make way for their going out, and an hour after to barricado the place again. Which because it could make no alteration to the hindrance of the service, the Lord Lieutenant thought good to grant. But Essex, having had some talk within a sally, and despairing of the success, and thinking better to yield himself, sent word that upon some conditions he would yield.

But the Lord Lieutenant utterly refusing to hear of capitulations, Essex desired to speak with my Lord, who thereupon went up close to the house; and the late Earls of Essex and Southampton, with divers other lords and gentlemen their partakers, presented themselves upon the leads: and Essex said, he would not capitulate, but entreat; and made three petitions. The first, *That they might be civilly used:* whereof the Lord Lieutenant assured them. The second, *That they might have an honourable trial:* whereof the Lord Lieutenant answered they needed not to doubt. The third, *That he might have Aston a preacher with him in prison for the comfort of his soul:* which the Lord Lieutenant said he would move to her Majesty, not doubting of the matter of his request, though he could not absolutely promise him that person. Whereupon they all, with the ceremony amongst martial men accustomed, came down and submitted themselves and yielded up their swords, which was about ten of the clock at night; there having been slain in holding of the house, by musket shot, Owen Salisbury, and some few more on the part of my Lord, and some few likewise slain and hurt on the Queen's part: and presently, as well the Lords as the rest of their confederates of quality were severally taken into the charge of divers particular lords and gentlemen, and by them conveyed to the Tower and other prisons.

So as this action, so dangerous in respect of the person of the leader, the manner of the combination, and the intent of the plot, brake forth and ended within the compass of twelve hours, and with the loss of little blood, and in such sort as the next day all courts of justice were open, and did sit in their accustomed manner; giving good subjects and all reasonable men just cause to think, not the less of the offenders' treason, but the more of her Majesty's princely magnanimity and prudent foresight in so great a peril; and chiefly of God's goodness, that hath blessed her Majesty in this, as in many things else, with so rare and divine felicity.

APPENDIX C

Francis Bacon's "Apology Concerning the Earl of Essex"

It may please your good Lordship: I cannot be ignorant, and ought to be sensible, of the wrong which I sustain in common speech, as if I had been false or unthankful to that noble but unfortunate Earl, the Earl of Essex: and for satisfying the vulgar sort, I do no so much regard it; though I love good name, but yet as an handmaid and attendant of honesty and virtue. For I am of his opinion that said pleasantly, *That it was a shame to him that was a suitor to the mistress, to make love to the waiting-woman*; and therefore to woo or court common fame otherwise than it followeth upon honest courses, I, for my part, find not myself fit nor disposed. But on the other side, there is no worldly thing that concerneth myself which I hold more dear than the good opinion of certain persons; amongst which there is none I would more willingly give satisfaction unto than to your Lordship. First, because you loved my Lord of Essex, and therefore will not be partial towards me; which is part of that I desire: next, because it hath ever pleased you to show yourself to me an honourable friend, and so no baseness in me to seek to satisfy you: and lastly, because I know your Lordship is excellently grounded in the true rules and habits of duties and moralities; which must be they which shall decide this matter: wherein (my Lord) my defence needeth to be but simple and brief: namely, that whatsoever I did concerning that action and proceeding, was done in my duty and service to the Queen and the State; in which I would not show myself false-hearted nor faint-hearted for any man's sake living. For every honest man, that hath his heart well planted, will forsake his King rather than forsake God, and forsake his friend rather than forsake his King; and yet will forsake any earthly commodity, yea and his own life in some cases, rather than forsake his friend. I hope the world hath not forgotten these degrees, else the heathen saying, *Amicus usque ad aras*, shall judge them. And if any man shall say that I did officiously intrude myself into that business, because I had no ordinary place; the like may be said of all the business in effect that passed the hands of the learned counsel, either of State or Revenues, these many years, wherein I was continually used. For, as your Lordship may remember, the Queen knew her strength so well, as she looked her word should be a warrant; and after the manner of the choicest princes before her, did not always tie her trust to place, but did sometime divide private favour from office. And I for my part, though I was not so unseen in the world but I knew the condition was subject to envy and peril; yet because I knew again she was constant in her favours, and made an end where she began, and specially because she upheld me with extraordinary access, and other demonstrations of confidence and grace, I resolved to endure it in expectation of better. But my scope and desire is, that your Lordship would be pleased to have the honourable patience to know the truth in some particularity of all that passed in this cause wherein I had any part, that you may perceive how honest a heart I ever bare to my Sovereign and to my Country, and to that Nobleman, who had so well deserved of me, and so well accepted of my deservings; whose fortune I cannot remember without much grief. But for any action of mine towards him, there is nothing that passed me in my life-time that cometh to my remembrance with more clearness and less check of conscience; for it will appear to your Lordship that I was not only not opposite to my Lord of Essex, but that I did occupy the utmost of my wits, and adventure my fortune with the Queen to have reintegrated his, and so continued faithfully and industriously till his last fatal impatience (for so I will call it), after which day there was not time to work for him; though the same my affection, when it could not work on the subject proper, went to the next, with no ill effect towards some others, who I think do rather not know it than not acknowledge it. And this I will assure your Lordship, I will leave nothing untold that is truth, for any enemy that I have to add; and on the other side, I must reserve much which makes for me, upon many respects of duty, which I esteem above my credit: and what I have here set down to your Lordship, I protest, as I hope to have any part in God's favour, is true.

It is well known, how I did many years since dedicate my travels and studies to the use and (as I may term it) service of my Lord of Essex, which, I protest before God, I did not, making election of him as the likeliest mean of mine own advancement, but out of the humour of a man, that ever, from the time I had any use of reason (whether it were reading upon good books, or upon the example of a good father, or by nature) I loved my country more than was answerable to my fortune, and I held at that time my Lord to be the fittest instrument to do good to the State; and therefore I applied myself to him in a manner which I think happeneth rarely amongst men: for I did not only labour carefully and industriously in that he set me about, whether it were matter of advice or otherwise, but neglecting the Queen's service, mine own fortune, and in a sort my vocation, I did nothing but devise and ruminate with myself to the best of my understanding, propositions and memorials of anything that might concern his Lordship's honour, fortune, or service. And when not long after I entered into this course, my brother Master Anthony Bacon came from beyond the seas, being a gentleman whose ability the world taketh knowledge of for matters of State, specially foreign, I did likewise knit his service to be at my Lord's disposing. And on the other side, I must and will ever acknowledge my Lord's love, trust, and favour towards me; and last of all his liberality, having infeoffed me of land which I sold for eighteen hundred pounds to Master Reynold Nicholas, and I think was more worth, and that at such a time, and with so kind and noble circumstances, as the manner was as much as the matter; which though it be but an idle digression, yet because I am not willing to be short in commemoration of his benefits, I will presume to trouble your Lordship with relating to you the manner of it. After the Queen had denied me the Solicitor's place, for the which his Lordship had been a long and earnest suitor on my behalf, it pleased him to come to me from Richmond to Twicknam Park, and brake with me, and said: Master Bacon, the Queen hath denied me yon place for you, and hath placed another; I know you are the least part of your own matter, but you fare ill because you have chosen me for your mean and dependance; you have spent your time and thoughts in my matters; I die (these were his very words) if I do not somewhat towards your fortune: you shall not deny to accept a piece of land which I will bestow upon you. My answer I remember was, that for my fortune it was no great matter; but that his Lordship's offer made me call to mind what was wont to be said when I was in France of the Duke of Guise, that he was the greatest usurer in France, because he had turned all his estate into obligations: meaning that he had left himself nothing, but only had bound numbers of persons

to him. Now my Lord (said I) I would not have you imitate his
course, nor turn your state thus by great gifts into obligations, for
you will find many bad debtors. He bade me take no care for that,
and pressed it: whereupon I said: My Lord, I see I must be your
homager, and hold land of your gift; but do you know the manner
of doing homage in law? always it is with a saving of his faith to the
King and his other Lords; and therefore, my Lord (said I), I can be
no more yours than I was, and it must be with the ancient savings:
and if I grow to be a rich man, you will give me leave to give it back
to some of your unrewarded followers. But to return: sure I am
(though I can arrogate nothing to myself but that I was a faithful
remembrancer to his Lordship) that while I had most credit with
him his fortune went on best. And yet in two main points we always
directly and contradictorily differed, which I will mention to your
Lordship because it giveth light to all that followed. The one was, I
ever set this down, that the only course to be held with the Queen,
was by obsequiousness and observance; and I remember I would
usually gage confidently, that if he would take that course constantly,
and with choice of good particulars to express it, the Queen would
be brought in time to Assuerus question, to ask, *What should be done
to the man that the King would honour:* meaning, that her goodness was
without limit, where there was a true concurrence; which I knew in
her nature to be true. My Lord on the other side had a settled
opinion, that the Queen could be brought to nothing but by a kind
of necessity and authority; and I well remember, when by violent
courses at any time he had got his will, he would ask me: Now Sir,
whose principles be true? and I would again say to him: *My Lord, these
courses be like to hot waters, they will help at a pang; but if you use them, you
shall spoil the stomach, and you shall be fain still to make them stronger and
stronger, and yet in the end they will lesse their operation;* with much other
variety, wherewith I used to touch that string. Another point was,
that I always vehemently dissuaded him from seeking greatness by a
military dependance, or by a popular dependance, as that which
would breed in the Queen jealousy, in himself presumption, and in
the State perturbation: and I did usually compare them to Icarus'
two wings which were joined on with wax, and would make him
venture to soar too high, and then fail him at the height. And I
would further say unto him: My Lord, stand upon two feet, and fly
not upon two wings. The two feet are the two kinds of Justice,
commutative and distributive: use your greatness for advancing of

merit and virtue, and relieving wrongs and burdens; you shall need no other art or fineness: but he would tell me, that opinion came not from my mind but from my robe. But it is very true that I, that never meant to enthral myself to my Lord of Essex, nor any other man, more than stood with the public good, did (though I could little prevail) divert him by all means possible from courses of the wars and popularity: for I saw plainly the Queen must either live or die; if she lived, then the times would be as in the declination of an old prince; if she died, the times would be as in the beginning of a new; and that if his Lordship did rise too fast in these courses, the times might be dangerous for him, and he for them. Nay, I remember I was thus plain with him upon his voyage to the Islands, when I saw every spring put forth such actions of charge and provocation, that I said to him: My Lord, when I came first unto you, I took you for a physician that desired to cure the diseases of the State; but now I doubt you will be like those physicians which can be content to keep their patients low, because they would always be in request: which plainness he nevertheless took very well, as he had an excellent ear, and was *patientissimus veri,* and assured me the case of the realm required it: and I think this speech of mine, and the like renewed afterwards, pricked him to write that Apology which is in many men's hands.

But this difference in two points so main and material, bred in process of time a discontinuance of privateness (as it is the manner of men seldom to communicate where they think their courses not approved) between his Lordship and myself; so as I was not called nor advised with, for some year and a half before his Lordship's going into Ireland, as in former time: yet nevertheless touching his going into Ireland, it pleased him expressly and in a set manner to desire mine opinion and counsel. At which time I did not only dissuade, but protest against his going, telling him with as much vehemency and asseveration as I could, that absence in that kind would exulcerate the Queen's mind, whereby it would not be possible for him to carry himself so as to give her sufficient contentment; nor for her to carry herself so as to give him sufficient countenance: which would be ill for her, ill for him, and ill for the State. And because I would omit no argument, I remember I stood also upon the difficulty of the action; setting before him out of histories, that the Irish was such an enemy as the ancient Gauls, or Britons, or Germans were, and that we saw how the Romans, who had such discipline to govern their soldiers, and such donatives to encourage them, and the whole world in a manner to levy them; yet when they came to deal with enemies which placed their felicity only in liberty and the sharpness of their sword, and had the natural and elemental advantages of woods, and bogs, and hardness of bodies, they ever found they had their hands full of them; and therefore concluded, that going over with such expectation as he did, and through the churlishness[1] of the enterprize not like to answer it, would mightily diminish his reputation: and many other reasons I used, so as I am sure I never in anything in my life-time dealt with him in like earnestness by speech, by writing, and by all the means I could devise. For I did as plainly see his overthrow chained as it were by destiny to that journey, as it is possible for any man to ground a judgment upon future contingents. But my Lord, howsoever his ear was open, yet his heart and resolution was shut against that advice, whereby his ruin might have been prevented. After my Lord's going, I saw how true a prophet I was, in regard of the evident alteration which naturally succeeded in the Queen's mind; and thereupon I was still in watch to find the best occasion that in the weakness of my power I could either take or minister, to pull him out of the fire if it had been possible: and not long after, methought I saw some overture thereof, which I apprehended readily; a particularity I think be[2] known to very few, and the which I do the rather relate unto your Lordship, because I hear it should be talked, that while my Lord was in Ireland I revealed some matter against him, or I cannot tell what; which if it were not a mere slander as the rest is, but had any though never so little colour, was surely upon this occasion. The Queen one day at Nonesuch, a little (as I remember) before Cuffe's coming over, I attending her, showed a passionate distaste of my Lord's proceedings in Ireland, as if they were unfortunate, without judgment, contemptuous, and not without some private end of his own, and all that might be, and was pleased, as she spake of it to many that she trusted least, so to fall into the like speech with me; whereupon I, who was still awake and true to my grounds which I thought surest for my Lord's good, said to this effect: Madam, I know not the particulars of estate, and I know this, that Princes' actions must have no abrupt periods or conclusions, but otherwise I would think, that if you had my Lord of

[1]*curlishness*, in original.
[2]So in original.

Essex here with a white staff in his hand, as my Lord of Leicester had, and continued him still about you for society to yourself, and for an honour and ornament to your attendance and Court in the eyes of your people, and in the eyes of foreign Embassadors, then were he in his right element: for to discontent him as you do, and yet to put arms and power into his hands, may be a kind of temptation to make him prove cumbersome and unruly. And therefore if you would *imponere bonam clausulam,* and send for him and satisfy him with honour here near you, if your affairs which (as I have said) I am not acquainted with, will permit it, I think were the best way. Which course, your Lordship knoweth, if it had been taken, then all had been well, and no contempt in my Lord's coming over, nor continuance of these jealousies, which that employment of Ireland bred, and my Lord here in his former greatness. Well, the next news that I heard was, that my Lord was come over, and that he was committed to his chamber for leaving Ireland without the Queen's license: this was at Nonesuch, where (as my duty was) I came to his Lordship, and talked with him privately about a quarter of an hour, and he asked mine opinion of the course was taken with him; I told him, My Lord, *Nubecula est, cito transibit;* it is but a mist: but shall I tell your Lordship, it is as mists are, if it go upwards, it may haps cause a shower, if downwards, it will clear up. And therefore good my Lord carry it so, as you take away by all means all umbrages and distastes from the Queen; and specially, if I were worthy to advise you (as I have been by yourself thought, and now your question imports the continuance of that opinion) observe three points: First, make not this cessation or peace which is concluded with Tyrone, as a service wherein you glory, but as a shuffling up of a prosecution which was not very fortunate. Next, represent not to the Queen any necessity of estate, whereby, as by a coercion or wrench, she should think herself inforced to send you back into Ireland, but leave it to her. Thirdly, seek access *importune, opportune,* seriously, sportingly, every way. I remember my Lord was willing to hear me, but spake very few words, and shaked his head sometimes, as if he thought I was in the wrong; but sure I am, he did just contrary in every one of these three points. After this, during the while since my Lord was committed to my Lord Keeper's, I came divers times to the Queen, as I had used to do, about causes of her revenue and law business, as is well known; by reason of which accesses, according to the ordinary charities of Court, it was given out that I was one of them that incensed the Queen against my Lord of Essex. These speeches, I cannot tell, nor I will not think, that they grew any way from her Majesty's own speeches, whose memory I will ever honour; if they did, she is with God, and *miserum est ab illis laedi, dequibus non possis queri.* But I might give this testimony to my Lord Cecil, that one time in his house at the Savoy he dealt with me directly, and said to me, Cousin, I hear it, but I believe it not, that you should do some ill office to my Lord of Essex; for my part I am merely passive and not active in this action, and I follow the Queen and that heavily, and I lead her not; my Lord of Essex is one that in nature I could consent with as well as with any one living; the Queen indeed is my Sovereign, and I am her creature, I may not leese her, and the same course I would wish you to take: whereupon I satisfied him how far I was from any such mind. And as sometimes it cometh to pass, that men's inclinations are opened more in a toy, than in a serious matter: A little before that time, being about the middle of Michaelmas term, her Majesty had a purpose to dine at my lodge at Twicknam Park, at which time I had (though I profess not to be a poet) prepared a sonnet directly tending and alluding to draw on her Majesty's reconcilement to my Lord, which I remember also I showed to a great person, and one of my Lord's nearest friends, who commended it: this, though it be (as I said) but a toy, yet it showed plainly in what spirit I proceeded, and that I was ready not only to do my Lord good offices, but to publish and declare myself for him: and never was so ambitious of any thing in my life-time, as I was to have carried some token or favour from her Majesty to my Lord; using all the art I had, both to procure her Majesty to send, and myself to be the messenger: for as to the former, I feared not to allege to her, that this proceeding toward my Lord was a thing towards the people very implausible; and therefore wished her Majesty, howsoever she did, yet to discharge herself of it, and to lay it upon others; and therefore that she should intermix her proceeding with some immediate graces from herself, that the world might take the knowledge of her princely nature and goodness, lest it should alienate the hearts of her people from her. Which I did stand upon, knowing very well that if she once relented to send or visit, those demonstrations would prove matter of substance for my Lord's good. And to draw that employment upon myself, I advised her Majesty, that whensoever God should move her to turn the light of her favour towards my Lord, to make signification to him thereof, that her Majesty, if she did it not in person, would at the least use some such mean as might not intitle themselves to any part of the thanks, as persons that were thought mighty with her, to work her, or to bring her about; but to use some such as could not be thought but a mere conduct of her own goodness: but I could never prevail with her, though I am persuaded she saw plainly whereat I levelled; but she had me in jealousy, that I was not hers intirely, but still had inward and deep respects towards my Lord, more than stood at that time with her will and pleasure. About the same time I remember an answer of mine in a matter which had some affinity with my Lord's cause, which though it grew from me, went after about in others' names. For her Majesty being mightily incensed with that book which was dedicated to my Lord of Essex, being a story of the first year of King Henry the fourth, thinking it a seditious prelude to put into the people's heads boldness and faction, said she had good opinion that there was treason in it, and asked me if I could not find any places in it that might be drawn within case of treason: whereto I answered: for treason surely I found none, but for felony very many. And when her Majesty hastily asked me wherein, I told her the author had committed very apparent theft, for he had taken most of the sentences of Cornelius Tacitus, and translated them into English, and put them into his text. And another time, when the Queen would not be persuaded that it was his writing whose name was to it, but that it had some more mischievous author, and said with great indignation that she would have him racked to produce his author, I replied, Nay Madam, he is a Doctor, never rack his person, but rack his stile; let him have pen, ink, and paper, and help of books, and be enjoined to continue the story where it breaketh off, and I will undertake by collecting[3] the stiles to judge whether he were the author or no. But for the main matter, sure I am, when the Queen at any time asked mine opinion of my Lord's case, I ever in one tenour said unto her; That they were faults which the law might term contempts, because they were the transgression of her particular directions and instructions: but then what defence might be made of them, in regard of the great interest the person had in her Majesty favour; in regard of the greatness of his place, and the ampleness of his commission; in regard of the nature of the business, being action of war, which in common cases cannot be tied to strictness of instructions; in regard of the distance of place, having

[3]So in original.

also a sea between, that demands and commands must be subject to wind and weather; in regard of a counsel of State in Ireland which he had at his back to avow his actions upon; and lastly, in regard of a good intention that he would allege for himself, which I told her in some religions was held to be a sufficient dispensation for God's commandments, much more for Princes': in all these regards, I besought her Majesty to be advised again and again, how she brought the cause into any public question: nay, I went further, for I told her, my Lord was an eloquent and well-spoken man, and besides his eloquence of nature or art, he had an eloquence of accident which passed them both, which was the pity and benevolence of his hearers; and therefore that when he should come to his answer for himself, I doubted his words would have so unequal passage above theirs that should charge him, as would not be for her Majesty's honour; and therefore wished the conclusion might be, that they might wrap it up privately between themselves, and that she would restore my Lord to his former attendance, with some addition of honour to take away discontent. But this I will never deny, that I did show no approbation generally of his being sent back again into Ireland, both because it would have carried a repugnancy with my former discourse, and because I was in mine own heart fully persuaded that it was not good, neither for the Queen, nor for the State, nor for himself: and yet I did not dissuade it neither, but left it ever as *locus lubricus.* For this particularity I do well remember, that after your Lordship was named for the place in Ireland, and not long before your going, it pleased her Majesty at Whitehall to speak to me of that nomination: at which time I said to her; Surely Madam, if you mean not to employ my Lord of Essex thither again, your Majesty cannot make a better choice; and was going on to show some reason; and her Majesty interrupted me with great passion: Essex! (said she); whensoever I send Essex back again into Ireland, I will marry you, claim it of me: whereunto I said; Well Madam, I will release that contract, if his going be for the good of your State. Immediately after the Queen had thought of a course (which was also executed) to have somewhat published in the Star-chamber, for the satisfaction of the world touching my Lord of Essex his restraint, and my Lord of Essex not to be called to it, but occasion to be taken by reason of some libels then dispersed: which when her Majesty propounded unto me, I was utterly against it; and told her plainly, that the people would say that my Lord was wounded upon his back,

and that Justice had her balance taken from her, which ever con-
sisted of an accusation and defence, with many other quick and
significant terms to that purpose: insomuch that I remember I said,
that my Lord *in foro famoe* was too hard for her; and therefore
wished her, as I had done before, to wrap it up privately. And
certainly I offended her at that time, which was rare with me: for I
call to mind, that both the Christmas, Lent, and Easter term following, though I came divers times to her upon law business, yet
methought her face and manner was not so clear and open to me as
it was at the first. And she did directly charge me, that I was absent
that day at the Star-chamber, which was very true; but I alleged
some indisposition of body to excuse it: and during all the time
aforesaid, there was *altum silentium* from her to me touching my
Lord of Essex causes.

But towards the end of Easter term, her Majesty brake with me,
and told me that she had found my words true: for that the proceeding in the Star-chamber had done no good, but rather kindled
factious bruits (as she termed them) than quenched them, and therefore that she was determined now for the satisfaction of the world,
to proceed against my Lord in the Star-chamber by an information
ore tenus, and to have my Lord brought to his answer: howbeit she
said she would assure me that whatsoever she did should be towards
my Lord *ad castigationem, et non ad destructionem;* as indeed she had
often repeated the same phrase before: whereunto I said (to the end
utterly to divert her), Madam, if you will have me speak to you in
this argument, I must speak to you as Friar Bacon's head spake, that
said first, *Time is,* and then *Time was,* and *Time would never be:* for
certainly (said I) it is now far too late, the matter is cold and hath
taken too much wind; whereat she seemed again offended and rose
from me, and that resolution for a while continued; and after, in the
beginning of Midsummer term, I attending her, and finding her
settled in that resolution (which I heard of also otherwise), she
falling upon the like speech, it is true that, seeing no other remedy, I
said to her slightly, Why, Madam, if you will needs have a proceeding, you were best have it in some such sort as Ovid spake of his
mistress, *Est aliquid luce patente minus,* to make a counsel-table matter
of it, and there an end; which speech again she seemed to take in ill
part; but yet I think it did good at that time, and help to divert that
course of proceeding by information in the Star-chamber. Nevertheless afterwards it pleased her to make a more solemn matter of

the proceeding; and some few days after, when[4] order was given that the matter should be heard at York-house, before an assembly of Counsellors, Peers, and Judges, and some audience of men of quality to be admitted, and then did some principal counsellors send for us of the learned counsel, and notify her Majesty's pleasure unto us, save that it was said to me openly by one of them, that her Majesty was not yet resolved whether she would have me forborne in the business or no. And hereupon might arise that other sinister and untrue speech that I hear is raised of me, how I was a suitor to be used against my Lord of Essex at that time: for it is very true that I, that knew well what had passed between the Queen and me, and what occasion I had given her both of distaste and distrust in crossing her disposition by standing stedfastly for my Lord of Essex, and suspecting it also to be a stratagem arising from some particular emulation, I writ to her two or three words of compliment, signifying to her Majesty, that if she would be pleased to spare me in my Lord of Essex cause, out of the consideration she took of my obligation towards him, I should reckon it for one of her highest favours; but otherwise desiring her Majesty to think that I knew the degrees of duties, and that no particular obligation whatsoever to any subject could supplant or weaken that entireness of duty that I did owe and bear to her and her service; and this was the goodly suit I made, being a respect that no man that had his wits could have omitted: but nevertheless I had a further reach in it, for I judged that day's work would be a full period of any bitterness or harshness between the Queen and my Lord, and therefore if I declared myself fully according to her mind at that time, which could not do my Lord any manner of prejudice, I should keep my credit with her ever after, whereby to do my Lord service. Hereupon the next news that I heard was, that we were all sent for again, and that her Majesty's pleasure was, we all should have parts in the business; and the Lords falling into distribution of our parts, it was allotted to me, that I should set forth some undutiful carriage of my Lord, in giving occasion and countenance to a seditious pamphlet, as it was termed, which was dedicated unto him, which was the book before-mentioned of King Henry the fourth. Whereupon I replied to that allotment, and said to their Lordships, that it was an old matter, and had no manner of coherence with the rest of the charge, being

[4]So in original.

matters of Ireland, and therefore that I having been wronged by bruits before, this would expose me to them more; and it would be said I gave in evidence mine own tales. It was answered again with good show, that because it was considered how I stood tied to my Lord of Essex, therefore that part was thought fittest for me which did him least hurt; for that whereas all the rest was matter of charge and accusation, this only was but matter of caveat and admonition. Wherewith though I was in mine own mind little satisfied, because I knew well a man were better to be charged with some faults, than admonished of some others: yet the conclusion binding upon the Queen's pleasure directly *volens nolens,* I could not avoid that part that was laid upon me; which part if in the delivery I did handle not tenderly (though no man before me did so in so clear terms free my Lord from all disloyalty as I did), that, your Lordship knoweth, must be ascribed to the superior duty I did owe to the Queen's frame and honour in a public proceeding, and partly to the intention I had to uphold myself in credit and strength with the Queen, the better to be able to do my Lord good offices afterwards: for as soon as this day was past, I lost no time, but the very next day following (as I remember) I attended her Majesty, fully resolved to try and put in ure my utmost endeavour, so far as I in my weakness could give furtherance, to bring my Lord again speedily into Court and into favour; and knowing (as I supposed at least) how the Queen was to be used, I thought that to make her conceive that the matter went well then, was the way to make her leave off there: and I remember well, I said to her, You have now Madam obtained victory over two things, which the greatest princes in the world cannot at their wills subdue; the one is over fame, the other is over a great mind: for surely the world be now, I hope, reasonably well satisfied; and for my Lord, he did show that humiliation towards your Majesty, as I am persuaded he was never in his life-time more fit for your favour than he is now: therefore if your Majesty will not mar it by lingering, but give over at the best, and now you have made so good a full point, receive him again with tenderness, I shall then think that all that is past is for the best. Whereat I remember she took exceeding great contentment, and did often iterate and put me in mind, that she had ever said that her proceedings should be *ad reparationem* and not *ad ruinam,* as who saith, that now was the time I should well perceive that that saying of hers should prove true. And further she willed me to set down in writing all that passed that day.

I obeyed her commandment, and within some few days brought her again the narration, which I did read unto her at two several afternoons: and when I came to that part that set forth my Lord's own answer (which was my principal care), I do well bear in mind that she was extraordinarily moved with it, in kindness and relenting towards my Lord, and told me afterwards (speaking how well I had expressed my Lord's part) that she perceived old love would not easily be forgotten; whereunto I answered suddenly, that I hoped she meant that by herself. But in conclusion I did advise her, that now she had taken a representation of the matter to herself, that she would let it go no further: For Madam (said I) the fire blazeth well already, what should you tumble it? And besides, it may please you keep a convenience with yourself in this case; for since your express direction was, there should be no register nor clerk to take this sentence, nor no record or memorial made up of the proceeding, why should you now do that popularly, which you would not admit to be done judicially? Whereupon she did agree that that writing should be suppressed; and I think there were not five persons that ever saw it. But from this time forth, during the whole latter end of that summer, while the Court was at Nonesuch and Oatlands, I made it my task and scope to take and give occasions for my Lord's reintegration in his fortune: which my intention I did also signify to my Lord as soon as ever he was at his liberty, whereby I might without peril of the Queen's indignation write to him; and having received from his Lordship a courteous and loving acception of my good will and endeavours, I did apply it in all my accesses to the Queen, which were very many at that time, and purposely sought and wrought upon other variable pretences, but only and chiefly for that purpose. And on the other side, I did not forbear to give my Lord from time to time faithful advertisement what I found, and what I wished. And I drew for him by his appointment some letters to her Majesty, which though I knew well his Lordship's gift and stile was far better than mine own, yet because he required it, alleging that by his long restraint he was grown almost a stranger to the Queen's present conceits, I was ready to perform it: and sure I am that for the space of six weeks or two months it prospered so well, as I expected continually his restoring to his attendance. And I was never better welcome to the Queen, nor more made of, than when I spake fullest and boldest for him: in which kind the particulars were exceeding many; whereof, for an example, I will remember to your Lordship one or two: as at one time, I call to mind, her Majesty was speaking of a fellow that undertook to cure, or at least to ease my brother of his gout, and asked me how it went forwards: and I told her Majesty that at the first he received good by it, but after in the course of his cure he found himself at a stay or rather worse: the Queen said again, I will tell you, Bacon, the error of it: the manner of these physicians, and especially these empirics, is to continue one kind of medicine, which at the first is proper, being to draw out the ill humour, but after they have not the discretion to change their medicine, but apply still drawing medicines, when they should rather intend to cure and corroborate the part. Good Lord Madam (said I), how wisely and aptly you can speak and discern of physic ministered to the body, and consider not that there is the like occasion of physic ministered to the mind: as now in the case of my Lord Essex, your princely word ever was that you intended ever to reform his mind, and not ruin his fortune: I know well you cannot but think that you have drawn the humour sufficiently, and therefore it were more than time, and it were but for doubt of mortifying or exulcerating, that you did apply and minister strength and comfort unto him: for these same gradations of yours are fitter to corrupt than correct any mind of greatness. And another time I remember she told me for news, that my Lord had written unto her some very dutiful letters, and that she had been moved by them, and when she took it to be the abundance of the heart, she found it to be but a preparative to a suit for the renewing of his farm of sweet wines: whereunto I replied, O Madam, how doth your Majesty conster of these things, as if these two could not stand well together, which indeed nature hath planted in all creatures. For there but two sympathies, the one towards *perfection,* other towards *preservation.* That to perfection, as the iron contendeth to the loadstone; that to preservation, as the vine will creep towards a stake or prop that stands by it; not for any love to the stake, but to uphold itself. And therefore, Madam, you must distinguish: my Lord's desire to do you service is as to his perfection, that which he thinks himself to be born for; whereas his desire to obtain this thing of you, is but for a sustentation. And not to trouble your Lordship with many other particulars like unto these, it was at the self-same time that I did draw, with my Lord's privity, and by his appointment, two letters, the one written as from my brother, the other as an answer returned from my Lord, both to be by me in secret manner showed to the Queen, which it pleased my Lord very strangely to mention at the bar; the scope of which were but to represent and picture forth unto her Majesty my Lord's mind to be such as I knew her Majesty would fainest have had it: which letters whosoever shall see (for they cannot now be retracted or altered, being by reason of my brother's or his Lordship's servants' delivery long since comen into divers hands) let him judge, specially if he knew the Queen, and do remember those times, whether they were not the labours of one that sought to bring the Queen about for my Lord of Essex his good. The troth is, that the issue of all his dealing grew to this, that the Queen, by some slackness of my Lord's, as I imagine, liked him worse and worse, and grew more incensed towards him. Then she, remembering belike the continual and incessant and confident speeches and courses that I had held on my Lord's side, became utterly alienated from me, and for the space of at least three months, which was between Michaelmas and New-year's-tide following, would not as much as look on me, but turned away from me with express and purpose-like discountenance wheresoever she saw me; and at such time as I desired to speak with her about law-business, ever sent me forth very slight refusals; insomuch as it is most true, that immediately after New-year's-tide I desired to speak with her; and being admitted to her, I dealt with her plainly and said, Madam, I see you withdraw your favour from me, and now that I have lost many friends for your sake, I shall leese you too: you have put me like one of those that the Frenchmen call *enfans perdus,* that serve on foot before horsemen, so have you put me into matters of envy without place, or without strength; and I know at chess a pawn before the king is ever much played upon; a great many love me not, because they think I have been against my Lord of Essex; and you love me not, because you know I have been for him: yet will I never repent me, that I have dealt in symplicity of heart towards you both, without respect of cautions to myself; and therefore *vivus vidensque pereo.* If I do break my neck, I shall do it in manner as Master Dorrington did it, which walked on the battlements of the church many days, and took a view and survey where he should fall: and so Madam (said I) I am not so simple but that I take a prospect of mine overthrow, only I thought I would tell you so much, that you may know that it was faith and not folly that brought me into it, and so I will pray for you. Upon which speeches of mine uttered with some passion, it is true her Majesty was exceedingly moved, and accumulated a number of kind and gracious words upon me, and willed me to rest upon this, *Gratia mea sufficit,* and a number of other sensible and tender words and demonstrations, such as more could not be; but as touching my Lord of Essex, *ne verbum quidem.* Whereupon I departed, resting then determined to meddle no more in the matter; as that that I saw would overthrow me, and not be able to do him any good. And thus I made mine own peace with mine own confidence at that time; and this was the last time I saw her Majesty before the eighth of February, which was the day of my Lord of Essex his misfortune. After which time, for that I performed at the bar in my public service, your Lordship knoweth by the rules of duty that I was to do it honestly, and without prevarication; but for any putting myself into it, I protest before God, I never moved neither the Queen, nor any person living, concerning my being used in the service, either of evidence or examination; but it was merely laid upon me with the rest of my fellows. And for the time which passed, I mean between the arraignment and my Lord's suffering, I well remember I was but once with the Queen; at what time, though I durst not tell directly for my Lord as things then stood, yet generally I did both commend her Majesty's mercy, terming it to her as an excellent balm that did continually distil from her sovereign hands, and made an excellent odour in the senses of her people; and not only so, but I took hardiness to extenuate, not the fact, for that I durst not, but the danger, telling her that if some base or cruel-minded persons had entered into such an action, it might have caused much blood and combustion; but it appeared well they were such as knew not how to play the malefactors; and some other words which I now omit. And as for the rest of the carriage of myself in that service, I have many honourable witnesses that can tell, that the next day after my Lord's arraignment, by my diligence and information touching the quality and nature of the offenders, six of nine were stayed, which otherwise had been attainted, I bringing their Lordships' letter for their say, after the jury was sworn to pass upon them; so near it went: and how careful I was, and made it my part, that whosoever was in trouble about that matter, as soon as ever his case was sufficiently known and defined of, might not continue in restraint, but be set at liberty; and many other parts, which I am well assured of [5] stood with the duty of an honest man. But indeed I will not deny for the case of Sir Thomas Smith of London, the Queen demanding my opinion of it, I told her I thought it was as hard as many of the rest: but what was the reason? because at that time I had seen only his accusation, and had never been present at any examination of his; and the matter so standing, I had been very untrue to my service, if I had not delivered that opinion. But afterwards upon a re-examination of some that charged him, who weakened their own testimony; and especially hearing himself *viva voce*, I went instantly to the Queen, out of the soundness of my conscience, and not regarding what opinion I had formerly delivered, told her Majesty, I was satisfied and resolved in my conscience, that for the reputation of the action, the plot was to countenance the action further by him in respect of his place, than they had indeed any interest or intelligence with him. It is very true also, about that time her Majesty taking a liking of my pen, upon that which I had done before concerning the proceeding at York-house, and likewise upon some other declarations which in former times by her appointment I put in writing, commanded one to pen that book, which was published for the better satisfaction of the world; which I did, but so as never secretary had more particular and express directions and instructions in every point how to guide my hand in it; and not only so, but after that I had made a first draught thereof, and propounded it to certain principal counsellors, by her Majesty's appointment, it was perused, weighed, censured, altered, and made almost a new writing,[6] according to their Lordships' better consideration; wherein their Lordships and myself both were as religious and curious of truth, as desirous of satisfaction: and myself indeed gave only words and form of style in pursuing their direction. And after it had passed their allowance, it was again exactly perused by the Queen herself, and some alterations made again by her appointment: nay, and after it was set to print, the Queen, who, as your Lordship knoweth, as she was excellent in great matters, so she was exquisite in small, and noted that I could not forget my ancient respect to my Lord of Essex, in terming him ever, My Lord of Essex, My Lord of Essex, in almost every page of the book, which she thought not fit, but would have it made Essex, or the late Earl of

Essex: whereupon of force it was printed *de novo*, and the first copies suppressed by her peremptory commandment. And this, my good Lord, to my furthest remembrance, is all that passed wherein I had part; which I have set down as near as I could in the very words and speeches that were used, not because they are worthy the repetition, I mean those of mine own; but to the end your Lordship may lively and plainly discern between the face of truth and a smooth tale. And the rather also because in things that passed a good while since, the very words and phrases did sometimes bring to my remembrance the matters: wherein I report me to your honourable judgment, whether you do not see the traces of an honest man: and had I been as well believed either by the Queen or by my Lord, as I was well heard by them both, both my Lord had been fortunate, and so had myself in his fortune.

To conclude therefore, I humbly pray your Lordship to pardon me for troubling you with this long narration; and that you will vouchsafe to hold me in your good opinion, till you know I have deserved, or find I shall deserve the contrary; and even so I continue

At your Lordship's honourable commandments very humbly.

APPENDIX D

"The Speech Intended To Be Made by George, Archbishop of Canterbury"

When it Came his Turn to Declare his Mind concerning the Nullity of the Marriage Between the Earl of Essex and the Lady Frances Howard.

[Seven of the Commissioners having before declared themselves that they would give Sentence for a Nullity, and great reason being to think, that the bishop of London, sir John Bennet, Dr. James, and Dr. Edwards, would give voices against the Nullity.]

My Lords, and you the rest of the Commissioners; I have had a great contention and deliberation within myself, in what manner I should utter my judgment in this present cause, since, after the speech of those three who first began, so great a stream and concurrence together of the rest (my lord excepted, who spoke last) have given their opinions for the annulling of the marriage. But yet I hold not myself concluded thereby, but that I may declare my judgment, having learned that *suffragia* among wise men are as well *appendenda* and *ponderanda*, as *numeranda*: and it was no shame for Phocion in Athens, upon good ground, to contradict the whole city; neither was Paphnusius in the council of Nice the less respected, when he stood against the whole Synod; nay, it was his honour, that by delivering of his sentence, he altered the resolution which that whole assembly had intended to take, which I freely acknowledge I have no hope to effect at this time. And yet, though I have not that hope, but might very well spare this labour, yet my conscience telleth me, that it becometh me to speak in a matter of this importance, because, not only, *Deum timeo*, I fear God, which I doubt not but all of this company doth; but I am afraid of God, lest he should be angry with me, if in this case I be silent. And I think it is expected of me, since I am here present, that I should not sit as an idol, and only fill a room; for that were to lay an imputation on myself, that I had undertaken a cause, which in public I durst not offer to maintain.

I must acknowledge, that in delivering of my mind in this business of so great weight, I do find two defects, that I cannot so pertinently speak unto the purpose as divers of the judges here: the one is, That I am no lawyer; and the other is, That I am no married man; by both which I am disabled, that I cannot speak with that confidence concerning some particulars, as most of you, the commissioners, are able to do; but in lieu thereof, I have endeavoured to furnish myself some other way concurrent to this purpose: as by reading, by conferring with some whom I do trust, with pondering thereupon, so that it hath lost me much sleep at several times, with frequent prayer unto God, that he would direct me aright; which I have more begged of God in this cause, than ever in any that was before me in judgment. And besides, I bring with me *animum eandidum,* a mind devoid of passion, or any perturbation, which inclineth to no part for fear or for favour, for spleen or for hatred: from which, I thank God, in pronouncing of sentence, I ever have been free, remembering that judges are in the place of God; and as Jehosaphat said, 2 Chron. xix. 'Non hominis judicia exercetis sed Domini, et quicquid judicaveritis in vos redundavit.' He then who sitteth in the place of God, and in pronouncing of sentence will vary from justice, he leaveth God, and sheweth himself worthy to lie in the flames of hell, for abusing of the trust which is committed unto him, which I hope I shall not do. And *cui bono?* To what end should I transgress in judgment for either side, when I have no reason to be partial for either, since it is indifferent to me, in any particular, whether this question receive one or other determination?

Where, lest I should be mistaken, I think it not amiss, as publicly I have done divers times before, to let the world know what my judgment is concerning the impotency of a husband towards his wife: that since marriage in young couples is for carnal copulation and procreation thereupon, and that it is the intendment of those which contract matrimony to receive satisfaction in that kind, that if this nobleman be not able to perform those marital rights unto his lady, he doth unto her a very great injustice to retain her as his wife; and we shall perform a great part of injury and cruelty towards her, if we do not free her from this burthen and yoke. We are bound in conscience to do it, since it is in truth no marriage, but a pretended matrimony, that consummation being wanting, which was one of the first things in intention when they two came together: for *impossibil-*

itas officii, by a received maxim, *solvit vinculum conjugii.* But the point is, that before the separation be pronounced, it must appear unto the church, that there is good cause for the same; which must not be upon light surmises, or questionable suggestions, but upon evident declarations and proofs, which may give full contentment to the conscience of the judge. The marriage was overt and in the face of the church, whereby they were joined into one; let the reason of separation be as clear as that was, if it possibly may be; or let it be so apparent, that the church may well know, that there is ground to stand upon for pronouncing of a Nullity. Now this is it which I doubt will not fall out in this case of my lord of Essex; there is not proof sufficient to inform the minds of the judges that this knot should be dissolved, and themselves set at liberty the one from the other. And then you understand what the general rule is, *Quod dubitas, ne feceris.* And in this controversy there seem in my judgment many reasons of doubting, that the separation desired ought not to be granted. You shall hear some few of them.

1. The first scruple which ariseth in my mind, is from the uncertainty of that proceeding, which we have had in this business. For in the handling of it formerly, we had it propounded, that there must be a Nullity *propter maleficium versus hanc.* That was it which we debated, and for the which we turned our books; that the counsel for my lady did still insist upon, not naming the words indeed, but by a periphrasis, or circumlocution, describing the same. And it cannot be forgotten, how Dr. Stuart, being told by one or more of the commissioners sitting then in court, that his whole speech did still point out *maleficium;* he answered, It is true, that is it which we intend. The authorities always brought out of the canonists were in direct terms upon *maleficium,* the proofs intended nothing else. And we all understand, that to have an impotency unto a man's own wife, and an ability unto other, and that incurably, and that for some latent reason, which cannot be known, is the case of *maleficium;* and that is the matter alleged in the libel, and whereupon my lord is examined. And yet, now since we sit upon the second commission, *maleficium* is disclaimed. One of my lords (my lord of Winchester) hath avowed it, that he dislikes that *maleficium;* that he hath read Del-Rio, the Jesuit, writing upon that argument, and doth hold him an idle and fabulous fellow; that he rather supposeth it to be God's own handy-work, than any thing from the devil. Another of my

lords (my lord of Ely) hath assented thereunto, and *maleficium* must be gone. Now I for my part will not absolutely deny, that witches by God's permission may have a power over men, to hurt all, or part in them, as by God they shall be limited; but how shall it appear that this is such a thing in the person of a man? The question is, *An factum sit,* and how it shall be discovered? But to make it a thing ordinary, as the Romish writers do beyond the seas, I take it to be a fable, acknowledging that for truth, which a bishop well versed in that argument did lately write, that maleficiation is the very garbage of popery; a thing so base, that we who have learnt Christ aright, should despise and contemn, allowing it no place amongst us. Which course it were a shame if we should not observe, since the papists themselves grow very weary of it; and that even in France, where there hath been more ado with this maleficiation than in any other country; for there the common sort, at the time of their marriages, were wont to be afraid to have the words of conjunction in matrimony to be spoken aloud, 'Quos Deus conjunxit, nemo separet;' or the benediction to be publicly given, lest some witch or sorcerer in the same instant should tie a knot upon a point, or play some other sorcering trick, whereby the new bridegroom, so long as that knot lasted, should be disabled from actual copulation with her whom he had married. And for avoiding of that hazard, they had therefore their matrimonies celebrated in the night-time, and in some private place, were none came but such friends as they dared to trust. This superstition grew so common, and men were so abused by the fright that came thereof, that the prelates of France, about thirty years since, in a council at Rheims, made this decree against it. 'Peccare graviter admonemus eos, qui noctu vel clanculum benedictionem nuptialem sibi dari procurant propter metum maleficii: Maleficium enim se vitare posse, credere debent, si eo pietatis affectu ad conjugium accedant, qui pro scribitur in sacris literis, videlicet, ut cum timore Domini, et amore filiorum, magis quam libidine impulsi copulentur, devote susceptis po nitentio et Eucharistio Sacramentis.' And the year after that, another council in that kingdom doth speak yet more plainly. 'Et quia Christiano nomine indignus error nostro secula inolevit, ut signationibus, consignotionibus, vinculis et nexibus matrimonia impediantur:—Hæc Synodus communione Ecclesiæ interdicit omnes eos, qui hujusmodi superstitionibus utuntur: monetque fideles, ne hujusmodi commentis fidem habeant, sed in Deo fiduciam certam constituant, nec idcirco matrimonia noctu fiant, sed in luce et frequentia hominum.' If it be rotton ripe in France; if it be 'error indignus, Christiano nomine;' if men must not 'fidem habere hujusmodi commentis;' what do we with it here in England? Let it be cast away as a rotten rag of popery. And yet I do now find, that in the very sentence which is this day to be given, it falleth directly upon the description of 'maleficium versus hanc.' So that what should I think of this case of my lord's, which is built on such a foundation as no man will stand to? We are on it, and off it, and avow it we dare not, yet fly from it we will not. This moveth scruple in me, how I should assent to that whereof I can learn no certainty from the counsel of my lady, nor from you that be the judges, who speak for this nullity: I dare not rest my building on such a sandy foundation.

2. Another matter which troubleth my mind, is the novelty of that which is now set on foot; a thing unheard of in our church, and unknown in our kingdom. We have many stories, old and new, of things done in this land: we have registers extant in every diocess; we have acts and records which specify those accidents which have fallen out in the days of our forefathers. I have caused search in many places to be made, and so I know have some of you, the Commissioners; and I have called upon you for the same, but I can have no precedent of any such example that hath passed in our kingdom. No memory of man can express unto me the name of that person, whose marriage was annulled for impotency towards his wife, when he found an ability of carnal copulation with any other woman. It is this year 1613, that hath set abroad this present imagination, for the former ages knew it not. It is safe walking in the ways which are treaded out unto us. We have great reason for our doings in these human actions, when we do those deeds which formerly were done by our predecessors. I have had many worthy men, which have gone before me in the place which I now hold, men learned, men judicious, great discoverers of impostures? Men that have done great services for the nation where we live; but of them never any had such a case before them, they never gave sentence for a nullity of marriage upon such an inability. I know not whether it be a happiness, or unhappiness, that I must be the first to sit in a Commission for determining such a controversy.

I know, to meet with this objection, it is whispered sometimes, that there is an example, and that is Bury's case, which is urged as a precedent unto this now in question. But, indeed, that is no pattern of this; the dissimilitude is great between the one case and the other; for Bury had his s—s stricken off with an horse, that nothing but a little of one of them remained. I will read you the very case, which if any man doubt of, shall be avowed unto him. Thus then it doth follow:

John Bury, esquire, was lawfully seized in his demesnes as of fee, of, and in divers manors, lands and tenements within the county of Devon. The said John Bury did, to 20th day of November, in the first year of queen Mary, marry one Willimot Gifford, and they lived together three years; and the said Bury could not *carnaliter cognoscere dictam Willimotam.*

Afterwards, viz. the 17th of May, 1561, the said Willimot called the said Bury before the ecclesiastical judge, and charged him to be 'impotentem ad coeundum cum dicta Willimota, propter vitium perpetuum, et incurabile impedimentum ad generationem, et ejus inhabilitatem,' &c. and thereupon desired to be divorced. In the proceeding before the judge, it was proved by divers witnesses, of which two were physicians, that the said Bury had but one little s—e, and that no bigger than a bean. It was also deposed by divers matrons, that the said Willimot Gifford remained a virgin, and incorrupt; and the said Bury confessed no less: upon which proof, and confession of John Bury, the ecclesiastical judge pronounced sentence of divorce, and did thereby separate them.

Afterward the said John Bury took to wife one Philippa Monjoy, his first wife, Willimot Gifford, being then alive; and the said Philippa had a son in the time of their continuing together, John Bury's first wife being alive.

Afterwards, the said Willimot being still living, the said Monjóy, of her own accord, without any sentence of divorce, forsook the said John Bury, and married one Langeden, with whom she continued. The said John Bury, and his first wife, Willimot, died; the said Monjoy and Langeden then living, married together.

The question is, Whether, John Bury being divorced from Willimot Gifford for impotency, the second marriage, solemized between the said John Bury and Monjoy, during which time the issue male was born, be in law a marriage or not?

It appeareth by the process made in the cause, and the words of the sentence grounded upon the same process, that the first marriage was pronounced to be void, 'propter defectum et vitium testiculorum,' which made the said John Bury 'impotentem et ineptum ad actum generandi, et coitum conjugalem.' And so in all respects this second marriage with Monjoy is void, and of no effect: for either this cause of the dissolution of the first matrimony is true, which is always to be presumed, until the contrary do appear, and then the same cause doth make the second marriage void also; or else, if it any ways appear, this cause of the dissolution of the first marriage to be false: 'Et ecclesia erat decepta, quia satis potens ad generandum, et quod in ipsa generavit.' And in that case the first marriage is good in law, 'et debet redire ad priora connubia:' And so the second marriage is utterly void.

We are of the opinion above laid down: John Loyde, Henry Jones, John Hone, Nicholas Stuart, Edward Crompton, Robert Fourth, William Farrand.

Whether this be true or no, I appeal to Dr. Stuart, who is here in presence, and of counsel for my lady, who, I know, will affirm it, because, not long since, being asked by me of it, he confessed the same. And here is Dr. Farrand, now of counsel for my lord, who was used for his advice in this case of Bury; and Dr. Hone is yet living, who can testify the same. For I will suppose that, that a man cannot forget such a famous case as that was wherein himself was employed: but if all these were dead, I know where records be, which still will continue. If this then were the matter in question touching Bury 'defectus testiculorum,' what is this to the great controversy now depending before us? and if this be the only precedent, that should be the inducement, that the sentence to be given in this cause is not new, but the like hath been heard of before; I am where I was: We are now to act a novelty, a thing strange, and unheard of in the church of England, whereof let other men be the managers, I may have no hand in it.

But perhaps it will be said, that in some other countries, and especially in France, these things are well known; and the examples of one kingdom, especially, being so near unto us, may be an inducement for us to do the like, since the reason is the same. My answer thereunto is, that I that live in England, am to frame myself to those things, which I find in the church of England, whereof I see no reason but there should be as great esteem, as of any church in the world. In the days of our forefathers, as our nation was held a very noble nation, so was the church of England held a very famous church. Ecclesia Anglicana, as might easily be shewed out of Mat-

thew Paris and by divers things in some later general councils, did
carry a greater sway. And why should we at this time, in any thing,
yield unto any church in the world, since it is a thing well known,
that the knowledge of divinity doth abound here beyond all other
nations? and men of this land have beat down the power of the
pope, and made evident divers questions in matters of theology,
beyond all the parts of Christendom: but beyond this, I do know,
that the customs of churches, even by the determination of the pope
himself, ought to be the rule of judgment in this nature. We have a
famous place interserted into the body of the law, written by pope
Alexander the 3rd, unto the bishop of Amiens in France. It is worth
your hearing: 'Quod sedem Apostolicam consuluisti super his, quæ
tibi dubia existunt, gratum gerimus et acceptum, et tua exinde fra-
ternitas non parum commendanda videtur. Ex tua siquidem parte
nobis est intimatum, quod quædam mulier tui episcopatus cuidam
viro nupserit, asserens quod ob utruisque inguinis rupturam, gen-
italia ejus abscissa fuissent, necdum ab eo cognita fuisset, qui utique
factus leprosus, se pariter et sua domui reddidit infirmorum. Mulier
vero ad domum patris reversa sicut asseris invenis, alio viro nubere
desiderat, et conjugali affectu conjungi. Unde licet Romana Ecclesia
non consueverit propter talem infirmitatem, vel propter alia
maleficia, legitimè conjunctos dividere, si tamen consuetudo generalis Gallicanæ Ecclesiæ habet, ut hujusmodi matrimonium dissolvatur;
nos patienter tolerabimus, si secundum eandem consuetudinem, ei-
dem multeri cui voluerit nubendi in Domino concesseris facultatem.'
By this we do find, that the church of Rome itself doth grant no
separations in matters of matrimony, where the church of France
doth; and if the pope permit, in France itself, that a divorce should
be made, it is but a toleration, and not this neither, but where it is,
'consuetudo generalis Ecclesiæ Gallicanæ;' which if you will apply
unto this cause in question, you must shew me, that in England it
hath been a general custom, that a nullity in marriage may be
pronounced 'propter impotentiam versus hanc;' which if you cannot
shew, as indeed you cannot, nor give any true example that ever
hath been of any such separation within this church, I may both in
law and conscience conclude, that I dare not introduce any novelty,
and so consequently pronounce for the nullity of this marriage.
Many things are done in France, whereof if we in England had the
examination, we should, peradventure, find the fact different from
that which they conceived; or if we agree in the fact, we should give

another sentence. It is not unknown how, within the space of one year, there hath been much ado in France about two women, Magdalen and Louyse, pretended to be possessed with a great many devils, and how Verrine, a principal spirit in one of them, hath avowed and maintained the mass, invocation of saints, adoration of images, and a great many other points of the grossness of popery; and a book hereof hath been printed and reprinted in Paris, with the approbation of the state, and allowance of learned men; in which the church of England would certainly dissent, and proclaim the whole business to be but an imposture; as the very like was in the days of queen Elizabeth, when the devils of Denham were said to possess Sarah Williams and her sister, and some other persons; and much ado was made of it, and divers fond people believing those knacks, turned papists thereupon; yet the issue of all was, that it proved no better than a shameful delusion, and a great abusing of credulous and light-believing persons.

3. But now to proceed farther; If it shall be said, it is not the novelty, nor the want of custom here in England, which should prejudice the truth; *valeat veritas* wheresoever or whensoever it appears: The Proofs are evident whereupon we do stand, and that will enforce the sentence. My answer thereunto is, Let that be made manifest, and clear, and perspicuous unto the conscience of an understanding man, and I shall concur with you: But how shall I find this in a matter of this quality? Because it is nothing else but truth which we do aim at, it were fit that all probations, if not which are possibly, yet at the least which reasonably may be had, should be got together to enforce a conclusion of this consequence. My books tell me, 'In valore matrimonii investigando quæcunque probationes possibiles adhibendæ sunt, et potius debent esse superfluæ quam dimimutæ.' It is Solomon's saying, Prov. xxv. It is the honour of a king to find out a thing. And wherein can judges bestow their time better in a point of difficulty, than to search and search again, by all honest and good means, to know what is the bottom of that which lieth secret, that they may satisfy their own conscience, and the conscience of others, in the sentence which they give, and leave no kind of scruple, which may trouble their own thoughts; Whether these things have been done in this present case, I appeal to your own consciences; whether the writers do not mention divers things; whether the counsel for my lord have not spoke of sundry matters;

whether we that be the judges, have not thought of divers courses convenient to be held; of all which no piece or parcel hath been permitted unto us. The proofs then which we have had, do arise only out of the depositions, and if there be not proof sufficient where shall we seek for it: Let us then consider them. I will tell you my opinion of them. I find nothing in them all, which is not in substance contained in the Answers of my lord of Essex: A noble personage saith, That in the hearing of divers things, the earl hath said, that he was not able to know his lady carnally; the earl thinking this to be true. But this is but a relation of wonder spoken extra-judicially; and therefore, for the understanding of the truth therein, we are to have recourse unto that, which by the said earl is judicially deposed. Divers witnesses do speak, that the earl and the lady have lived and lain together for divers years; my lord doth acknowledge it in his answer; the matrons and midwives do declare, that in their judgment my lady is a virgin, and therefore, that she was never known carnally by the earl; himself confesseth that he did never know her. So that now, all in substance depending upon his lord-ships answer, it ought to be our labour to scan that exactly, and to judge of it circumspectly. Doth not he then say, *in responsione ad quartum,* That though divers times, in the first year of their cohabita-tion, he did attempt to know her, (which divers times may be twice or thrice, and no more) yet in the two latter years he did never attempt it? But doth he not say plainly, *responsione ad tertium,* That since the time of his marriage, he had not, nor hath any sickness or impediment to hinder him, but that he might have had, and may have, carnal knowledge with a woman? This is for the general, that he hath no impediment: But, *in responsione ad quintum,* doth he not descend more particularly unto his own lady: that it is true that he did never carnally know the said lady Frances? Mark now what followeth; but that to the act of carnal copulation he did not find any defect in himself. Indeed he was not able to penetrate into her body; but he layeth the fault of that upon her, as may be seen in his answer unto the 7th article. And it may not be forgotten, that in the end of the answer to the 4th article, he saith, That sometimes she refused him. These things are evident, and cannot be denied. The only matter which maketh shew against this is, that lie acknowledgeth that he hath lain by her, and hath had no motion to have carnal knowl-edge of her; but especially, that in the end of his answer unto the 6th article, "And believeth he never shall." These words are the shield and buckler of the contrary part; but how easily do they vanish away, or fall to the ground! For I appeal unto you all, who were present at the examinations, (and those were ten of us in number, who now sit here present) whether the earl did not openly subjoin that to his answer; "When I came out of France, I did love her; but I do not so now, neither ever shall I." I appeal unto the conscience of you all, except my lord of Winton, and my lord of Rochester, who were not then commissioners, whether this be so or no: Here then is the matter, it is the want of love, which restraineth all motions of carnal concupsicence, and not any impotency; it is *defectus voluntatis,* and not *defectus potestatis.* Let discontentment be removed, and there will be an end of all the inability: Married men best know these things; but out of common reason, there can be no great longing, where there is no great liking: many things they say fall out between man and wife, that for some good space of time there is no carnal conjunction, and yet no impotency concluded thereby may be. The case is famous of Pulcheria, sister unto the emperor Theodosius the younger, who having vowed virginity, was notwithstanding afterward, for great reason of state, thought fit to be married unto Martianus, who thereupon was chosen emperor; she would not condescend thereunto, till she had promise from him, that her virginity should be preserved, and with such a promise he did marry her; so that they lived together in shew as man and wife, but indeed as a brother and a sister. Our stories do make mention, that he who was called saint Edward in England, I mean king Edward the confessor, did marry a lady, the knowledge of whose body he never had, neither did this wedded couple ever endeavour to break their virginity. The writers do declare no other reason hereof, but that they had an opinion, that to live in virginity was the more meritorious, according to the superstition of those times. Now were it not a strange argument, to conclude in this manner, that because Martianus had not conjugal copulation with Pulcheria, therefore he was a man impotent; or because king Edward had not carnal knowledge of his wife, therefore he could not know her? I know the circumstances of this present question do differ from those, but the ground of the argument is the same. Want of act, upon private reason, will never enforce a want of power. And this is our case, as I understand it which maketh me unwilling to consent to this nullity.

4. There followeth now another argument, which I shall deliver briefly. We have always agreed, that the chapter in the law which containeth our case, is the chapter 'Litera de Frigidis et Maleficiatis;' for if it be not there, it is no where to be found. When we have delivered many things appertaining to this cause out of the best writers of the former ages, or of our own time; as that my lord should be inspected, or that physicians should use their art to discern and remove impotency, if any were to be found, or that fasting, prayer, and alms, should be exercised to overcome this evil, and divers other points of like nature; it hath still been answered to us, So say the interpreters, but it is not in the law; or it is in the decrees which bind not, but it is not in the decretals; or it is a counsel and exhortation, but it is no mandate or injunction. I now therefore mention something, which is in the law, and in the very body of this law, and it is the Pope's mandate; and that is, that my lord should have given his *juramentum cum septima manu,* as well as my lady: for want whereof, the whole proceeding is annullated. This is the pope's commandment, 'quocirca mandamus;' and it requireth the oath of both, 'ipsis cum septima propinquorum manu firmantibus juramento, se commisceri carnaliter nequivisse,' then 'proferatis divortii sententiam inter cos.' This is a thing so clear, that when on Thursday last, by chance there fell mention of it; the counsel for my lady (Dr. Stuart and Dr. Bird) were so far from giving answer to it, that to speak plainly, they stood as men blasted or blighted with lightning, and knew not which way to turn them: as was manifest not only unto us, but to all the standers-by; which I do not utter to do them any wrong, for they are worthy men, both learned and faithful to the cause which they undertake; but the note is, that this objection can receive no true answer. I know, that since that time there hath been labour made, to give a salve to this sore, but no man's wit can do it. I said, and say still, that no man's loquence, neither any man's eloquence, can persuade me, that 'ipsis firmantibus juramento' is of the singular number. I know there hath been tumbling and turning of books, to find some shew to meet with this objection; but nothing can be found which will hold out this water. The proceeding therefore doth appear to be unperfect and defective in that, which is mainly required by the law, which makes me to conclude in this fashion against some unperfect speech touching my lord of Essex his affirming or denying of his own inability towards my lady; that

either he doth confess it, or deny it: If he do acknowledge it, where is then his oath 'cum septima manu,' which the law imposeth? If he do deny it, where is then your proof of his inability, since you ground the whole substance of the nullity upon his lordship's answer, That he could not know her carnally?

5. I must yet crave patience to go a little farther. One other exception which I take unto this nullity, is the manner of the sentence, which by us is to be given, which hath ever been resolved should be in general, not expressing any reason particular wherefore we do give it. To say that my lord is 'impotens in genere versus hanc,' and not to tell wherein, is to propound a riddle to the world, which no man understandeth. It were a strange thing in learning to say, that such a creature is animal, and not to tell whether it be a man, or a horse, or a fish, or a bird. And although it hath been said, and strongly maintained (by sir Julius Cæsar and sir Daniel Dun), 'That it is enough in a sentence to pronounce a thing in general, and that the judge is bound to give no reason of it;' yet I would be glad to know whether, howsoever I will conceal the particular reason from the hearers or standers-by, yet were it not fit, that I who am the judge, and must give the sentence, or at least consent unto it, should know the ground whereupon I do give it? Give me leave to speak my conscience; I think a sentence, 'propter latens aliquod impedimentum,' which is 'perpetuum et incurabile versus hanc,' is nothing but a device to serve a present turn, which we must deliver in such obscure words, to blind posterity that comes after, and to amuse those which will enquire into it, as if we had known something which we held not fit to utter, when in truth we know nothing. I find the texts of the law do still set down the reason, and give a case particular, as frigidity, or section, or unfitness of the generative part, or some such other matter; but for an inability, 'propter latens impedimentum,' my dullness is such, that in the whole book I cannot discover: And it is a mystery that cannot enter into me, how a man should be potent unto other women, and impotent to his wife, if it be not in case of phrensy, which is not 'latens impedimentum,' and which also findeth 'lucida intervalla.' It was the assertion of him in the law, (Cap. Literæ) 'That he did not know his wife, but that he had a power to know other women.' But what wise man doth believe him? Or what is there in the text which doth declare it to be true? I will end this point with that of our Saviour in the 29th of St.

Matthew, That there are three sorts of Eunuchs, or men unfit to marry; the one is of God's making, the second is of men's making, and the third is of their own making. The first are they that are past from their mother's belly, who either are *frigidi,* or such as have not members fit for generation, or some apparent debility. The second are those who are castrated by men, or by some violence have that hindred in them, whereunto by nature they are fit in respect of procreation. I will not here dispute that idle *maleficium,* because yourselves are flown from it. The third hath no coherence with this nobleman. Let me know then, in which of the former two you do place it. Is he past from his mother's womb? Why then do you give him leave to marry again, that he who hath deluded and frustrated one, may also delude another? If he be in the second rank, why do you not tell us what the violence is which he had sustained from men, or from any other creature? Let us have, I pray you, some kind of satisfaction, and let not this ænigma in general blind us, lest the world should say, that wilfully we shut our eyes against the truth.

6. One reason I have more, why I yield not to this nullity, and then I have done. It is drawn from the inconveniences which will follow thereupon, if we dissolve the matrimony in such case as is now desired. I look first on the detriment and harm which will follow, if the marriage do continue in force and in vigour, and I do find, that all the inconvenience doth redound but to one person. Between a lady and her husband there is some discontentment, which time and God's grace may easily remove: There is then an end of that controversy. Or, if the disagreement shall never be appeased, it is no more but one lady doth want that solace which marital conjunction would afford unto her; which many a good woman is enforced to endure, and yet commits no sin, neither labours to violate the laws of the church: For suppose the husband be sick of some long disease, or languishing weakness, must not the wife sustain it with patience and quietness? Suppose the husband be captive in some foreign nation, or prisoner in his own country, whereby occasion of marital connexion is taken from the wife, no divine will pronounce, that a separation is in this case to be sought. Let a woman do that in modesty, which others are enforced to do out of necessity; and let her expect God's leisure, in fasting and in prayer, and in other humiliation. This is all the inconvenience which ariseth to one person, if she have not the performance of conjugal duty.

But look on the other side, what are the incongruities, or other absurdities, which will easily follow, if such dissolutions of marriages be permitted. I will name only two. The first is the hazard of violating and annulling of marriage by an ordinary practice; for if the gap be open, who will not run in? And the judge must dispense the law indifferently to all, if the proofs be accordingly; for we may not say, that it is for noble personages, and great peers in the state, and not for others of inferior rank. Whatsoever couple therefore have no children, and live discontented, come presently to take part of this general jubilee: And albeit they know in their consciences, that it which they attempt is unlawful; yet, to satisfy their fancy, they will collude the one with the other, and enter a prosecution secretly agreed upon, howsoever in open shew they seem to differ the one from the other: And who can doubt, but for money or favour, they may procure witnesses, and others who are to be used by the formality of the law, to testify and depose so much as serves the turn? By which means we are at a fair pass, when not only the marriage-bed shall be defiled, and adulteries made frequent, which is against the second table of the law, but perjury shall be committed, and God's name taken in vain, which is repugnant unto the first table.

A second inconvenience is the danger, lest both parties which are freed from their matrimony, should divers years after be returned to it again, when perhaps the husband by a second wife hath children, and the wife by a second husband hath store of issue also; for there is no doubt in the law, but if a man supposed to be *frigidus,* and therefore divorced, shall afterwards marry, and by begetting of children shew himself not to be impotent, but apt for generation, this man is to be taken from his second woman, and returned to his first wife; and the woman for whose marriage a nullity was pronounced in respect of the insufficiency of her mate, must be now taken from her second companion, and returned to the first. Of this the reason is apparent, *quia decepta est ecclesia;* they adjudged him to be impotent upon wrong information, whom experience and truth hath declared to be potent. And what man can foretel, how variety of times may produce other judgments? There may be question of land or inheritance, of legitimation or illegitimation; and a wise man would be unwilling to bring it on the stage when he is dead and gone, and to make it the fable of the world, whether his children be born lawfully, or to be reputed in the rank of bastards. The world is subject to much mutability, and judges of future times may peradventure be led with the power of some great persons, and perhaps may think upon other considerations, that it is but a conceit, that a man should be potent unto another woman, and impotent to his wife; or that the common law doth not know any *maleficiam;* or that they do not believe, that there may be 'latens impedimertum, perpetuum et incurabile versus hanc,' when they see that the husband is, in shew of the world, a lusty able man, and hath well proved his potency, by begetting three, or five, or seven, or ten children upon another woman. These are pretty things, if a man do well consider them, and will serve to make distraction between kinsman and kinsman, and make work for the lawyers, and keep the courts at Westminster that they shall not be idle; which if we could not learn otherwise, yet Bury's case before remembered doth teach us, who was divorced from his wife in the third or fourth year of queen Elizabeth; and when his brother had enjoyed his land until the fortieth year of the said queen, then was he thrust out of it, and the questioned son, or his heir, was put into possession of it by trial of law; a great deal of money being spent in that contention, and both civilians and common lawyers in great numbers were entertained of both sides; and yet the controversy was not so appeased, but that of my certain knowledge, within these three years it had been raised again, and a strong device was laid how to bring this about again; only myself withstood it, and would not give way unto it, when I was divers times consulted thereabout; conceiving very well that it would not be long before some prohibition would come out of some of the king's courts, because the common law disliked, that men's inheritance, especially after judgments, should be disturbed, when the parties whom most of all it concerned, are dead long before, and cannot answer for themselves; whereas, peradventure, if themselves had been living, they could have answered that for themselves which other men knew not. And there ought to be a settled course in all things appertaining to inheritance.

By this time, I hope you see, that it is not out of wilfulness, or prejudicate conceit, that I have impugned this nullity, but out of ground of reason, and out of scruple of conscience, which is it that must accuse me, or excuse me before the ever-living God. I know you have answered for themselves. Upon all which grounds I make this conclusion, That howsoever this matter of separation with great earnestness hath been pursued, yet it is the surer and the safer way to leave it as we find it, and in no case to dissolve it. I oft remember that saying, which is frequent among the canonists, 'Tolerabilius est aliquos contra statuta hominum dimittere copulatos, quam conjunctos legitimè contra statuta Domini separare.' That concerneth us who be the judges; and for the parties themselves, who perhaps can be content to be severed, and to marry elsewhere, let them know this from me, that they may best expect a blessing from God when they live in that state where fewest scruples shall arise in their mind: From which whether they shall be free in leaving their old conjunction, and betaking themselves unto a new, I refer to their wiser thoughts, when in all probability, if any cross or thwart shall arise in their new-intended matrimony, this perplexity and anguish will still follow their souls, that they have done that whereof in their truest meditations they have no ground of conscience, and therefore that it is the hand of God upon them, who giveth not a blessing unto that which was unduly sought.

You have thus at large heard my opinion against the annullation of this marriage. Now, if you ask me, What would you then have done concerning this couple of noble personages? My answer is, That I would have a reconciliation by all means to be laboured; and although that be difficult to bring about, yet it is the more honour when it is effected. Charity will forgive and forget the highest offences. It is St. Augustine's judgment, "That in the greatest breaches between man and wife, reconciliation is the best; and the worthiest pains that can be bestowed, is to bring that about." There wanteth only one or more good mediators, and then great things will be compassed. The disagreement was inconceivable between God and man, yet Chirst, that great mediator, did take it away. The breach was very bitter between England and Spain, yet our most blessed sovereign, as a gracious intercessor, did give an end unto it. Let divines be used now, as much as lawyers have been used heretofore. Take the godly counsel of the one, which will be given freely, as you have taken the advice of the other with much expence of money. This I wish for, this I pray for; and if my counsel had been used, before things grew to this height, I would have used my best means to have wrought an atonement. But because there is no hope thereof, and this doth expect a legal decision, proceed you that please unto this separation. Give your sentence *in scriptis* as you have declared your opinion *in verbis*. Five might have served the turn by the words of the Commission, if seven had dissented; but you have seven suffrages, and therefore proceed; only this I crave of the register, that he do make his act, that this sentence is given, Joanne Episcopo London.; D. Joanne Bennet milite; D. Francisco James; D. Thoms Edwards; dissentientibus, potissimum verò Georgio Archiepiscopo Cantauriensi renitente.

This is the substance of that matter which the Archbishop of Canterbury, out of certain Notes which he had drawn up, was ready to have uttered, and no one material point is added thereunto, as appeareth unto me, the writer hereof, comparing it with the Notes at such time as I ended the writing of this, which was on the 28th Sept. 1613, three days after the time when it should have been spoken.

APPENDIX E

King James's Reply to the Argument of the Archbishop of Canterbury

My Lord; After I had received, and read your papers, which the bishop of Litchfield brought me, I found it very necessary that I should make answer thereunto at my first leisure: for whereas, before, at my last meeting with you, ye secured to me to be only as yet unresolved what sentence to give in this business, till you had heard it thoroughly disputed, that by that means ye might be fully informed of the state of the cause; it appears now by these papers, that you have, after your last day's consultation, put on a negative resolution, grounded upon fundaments of divinity and conscience, as you think, which hath moved me to send you herewith my judgment upon your arguments, in regard that I did ever hold it necessary, that in a matter of this weight all my commissioners should be as near of one mind, as might be; and therefore I would be sorry that your private conceits should so blind your judgment, as to make you and your followers draw the catharrows (perplex or torment) against your yoke-fellows; for that I may now open plainly my heart unto you, at my first reading of your papers from the bishop, I chanced to cast mine eye first upon the paper of your arguments, before I had looked upon your letter, and lighting upon your first words, 'Inasmuch as we do firmly believe, &c.' I protest I thought it had been some strange confession of faith, that you had intercepted amongst some of the sectaries; but when I had read out the rest of that first article, God is my judge, I thought that paper had been some pasquil made against this divorce, which coming to your hands ye had sent me, and therefore without reading any farther therein, I looked upon your letter, which resolved me of all these doubts; but after that I had fully perused, and rightly considered of all your papers, I found your principles so strange, and your doubts so far sought, that I thought it necessary, as I have already said, to set down unto you my observations upon them. But to conclude my letter with that plainness that becometh one of my quality, I must

326

freely confess, that I find the grounds of your opposition so weak, as I have reason to apprehend, that the prejudice you have of the persons is the greatest motive of breeding these doubts into you; which prejudice is the most dangerous thing that can fall in a judge for misleading of his mind. And the reason moving me to this apprehension, is partly grounded upon your last words to me at your parting from Windsor, and partly upon a line scraped out in your paper of doubts: for I am sure you think me not so blunt a secretary, but that I can read a line so scraped out. In your last speeches with me, you remember you told me what assurance you had of the earl's ability out of his own mouth, which you said you could not but trust, because he was so religious a nobleman. But when I told you of the other party's contrary affirmation, you remember how you used the word of iniquity; and how far your interlined line seems to have a harmony with this word, yourself can best judge. Now then, if I would ask you what proof you have of the one's religion more than the other's, you must answer me, by judging upon the exterior; and how deceivable that guess is, daily experience teaches us — But with a holy protestation that I never knew anything but good in the young earl. Was not this the ground of master Robert Bruse's incredulity, because he knew the earl of Gowry to be truly religious; and did not beg a register. See Bothwell in his preface of his book 'De viris illustribus.' And as for your judgment of the other party, Christ's precept is the best answer unto you, 'Nolite judicare.' But if the question were to judge of the earl's inclination, whether is it likely that you or I could best judge of it; I, he having been bred with my late son, and served him so long; or you, that never spoke with him but once or twice in your life, and never knew either good or evil of him but out of his own mouth? I will conclude, therefore, with inverting the argument; that if a judge should have a prejudice in respect of persons, it should become you rather to have a kind of faith implicit in my judgment, as well in respect of some skill I have in divinity, as also that I hope no honest man doubts of the uprightness of my conscience; and the best thankfulness that you that are so far my creature, can use towards me, is, to reverence and follow my judgment, and not to contradict it, except where you may demonstrate unto me that I am mistaken, or wrong informed; and so farewel.

JAMES R.

APPENDIX F

The Remarkable Letter Written by James I to Robert Carr in the Tower of London

First, I take God, the searcher of all hearts, to record that in all the time past of idle talk, I never knew nor could, out of any observation of mine, find any appearance of any such Court faction [backing Villiers against Carr] as you have apprehended, and so far was I ever from overseeing or indirectly feeling of it (if I had apprehended it) as, I protest to God, I would have run upon it with my feet, as upon fire, to have extinguished it, if I could have seen any sparkle of it. As for your informations, you daily told me so many lies of myself that were reported unto you, as (I confess) I gave the less credit to your reports in other things, since you could not be an eye-witness of it yourself.

Next, I take the same God to record, that never man of any degree did directly or indirectly let fall unto me anything that might be interpreted for the lessening of your credit with me, or that one man should not rule all, and that no man's dependence should be put upon the King, or any such like phrase; which, if I had ever found, then would I have behaved myself as became so great a king, and so infinitely loving a master.

Thirdly, as God shall save me, I meant not in the letter I wrote unto you to be sparing, in the least jot, of uttering my affection towards you, as far as yourself could require; my differing from your form in that point being only to follow my own style, which I thought the comeliest; so as having delivered my mind as fully to May as you could have wished — having written this letter, — having quite turned my countenance from Graham, — the like whereof I never did to any man without a known offense — I having received your nephew in my bedchamber, the fashion thereof being done in a needless bravery of the Queen, I did surely expect that the idle talk would wear out like the pope's cursing; especially seeing my own heart knew it to be without a ground. For I am far from thinking of any possibility of any man ever to come within many degrees of your trust with me, as I must ingenuously confess you have deserved more trust and confidence of me than ever man did, — in secrecy above all flesh, in feeling and impartial respect, as well to my honor in every degree as to my profit. And all this, without respect either to kin or ally, or your nearest and dearest friend whatsoever; nay unmovable in one hair that might concern me against the whole world. And in those points I confess I never saw any come towards your merit: I mean in the points of an inwardly trusty friend and servant.

But, as a piece of ground cannot be so fertile, but if either by the own natural rankness or evil manuring thereof it becomes also fertile of strong and noisome weeds, it then proves useless and altogether unprofitable; even so, these before rehearsed rich and rare parts and merits of yours have been of long time, but especially of late, since the strange phrenzy took you, so powdered and mixed with strange streams of unquietness, passion, fury and insolent pride, and (which is worst of all) with a settled kind of induced obstinancy, as it chokes and obscures all these excellent and good parts that God hath bestowed upon you. For, although I confess the greatness of that trust and privacy betwixt us will very well allow unto you an infinitely great liberty and freedom of speech unto me, yea even to rebuke me more sharply and bitterly than ever my master durst do, yet, to invent a new act of railing at me — nay, to borrow the tongue of the devil — in comparison whereof all Peacham's book is but a gentle admonition, that cannot come within the compass of any liberty of friendship. And do not deceive yourself with that conceit, that I allowed you that sort of licentious freedom till of late. For, as upon the one part, it is true you never passed all limits therein till of late; so, upon the other, I bore, God Almighty knows, with those passions of yours, of old dissembling my grief thereat, only in hope that time and experience would reclaim and abate that heat, which I thought to wear you out of, by a long suffering patience and many gentle admonitions; but the circumstances joined to the . . . [illegible] made them relish ten times worse to my taste than otherwise they would have done if they had only remained *in puris naturalibus* of passions.

For, first, being uttered at unseasonable hours, and so bereaving me of my rest, was so far from condemning your own indiscretion therein, as by the contrary it seemed you did it of purpose to grieve and vex me. Next, your fiery boutades were coupled with a continual dogged sullen behaviour, especially shortly after your fall, and in all the times of your other diseases. Thirdly, in all your dealings with me you have many times uttered a kind of distrust of the honesty of my friendship towards you. And fourthly (which is worst of all) and worse than any other thing that can be imagined, you have, in many of your mad fits, done what you can to persuade me that you mean not so much to hold me by love as by awe, and that you have me so far in your reverence as that I dare not offend you or resist your appetites. I leave out of this reckoning your long creeping back and withdrawing yourself from lying in my chamber, notwithstanding my many hundred times earnestly soliciting you to the contrary, accounting that but as a point of unkindness.

Now, whether all your great parts and merits be not accompanied with a sour and distasteful sauce, yourself shall be judge. Consider likewise of the difference of the things that you lay to my charge and that I lay to yours. Here is not, "he said," or "she said," no conjectural presumptions; I charge you with nothing but things directly acted or spoken to myself. I wish to God, therefore, and I shall both pray for it and hope it, that you may make good use of this little mirror of yourself, which herein I present unto you; it is not like Sir Walter Raleigh's description of the kings that he hates, of whom he speaketh nothing but evil; for this lays plainly and honestly before you both your best and worst parts.

To conclude, then, this discourse proceeding from the infinite grief of a deeply wounded heart, I protest in the presence of the Almighty God, that I have borne this grief within me to the uttermost of my ability, and as never grief since my birth seated so heavily upon me, so have I borne it as long as possibly I can; neither can I bear it longer without admitting an unpardonable sin against God in consuming myself wilfully, and not only myself, but in perilling thereby not only the good estate of mine own people, but even the state of religion through all Christendom, which almost wholly, under God, rests now upon my shoulders. Be not the occasion of the hastening of his death through grief, who was not only your creator under God, but hath many a time prayed for you, which I never did for any subject alive but for you. But the lightening my heart of this burden is not now the only cause that makes me press you undelayedly to ease my grief; for your own furious assaults upon me at unseasonable hours hath now made it known to so many that you have been in some cross discourse with me, as there must be some exterior signs of the amendment of your behaviour towards me. These observations have been made and collected upon your long being with me at unseasonable hours — loud speaking on both parts — and their observation of my sadness after your parting, and want of rest.

What shall be the best remedy for this I will tell you — be kind. But for the easing of my inward and consuming grief, all I crave is, that in all the words and actions of your life you may ever make it appear to me that you never think to hold grip of me but out of my mere love, and not one hair by force. Consider that I am a free man, if I were not a king. Remember that all your being, except your breathing and soul, is from me. I told you twice or thrice, you might lead by the heart and not by the nose. I cannot deal honestly, if I deal not plainly with you. If ever I find that you think to retain me by one sparkle of fear, all the violence of my love will in that instant be changed into as violent a hatred. God is my judge, my love hath been infinite towards you; and only the strength of my affection towards you hath made me bear with these things in you, and bridle my passions to the uttermost of my ability. Let me be met, then, with your entire heart, but softened by humility. Let me never apprehend that you disdain my person and undervalue my qualities; and let it not appear that any part of your former affection is cold towards me. A king may slack a part of his affections toward his servant upon the party's default and yet love him; but a servant cannot do so to his master, but his master must hate him.

Hold me thus by the heart; you may build upon my favour, as upon a rock that never shall fail you, that never shall weary to give new demonstrations of my affection towards you; nay, that shall never suffer any to arise in any degree of my favour, except they may acknowledge and thank you as a furtherer of it, and that I may be persuaded in my heart, that they love and honor you for my sake; not that any living shall come to the twentieth degree of *your* favour.

For, although your good and heartily humble behaviour may wash quite out of my heart your past errors, yet shall I never pardon myself, but shall carry that cross to the grave with me, for raising a man so high, as might make him presume to pierce my ears with such speeches.

To make an end, then, of this unpleasing discourse, think not to value yourself so much upon other merits, as by love and heartily humble obedience. It hath ever been my common answer to any that would plead for favour to a puritan minister by reason of his rare gifts, that I would rather have a conformable man with but ordinary parts, than the rarest men in the world, that will not be obedient; for that leaven of pride sours the whole loaf. What can or ever could thus trouble your mind? For the exterior to the world — what can any servants express of their prince but countenance or reward? Do not all courtesies and places come through your office as chamberlain, and rewards through your father-in-law as treasurer? Do not you two (as it were) hedge in all the Court with a manner of necessity to depend upon you? And have you not besides your infinite privacy with me, together with all the main offices you possess, your nephew in my bedchamber? — besides another far more active than he in Court practices? And have you not one of your nearest kinsmen that loves not to be idle in my son's bedchamber? With this should you have silenced these news-bringers and makers of lies. For no other thing is left you behind but my heart, which you have neither cause to doubt, nor, if it did need, could they counsel or advise you how to help.

Thus have I now set down unto you what I would say, if I were to make my testament; it lies in your hands to make of me what you please — either the best master and truest friend, or if you force me once to call you ingrate, which the God of heaven forbid, no so great earthly plague can light upon you. In a word, you may procure me to delight to give daily more and more demonstrations of my favours towards you if the fault be not in yourself.

APPENDIX G

Letter Written by Somerset to James I
After Somerset's Conviction and Reprieve
Requesting Redress and Restitution of Property

May it please your Majesty: By this gentleman, your Majesty's
Lieutenant, I understand of some halt you made, and the cause of it,
at such time as he offered to your Majesty my letters; but soon after
your Majesty could resolve yourself, and behold me nothing so
diffident of you, but in humble language petitioning your favour;
for I am in hope that my condition is not capable of so much more
misery, as I need to make my passage to you by such way of
intercession.

This which follows after, I offer your Majesty, though not as to
yourself, for upon less motive you can find favour for me. Now, I
need only move, not plead, before your Majesty, as my case doth
stand; for what I seek to have done, follows upon what you have
already done, as a consequence and succeeding growth of your own
act. But to the intent that your Majesty may see that there is enough
to answer those (if any such there be) as do go about to pervert the
exercise of your power, and to turn it from its own clear excellency,
for to minister unto their passions; I have presumed to this end to
awake your Majesty's own conceit upon the subject, which can gather
to itself better and more able defences in my behalf upon this view.
For though the acts of your mercy which are not communicable, nor
the causes of them with others, as derived from those secret motives
which are only sensible and privy to your own heart, and admit of
no search or discovery to any general satisfaction; and that under
the protection I might guard my particular sufficiently; yet my case
need not hide itself, but attend the dispute with any, that would put
upon it a monstrous and heavy shape; though . . . I must acknowledge that both life and estate are forfeited to you by law; yet so
forfeited, that the same law gives you the same power to preserve as
it doth to punish, whereby your Majesty's higher prerogative doth

not wrestle with it, nor do you infringe those grounds by which you have ever governed, so as the resistance is not great, that your Majesty hath for to give life, and which is less in the gift of estate, for that the law casts wholly upon yourself, and yields it as fit matter for exercise of your goodness.

Once it was your Majesty's gift to me, so it may be better not taken, for to avoid to take that which hath been once their own; and I may say farther, that the law hath not been severe upon the ruin of innocent posterity, nor yet cancelled nor cut off the merits of ancestors, before the politic hand of state had contrived it into these several forms, as fitted to their ends of government. To this I may add, that whereupon I was judged, even the crime itself might have been none, if your Majesty's hand had not once touched upon it, by which all access unto your favour was quite taken from me. Yet as it did at length appear, I fell rather for want of well defending, than by the violence or force of any proofs; for I so far forsook myself and my cause, as that it may be a question whether I was more condemned for that, or for the matter itself, which was the subject of that day's controversy.

Then thus far nothing hath appeared, wherein your Majesty hath extended for me your power, beyond the reasonable bound; neither doth anything stand so in the way of your future proceedings, but rather make easy your Majesty's favour for my relief. What may then be the cause that malice can pitch upon, wherefore your Majesty should not proceed to accomplish your own work? Aspersions are taken away by your Majesty's letting me loose to the utmost power of law, with the lives of so many offenders, which yieldeth the world subjects of sorrow rather than appetite to more blood. But truth and innocency protect themselves in poor men, much more in kings, neither was there such aspersion (God knows) in any possibility towards your Majesty, but, among those who would create these pretenses to mislead your Majesty, and thereby make me miserable; if not this (whereof the virtue and use was in the former time, and is now determined) there is not any but your pleasure.

It is true, I am forfeited to your Majesty, but not against you by any treasonable or unfaithful act; besides, there is to be yielded a distinction of men, as in faults; in which I am of both under the nearest degrees of exception. Yet your Majesty hath pardoned life and estate to traitors and strangers, sometimes the one, sometimes the other; nay, to some concerned in this business, wherein I suffer, you have pardoned more unto them, than I desire, who (as it is reputed) if they had come to the test, had proved copper, and should have drunk of their bitter cup as well as others. But I do not by this envy your favours to any persons, nor seek I to draw them into the yoke with myself, but applaud your Majesty's goodness, being in that respect in a near possibility to come at me; besides this, to Elwes your Majesty has given an estate (which is a greater gift than life, because it extends to posterity), who was the worst deserver in this business, an unoffended instrument, who might have prevented all after-mischief, but for his own ends suffered it, and by the like arts afterwards betrayed it. To this I may add Tresham in the powder treason, upon whose successors I do not cast any of his infamy, yet he preserved himself to posterity; so as what he, or others such as he, have defrauded by the arts of law, and whom their own unfaithfulness made safe; I have much ado to hold my ingenuity and confidence, how it may be, because I distrusted not your Majesty, or because it returned in your power from whom I had it. Is it in danger to be broken or dismembered? Let me hope that there is nothing, which by favour may be excused, or by industry might have been avoided, that will fail me, where your Majesty is to determine.

It is not I, that put your Majesty in mind opportunely, it is he, that was your creature; it is Somerset, with all your honours and envious greatness, that is now in question. Kings themselves are protected from the breach of law, by being favourites and God's anointed; which gives your Majesty like privilege over yours, as I took from Dr. Donne his sermon, that the goodness of God is not so much acknowledged by us in being our Creator, as in being our Redeemer: Nor in that he hath chosen us, as that nothing can take us out of his hand; which in your Majesty's remembrance let me challenge and hope for: For the first accesses of favour, they may be ascribed unto one's own pleasing themselves, but that appears to be for our sakes, and for our good, when the same forsake not our civil desires. This redemption I crave, not as to my own person, but with your benefits once given; nor do I assume them very deep, for I have voluntarily departed from the hopes of my pension, place, office; I only cleave to that which is so little, as that it will suffer no parting or diminution.

And as in my former letters, so by this, I humbly crave of your Majesty not to let the practices of Court work upon your son the

Prince, not fearing the suffering of my loss in that particular so much (for I cannot lose it but willingly all with it), as for to take off the stage, that which in the attempt may prove inconvenient. But if your Majesty have any respects to move you to suspend your goodness towards me, let that which is mine rest in your own hands, till that you find all opposite humours conformed to your purpose. I have done wrong to myself, thus to entertain such a doubt of your Majesty; but the unrelenting of adversaries, which, when you will have them, will soon alter; and that all the while I have received nothing of present notice for direction, or to comfort me from your Majesty, hath made me to expostulate with myself thus hardly: For God is my judge, sir, I can never be worthy of it, if I have these marks put upon me of a traitor, as that tumbling and disordering of that estate, would declare. The divorce from your presence, lays too much upon me, and this would upon both. I will say no further, neither in that which your Majesty doubted my aptness to fall into; for my cause nor my confidence is not in that distress, as for to use that mean of intercession or anything besides; but to remember your Majesty that I am the workmanship of your hands, and bear your stamp deeply imprinted in all the characters of favour; that I was the first plant engrafted by your Majesty's hand in this place, therefore not to be unrooted by the same hand, lest it should taint all the same kind with the touch of that fatalness; and that I was even the son of a father, whose services are registered in the first honours and impressions I took of your Majesty's favour, and laid there as a foundation stone of that building. These and your Majesty's goodness for to receive them is what I rely upon, praying for your Majesty's prosperity; I am in all humbleness, your Majesty's loyal servant and creature, R. SOMERSET.

BIBLIOGRAPHY

To enhance its usefulness, most material examined is listed in this bibliography, even though lack of space prevented use of a few items. Where several editions were examined, I have listed here the edition ordinarily most available. Spelling is modernized and footnote references in the text are to the first word or two appearing in each listing below. As is customary, Roman numerals in the footnote references designate volume numbers and Arabic numerals designate page numbers. Where a cited reference includes more than one page, only the first page number is given. Frequently I have added to the listing a few words to suggest the reliability of the author or circumstances putting him peculiarly in position to know whereof he wrote.

Abbott, E. A. "Bacon and Essex." London, 1877.

Abbot, George, Archbishop of Canterbury. "The Case of Impotency." London, 1719. Abbot, made archbishop by James I in spite of his Puritan leanings, was renowned for his theological studies. He was disliked by and unfriendly to the Howards and Lord Coke and served as a commissioner in the Howard-Essex annulment proceedings.

Aikin, Lucy. "Memoirs of the Court of King James the First." London, 1823.

Akrigg, G. P. V. "Jacobean Pageant." Cambridge, 1962.

Amos, Andrew. "The Great Oyer of Poisoning." London, 1846. Amos was accepted as the great nineteenth-century authority on British Criminal Law.

"Archaelogia." A long series of publications by the Society of Antiquarians of London; various dates.

Aubrey's "Brief Lives." Various editions.

"Aulicus Coquinariae, or the Character of him who Satirized King James and his Court." Probably written by William Sanderson in 1651 from material collected by Bishop Goodman and reprinted in 1811 as Part 3 of "The Secret History of the Court of James the First," which has been used for the footnote references. Part 1 of this useful two-volume work contains Osborne's "Memoirs," first published in 1658, and Part 2 contains Anthony Weldon's "The Court and Character of King James," originally published in 1651. Part 3 is supposed to be in part a rebuttal of Part 2, the name "Aulicus Coquinariae" referring to Weldon's early employment as clerk of the kitchen under James I.

Bacon, Francis. "His Apology in Certain Imputations Concerning the Late Earl of Essex," London, 1605.

Bagenal, P. H. "Vicissitudes of an Anglo-Irish Family." London, 1925.

Bassett, Thomas (Publisher or Printer). "The Popish Plot Trials." London, 1679.

Bibliography of British History (Tudor Period). 2nd Ed. Oxford, 1959.

Birch, Thomas. "Letters, Speeches . . . of Francis Bacon." London, 1763. Birch, Secretary of the Royal Society, was a scholarly early eighteenth-century historian and biographer whose works are indispensible to the student of history; his books and manuscripts in the British Museum contain many valuable documents copied from the originals at his expense. However, his difficult style caused Samuel Johnson to say, "Tom Birch is as brisk as a bee in conversation, but no sooner does he take a pen in his hand than it becomes a torpedo to him and numbs all his faculties."

Birch, Thomas. "Life of Henry Prince of Wales." London, 1760.

Birch, Thomas. "Memoirs of the Reign of Queen Elizabeth." London, 1754. Footnote references to "Birch" are to this work unless otherwise indicated.

Blackstone's "Commentaries." (Chase's edition.) New York, 1878.

Brydges, S. E. "Memoirs of the Peers of England during the Reign of James the First." London, 1802.

Burnet, G. "The History of the Reformation of the Church of

England." London, 1679, 1681 and 1714. Burnet, Bishop of Salisbury, born in 1643, was a lifelong writer, statesman and churchman.

"Cabala (Mysteries of State and Government in Letters)." London, 1694.

Camden, William. "The Life and Reign of Queen Elizabeth, newly done into English" and "The Life and Reign of King James I." Both appear in Volume 2 of "A Complete History of England . . .," edited by Hughes and Kennet and published in London in 1719 (2nd Ed.). Camden lived during the reigns of Elizabeth and James I and was a close observer of what went on at Court. He wrote the portion of the history relating to Queen Elizabeth's reign, edited by John Hughes; he left only a brief outline in diary form of events under James I – this was amplified by Arthur Wilson and was edited by Hughes. Camden was a dedicated lifelong antiquarian, encouraged and assisted by Bishop Goodman, Sir Philip Sidney and the two Carews.

"Camden Miscellany." Camden Society. Published by The Royal Historical Society in London. Pertinent material appears in several volumes, e.g. old poems about Elizabeth and Essex in Volume 3 and papers relating to the Devereux in Volume 13.

Campbell, John. "The Lives of the Chief Justices of England." New York, 1894. In addition to being a legal biographer, Campbell was successively lord chief justice and lord chancellor of England.

Carte, Thomas. "A General History of England." 4 v. 1747-55. Carte (born 1686) criticized existing histories of England as making insufficient use of source material so wrote his own; his history, based on tremendous research financed by many sources, enjoys high regard.

Cecil, Robert. "Letters to Sir George Carew." Camden Society, 1864. During and preceding his tenure as secretary of state, Cecil wrote many letters to Carew. His intimate participation in all matters of state during his long life makes these letters most valuable; his son married the sister of Frances Howard, Lady Essex.

Chamberlain, John. "The Letters of John Chamberlain." McClure, N. E., Ed. American Philosophical Society. Philadelphia, 1939. Chamberlain, an indefatigable and famous letter-writer and friend of the eminent men of his period, was in close touch with Court circles during the entire period covered by this book and was known as the Horace Walpole of his day.

Chambers, Robert. "The Life of King James the First." Edinburgh, 1830. Chambers, a nineteenth-century writer of Scottish history, including this biography, enjoys a wide reputation for his histories.

Coke, Edward. "Institutes of the Laws of England." (Third and Fourth Parts). 6th Ed. London, 1680.

Coke, Roger. "A Detection of the Court and State of England During the Four Last Reigns." London, 1694. Roger Coke was the grandson of Sir Edward Coke; his "Detection" contains considerable information based on family sources.

Collier, John Payne, Ed. "Mss. Collection Relating to Robert Devereux, Earl of Essex." 2 v. 1840. Lords Egerton and Ellesmere gave Collier access to the rich collection of papers at Bridgewater House, which he partially catalogued. A selection was published by him in 1840 as "The Egerton Papers" (see below); later he contributed to the two volumes of the "Trevelyan Papers" (see below). The papers in the "Mss. Collection" are entirely in handwriting—most are photographed originals, but some are photographs of copies.

Cotton (Binder's Author.) "A Brief Discourse Concerning the Power of the Peers and Commons of Parliament, in point of Judicature, Written by a Learned Antiquary at the Request of a Peer of this Realm. Printed in the year/That Sea-Coal was exceeding dear,/1640."

"Criminal Law Review." A monthly English publication on Criminal Law.

Cross, Rupert. "Introduction to Criminal Law." London.

D.N.B. This abbreviation is used for the British "Dictionary of National Biography." Material is classified alphabetically under the names of the persons whose biographies are included. Both the 1922 and 1960 editions were used, but the texts are identical.

D.S.P. This abbreviation is used for "State Paper Office, Domestic Papers." The documents in the collection are classified by date and numbered in chronological order.

Devereux, Walter B. "Lives and Letters of the Devereux, Earls of Essex." London, 1853.

DeFord, Miriam. "The Overbury Affair." Philadelphia, 1960.

D'Ewes, Simonds. "The Autobiography and Correspondence of Sir Simonds D'Ewes, Bart." London, 1845. D'Ewes (1602-50) spent his life studying old manuscripts and muniments which throw light on English history; with the encouragement of Selden and Sir Robert Cotton, he kept elaborate diaries covering the events of his day.

Dicey, A.V. "Law and Public Opinion in England." London, 1905.

D'Israeli, Isaac. "Miscellanies of Literature." Paris, 1840, London, 1856. This book, based upon D'Israeli's lifelong research in the British Museum, went through twelve editions during his lifetime.

Durant, Will. "The Age of Reason Begins." New York, 1961.

E.H.R. This abbreviation is used for "English Historical Review." (Annual volumes numbered consecutively, well indexed. Volumes 18, 37, 38 and 75 particularly pertinent here.)

"Egerton Papers." J. P. Collier, Ed. Camden Society. London, 1840. (See "Collier" above.)

Ewald, A. C. "Stories from the State Papers." London, 1882.

Folsom, George. "A Catalog of Original Documents in the English Archives Relating to the Early History of the State of Maine." New York, 1858. Pages 109 to 135 include the "Defense of Sir Ferdinando Gorges," included in Folsom's volume because Gorges was lord proprietor of Maine in 1639.

Forman, Simon. "The Autobiography and Diary of Simon Forman." London, 1849.

Froude, James A. "History of England." London, 1856-70.

Gairdner, James, and Spedding, James. "Studies in English History." Edinburgh, 1881.

Gardiner, Samuel. "History of England, 1603-1642." 3rd Ed. London, 1889. Nineteenth-century historian noted for his methodical and strenuous industry in examining systematically every possible source of information as well as for his breadth of view. Studied all papers relevant to Stuart reigns in all European archives; many honorary distinctions at home and abroad.

Gibbs, Philip. "King's Favorite." London, 1909.

Goodman, Godfrey. "The Court of King James the First." London, 1839. Goodman, born in 1583, became Bishop of Gloucester; the manuscript of his "Court of King James" is in the Bodleian Library and is a temperate defense of James in answer to Weldon. Although Goodman's kindly goodness tends to restrain his criticisms, this manuscript is a valuable authority for the reign.

H.M.C. This abbreviation is used for the reports of the Royal Commission on Historical Manuscripts. The 4th Report (London, 1874) is particularly pertinent here.

Hale, Matthew. "Jurisdiction of the Lord's House." London, 1796.

Hallam, Henry. "Constitutional History of England." 2 v. London, 1846.

Halliwell, James O. "Letters of the Kings of England." London, 1846. Halliwell began to collect manuscripts at 15 and never stopped. He was a steady contributor to "Archaeologia" and was elected to the Royal Society at 18.

Harleian Mss. Valuable material in the British Museum classified by number and folio.

"Harleian Miscellany, The." London. (Many volumes, variously dated.)

Hargrave, Francis. "A Complete Collection of State Trials and Proceedings . . . " 4th Ed. London, 1776.

Harrington, John. "Nugae Antiquae." London, 1804. Harrington was Queen Elizabeth's godson (his father and Elizabeth had been imprisoned in the Tower at the same time) and Lord Burghley was his protector. Harrington was a popular and somewhat indecent wit at Court; nevertheless, his "Nugae Antiquae" contains much material of value to the historian.

Harris, William. "An Historical and Critical Account of the Life and Writings of James the First, after the Manner of Mr. Bayle." London, 1753. Harris was the biographer of the Stuarts; although he was a nonconformist and not impartial, his notes are full of information from sources not easily accessible. Thomas Birch assisted him in his writing.

"Hatfield House Papers." Murdin, William, Ed. London, 1759.

Haynes, Samuel. "Collection of State Papers left by William Cecil, Lord Burghley." London, 1740-59.

Hogue, A. R. "Origins of the Common Law." Bloomington, Ind., 1966.

Holdsworth, W. S. "A History of English Law." 3rd Ed. London, 1922. Lawyer and historian of law; as Professor of Law at Oxford, rated second only to Blackstone; colossal output.

Howell, T. B. "A Complete Collection of State Trials . . ." London, 1816.

Hume, Martin. "Courtship of Queen Elizabeth." London, 1896. (The 1928 edition was used here.) Writer of many scholarly works as well as (in later life) some books designed to appeal to the public; contributor to Cambridge Modern History; honorary M.A. from Cambridge.

Hume, Martin. "Treason and Plot." New York, 1901.

"Huntington Library Quarterly." v. 5.

Huth Library. "The Bloody Downfall of Adultery, Murder, Ambition." London, 1615.

Jardine, David. "Criminal Trials." (Published in v. 1 of "Library of Entertaining Knowledge." London, 1832.) Writer on various legal matters, including the admirable "General Index to Howell's State Trials."

Jenkins, Elizabeth. "Elizabeth the Great." New York, 1959.

Jesse, J. H. "Memoirs of the Court of England During the Reign of the Stuarts." Boston (no date).

Jeudwine, John W. "Tort, Crime and Police in Medieval Britain." London, 1917.

Jonson, Ben. "Works." London, 1875. The material here used is taken from the "Conversations with William Drummond" in v. 9; these are notes made by Drummond of his conversations with Jonson, discoverd and copied by an Edinburgh antiquary around 1700. Drummond, related to the Stuart kings, was wellknown and highly regarded in his day.

"Journal of Criminal Law." London, various dates.

Knight, Charles. "Criminal Trials." London, 1832.

"Letters of James VI." (Printed from the originals in the Library of the Faculty of Advocates.) Edinburgh, 1835.

McElwee, W. L. "The Murder of Sir Thomas Overbury." New York, 1952.

McElwee, W. L. "The Wisest Fool in Christendom." London, 1958.

McKecknie, W. S. "Magna Carta." 2nd Ed. Glasgow, 1914.

Nauton, Robert, "Fragmenta Regalia." London, 1641. Nauton was a protégé of Essex II and of Buckingham, advancing to the position of secretary of state in 1618; he left unpublished a valuable account of the chief courtiers of Queen Elizabeth and interesting reminiscences of her Court—this manuscript was carelessly published in 1641 as the "Fragmenta."

Niccols, R. "Sir Thomas Overbury's Vision." London, 1616.

Nicolas, Harris. "The Life and Times of Sir Christopher Hatton." London, 1847.

Nichols, John. "Bibliotheca Topographica Britannica." London, 1780-1808.

Northall, G. F. "English Folk-Rhymes." London, 1892.

Osborne, Francis. "Traditional Memoirs." (See "Aulicus Coquinariae" above for the most readily accessible edition.) Osborne, born in 1593, a friend of Hobbes, worked some time in the lord treasurer's office but spent the last years of his life at Oxford writing historical, ethical and political tracts: Issac D'Israeli called Osborne "a misanthropical politician, who cuts with the most corroding pen that ever rottened a man's name."

Overbury. "A True and Historical Revelation of the Poisoning of Sir Thomas Overbury." London, 1651.

Overbury, Thomas. "The Miscellaneous Works in Verse and Prose of Sir Thomas Overbury, with Memoirs of his Life." 10th Ed. London, 1756.

Parry, E. A. "The Overbury Mystery." London, 1925.

Pike, Luke. "A History of Crime in England." 2 v. London, 1873.

Plucknett, F. T. "Concise History of the Common Law." 5th Ed. Boston, 1956.

Pricket, Robert. "Honor's Fame in Triumph Riding." London, 1604, Manchester, 1881.

Pulton, Ferdinando. "De Pace Regis et Regni." London, 1623. (The intriguing subtitle explains the character of the work: "A Treatise on Crimes and Criminal Procedure Collected from the Reports and Statutes and out of the Painful Works of the Judges and Law Writers.")

R.H.S. This abbreviation is used for "Transactions of the Royal Historical Society." (3rd Series, No. 5, published in 1911, is especially pertinent here.)

Rimbault, E. F. "Miscellaneous Works and a Biography of Sir Thomas Overbury, Knight." London, 1856.

Roughead, William. "The Fatal Countess." Edinburgh, 1924.

Salmon, Thomas. "A New Abridgement and Critical Review of the State Trials, 1388-1736." Dublin, 1737. Although his comments do not show it, Salmon was not a lawyer but a well known writer of history.

Sanderson, William. "The Reign and Death of James of Great Britain." (Part of "A Complete History of Mary Queen of Scotland and of her Son and Successor James.") London, 1656. Sanderson, born in 1586, was a noted historian; he utilized both his own observations and material gathered by Bishop Goodman.

"Secret History of Elizabeth and the Earl of Essex." (Author unknown.) London, 1699.

Selden, John. "Brief Discourses . . . ." London, 1640. Selden was a noted English jurist and legal antiquary who was born in 1584 and died in 1654. Many of his numerous writings afford interesting sidelights on the history of his period.

Selden, John. "The Privileges of the Baronage of England . . ." London, 1642.

Selden, John. "Of the Judicature in Parliaments." London, 1681.

Selden, John. "Tracts." London, 1683.

Selden Papers. (Publications of the Selden Society. 79 v. plus index.)

Selden Society. "Royal Writs in England from the Conquest to Glanville." (v. 77 of Selden Papers.) 1959.

Sidney Papers. ("Letters and Memorials of State . . . Written and Collected by Sir Philip Sidney.") London, 1746.

Sloane Mss. (British Museum.)

Smith, Logan P. "The Life and Letters of Sir Henry Wotton." Oxford, 1907.

"Somers Tracts." Sir Walter Scott, Ed. 2nd Ed. 13 v. London, 1809-15.

Sparke, M. (Printer.) "Truth Brought to Light by Time." London, 1651.

Spedding, James. "The Life and Letters of Francis Bacon." London, 1861-74.

Steeholm, Clara. "The Wisest Fool in Christendom." London, 1938.

Stephen, Harry. "The State Trials, Political and Social, Second Series." London, 1902.

Stephen, James Fitzjames. "A History of the Criminal Law of England." 3 v. London, 1883.

Stephen, James Fitzjames. "A General View of the Criminal Law of England." London, 1890.

Strachey, Lytton. "Elizabeth and Essex." New York, 1928.

Strype, John. "Annals of the Reformation . . . During Queen Elizabeth's Happy Reign." London and Oxford, 1709 and 1824. An ecclesiastical historian and biographer, most of Strype's materials were derived from the magnificent collection of charters, letters, state papers, etc., acquired "under very questionable circumstances" from the great-grandson of Lord Burghley's secretary, who had preserved the Burghley Papers. Strype's works were published beginning in 1694 but were reprinted at Oxford in 19 volumes, the last in 1824; the books are invaluable to the student of sixteenth-century English ecclesiastical and political history.

Strype, John. "The Life and Acts of John Whitgift." London and Oxford, 1718 and 1822.

"T.G." "The Secret and Tragical History of Queen Elizabeth and the Unfortunate Earl of Essex." London, 1712. (Possibly first printed in 1680; author unknown; if not published until 1712, it could have been written by Thomas Gent, who in 1711 was in London working for Edward Midwinter of Pie Corner, Smithfield, publishing broadsides.)

"Trevelyan Papers." (The volumes here pertinent edited by J. Payne Collier.) Camden Society. London, 1857-72.

"True and Historical Relation of Poisoning of Sir Thomas Overbury." (Author unknown.) London, 1651.

Weldon, Anthony. "The Court and Character of King James, Written and taken by Sir A. W., being an eye and ear witness." London, 1650. (Printed in London in 1817 in Volume One of Smeeton's "Historical and Biographical Tracts." Footnote references are to this edition.) Weldon was closely associated with James I throughout his reign and was fully possessed of the facts he needed for his work but worked zealously for Parliament when Parliament broke with the Stuarts and was twice voted substantial grants for his services, his impartiality hence being subject to question; he has been accused of copying part of his work on King James from the similar work by Arthur Wilson.

Whibley, Charles. "Essays in Biography." London, 1913.

Will With the Whip (Publisher), "The Secret History of the Duke of Alençon and Queen Elizabeth." London, 1691. A curious little book, presumed written by a gentleman servitor of Princess Marianna (daughter of Catherine by Henry VIII, born after Henry had exiled her), of whom Elizabeth is said to have been more jealous than she was of Mary, Queen of Scots. Alençon, Elizabeth's suitor, later became Duke of Anjou and still later Henri III of France. The book should probably be classified as fiction, although many of its statements can be substantiated as fact.

Williams, R. F. "The Court and Times of James the First." London, 1848.

Willingham, George. "A Historical Narrative of the First Fourteen Years of King James." London, 1651. (The title page of the printed volume contains no author's name, but there was added to the copy I used, in faded black ink and very old script, "By George Willingham.")

Wilson, Arthur. "The Life and Reign of King James the First." London, 1653. After his discharge from the Exchequer for quarrelsomeness, Wilson was employed by and traveled extensively with Essex III; when discharged by Essex's second wife he went first to Oxford and then worked for the Earl of Warwick. His work is valuable but influenced by his prejudice against the Stuarts. Also, see above, under "William Camden."

Willson, David H. "King James VI and I." London, 1956.

Winwood, Ralph. "Memorials of Affairs of State in the Reigns of Queen Elizabeth and King James I." London, 1725.

Wood, Anthony A. "Athenae Oxonienses." Bliss, Ed. London, 1721. Wood, born in 1632, was a prime example of a dedicated antiquarian; he spent his life in two rooms across from Merton College Gate. With access to all the manuscripts held by the University and Bodleian Library as well as local antiquarian bookshops, parish and other official records, his "Athenae," which is a biographical history of Oxford-educated writers and bishops, became a mine of information.

Wotton, Henry. "Reliquae Wottonianae." 4th Ed. London, 1685. Wotton became secretary to Essex II in 1595 and enjoyed his full trust as agent, diplomat and general assistant. At the accession of James I Wotton entered his employ, then entered the House of Commons and finally after numerous diplomatic missions became Provost of Eton College; he maintained to the end of his life a highly valuable correspondence.

CHAPTER NOTES

Chapter One

1. Devereux I 1
2. D.N.B.
3. Harleian Miscellany I 218
4. Hatfield House Papers 300
5. Hatfield House Papers 317
6. D.N.B.
7. Abbott 2
8. Durant 41, citing Spedding, J., "Life and Times of Francis Bacon" I 179
9. H.M.C., 4th Report 338
10. Camden II 637
11. Abbott 27
12. Carte III 687
13. Jardine I 293
14. Jenkins 28
15. Jonson IX 395
16. Durant 10, citing Froude
17. Hume (Courtships) 349
18. Carte III 567
19. D.N.B.
20. Nicolas 15
21. Hume (Courtships) 357
22. Hallam I 125
23. Hume (Courtships) 336

Chapter Two

1. R.H.S., 3rd Ser., No. 5. (1911)
2. Chamberlain I 71
3. Chamberlain I 84
4. Aulicus Coquinariae II 139
5. Birch II 432
6. Trevelyan Papers II 101
7. Abbott 133
8. Sidney Papers II 127
9. Sidney Papers II 129
10. Sidney Papers II 131
11. Birch II 436
12. Harrington I 356
13. Sidney Papers II 151
14. Sidney Papers II 166
15. Sidney Papers II 181, 187, 193
16. Birch II 443
17. Birch II 444
18. Birch II 447
19. E.H.R., v. 37 P. 340 (1922)
20. Abbott 169
21. Birch II 447
22. Stephen (History) I 170; Holdsworth I 47; Plucknett 182
23. E.H.R., v. 37, pp. 340, 516
24. Stephen (General View) 34
25. Hallam I 230
26. Stephen (History) I 176
27. Plucknett 80
28. Jeudwine 111

Chapter Three

1. H.M.C., 4th Report 334
2. Collier I 124
3. Cecil-Carew Letters 23
4. Sidney Papers II 213
5. T.G. 12
6. Camden II 628
7. Camden II 628
8. Camden II 628
9. Devereux II 131
10. Wotton 192
11. Harrington I 179
12. Birch II 463
13. Camden II 629
14. Carte III 684
15. Carte III 684
16. Cecil-Carew Letters 65
17. Carte III 686
18. Strype (Annals) IV 495
19. Abbott 235
20. Birch II 479n
21. Wotton 192
22. Collier I 101
23. Amos 59

Chapter Four

1. McKecknie 377, 379
2. Sanderson 414

3. Strachey 79

4. Hallam I 158, 231

5. Stephen (History) I 302

6. Plucknett 433

7. Blackstone 1025

8. Hallam I 371

9. Pike II 90

10. Camden II 634

11. Folsom 118, quoting Cotton Mss. Julius F. VI, fol. 423

12. Salmon I 43

13. Spedding II 227

14. Howell I 1355

15. Chamberlain I 120

16. Cecil-Carew Letters 67

17. Camden II 635

18. Howell I 1358

Chapter Five

1. Campbell I 357

2. Collier I 99

3. Abbott 237

4. Abbott 127

5. Goodman II 17

6. Birch II 475

7. Camden II 636

8. Amos 198

9. T.G. 93

10. Strachey 268

11. Camden II 637

12. Pricket

13. Howell I 1417n

Chapter Six

1. Birch II 486
2. Hallam I 331
3. Jesse I 79
4. Durant 137
5. Hallam I 333
6. Gardiner II 34
7. Aikin I 20
8. Hallam I 331n, "Nugae Antiquae" I 348
9. Willingham 4
10. D'Israeli 352
11. Ewald II 44
12. Osborne, Francis. "Some Traditional Memorials on the Reign of King James," in "The Works of Francis Osborne," 9th Ed., London, 1689. P. 476
13. Goodman II 379
14. Willingham 7
15. Camden II 689
16. Camden II 689n
17. Camden II 686
18. Camden II 686
19. Jesse I 264
20. D'Ewes I 74
21. D'Ewes I 90
22. Gibbs 11, citing "Nugae Antiquae"
23. Chamberlain I 548
24. Gibbs 98
25. Winwood III 453
26. Gibbs, citing Harleian Ms. 6908, fol. 4
27. Camden II 686
28. Harleian Miscellany I 219

29. Carte IV 7

30. D'Ewes I 89

31. Camden II 687

32. Weldon I 21

33. Sanderson (Proem to the "Reign and Death")

34. D'Israeli 349n

35. Camden II 687

36. Coke, Roger 67

37. Forman

38. Strype (Whitgift) II 457

39. Camden II 687

40. Camden II 687

41. Camden II 691

42. Osborne (Secret History) II 53

43. Goodman I 215

44. Gibbs 126, citing D.S.P.

45. Goodman I 221

46. Sanderson 385

47. Whibley 3

48. Gibbs 54, citing "A Book Touching Sir Thomas Overbury . . . ," "ghost-written" for Overbury's father.

49. Sanderson 416

50. Carte IV 10

51. Whibley 7, 10

52. Sanderson 417

53. Weldon 21

54. Coke, Roger 69

55. Camden II 691

56. Sanderson 393

57. D'Ewes I 71

58. Camden II 691

59. Jesse I 266

60. Chamberlain I 443
61. Weldon 22
62. Coke, Roger 74
63. Goodman I 216
64. Ewald II 54
65. D'Ewes I 73
66. Wotton 413
67. Winwood III 455
68. Sanderson 418

Chapter Seven

1. Camden II 692
2. Plucknett 80
3. Carte IV 7
4. Gardiner II 171
5. See Appendix
6. Gardiner II 174
7. Chamberlain I 461
8. Weldon 25
9. Camden II 692
10. Carte IV 8
11. Goodman I 221
12. Chamberlain I 478
13. Winwood III 475
14. Hallam I 318
15. Goodman II 152

Chapter Eight

1. Gibbs 155, citing S.P.O.
2. Rimbault li, citing Harl. Ms. 7002

3. Amos 162, 167

4. Weldon 23

5. Camden II 693

6. Camden II 694

7. D.N.B. on Killigrew, citing Gardiner II 182

8. Sanderson 419

9. Amos 173, referring to Cotton Mss., Titus C. vii., fol. 107 back. British Museum

10. Winwood III 482

11. Winwood III 481

12. Amos, citing D.S.P., 1615, Oct. 1 (No. 159)

13. D'Ewes I 77

14. Wood II 135

15. Camden II 693

16. Camden II 693

17. Weldon 28

18. Goodman I 385

19. Camden II 698

20. Coke, Roger 84

21. Halliwell II 126

22. Weldon 30

23. Camden II 698

24. Spedding V 208

25. Weldon 29

26. D'Ewes I 70

27. D.S.P., 1615, Oct. 5; Whibley 42

28. Spedding V 208; Howell II 956

29. Coke, Roger 86

30. Amos 36 (quoting Weldon)

31. Camden II 698

32. Amos 36 (quoting Weldon)

33. D.S.P., 1615, Oct. 17 (Nos. 201, 202, 203, original draft of Nos. 202, 203 in Lord Coke's hand); Amos 40

34. D.S.P., 1615, Oct. 18 (No. 204, original draft in Coke's hand); Amos 38

Chapter Nine

1. Stephen (General View) 38
2. Holdsworth I 335
3. Stephen (General View) 19
4. Blackstone 1028
5. Blackstone 1025
6. Pulton 184
7. Holdsworth I 337
8. Hogue 155
9. Coke, Edward 49, 136
10. Salmon I 59
11. Spedding V 210
12. Spedding V 212
13. Gibbs 301, citing D.S.P., 1615, Oct. 22
14. Gibbs 301, citing D.S.P., 1615, Oct. 22
15. Coke, Edward 49
16. Camden II 699; Spedding V 211
17. Whibley 9
18. Amos 219, citing D.S.P., 1615, Nov. 10, 11, 14 (Nos. 282, 283, 290)
19. Camden II 688
20. Goodman II 146

Chapter Ten

1. Howell II 937n
2. Stephen (History) I 332
3. Amos 213, citing D.S.P., 1615, Nov. 18 (No. 305, in Coke's handwriting)

4. Goodman II 147

5. Camden II 699

6. Amos 216; Goodman II 148

7. Amos 225, citing D.S.P., 1615, Dec. 9 (No. 355, in Coke's handwriting)

8. Egerton 473

9. Spedding VI 118

10. Weldon 36

11. Wilson 89

12. Spedding V 229

13. Spedding VI 118

14. Camden II 702

15. Chamberlain I 623

16. Hallam I 334

17. Plucknett 243

18. Durant 138n

19. Campbell I 422; II 1; 18 E.H.R. 664

20. Chamberlain II 1

21. Ewald II 58

22. Camden II 699

23. DeFord 97

24. Sanderson 419

Chapter Eleven

1. Spedding V 292

2. Weldon 37

3. Spedding V 275

4. Spedding V 282

5. Spedding V 286

6. Spedding V 296

7. Northall 542

8. Amos 247

9. Amos 272

10. Spedding V 312n

11. A definition and example kindly suggested to me by Norval Morris, Director of the University of Chicago Center for Studies in Criminal Justice

12. Amos 176

13. Gardiner II 350

14. Salmon I 64

15. Coke, Edward 49

Chapter Twelve

1. Halliwell 137

2. Hallam I 352 and note

3. Weldon 38

4. Rimbault lxi n

5. Rimbault lxiii n

6. Weldon 36

7. Weldon 37

8. Chamberlain II 6

9. Goodman II 153

10. Carte IV 34

11. Hallam I 353n, citing "Archaelogia" XVII 280

12. Camden II 699

13. D.N.B.

14. Salmon I 64

INDEX

Writers are included in the index only where they were contemporaries and figure in the action

108, 111-14, 156, 221

Howard, Catherine (Countess of Nottingham), 73-74

Howard, Charles (Earl of Nottingham, Lord Admiral), 6, 19, 33, 42, 63-64, 71, 73, 75, 79-80, 85, 87, 97

Howard, Elizabeth (Lady Knollys), 255

Howard, Frances (Countess of Essex, later Countess of Somerset): arrested, 145; birth of daughter, 201; character, 98-99; delay of trial, 201; death, 258; divorce action, 115-29; explanation of "letters," 238; fabricated proof of virginity, 123-25; letters from Carr regarding Overbury, 192; letters to Elwes, 234, 237; life and marriage of Anne, her only child, 257; life subsequent to murder trial, 255-58; life with Essex, 101-105; marriage to Essex, 97-98; married to Carr, 137-38; pardoned, 256; plots to free her from Essex, 105-106, 109-11; property partly confiscated, 255-56; removal to country, 256; trial for murder, 202-209; other mention, 92, 108, 112-13, 141-42, 152, 154, 156-58, 160, 162-65, 168-70, 173, 176-79, 181, 183-84, 187-88, 192-93, 208, 212-15, 221, 223, 225, 228-31, 234, 236-41, 243-44, 252; for names of officials and peers in attendance at trial, *see* pages 202-203

Howard, Henry (Earl of Northampton): conduct while Overbury was in Tower, 132-35; referred to in Carr's trial for murder, 226, 228, 230, 233-35, 240, 243, 245; petitions James for divorce for Frances, 115; other mention, 30, 97-99, 101, 112, 121, 131, 144, 181-84, 188, 190

Howard, Katherine (sister of Frances), 120

Howard, Katherine (Countess of Suffolk, wife of Lord Thomas Howard), 98, 121, 125, 182

Howard, Thomas (Earl of Suffolk), 38, 67, 76, 97-100, 102, 121, 138, 174, 185, 187, 194-95, 197, 235, 245

Huic, Dr. (Elizabeth's physician), 9

Hunsdon, Lord Henry, 79

Hyde, Sir Lawrence, 156, 166, 173, 197, 203

I

Ireland, 2, 11-12, 15, 20, 22, 32, 73, 82, 90

Irish expedition, 11-14

J

James I (King of England, King

R

S